Collective Preferences in Democratic Politics

How useful can opinion surveys be as inputs to the political process when most people know little about politics but are nevertheless willing to give opinions on even the most esoteric policy issues when asked to do so by pollsters? This study, the first comprehensive treatment of the relationship between knowledge, representation, and political equality in opinion surveys, suggests some surprising answers. Knowledge does matter, and the way it is distributed in society can cause collective preferences to reflect disproportionately the opinions of some groups more than others. Sometimes collective preferences seem to represent something like the will of the people, but frequently they do not. Sometimes they rigidly enforce political equality in the expression of political viewpoints, but often they do not. The primary culprit is not any inherent shortcoming in the methods of survey research. Rather, it is the limited degree of knowledge held by ordinary citizens about public affairs and the tendency for some kinds of people to be better informed than others. Accounting for these factors can help survey researchers, journalists, politicians, and concerned citizens better appreciate the pitfalls and possibilities for using opinion polls to represent the people's voice.

Scott L. Althaus earned his Ph.D. in Political Science at Northwestern University and is associate professor of Speech Communication and associate professor of Political Science at the University of Illinois, Urbana-Champaign. His research interests center on the communication processes that equip ordinary citizens to exercise popular sovereignty in democratic societies, as well as on the communication processes by which the opinions of these citizens are conveyed to government officials. His research has appeared in the *American Political Science Review*, the *American Journal of Political Science*, *Communication Research*, *Journalism and Mass Communication Quarterly*, the *Journal of Broadcasting & Electronic Media*, and *Political Communication*.

Collective Preferences in Democratic Politics

Opinion Surveys and the Will of the People

SCOTT L. ALTHAUS
University of Illinois

CAMBRIDGE
UNIVERSITY PRESS

PUBLISHED BY THE PRESS SYNDICATE OF THE UNIVERSITY OF CAMBRIDGE
The Pitt Building, Trumpington Street, Cambridge, United Kingdom

CAMBRIDGE UNIVERSITY PRESS
The Edinburgh Building, Cambridge CB2 2RU, UK
40 West 20th Street, New York, NY 10011-4211, USA
477 Williamstown Road, Port Melbourne, VIC 3207, Australia
Ruiz de Alarcón 13, 28014 Madrid, Spain
Dock House, The Waterfront, Cape Town 8001, South Africa

http://www.cambridge.org

First published 2003

Printed in the United States of America

Typeface Sabon 10/13 pt.   *System* LaTeX 2_ε [TB]

A catalog record for this book is available from the British Library.

Library of Congress Cataloging in Publication data

Althaus, Scott L., 1966–
Collective preferences in democratic politics : opinion surveys and the will of the people /
Scott L. Althaus.
  p. cm.
Includes bibliographical references and index.
ISBN 0-521-82099-5 – ISBN 0-521-52787-2 (pb.)
1. Public opinion – United States. 2. Public opinion. 3. Democracy.
4. Political participation. I. Title.
HN90.P8A47 2003
303.3′8′0973–dc21   2003041961

ISBN 0 521 82099 5 hardback
ISBN 0 521 52787 2 paperback

For Ellen

Acknowledgments

This book is an attempt to conduct public opinion research in what Paul Lazarsfeld (1957) called the "classical tradition": using empirical methods to pursue and refine the foundational questions about popular sovereignty raised by political theorists. If this effort meets with the reader's approval, it is in no small part because of the many people who have either shaped my thinking or tangibly contributed to this project along the way.

It all began on April 20, 1992, when, as a first-year master's student at Northwestern University, I was introduced by Benjamin Page to *The Rational Public* in his graduate seminar on public opinion. Ben encouraged me from the beginning to forge ahead on a project that eventually became my doctoral dissertation, knowing that it was often critical of his own work. His first priority in research is the pursuit of truth, and he is a worthy role model for all who would devote themselves to the life of the mind. It was also during that momentous April that I was first introduced to Susan Herbst, whose vision for integrating contemporary public opinion research with its historical roots has been a profound influence. The toughest questions always came from Susan, and I am especially grateful to her for reminding me to look toward the bigger picture that lies beyond disciplinary boundaries. My early work on this project was also influenced by Jane Mansbridge, who spurred me to think about political interests in addition to preferences, and by Patricia Conley, whose command of econometrics and patience with my repeated questions made her an indispensable resource.

Over the course of what turned out to be a 10-year project, I have also benefited from the comments, suggestions, and assistance of Allen

Barton, Jim Beniger, Stephen Bennett, Joan Black, Dennis Chong, Ken Corioso, Michael Delli Carpini, Robert Eisinger, Tim Fedderson, Kathy Frankovic, Brian Gaines, Doris Graber, Paul Gronke, Michael Hagan, Herbert Jacob, Ken Janda, Scott Keeter, Steven Klepper, Jon Krosnick, Jim Kuklinski, Kurt Lang, Paul Lavrakas, Robert Luskin, Elizabeth Martin, Peter Miller, Jennifer Oats-Sargent, Thomas Patterson, Sam Popkin, Paul Quirk, Brian Roberts, Daniel Robinson, Frank Rusciano, Arthur Sanders, Jacob Shamir, Tom Smith, David Tewksbury, Robert Weissberg, Chris Wlezien, the many graduate students in my public opinion seminars who commented on earlier drafts of the book, and the anonymous reviewers of various manuscripts stemming from this project.

I am especially grateful to Michael Delli Carpini and Robert Entman, who read the manuscript in its entirety and whose excellent advice greatly improved the final product, and to Guido Schuster for his generous assistance in writing, editing, and compiling the simulation program used in Chapter 2. Lewis Bateman, the political science editor at Cambridge University Press, Sarah Gentile, Lauren Levin, Regina Paleski, Teresa Barensfeld, and Eric Schwartz provided invaluable assistance throughout the publishing process. I am also indebted to the University of Michigan's Center for Political Studies for collecting the American National Election Studies data used in this project, and to the Inter-University Consortium for Political and Social Research, for making the data available to the scholarly community.

There is a special group of people who deserve my highest thanks, for this project never would have been started or completed were it not for the family members, friends, and mentors who encouraged me to enter graduate school and supported me along the way. My family has always been my biggest supporter. I am especially thankful to my parents, Sean and Sandy Althaus, for keeping me in good humor and for raising me to respect the value of an education. My long hours spent on this project have tested the patience of my children, Colin, Kyra, and Curtis, and I thank them for keeping me focused on what is really important in life. More than anyone else, my biggest debt of thanks is due to my wife, Ellen, for her loving companionship, constant support, readiness to listen, and daily sacrifices of time and attention that freed me to focus on the book. This volume is as much the product of her efforts as it is of mine.

Soli Deo Gloria

Chapters 3 and 4 update and expand arguments that originally appeared in Althaus, Scott L. 1996. "Opinion Polls, Information Effects, and Political Equality: Exploring Ideological Biases in Collective Opinion," *Political Communication* 13 (1): 3–21 and in Althaus, Scott L. 1998. "Information Effects in Collective Preferences," *American Political Science Review* 92(3): 545–58. Excerpts from these articles are reproduced by permission of Taylor & Francis, Inc. (http://www.routledge-ny.com), and the American Political Science Association, respectively.

1

Introduction

> The more completely popular sovereignty prevails in a country, so much the more important is it that the organs of opinion should be adequate to its expression.
>
> – James Bryce, *The American Commonwealth*

There are only three questions of any lasting importance to the study of what has since the 18th century been called public opinion. The entire corpus of human knowledge on the subject, from the philosophical inquiries of the ancient Greeks to the most modern statistical analyses, can be seen to unfold from just three enduring points of inquiry and contention: What is public opinion, or in what form ought the concept of public opinion be recognized? What is its nature, or what characteristics should public opinion possess? What kind of political power does it have, or what kind of power should it be given? Although a focus on the *is* became the hallmark of modern research on public opinion even as the work of previous generations emphasized the *ought*, the course of scholarship on public opinion continues to be set by these deceivingly profound and complex pole stars. It is a testimony to the knottiness of these questions that definitive answers to them seem as elusive today as they were to the contemporaries of Socrates and Protagoras.

This book is concerned with a particular definition of public opinion that has become generally accepted in recent years, a shortcoming in the nature of this public opinion that calls into question its usefulness in democratic politics, and the potential for this kind of public opinion to reflect the interests of the citizens it is taken to represent. Although the role of public opinion in democratic governance has been a concern of political theorists since the time of Plato and Aristotle (Minar 1960), the recent tendency toward equating public opinion with the results of opinion surveys has raised new concerns among social scientists and political philosophers about the role of public opinion as a rudder for the ship of state. How useful can opinion surveys be as inputs to the political process, when most people know little about politics but are nonetheless willing to give opinions on even the most esoteric policy issues when asked to do so by survey researchers?

Given the mass public's dual tendencies toward innocence and glibness on matters of public affairs, it is natural to ask whether the effluence of information about citizen preferences that is produced by opinion polling advances or hinders the progress of democratic rule. At the root of this question is nothing less than the meaning of democracy, for rule by the people is merely a slogan until we clarify how a polity is to recognize the people's will, by which we mean their political interests. All theories of democracy hold at least minimally to the idea that the people's own voice – that is, information provided by the people about their preferences – should have a central role in organizing and overseeing the processes of governance. Yet they offer little guidance on how the voice of the people should be recognized or in what forms it might be embodied.

Most public opinion scholars agree that opinion surveys are useful for mass democracies precisely because they can reveal what the people are thinking. Some go farther, suggesting that opinion surveys are indispensable to democratic politics. Sidney Verba (1996), who has built a career out of analyzing the deficiencies of citizen input to democratic systems, concludes that opinion surveys help compensate for the inherent shortcomings of citizen participation in politics:

Surveys produce just what democracy is supposed to produce – equal representation for all citizens. The sample survey is rigorously egalitarian; it is designed so that each citizen has an equal chance to participate and an equal voice when participating. (3)

Likewise, in their path-breaking book on collective opinion, Benjamin Page and Robert Shapiro (1992) conclude that the traditional understanding of public opinion as volatile and capricious is incorrect. Collective policy preferences, they argue, have emergent properties that make collective opinion "stable (though not immovable), meaningful, and indeed rational" (14) by compensating for the sometimes erratic opinions of individual respondents. This means that

> Democracy is not made impossible by default, by public opinion being nonexistent or unknowable or irrelevant. An attentive reader of polls and surveys can get a good deal of coherent guidance about policy. (385)

Lawrence Jacobs and Robert Shapiro (2000) go further, arguing that democracy suffers when *Politicians Don't Pander* to the polls:

> The public's [surveyed] preferences offer both broad directions to policymakers (e.g., establish universal health insurance) and some specific instructions (e.g., rely on an employer mandate for financing reform). *In general, policymakers should follow these preferences....* What concerns us are indications of declining responsiveness to public opinion and the growing list of policies on which politicians of both major political parties ignore public opinion and supply no explicit justification for it. The practice of American government is drifting from the norms of democratic responsiveness. (xv, xviii; emphasis added)

Even the most optimistic supporters of opinion surveys recognize that polls are not without their problems as indicators of the people's voice. Slight changes in the wording of a question can sometimes lead to drastically different response patterns. Sampling problems and nonresponse error are well-known pitfalls to survey researchers, and the questions that are used in surveys may fail to capture the public's real concerns. While these problems are worthy of serious attention, there is an even greater problem about which few seem aware or concerned: the public's low levels and uneven social distribution of political knowledge diminish the quality of political representation provided by opinion surveys. Despite all appearances to the contrary, this problem is so pervasive as to call into question whether opinion surveys can tell us reliably what the people really want.

The timeworn finding of nearly a half century of survey research is that "textbook" information about the political process is scarce and unevenly distributed to the mass public. "There now seems to be a consensus," notes Robert Luskin, "that by anything approaching elite standards most citizens think and know jaw-droppingly little about politics" (2002: 282). Since so few people appear knowledgeable about public affairs, one might wonder whether collective policy preferences revealed in opinion surveys accurately convey the distribution of voices and interests in a society.

To date, this vital question has received only indirect attention from social scientists and survey researchers. This study, the first comprehensive treatment of the relationships among knowledge, representation, and political equality in opinion surveys, suggests some surprising answers. Knowledge does matter, and the way it is distributed in society can cause collective preferences to reflect disproportionately the opinions of some groups more than others. To the extent that opinion polls influence democratic politics, the uneven social distribution of political knowledge may impair the responsiveness of governments to their citizens.[1]

OPINION SURVEYS AS THE VOICE OF THE PEOPLE

The public's surveyed opinions on policy issues are often used to hold elected officials accountable to their constituents, as a feedback loop between governments and citizens, and as a medium for the mass public to communicate with itself. They may also provide an important channel for political representation by conveying information to political leaders about the mind of a populace so vast and varied as to be inscrutable save through the medium of the sample survey.

Before the middle of the 20th century, the voice of the people was commonly discerned through election results, the activities of organized groups, and the attentions of the press. Yet the ambiguous nature of these "organs of public opinion" (Bryce 1891) limited their usefulness as mirrors of the public mind. For example, while the popular vote has long served as a formal mechanism for registering the people's will, election results are inherently contestable as indicators of the people's voice. Does a victory for one candidate over another indicate support for the winner's policy positions, dislike for the losing candidate, satisfaction with the status quo, or something else? Added to the range of possible meanings that can be assigned to elections is the problem of nonparticipation. Bill Clinton won the American presidency in 1992 with 43% of the vote in an election where only 55% of those eligible turned out to cast a ballot. Consequently, Clinton was elected to preside over a nation in which 76% of the adult population either voted against him or failed to vote at all. While we are in the habit of recognizing the results of free and fair elections as binding and legitimate, the nonparticipation problem makes it difficult to know whether a procedure that could somehow reflect the will of every

---

[1] By *opinion poll* or *survey* I mean specifically those that measure self-reported opinions about political topics. We know that surveys can be a very useful tool for measuring past behavior in a population, and a reasonable tool for assessing potential behavior (like the propensity to vote), but the focus in this book is more narrowly on the use of survey methods to measure attitudinal information that might subsequently be employed as an indicator of that contested concept we call public opinion.

citizen might produce a different outcome. The natural advantages accruing to wealthy and privileged interests in group politics have likewise cast doubt on the likelihood that all relevant voices are properly represented in the group system, or that any particular group properly represents the people in whose interests it claims to act. In similar ways, the commercial motives of the press and its lack of formal accountability to citizens limit its ability to represent the people's voice.

While elections and the activities of groups may remain the most decisive channels of public opinion in democratic societies, since the 1930s there has been a growing acceptance of opinion polling as a superior channel for conveying or representing the voice of a people (J. M. Converse 1987; P. E. Converse 1987). Because opinion surveys solicit views from a representative sample of a population and are intended to be nonideological and scientific, they provide what many believe to be a clearer and more inclusive indicator of a public's will than had been available through more traditional indicators of public opinion. This view of opinion polling was championed by influential pioneers of survey research like George Gallup, Archibald Crossley, Harold Gosnell, and Elmo Roper, who promoted opinion surveys as a corrective to the problems inherent in using election results and group activity as indicators of what the people want from government (e.g., Gallup and Rae 1940; Gosnell 1940). Although opinion surveys are unlikely to rival the legitimacy of elections as formal expressions of the public will, they are unique in their ability to serve as a communication medium linking citizens to representatives: they allow the individual members of a polity to speak in a collective voice *as* a public on important issues of the day. As a consequence, opinion surveys may be the mass public's clearest and most influential voice in the routine conduct of democratic politics that occurs between infrequent elections.

All theories of democracy regard free and fair elections as crucial for realizing popular sovereignty (Dahl 1989; Held 1987; Manin 1997), and many theories posit that the common good arises out of the competition for power among organized groups (e.g., Dahl 1956; Sartori 1987; Schattschneider 1960; Schumpeter [1942] 1976). But while elections and groups are standard elements of most models of democracy, political philosophers have provided little guidance about whether the opinion polls that are so commonplace today might serve useful purposes in democratic politics. The preferences of ordinary citizens play important foundational roles in most models of democracy, but the communication processes by which those preferences are represented to governing officials and institutions have received little sustained attention from political scientists, communication researchers, and democratic theorists. To borrow a phrase from Walter Lippmann (1922: 239), it would seem in the case of opinion polling that "the practice of democracy has been ahead of its theory."

The problem is that opinion polling makes it possible to distinguish collective decisions from collective preferences. Elections produce collective decisions, which are the legitimate, binding, and constitutionally recognized forms of popular sovereignty. Elections also produce collective preferences about what the people want. American voters in 1992 elected a Democratic president after 12 years of Republican leadership, which indicates a collective preference for change of some sort. While decisive, election results have always provided ambiguous and contestable signals about the reasons why the people voted this way or that, and the vast scale of modern democratic institutions added to the difficulty of sorting out what the people collectively desired from what the people collectively did on election day. The rise of the sample survey made it possible not only to clarify the meaning of collective decisions through exit polling but, more important, to separate information about collective preferences from the activity of collective decisions. Opinion polling introduced the collective preference as a new form of popular sovereignty, but after half a century there is still no clear standing within democratic theory for the voice of a people divorced from its vote.

This gap between theory and practice may stem in part from the tendency among political theorists in the liberal tradition to focus on institutional design and structures of representation as keys to successful governance by the people. Pure democracy was controversial even among the ancient Athenians, and modern research on social choice theory has concluded that aside from the problems of political instability inherent in "rule by the mob," there are no methods for aggregating individual preferences that can satisfy even the minimal requirements one would expect for democratic rule (Arrow 1963; Riker 1982).[2] While at least one scholar has founded a justification for democratic rule on the idea of random sampling (Swabey 1937), and while the utilitarianism of Bentham and Mill has made important contributions to democratic thinking, it is safe to characterize the broadest currents of work in democratic theory as suspicious of the potential for simple preference aggregation to reveal the common good, which by extension implicates polling. Much

---

[2] However, this problem may be less serious than it sounds. See my discussion on this point in Chapter 7.

of this doubt is cast by critics of liberal conceptions of democracy (e.g., Arendt 1958; Barber 1984; Habermas 1989, 1996a), but the premise that all preferences are created equal has come under fire even from defenders of the liberal tradition, who recognize that a citizen's interests can be at odds with her preferences (e.g., Bachrach 1967, 1975; Dahl 1989; Sunstein 1991). So while political philosophers have said little about the ability of surveys to convey the voice of the people, what they do say indirectly about the theoretical rationale underlying opinion polling reflects poorly on the potential for survey results to represent the will of the people.

In contrast to the philosophical literature relevant to opinion polling, empirical work on public opinion has tended to accept opinion surveys as an important indicator of the people's voice, but also to conclude that what individuals say through opinion polls is often shallow, coarse, vacillating, and illogical. So widely accepted is this premise that in recent years only two theoretical arguments have been successfully advanced to support the idea that the voice of the people conveyed through polls or elections can be reasonable, adaptive, meaningful, and consistent. The first of these, an obscure application of statistical probability theory known as the Condorcet Jury Theorem, was developed more than 200 years ago (Condorcet 1785, 1995) but had been regularly forgotten and rediscovered until its potential value to democratic theory was clarified by social choice theorists in the last 20 years. The second of these arguments points to the error-reducing properties of statistical aggregation and is most fully elaborated in the collective rationality models of Page and Shapiro (1992) and Philip Converse (1990).[3] As detailed in Chapter 2, the Condorcet Jury Theorem and collective rationality arguments posit that so long as the preferences of individuals share certain plausible distributional characteristics, collective preferences should be good indicators of what the people want from government, even if individuals are as loose in their thinking as the empirical literature often reveals. In addition to rehabilitating survey results as useful organs of the people's voice, these arguments raise the possibility that something like the will of the people might be discerned through the results of opinion surveys.

Yet we still do not know whether these arguments explain what actually happens when individual opinions are aggregated into collective preferences. While these theoretical accounts of the superiority of collective

---

[3] The term *collective rationality* comes from Page and Shapiro, but as the statistical logic used by Converse is so similar, I use the term to describe both models.

preferences over individual opinions have been widely accepted by social scientists, there is little direct evidence that the mechanics of aggregation at the heart of these arguments actually produce collective opinions more worthy of political consideration than the individual preferences of which they are composed.

Another important limitation in the literature on opinion surveys in democratic politics is that regardless of whether the potential impact of polls is being criticized or praised, the debate on these points rarely ventures beyond the narrow question of whether polls are generally good or generally bad for democracy.[4] This focus has contributed to a polarized debate that seems to impel participants toward the boundaries of Panglossian cheer or Jerimanic gloom. In the literature on the Condorcet Jury Theorem, terms like "perfection" (Miller 1986: 175) and "infallible" (Ladha 1992: 619) are commonly used to salute the apparent competence and wisdom of majority decisions made by large groups. Likewise, the statistical logic of Page and Shapiro's collective rationality argument leads them to deduce that the mass public's collective opinions on subjects as arcane as the number of missiles needed for effective nuclear deterrence should be just as robust and sensible as its opinions on more familiar subjects like prayer in the schools or affirmative action policy (1992: 19–23). At the other extreme are critics like Charles Salmon and Theodore Glasser, who conclude that "When used as a gauge of 'public opinion,'. . . polls not only miss the mark but shift the target. . . . Polls offer at best a naïve and narrow view of democracy" (1995: 449). Likewise, Benjamin Ginsberg argues that the widespread use of polling alters the nature of public opinion by drawing attention away from the threat of actions by organized citizen groups, thereby "robbing opinion of precisely those features that might maximize its impact on government and policy" (1986: 83). Sociologist Pierre Bourdieu (1979) concludes bluntly that "public opinion does not exist," and that polls construct a fictitious public mind to serve the symbolic ends of the powers that be. While broad claims such as these serve to clarify the points of contention, they are somewhat less helpful in advancing the debate about polls into more fruitful territory. Opinion surveys might produce some negative consequences for democracy, but that should not prevent us from exploring whether there are better techniques

---

[4] For some exceptions to the tendency for scholars to divide themselves on the question of whether polls are generally good (e.g., P. E. Converse 1987; Converse 1996; Jacobs and Shapiro 2000; Page and Shapiro 1992; Verba 1996; Warren 2001) or bad for democracy (Bourdieu 1979; Ginsberg 1986; Herbst 1993; Rogers 1949; Weissberg 2002a; Wheeler 1976), see Geer 1996; Price and Neijens 1997; Yankelovich 1991.

of polling or more appropriate roles for surveys to fill. Opinion surveys might provide some benefits to democracy, but that should not distract us from the potential for surveys to undermine government responsiveness and confound the workings of Leviathan.

In light of the uses to which opinion polls are routinely put in modern democracies, this book explores two critical areas of concern. First, do citizens have enough knowledge about the political world to regularly formulate policy preferences that are consistent with their needs, wants, and values? And second, is the quality of political representation provided by opinion surveys adequate for the uses to which they are put in democratic politics? One aim of the book is to put the power of aggregation to the test, first by providing a comprehensive assessment of the information-pooling properties of collective opinion (Chapter 2), and then by examining whether the opinions expressed in sample surveys possess the critical characteristics necessary for collective rationality to work (Chapter 3). Another goal is to clarify how the low levels and uneven social distribution of political knowledge affect the quality of representation afforded by collective preferences (Chapters 4–6). By demonstrating how information effects can influence the usefulness of survey results in democratic politics, this book also seeks to chart a middle course between the champions and skeptics of the polling enterprise by detailing how the use of surveys to represent the voice of the people can be inherently problematic while at the same time acknowledging the potential for this unique medium of citizen communication to enhance the practice of democracy (Chapter 7 and 8).

As other observers of this debate have pointed out (Jacobs and Shapiro 2000; Kuklinski and Quirk 2001; Price and Neijens 1997; Yankelovich 1991), what is needed to move the discussion forward are clear normative standards for assessing the usefulness of surveyed opinion as an input to democratic governance. Toward this end, this book examines the quality of political representation provided by surveys. It does so through a statistical analysis of representation in surveys where quality is analyzed from the standpoint of two foundational concepts in democratic theory: the degree to which surveys regard and promote the political equality of all individuals in a population, and the likelihood that surveys represent the political interests of all individuals in a population.

The following chapters suggest that sometimes collective preferences seem to represent something like the will of the people, but frequently they do not. Sometimes they rigidly enforce political equality in the expression of political viewpoints, but often they do not. In the final analysis, the primary culprit is not any inherent shortcoming in the methods of survey research. Rather, it is the limited degree of knowledge held by ordinary citizens about public affairs and the tendency for some kinds of people to be better informed than others.

POLITICAL KNOWLEDGE AND PUBLIC OPINION

One long-standing concern about the usefulness and validity of survey data as an input to the political process arose from the finding that Americans habitually ignore the world of public affairs (Almond 1950; Berelson, Lazarsfeld, and McPhee 1954; Campbell, Converse et al. 1960; Converse 1964; Key 1961; Patterson 1980). The following pages present a brief review of this controversy as well as the reasons why many scholars are less concerned today about the public's knowledge of politics than they were a decade ago.

Overall Levels of Political Knowledge Are Low

Survey after survey has shown that citizens are often at a loss to relate basic facts about the players, issues, and rules of the game that structure American political life (Bennett 1988; Berelson, Lazarsfeld, and McPhee 1954; Converse 1964, 1970; Delli Carpini and Keeter 1996; Neuman 1986; Page and Shapiro 1992; Popkin and Dimock 1999; Price 1999; Smith 1989). For example, the 1992 American National Election Studies included a wide array of questions designed to measure the public's knowledge of politics. The ability of respondents to answer these questions correctly is, to put it mildly, underwhelming (for similar results from other years, see Appendix A). Table 1.1 shows that while nearly 9 in 10 respondents were able to identify Dan Quayle as the vice president of the United States (up from 74% in 1989), only a quarter could identify Tom Foley as Speaker of the House. Just 6 in 10 were able to say that the president nominates federal judges and that the Supreme Court, rather than Congress or the president, decides the constitutionality of laws. While 57% of respondents could identify the Republican Party as being more conservative than the Democratic Party, only about half could say that the Republican Party favored reducing government services and increasing defense spending more than the Democratic Party. Flipping a coin would have produced comparable results. The public hardly fared better when identifying important policy positions staked out by the candidates. Fewer than two-thirds of respondents were able to locate George Bush

TABLE 1.1. *Low levels of knowledge about politics*

	% Correct among All Respondents	Average% Correct among Highest Knowledge Quartile	Average% Correct among Lowest Knowledge Quartile
More conservative party	57.0	93.4	13.1
Office held by Quayle	87.6	99.7	58.2
Office held by Rehnquist	8.4	26.6	0.0
Office held by Yeltsin	44.8	79.9	8.0
Office held by Foley	25.7	61.9	1.3
Which branch decides constitutionality of laws	57.6	94.4	19.1
Which branch nominates federal judges	57.9	90.7	15.0
Majority party in the House	59.2	94.8	12.2
Majority party in the Senate	51.0	85.8	9.7
Relative ideological location of:			
Republicans/Democrats	58.6	96.3	12.0
Bush/Clinton	63.3	97.5	17.9
Relative position of:			
Parties on government services	53.9	94.8	15.2
Bush/Clinton on government services	49.7	93.1	9.7
Parties on defense spending	51.6	90.1	12.2
Bush/Clinton on defense spending	50.9	88.2	12.9
Parties on job assurance	57.8	92.8	7.2
Bush/Clinton on job assurance	51.5	93.3	11.6
Bush/Clinton on abortion	58.9	90.7	17.1

Source: 1992 American National Election Studies.

to the ideological right of Bill Clinton on a scale ranging from strongly conservative to strongly liberal. Even on a contested and highly salient issue such as abortion rights, only 59% of respondents were able to say that Bill Clinton was relatively more prochoice than George Bush.

Philip Converse observes that "the two simplest truths I know about the distribution of political information in modern electorates are that the mean is low and the variance high" (Converse 1990: 372). Just how high is made clear when we add up the number of correct answers to these questions and divide respondents into knowledge quartiles. While people in the highest knowledge quartile averaged 15.6 correct answers out of 18 possible, those in the lowest averaged only 2.5 correct answers. Among this lowest quartile, slightly more than half of respondents could identify the vice president when presented with his name and only about 1 in 10 were able to place the Republicans to the ideological right of the Democrats. If ignorance is bliss, then the pursuit of happiness seems alive and well in American society.

Similar findings in several early and influential studies pointed to the conclusion that while the mass public's knowledge deficit could produce important social benefits (Moore and Tumin 1949), its views on political affairs were fickle and not to be trusted (Almond 1950; Berelson, Lazarsfeld, and McPhee 1954; Converse 1964, 1970). These findings forced opinion scholars to come to grips with a paradox between the knowledgeable and astute public apparently presumed by democratic theory and the frequently inattentive and ill-informed[5] public revealed in opinion surveys (Berelson, Lazarsfeld, and McPhee 1954; Neuman 1986). Most opinion scholars today consider this paradox resolved for two reasons. First, as mentioned earlier, it is thought that the process of statistical aggregation can create collective public opinion that is meaningful even when many respondents provide answers that are ill-informed, ambivalent, uncertain, or even arbitrary (Converse 1990; Erikson, MacKuen, and Stimson 2002; Erikson, Wright, and McIver 1993; Feld and Grofman 1988; Grofman and Owen 1986b; Kinder and Herzog 1993; MacKuen, Erikson, and Stimson 1992; Miller 1996; Page and Shapiro 1992, 1993, 1999; Seeley 2001; Stimson 1990, 1991; Wittman 1989, 1995; although see Althaus 1998, 2001; Bartels 1996; Delli Carpini and Keeter 1996; Duch, Palmer, and Anderson 2000).[6] When aggregated, this argument goes, the more or less random responses from ill-informed or unopinionated respondents should tend to cancel each other out, leaving the nonrandom views of informed and opinionated respondents reflected in collective opinion. The related argument from Condorcet's jury theorem reaches similar conclusions (Condorcet 1785; Grofman and Owen 1986b; Ladha 1992; Miller 1986; although see Austen-Smith and Banks 1996).

---

[5] Throughout this study I use the term *ill informed* to refer to people who are either misinformed (Kuklinski, Quirk et al. 2000) or who have low levels of general knowledge about politics. *Well-informed* people are those who have relatively high levels of the kinds of political knowledge discussed here. My use of these terms is in a relative rather than absolute sense; ill-informed people are less knowledgeable than well-informed people, but these terms do not connote any precise degree of difference.

[6] For recent reviews of the debate surrounding this claim, see Grofman and Withers 1993; Kinder 1998; Luskin 2002; Somin 1998.

In the view of these perspectives, it is the aggregation process itself that generates meaningful public opinion.

Second, recent studies influenced by developments in social psychology have shown that although most people are ill informed about public affairs, they are nevertheless able to form opinions consistent with their predispositions by basing preferences on heuristic shortcuts – interpretive schema or cues from political elites – in place of factual knowledge (Carmines and Kuklinski 1990; Gigerenzer and Selten 2001; Gigerenzer, Todd, and Group 1999; Graber 1988; Iyengar 1990; Lupia 1994; Lupia and McCubbins 1998; McKelvey and Ordeshook 1990; Mondak 1993a, 1993b, 1994a, 1994b; Ottati and Wyer 1990; Popkin 1991, 1993; Schlesinger and Lau 2000; Smith and Squire 1990; Stimson 1990; although see Cutler 2002; Kuklinski and Hurley 1994; Kuklinski and Quirk 2000; Lau and Redlawsk 2001; Luskin 2002; Nisbett and Ross 1980; Popkin and Dimock 1999; Sniderman 2000; Sniderman, Brody, and Tetlock 1991). From this perspective, the public's low levels of information may not be a significant problem since many citizens apparently can compensate for their lack of knowledge with information shortcuts.

Further support for these two views comes from experimental studies suggesting that the common methods used to measure information about politics may actually test recall ability rather than knowledge-in-use. Arising from research on "impression-driven" or "on-line" information processing, this view suggests that many people process information at the time they are exposed to it, update their opinions based on the new information, and then quickly forget the information itself while retaining the updated summary judgment (Hastie and Park 1986; Lodge and McGraw 1995; Lodge, McGraw, and Stroh 1989; Lodge, Steenbergen, and Brau 1995; more generally, see Nisbett and Wilson 1977). Thus people may express preferences that are informed despite being unable to recall the actual information used to shape their preferences. From this perspective, the public's apparently low levels of political knowledge are a red herring. Citizens may be much more informed than they appear on knowledge tests.

Each of these "revisionist" perspectives discounts the importance of factual political knowledge to the quality of survey results and election returns. Not that any of the defenders of these perspectives suggest that such knowledge is irrelevant. It is merely, in their view, that individuals and groups may be able to compensate for these low levels of knowledge in ways that help them arrive at opinions similar to those they might give if they were better informed. Yet the weight of evidence in support of these claims is quite modest. A number of studies have detailed how people *can* use on-line processing and various information shortcuts to make up for a lack of hard knowledge. But their conclusions have tended to rely almost exclusively on experimental data covering a small number of issues at particular points in time. There is surprisingly little evidence to support the notion that large numbers of people in fact *do* use these shortcuts effectively, on a regular basis, and across a wide range of issues. There is even less evidence that shortcutting strategies help people to express opinions similar to those they would give if they were better informed about politics (see Lau and Redlawsk 2001). More glaring is the lack of evidence bearing on the collective rationality hypothesis. While this idea has been subject to a great deal of conjecture, only a few studies have attempted to test this hypothesis on survey data, with mixed results (Althaus 1998, 2001; Bartels 1996; Duch, Palmer, and Anderson 2000; Feld and Grofman 1988; Miller 1996). Aside from these studies and from formal work on Condorcet's jury theorem (e.g., Grofman and Owen 1986a; Ladha 1992; Miller 1986), the hypothesis that simple aggregation can redeem an ill-informed public never has been tested systematically with empirical data.

Not only is there little systematic evidence to show that low levels of political knowledge are relatively benign to democratic processes, but these revisionist perspectives tend to overlook an important fact: low information levels are only half the problem. Just as important is the observation that some kinds of people tend to be better informed than others.

Political Knowledge Is Distributed Unevenly

It is no surprise why so many are so in the dark about public affairs. For most of us, the time and effort it takes to become informed outweighs any likely benefit we might gain from the exercise (Downs 1957; Popkin 1991). I can cast my vote based on careful consideration of the issues, or on party ties, or on the toothiest smile, and my choice will almost never affect the outcome of the election any differently than if I hadn't bothered to vote at all. If I read the *New York Times* faithfully, and understand the federal budget process, and hold opinions about the Portuguese revolution and the Agricultural Trade Act of 1978, but do not have special access to my representative's full attention, my knowledge gains me little unless it impresses my friends. On top of that, acquiring this knowledge costs me plenty, in lost opportunities to pursue other goals and in lost resources of time and money that could have been put to more rewarding uses. Given that few people have time or money to squander, most of us find that these high opportunity costs make it irrational to become informed on matters that may be important to the larger society but remain tangential to everyday living.

Yet some people are better informed than others despite the costs involved. Much of the variation in knowledge levels can be traced back to individual differences in motivation, ability, and opportunity (Bennett 1995a; Delli Carpini and Keeter 1996; Luskin 1990; Marcus, Neuman, and MacKuen 2000; Neuman 1986). Motivation to become informed is influenced by such things as a person's interest in politics, sense of civic duty, and anxiety about the future. A person's ability to process political knowledge is enhanced by years of formal education and by routine exposure to news of the day. Opportunities to become informed vary with mobilization efforts by political parties, a person's geographical location relative to nearby media markets, as well as on the content and breadth of available news coverage. Because motivation, ability, and opportunity are distributed unevenly in society, some people come to be more knowledgeable about politics than others.

The extent of these differences is made clear when the demographic characteristics of the most knowledgeable survey respondents are compared with the characteristics of all respondents taken together (Table 1.2).[7] If political knowledge were evenly distributed throughout a population, then the highest knowledge quartile should contain roughly the same percentage of each demographic group as is found in the population as a whole. The actual distribution tells quite a different story.

Knowledge of politics tends to be concentrated among those who are politically and socially advantaged. College graduates make up nearly 25% of total survey respondents in the National Election Studies (column 1) but 55% of the most knowledgeable ones (column 2), a difference of 31 percentage points (column 3). In other words, there are 2.25 times as many college-educated respondents in the ranks of the well informed than

---

[7] The knowledge index for the 1992 American National Election Studies was formed by summing the number of correct responses to the questions in Table 1.1, along with the interviewer's subjective rating of the respondent's level of knowledge. A similar set of questions was used to form political knowledge indices for the 1988 and 1996 American National Election Studies (ANESs). Respondents from the 1988, 1992, and 1996 ANESs were grouped into information quartiles based on their knowledge scores and then pooled into a common data set. See Appendix A for more information on these indices.

TABLE 1.2. *The social distribution of political knowledge*

	(1) % of All Respondents	(2) % of Highest Knowledge Quartile	(3) (2) – (1)	(4) (2) ÷ (1)
Educational attainment				
College degree	24.5	55.2	+30.7	2.25
High school diploma	57.5	42.3	−15.2	.74
Less than H.S. diploma	18.1	2.5	−15.6	.14
Income				
Top quartile	26.8	43.2	+16.4	1.61
Upper middle quartile	24.7	30.8	+6.1	1.25
Lower middle quartile	23.7	19.3	−4.4	.81
Bottom quartile	24.8	10.3	−14.5	.42
Occupation				
Executive/Professional	20.8	41.4	+20.6	1.99
Technical/Sales	9.1	12.0	+2.9	1.32
Clerical	9.7	7.4	−2.3	.76
Retired	16.1	11.9	−4.2	.74
Homemaker	9.3	4.7	−4.6	.51
Other occupation	34.9	22.6	−12.3	.65
Party identification				
Republican (inc. leaners)	39.1	50.8	+11.7	1.30
Independent	11.4	5.2	−6.2	.46
Democrat (inc. leaners)	49.4	43.9	−5.5	.89
Age				
17–34	30.7	25.2	−5.5	.82
35–54	37.9	48.8	+10.9	1.29
55 and older	31.4	25.9	−5.5	.82
Unmarried	44.6	36.3	−8.3	.81
Renter	35.3	28.4	−6.9	.80
Financially worse off	30.7	27.5	−3.2	.90
Parent of minor child	35.8	35.6	−0.2	.99
Union household	17.6	16.9	−0.7	.96
Black	12.1	4.6	−7.5	.38
Female	55.1	36.3	−18.8	.66
Region				
West	19.4	26.8	+7.4	1.38
East	17.4	19.1	+1.7	1.10
Midwest	27.4	25.6	−1.8	.93
South	35.8	28.6	−7.2	.80
Locality				
Urban	39.1	43.8	+4.7	1.12
Suburban	32.7	36.5	+3.8	1.12
Rural	28.2	19.8	−8.4	.70

Note: The pooled data contain a total of 5,564 respondents, and the highest knowledge quartile in these pooled data contains 1,412 respondents.

Source: Pooled data from the 1988, 1992 and 1996 American National Election Studies.

there are in the general population (column 4).[8] By contrast, respondents with less than a high school diploma constitute nearly a fifth of respondents overall but just one-fortieth of the most knowledgeable respondents, leaving them with 14% of the numbers they would have in the highest knowledge quartile if political information were distributed evenly across society. In the same way, the most informed quartile of survey respondents is disproportionately affluent, with less than a third of respondents in the top knowledge quartile coming from the lowest two income quartiles, and disproportionately from high status occupations, with executives and professionals comprising 41% of the most knowledgeable respondents but only 21% of the general population.

Political knowledge also tends to be distributed unevenly among groups with distinctive and potentially competing political interests. Although a plurality of the general population aligns itself with the Democratic Party, Republican identifiers constitute a majority of the most knowledgeable respondents, and only half as many self-declared independents are found in the ranks of the well informed as in the ranks of all survey respondents taken together. Likewise, relative to the general population, the most knowledgeable citizens are disproportionately white,[9] male, middle-aged,[10] and married. The ranks of the well informed also overrepresent urban and suburban residents relative to their rural counterparts, and people from western and eastern states relative to those from midwestern and southern states. The only demographic characteristics in Table 1.2 that are represented among the politically knowledgeable at roughly the same levels as in the general population are parental status, current financial status, and union affiliation.

KNOWLEDGE AND POLITICAL REPRESENTATION

It is the central argument of this study that these group differences in knowledge, along with the public's rather modest average level of political

---

[8] This table reproduces the format developed by Wolfinger and Rosenstone (1980) to describe demographic differences between the general population and voters in presidential elections.

[9] While this conclusion holds for national issues, the reverse seems to be true in the case of local political issues, where African Americans tend to be more knowledgeable than whites (Delli Carpini and Keeter 1996: Chapter 4).

[10] Using a more sophisticated data set, Delli Carpini and Keeter (1996) found a linear association between age and knowledge: the older people were, the more informed they tended to be.

information, can cause significant distortions in the quality of representation provided by collective preferences. When survey researchers and
pollsters think about representation problems in opinion surveys, they
tend to focus on how well a sample represents significant characteristics
of a population. Two problems in particular have drawn the attention
of survey researchers: sampling error and nonresponse error. Sampling
error can occur when the selection procedure for drawing a sample of
respondents unintentionally biases the characteristics of the sample. For
instance, since the 6% to 10% of American adults who lack telephone
service tend to be young, poor, and members of minority groups, samples
drawn using random-digit-dialing techniques will tend to underrepresent
these groups (Groves 1989; Schuman and Presser 1981). Nonresponse error can occur when certain kinds of respondents refuse to be interviewed,
fail to complete their interviews, or are never contacted in the first place.
This sort of error causes the General Social Surveys and National Election
Studies to overrepresent older people, poor people, and African Americans (Brehm 1993). To the extent that sampling and nonresponse errors
can be minimized or corrected, surveys are often considered to be representative. Indeed, a perfectly random sample is customarily thought of as
the defining quality of a representative survey.

   This custom is misleading and wrong. Although survey researchers
have developed sophisticated methods to deal with sampling and nonresponse error, they have given almost no attention to other aspects of
representation in opinion surveys. The demographic correspondence between a population and a sample is only one facet of representation. Just
as important is the demographic correspondence between a population
and the members of the sample who actually give opinions. It is also worth
wondering how accurately the opinions registered in surveys represent the
interests of opinion givers. Some people may tend to give opinions that,
for various reasons, are inconsistent with their needs, wants, and values. If
this is the case, then some interests may be better represented than others
in opinion surveys.[11]

   The single most important influence on these other aspects of representation is political knowledge. Following Delli Carpini and Keeter, I use

---

[11] Of course, many interests won't be represented in surveys because relevant questions or
response options are never posed to survey participants (Bourdieu 1979; Ginsberg 1986;
Lipari 2001). The decision to allow citizens to express opinions on some questions rather
than others is itself an important form of political power (Bachrach and Baratz 1962)
rarely considered in the survey research literature. For a compelling discussion of these
issues, see Lewis 2001.

the term *political knowledge* to refer to "the range of factual information about politics that is stored in long-term memory" (Delli Carpini and Keeter 1996: 10).[12] There are obviously other ways of thinking about information that is relevant to political life – such as what people actually do know about politics[13] – but this definition seems a reasonable place to start. People who can recall this sort of "textbook" knowledge are likely to have a good grasp of other kinds of information relevant to politics. Although there is some support for the "issue publics" hypothesis (Almond 1950; Converse 1964; see Iyengar 1986, 1990; Krosnick 1998; Krosnick, Berent, and Boniger 1994; Neuman 1998), which suggests that people may be highly informed about the few issues that are important to them and ignorant about others, researchers tend to conclude that people are generalists rather than specialists when it comes to knowledge about politics (Delli Carpini and Keeter 1996; Fiske, Lau, and Smith 1990; Neuman 1986; Price and Zaller 1993; Zaller 1985). As a consequence, even though the sorts of knowledge questions shown in Table 1.1 may seem rather limited in scope, an index made up of these questions provides an accurate estimate of media use and thus of exposure to a broader range of political information (Delli Carpini and Keeter 1996; Price and Zaller 1993; Zaller 1992a). More important, recent work by Michael Delli Carpini and Scott Keeter (1996) shows that this sort of political knowledge is a vital resource for developing, expressing, and acting on political opinions. Simple bits of factual information about the parties and players in politics, the rules of the political game, and the issue positions taken by various actors help to orient people in the world of politics. They are also crucial in helping people arrive at opinions that conform to their political predispositions and are internally consistent with other opinions. So despite the optimistic assessments of those who champion the presumed benefits of information shortcuts and collective rationality, there is good reason to doubt that the public's low levels of knowledge are as innocuous as they are sometimes made to appear.

[12] In this study I use *political knowledge* interchangeably with *political information*, although the latter term can also refer to factual information that has yet to be received and translated into knowledge. My use of these terms is synonymous with what other scholars have labeled political awareness (Zaller 1992a) and political sophistication (Luskin 1987). While these various terms are sometimes used in ways that assume fine differences in meaning, they are all based on roughly similar measures and are interpreted here as referring to essentially the same thing.

[13] This definition of political knowledge is common to "constructionist" approaches that seek to understand why people happen to know what they know about politics. For examples of this approach, see Neuman, Just, and Crigler 1992 and Bennett 1993.

The mass public's low levels of political knowledge and the differences in knowledge levels among groups composing the mass public have two consequences for the quality of political representation in opinion surveys. The first comes from the finding that people who are knowledgeable about politics tend to give opinions more frequently than those who know little about the political world (Althaus 1996; Faulkenberry and Mason 1978; Krosnick and Milburn 1990; Zaller 1991). This means that the social distribution of political knowledge affects which voices get represented in the ranks of opinion givers. Survey results tend to underrepresent the voices of the poor, the young, women, and African Americans because these people tend to be ill informed about politics (Althaus 1996; Bishop, Tuchfarber, and Oldendick 1986; Francis and Busch 1975; Krosnick and Milburn 1990). A second consequence follows the observation that people who are well informed about politics are better able to form opinions consistent with their political predispositions (Delli Carpini and Keeter 1996; Galston 2001; Nie, Junn, and Stehlik-Barry 1996; Zaller 1992a). This means that opinion givers who are ill informed may be mistaken about their needs, wants, and values: they might give opinions that they wouldn't give if they were more knowledgeable about politics. Thus besides affecting the representation of voices, information asymmetries may also influence the representation of interests.

These two dynamics can create information effects in measures of public opinion. An *information effect* is a bias in the shape of collective opinion caused by the low levels and uneven social distribution of political knowledge in a population. While others have examined the individual-level effects of political knowledge on response stability (e.g., Delli Carpini and Keeter 1996; Feldman 1989, following Converse 1964) and the role of political knowledge as a link between political predispositions and policy or voting preferences (e.g., Bartels 1988; Bennett 1995a; Delli Carpini and Keeter 1996; Zaller 1992a), the focus here is more narrowly on the macro-level impact of these effects on collective opinions. By *collective opinion* I mean any aggregation of individual preferences, including (but not limited to) survey results and election returns. Information effects can be estimated for individuals, but their political impact is realized only when individual preferences are aggregated together. By *bias* I mean a distortion away from what collective opinion might look like if all relevant groups in a population were equally and optimally well informed about politics.[14]

---

[14] Two points are worth noting about this standard. While it is possible to directly observe differences between groups, there is obviously no absolute standard of what constitutes

Information effects can influence the direction of majority opinion as well as the extent of support for a policy. Sometimes majority opinions are driven by the opinions of a small number of respondents who have intense and unified views, as will be shown in the case of African Americans on affirmative action. Sometimes majority opinions are driven by the most knowledgeable opinion givers, as will be shown to occur on certain foreign policy issues. But frequently the people's collective preferences are determined by the one-sided opinions of those who are least informed about politics. Not only is majority opinion often an unreliable indicator of a population's informed preferences, but there is no way to evaluate the quality of a collective opinion just by looking at its marginal percentages. Sometimes strong and stable majority opinion is an artifact of information asymmetries; at other times it is an accurate reflection of informed preferences.

Distortions in collective preferences produced by information effects have profound consequences for democratic politics. There is a strong link between the preferences of those citizens who are active in politics – whether through voting, letter writing, or other forms of participation – and the policies that local, state, and federal governments come to adopt (Erikson, Wright, and McIver 1993; Hill and Hinton-Andersson 1995; Hill and Leighley 1992; Mebane 1994; Verba and Nie 1972: 309–18). For example, when citizens from lower socioeconomic classes are mobilized to vote, the addition of their political views to the electoral field causes elected officials to revise their own policy preferences (Hill and Hinton-Andersson 1995; Hill and Leighley 1992). While the centrality of elections to democratic representation is obvious, there is a sizable body of evidence suggesting that elections are not the only important channel for political representation. Political elites are also responsive to changes in public opinion between elections. When public opinion shifts in significant

optimal levels of political knowledge. Thus the direction of any population's average knowledge level (high or low) is relative to whatever scale of political knowledge happens to be used. This is not to say that all scales are equally valid: the public could achieve uniformly high or abysmally low scores on scales that have poor discriminating power. It is nevertheless important to recognize that this definition of information effects refers to an absolute standard of political knowledge that remains unspecified. The second point to mention about this standard is that the opinions of knowledgeable people are sometimes more susceptible to media effects such as priming than are the opinions of people who are relatively less informed about politics (Krosnick and Brannon 1993). This implies that, under certain circumstances, high levels of knowledge may be less normatively desirable than low levels. My presumption is that under optimal conditions, more knowledge about politics is better than less.

ways, it is often the case that government policy soon follows (Bartels 1991; Erikson, MacKuen, and Stimson 2002; Hartley and Russett 1992; Monroe 1979; Page and Shapiro 1983; Stimson 1991; Stimson, MacKuen, and Erikson 1995; Weissberg 1976; Wlezien 1995a, 1995b; although see Jacobs and Shapiro 2000; Monroe 1998). The complication introduced by information effects is that political leaders may sometimes be reacting to an "airy nothing," as Shakespeare put it. Despite all appearances to the contrary, subsequent chapters will show that strong and stable majority opinion can often be a figment of the public's misinformation.

This is especially troubling since public opinion surveys are widely thought to provide the most representative gauge of the public's pulse. It is well known that the interest group system gives a disproportionate voice to moneyed interests (Schattschneider 1960), and that the views of party elites are more extreme than those of their rank-and-file members (Baer and Bositis 1988; Miller 1988; Miller and Jennings 1987). Likewise, people from higher socioeconomic status groups tend to dominate the various alternative channels of public opinion – such as contacting public officials, volunteering for campaigns, and contributing to political causes – because these participatory activities require resources such as time, skills, and money that other people lack. Since they have different personal experiences and priorities for government action than members of lower socioeconomic groups, this inequality distorts the content of communications from the public to political leaders (Verba, Schlozman et al. 1993; Verba, Schlozman, and Brady 1995; see also Mansbridge 1999b). The special value of the sample survey as a channel for political communication comes from its reputation as a representative measure of public opinion. I will argue in the following chapters that opinion surveys may not always be as representative as commonly thought. The presence of information effects suggests the need to reconsider how opinion surveys are used in the political process.

Chapter 2 explores what Philip Converse has called the "hidden power," "magic," and "miracle" of aggregation. A common hypothesis in the collective opinion literature is that the process of aggregating large numbers of opinions together – in sample surveys or in election returns – should reveal the preferences of the informed public even when the opinions expressed by most individuals are unstable, impulsive, or randomly determined. In this chapter I argue that collective rationality models contain several conceptual problems that limit their applicability to survey results. I then provide a systematic test of collective rationality in action. Using a computer simulation of nearly 28,000 unique opinion distributions, this chapter shows that marginal percentages and the relative location of means and majority preferences provide unreliable estimates of informed opinion when the size and shape of the "noise" distribution are unknown. The purported information-pooling benefits of aggregation turn out to be more illusion than magic.

Not only are collective rationality mechanisms less useful for pooling information than is commonly supposed, but Chapter 3 shows that the assumptions of these models are usually violated in the opinion distributions of actual survey respondents. In contrast to collective rationality models described by Converse and by Page and Shapiro, this chapter develops a theory of information effects in collective preferences that explains why these violations occur. I suggest that the social distribution of political knowledge can undermine political equality in opinion surveys because the ill informed are more likely than the well informed to remove themselves from the pool of opinion givers by answering "don't know" or "no opinion." In this way, the uneven social distribution of political knowledge tends to deplete the ranks of less knowledgeable demographic groups from among the voices making up a collective preference. Yet while the opinions of well-informed respondents tend to be overrepresented numerically in collective preferences, the opinions of ill-informed respondents are often amplified in collective preferences because they tend to be more like-minded in their answers than knowledgeable respondents.

Chapter 4 outlines a method for estimating the impact of information effects on collective preferences. Using data from the 1988, 1992, and 1996 American National Election Studies, I model what collective preferences might look like if all respondents were as well informed about politics as the most knowledgeable ones. Statistically correcting for information asymmetries reveals that the mass public's low levels and uneven social distribution of political knowledge often cause surveys to misrepresent the mix of viewpoints in a society, with simulations suggesting that one in four collective opinions might have a different preference order if all citizens were equally well informed about politics. But it is not merely that the public's low levels of political knowledge sometimes cause collective preferences to differ from the preferences that a hypothetical "fully informed" public might have. More important, the direction and magnitude of these distortions fall into predictable patterns: collective opinions consistently appear more progressive on some issues and more conservative on others than they might if all citizens were equally well informed about politics. After controlling for information effects, collective opinion tends to become less approving of presidents and Congress, more dovish and interventionist on foreign policy, less conservative on social, environmental, and equal rights issues, and more conservative on morality issues and questions about the proper limits of government activity.

Chapter 5 explores why information effects should be large in some kinds of collective preferences and small in others. Focusing first on the relative impact of the two mechanisms expected to produce information effects, this chapter reveals that correcting for asymmetries in political knowledge has its nearly full effect through changing the views of opinion givers who were poorly informed. Demographic misrepresentation in the pool of opinion givers appears at first glance to make little difference to the size of information effects. Further inspection reveals that higher levels of inequality occur in questions that arc more cognitively demanding, and this confounding relationship makes it difficult to specify the unique impact of demographic misrepresentation on the size of information effects. The chapter goes on to examine why ill-informed people often hold different opinions than the people who share their demographic characteristics but are better informed about politics. The consistent patterns of ideological bias in collective preferences are neither artifacts of the survey instrument nor of the particular topics posed to respondents. Instead, differences in opinion between ill- and well-informed citizens are shown to arise from both social and psychological factors that influence how people establish and update their political preferences.

Chapter 6 continues this analysis into the causes of information effects by considering how gaps between surveyed and fully informed collective preferences evolve over time. Using time series data to assess the development of information effects in selected questions over an 18-year period from 1980 to 1998, this chapter demonstrates how psychological and social processes influence the evolution of information effects. Information effects tend to grow smaller when the political environment motivates citizens to process information more systematically, although many of these changes turn out to be short-lived. Information effects also tend to grow larger over time among questions with higher levels of inequality among respondents, confirming that the degree of demographic correspondence between opinion givers and the population they are supposed to represent is an important indicator of representational quality. Controlling for information effects in collective preferences can also clarify future trends in surveyed opinion. Gaps between the collective opinions of ill- and well-informed citizens tend to persist over time, but once these groups arrive at a similar mix of opinions, information effects usually remain small. As a result, simulated measures of fully informed opinion are quite accurate when predicting that collective policy preferences will remain stable. They are decidedly less accurate in predicting when surveyed opinion will change in significant ways. This analysis shows that while statistical simulations of fully informed opinions can shed important light on the relationship between political knowledge and opinions, they do not represent the latent political interests of a population any better than the expressed views of that population.

Chapter 7 places the empirical findings of previous chapters into a normative context by exploring how information effects complicate the use of opinion surveys in political decision making. I argue that survey results are often less representative than they appear, primarily because survey researchers tend to conceive of representation in relatively narrow terms as the degree of demographic correspondence between a sample and the population from which it is drawn. This view neglects the uneven rates of "don't know" and "no opinion" responses that cause opinion givers to misrepresent the demographic characteristics of the sample itself, as well as the tendency for ill-informed opinion to exert a disproportionate influence on the shape of collective preferences. I argue that collective preferences are least troubled by representation problems when two conditions are met: when the survey respondents who give substantive opinions have essentially the same mix of relevant demographic characteristics as the population they are supposed to represent, and when the people who are especially knowledgeable about politics give essentially the same mix of opinions as the people who appear to know little about public affairs. The absence of information effects, however, should not be taken as a sign of enlightened preferences. Instead, the absence of information effects confirms only that a collective preference provides good information about what the people want, rightly or wrongly.

The systematic biases in the public's voice as communicated by opinion polls call into question many of the ways opinion data are used by political leaders, journalists, and the mass public. Yet because the failings of surveys are detectable and to some extent predictable, it may be possible to take these problems into account in a way that suggests useful roles for collective preferences in democratic politics. Chapter 8 summarizes the main findings of this study and outlines some new directions for inquiry on the political uses of opinion surveys in democratic politics.

PART I

ILLUSIONS OF AGGREGATION

2

The Power of Noise

Individual voters today seem unable to satisfy the requirements for a democratic system of government outlined by political theorists. But the *system of democracy* does meet certain requirements for a going political organization. The individual members may not meet all the standards, but the whole nevertheless survives and grows. This suggests that where the classic theory is defective is in its concentration on the *individual citizen*. What are undervalued are certain collective properties that reside in the electorate as a whole and in the political and social system in which it functions.

– Berelson, Lazarsfeld, and McPhee (1954: 312)

We concur with the usual empirical assessments regarding the bleak distribution of political awareness, interest, and sophistication within the American electorate. This book offers no claim that individual citizens are any more capable than the experts say to be the case. Our claim instead is that macro-level dynamics are driven by an electorate where, in the aggregate, the more politically capable citizens possess dominant influence.... A major part of the argument is the reduction of noise due to the "miracle" of aggregation.

– Erikson, MacKuen, and Stimson (2002: 428–9)

In almost every political theory there is an inscrutable element which in the heyday of that theory goes unexamined. Behind the appearances there is a Fate, there are Guardian Spirits, or Mandates to a Chosen People, a Divine Monarchy, a Vice-Regent of Heaven, or a Class of the Better Born. The more obvious angels, demons, and kings are gone out of democratic thinking, but the need for believing that there are reserve powers of guidance persists.

– Walter Lippmann (1922: 162)

This chapter explores what some have called the "hidden power," "magic," and "miracle" of aggregation (Converse 1990). A common hypothesis in the collective opinion literature is that the process of aggregating large numbers of opinions together – in sample surveys, for instance, or in election returns – should reveal the preferences of the informed public even when the opinions expressed by most individuals are unstable, impulsive, or randomly determined. Converse (1990) describes this process using the metaphor of signal and noise: when aggregated, the more or less random responses from ill-informed respondents (the "noise") should tend to cancel each other out, leaving the nonrandom views of informed respondents (the "signal") reflected in the means of collective opinion distributions. Page and Shapiro (1992) provide an alternative account of what they call "collective rationality." They argue that respondents' opinions have both random and nonrandom components, and when aggregated, the underlying central tendencies of these opinions become reflected in the aggregate parameters – means, marginal percentages, and majority and plurality choices – of collective opinions.

Although the idea of collective rationality is widely acknowledged in the collective opinion literature, very little is known for certain about the information-pooling properties of collective opinion. This chapter presents a comprehensive effort to test the information-pooling qualities of collective opinion. After a brief history of the "collective rationality" concept, I explore two critical assumptions underlying the notion of collective rationality: that errors are random, and that random error cancels out when aggregated. The remaining part of the chapter examines what signals look like when refracted through aggregate parameters, the conditions required for collective opinions to accurately convey signals from informed opinion givers, and how accurately means, plurality choices, and marginal percentages reflect the direction and shape of informed opinion.

THE ENDURING CONCEPT OF COLLECTIVE RATIONALITY

The most significant work to date on the nature and dynamics of collective opinion has been Page and Shapiro's (1992) *Rational Public*, which presents a detailed exposition on why collective policy preferences should have emergent properties that make up for the deficiencies of individual opinion givers. Framed as a response to the charge that public opinion is capricious, fickle, and volatile, Page and Shapiro studied all available national surveys of policy preferences administered from the late 1930s to 1990 and found, contrary to earlier studies based on individual-level data, that "the American public, as a collectivity, holds a number of real, stable, and sensible opinions about public policy and that these opinions develop and change in a reasonable fashion, responding to changing circumstances and to new information" (1). Summarizing their findings, the authors write:

> While we grant the rational ignorance of most individuals, and the possibility that their policy preferences are shallow and unstable, we maintain that public opinion as a *collective* phenomenon is nonetheless stable (though not immovable), meaningful, and indeed rational in a higher, if somewhat looser, sense; it is able to make distinctions; it is organized in coherent patterns; it is reasonable, based on the best available information; and it is adaptive to new information or changed circumstances, responding in similar ways to similar stimuli. Moreover, while we grant that recorded responses of individuals to survey questions vary from one interview to another, we maintain that surveys accurately measure this stable, meaningful, and reasonable collective public opinion. (14, emphasis in original)

While Page and Shapiro's book was conceived as a direct response to the Michigan School's portrayal of an ignorant and capricious public (Berelson, Lazarsfeld, and McPhee 1954; Campbell, Converse et al. 1960; Converse 1964, 1970), in a larger sense it is one of the most recent (and most empirical) contributions to a venerable dialogue about the extent to which ordinary citizens can and should play a direct role in democratic governance. Arising among the ancient Greeks as a controversy about the wisdom of collective decisions, this debate simmered through the centuries until it was actively resurrected among the political philosophers of 18th-century France and England (Habermas 1989; Palmer 1936). It has since taken on new importance with the rise of quantitative methods to measure the public's opinions, beginning with the advent of straw polls in the early 19th century and becoming more pressing with the rise of modern sample surveys in the late 1930s (Herbst 1993). While today the importance of popular elections is a settled issue, the controversy over the wisdom of collective preferences is far from resolved.

The argument against giving the opinions of the mass public undue credulity, familiar to all students of public opinion, was aptly stated by Alexander Hamilton: "The voice of the people has been said to be the voice of God: and however generally this maxim has been quoted and believed, it is not true in fact. The people are turbulent and changing;

they seldom judge or determine right."[1] The earliest recorded version of this argument is found in the writings of Plato (Minar 1960), and it is no coincidence that Walter Lippmann opened his famous (1922) critique of populism by quoting Plato's analogy of the cave. Empirical support for the apparent capriciousness of public opinion was provided by several early and influential studies in the political science discipline (Almond 1950; Berelson, Lazarsfeld, and McPhee 1954; Campbell, Converse et al. 1960; Converse 1964). These studies revealed that only a small proportion of the general public was attentive to or knowledgeable about politics. The verdict on surveys as an enlightened source of guidance seemed clear: by diluting the preferences of the informed in a sea of "doorstep opinions," surveys should generally fail to communicate the views of this small but knowledgeable group of citizens (Key 1961: 536). Summarizing this perspective, Benjamin Ginsberg (1986: 65) writes that "Polls, in effect, submerge individuals with strongly held views in a more apathetic mass public.... Indeed, relative to ... other modes of public expression, polled opinion could be characterized as a collective statement of permission."

Yet along with these criticisms has come a persistent and spirited defense of the wisdom and even beneficence of collective opinion. Aristotle was the first to make this claim,[2] but the modern defense of collective preferences was founded by a pair of 18th-century French contemporaries: Jean-Jacques Rousseau, the man credited by some with coining the term "public opinion" (Noelle-Neumann 1984: 80), and Marie Jean Antoine Nicolas Caritat, Marquis de Condorcet, a mathematician with a well-exercised talent for designing political and juridical institutions.

Rousseau held that citizens were guided in their preferences by two conflicting sources of direction: the general will, which he identifies as the will people would have if the common good was their only desire, and the

---

[1] From *Selected Writings and Speeches of Alexander Hamilton*, Morton J. Frish, ed. Washington D.C.: American Enterprise Institute, 1985: 108. This quote was brought to the author's attention by Robert Eisinger.

[2] Aristotle writes: "It is possible that the many, no one of whom taken singly is a good man, may yet taken all together be better than the few, not individually but collectively, in the same way that a feast to which all contribute is better than one given at one man's expense. For where there are many people, each has some share of goodness and intelligence, and when these are brought together, they become as it were one multiple man with many pairs of feet and hands and many minds. So too in regard to character and the powers of perception. That is why the general public is a better judge of works of music and poetry; some judge some parts, some others, but their joint pronouncement is a verdict upon the whole. And it is this assembling in one what was before separate that gives the good man his superiority over any individual man from the masses." From *The Politics*, T. A. Sinclair, ed. and trans. Baltimore, MD: Penguin Books, 1962, p. 123.

individual wills that people actually have, in which considerations of the public good are mixed with self-interested concerns. Rousseau argued that while the general will was obscured in any one individual, it could nevertheless emerge from the aggregation of particular wills:

> There is often a great deal of difference between the will of all and the general will; the latter considers only the common interest, while the former takes private interest into account, and is no more than a sum of particular wills: but take away from these same wills the pluses and minuses that cancel one another, and the general will remains as the sum of the differences. If, when the people, being furnished with adequate information, held its deliberations, the citizens had no communication one with another, the collective total of the small differences would always give the general will, and the decision would always be good. ([1762] 1973: 202)

Rousseau's novel argument[3] seems to have been the first detailed exposition of what Page and Shapiro would later call "collective rationality."

Rousseau's optimistic view of mass opinion was not shared by Condorcet, who as a republican believed that the only proper way for the unenlightened masses to express themselves politically was through the election of representatives from among the nation's elite (Cranston 1991). Yet Condorcet was able to prove using the new science of probabilities that, under certain conditions, majority decisions of groups could be more enlightened than any individual's choice. Condorcet supplied a mathematical proof in his *Essai sur l'application de l'analyse à la probabilité des décisions rendues à la pluralité des voix* (1785, significant portions of which have been excerpted in McLean and Urken 1995) that showed how, in the case of dichotomous choices where one option was correct and the other incorrect, juries made up of three or more members, each having a probability greater than chance of choosing the correct alternative, were more likely to make the right decision than any single member choosing alone. Moreover, as the number of jurors increased, majority decisions became nearly infallible. (For a brief introduction to the mathematics of the Condorcet Jury Theorem, see Grofman and Owen 1986a; for a detailed analysis, see Black 1958: 159–180). Condorcet shows that the theorem holds if four assumptions are satisfied: (1) the decision must be between two options, (2) one of the options must be correct and the other incorrect, (3) votes must not be correlated with one another, and (4) each voter must have a probability greater than .5 of making the right

---

[3] Found mainly in Book II, Chapter 3, and Book IV, Chapters 1, 2, and 3 of the *Social Contract*.

choice. Condorcet believed that his jury theorem could be extended to decisions made by assemblies of any sort, and part of his *Essai* is devoted to a probabilistic theory of enlightened elections with multiple candidates.[4]

Condorcet's insight was quickly lost on his peers, however, in part because his *Essai* dealt with topics far beyond the scope of 18th-century probability theory and in part because "even allowing for the difficulty of the thought, his exposition is unduly obscure" (Black 1958: 162). His ideas would be rediscovered several times over the next two centuries, but Condorcet's claim that his jury theorem could be applied to decisions outside the realm of law fell on critical ears. One problem with the theorem was its premise that all voters must have a greater than chance probability of making the right choice: certainly some people might have strong prior beliefs that would give them less than an even chance of choosing correctly. A second difficulty was in assuming perfect independence of votes, which makes no allowance for shared worldviews or common sources of information. The main problem, however, was with the assumption that the outcomes of political decisions could be properly considered right or wrong. In legal matters, the correctness of a decision is defined by the agreed-upon letter of the law. "But in the case of elections," writes Duncan Black, "no such test is conceivable; and the phrase 'the probability of the correctness of a voter's opinion' seems to be without definite meaning." Black concludes: "Truly this is an unpromising start" (1958: 163).

Nevertheless, several recent advances have established the applicability of the jury theorem, under certain limited conditions, to political decision making. Owen, Grofman, and Feld (reported in Grofman and Owen 1986a) have shown that each voter can have any probability of choosing the correct alternative so long as the average probability of voters is greater than chance. And a further extension by Krishna Ladha (1992) shows that the theorem can hold even when votes are highly correlated, so long as the range of views expressed through voting is evenly balanced and especially broad. Black's assessment of Condorcet's jury theorem has been challenged by Nicholas Miller (1986), who found that the theorem holds if people vote in their own correct interests rather than in the interests of society as a whole. While this represents an important development for the applicability of the jury theorem to political decision making, Miller points out that the "correctness" of majority decisions is highly dependent on a fairly even distribution of information among voters. Referring to

---

[4] For a comparison of Condorcet's theorem with Rousseau's concept of the general will, see Grofman and Feld 1988 and Estlund et al. 1989.

the tendency for majority decisions to become infallible as the number of voters increases, Miller concludes that "this optimistic conclusion cannot be sustained if there are substantial inequalities (of a particular sort) in the distribution of information in the electorate" (191). As will be demonstrated throughout this book, such inequalities should be the norm among citizens of any large-scale democratic society.

Another thread of the collective rationality thesis started with the migration of the rational actor paradigm from economics to political science, which led to renewed interest in the dynamics of collective decision making and several important studies on the logic of collective behavior (see, e.g., Arrow 1963; Black 1958; Downs 1957; Olson 1965). But although it had been suggested early on in the political science literature that collective decisions had emergent properties that made up for individual deficiencies (see, e.g., Berelson, Lazarsfeld, and McPhee 1954: 312), little attention was given in the empirical literature to studying the nature of collective policy preferences until Page and Shapiro began their line of research in the early 1980s.

ASSUMPTIONS ABOUT THE AGGREGATION PROCESS IN COLLECTIVE RATIONALITY MODELS

Two models of collective rationality have been proposed in recent years to support arguments that aggregate measures of opinion can be meaningful even when the individual opinions that make them up are not. Philip Converse (1990) bases his on the "black-and-white" model of the survey response introduced in an early and influential paper (Converse 1964). Because it posits only two kinds of opinion givers – those reporting real and stable attitudes, and those reporting completely random nonattitudes – this model has come under criticism for failing to fit empirical data. Nevertheless, the statistical logic behind this model of collective rationality is quite similar to that used in Page and Shapiro's (1992) more widely noted model.

Instead of suggesting that people's opinions are either perfectly random or perfectly meaningful, Page and Shapiro posit that each respondent's opinions have both random and nonrandom components, and when aggregated, the underlying central tendencies of these opinions become reflected in the aggregate parameters of collective opinions. Although Page and Shapiro claim that their collective rationality argument does "not depend upon any particular theory of exactly how individuals form and change opinions, process knowledge, or give survey responses" (17), the rationale underlying their argument rests on a set of assumptions derived from measurement-error theories of the survey response. Measurement-error models of the survey response (e.g., Achen 1975; Heise 1969; Lord and Novick 1968; Wiley and Wiley 1970; for reviews of this literature, see Converse 2000; Feldman 1989, 1995; Groves 1989) conceive of the survey response as consisting largely of two components, true attitudes and random error. These models take the general form:

Surveyed Opinion = True Attitude + Random Error

In this perspective, all respondents are presumed to possess "true" attitudes about the objects of survey questions. These true attitudes are defined as the central tendency of a group's opinion at one point in time or an individual's opinion measured independently at several points across time. Measurement-error theories are based on the idea that the process of measuring opinions in surveys introduces errors into the reports that people give about their true attitudes. These errors may be produced by, among other things, poorly worded questions, guessing, indifference, conflicting values, or when low levels of knowledge or sophistication lead respondents to see greater ambiguity in a question. The important point is that measurement-error models define these errors as perfectly random and independent from the errors of other respondents. When errors are defined in this way, the process of aggregating opinions together should cause an error in one direction to offset an error in the other. Because perfectly random errors are thought to cancel out when aggregated, the unobserved true attitudes can be measured as the central tendencies of collective opinions (Lord and Novick 1968) and should also be reflected in other aggregate parameters of collective preferences (Erikson, MacKuen, and Stimson 2002; MacKuen, Erikson, and Stimson 1992; Page and Shapiro 1992; Russett 1990; Stimson 1990, 1991). These assumptions about the nature of survey responses form the theoretical core of Page and Shapiro's collective rationality argument:

So long as the measurement errors in different individuals' opinions are not systematically related to each other, . . . a survey can produce a highly reliable estimate of collective preferences, as of the moment of interviewing. And so long as the bits of knowledge temporarily affecting different individuals at the time of their interviews are also random, then these will also be reliable estimates of stable *long-term collective preferences*: collective preferences as defined in terms of the individual's long-term preferences. (1992: 20–1, emphasis in original)

This approach suggests that errors or noise in the aggregate responses of a population should cause the distribution of surveyed opinions to be relatively more dispersed across response options than is the underlying distribution of true attitudes. The larger the error component in surveyed opinions, the flatter the distribution of opinions. And because the opinions of politically knowledgeable respondents tend to have less measurement error than those of ill-informed respondents (Alwin and Krosnick 1991; Delli Carpini and Keeter 1996; Feldman 1989), it follows that ill-informed opinions should tend collectively to disperse more evenly across response options than well-informed opinions. In this way, the differences between the opinion distributions of well- and ill-informed people predicted by the Page and Shapiro model are quite similar to those predicted by the Converse model. In both cases, ill-informed opinion should tend to have more variance than well-informed opinion.

The validity of the collective rationality hypothesis therefore depends on the extent to which the opinion distributions of ill- and well-informed people conform to either the black-and-white model of political attitudes or the logic of measurement-error theories. Given the serious challenge to the former view by information processing models of the survey response (Chaiken 1980; Chaiken, Liberman, and Eagly 1989; Fiske and Taylor 1991; McGuire 1969; Petty and Cacioppo 1986; Zaller 1992a; Zaller and Feldman 1992) and to the latter view by subsequent empirical work that has modified the assumptions of classical test score theory (Converse 2000; Feldman 1995; Hill and Kriesi 2001), the validity of collective rationality models seems increasingly open to question. In particular, two assumptions about the nature of aggregate noise are critical to both versions of the collective rationality hypothesis: individual "errors" or deviations from "true" attitudes are randomly distributed, and if random, these errors cancel out when aggregated together. As some readers may recognize, these assumptions are germane not only to work by Converse and by Page and Shapiro, but also to several other important studies of collective opinion (see, e.g., the discussions of collective rationality in Erikson, MacKuen, and Stimson 2002; Erikson, Wright, and McIver 1993: Chapter 10; MacKuen, Erikson, and Stimson 1992; Russett 1990: 87–118; Stimson 1990, 1991: 125). Because these two assumptions are central to much of the literature on collective opinion, it is important to examine the implications of each in turn.

Error is Random

Individual opinions on some issues can be so unstable over time that they appear to be completely random "nonattitudes" (Converse 1964; Converse 2000; Markus and Converse 1979; Neuman 1986; although see Achen 1975; Nie and Andersen 1974). The theoretical implications of this finding are explored in classical test score theory, where individual deviations from true scores are by definition randomly distributed around a mean of zero (Lord and Novick 1968).[5] But use of the term *random* is misleading because it obscures at least three different kinds of distributions: those in which noise is distributed with equal probability into each response category, those in which noise takes an approximately normal distribution, and those in which noise skews to one side or another of the range of responses. All three can be generated by random processes, but Converse's model presumes the first, Page and Shapiro's the second, and neither accounts for the third. As will be detailed later, the shape of the noise distribution is an important determinant of how well aggregate parameters reflect the "signal" distribution of informed responses.

The equiprobable or uniform random noise distribution is most closely associated with Converse's (1970) black-and-white model of opinionation. But positing that noise distributes evenly across the range of response categories entails the improbable assumption that for people who lack "real" or stable opinions, responses at the extreme ends of a scale are just as likely as middling ones. The survey research literature indicates to the contrary that respondents lacking well-developed or intense opinions who nonetheless answer survey questions tend to choose middle responses (Asher 1988: 21–37; Presser and Schuman 1980), suggesting that noise might frequently conform to an approximately normal distribution.

While uniform random noise has desirable properties from a collective rationality standpoint, there is good reason to expect that the distribution of noise often will be biased in one direction or another (Bartels 1996; Kuklinski and Quirk 2000).[6] This sort of bias can result from question

---

[5] "True scores" in classical test score theory refer to constructs that are neither directly observable nor directly measurable (Feldman 1995). Lord and Novick (1968: 30) define true score as "the expected observed score with respect to the propensity distribution of a given person on a given measurement," where the propensity distribution is "a cumulative distribution function defined over repeated statistically independent measurements on the same person." True score is seen in classical test score theory as a constant that is revealed (1) through repeated measurements of individuals and (2) through the central tendencies of populations. By this definition, error is simply the difference between an individual's true score and observed score. Since the true score is by definition a constant, the error score must be randomly distributed with a mean of zero. The terms *ability* and *standard error of measurement* identify the complementary concepts for true score and error score in item response theory, as detailed in Lord 1980. For an overview of the concept of error in psychometric theories, see Groves 1989: 18–27.

[6] Such bias has been demonstrated in split-ballot surveys using variously worded filter questions designed to reduce noise (Bishop, Oldendick, and Tuchfarber 1983); in retrospective

wording and question order effects, response set bias, and social desirability effects (Schuman and Presser 1981). It can result from the information processing styles used by respondents who are unable or disinclined to answer survey questions (Krosnick 1991; Krosnick and Fabrigar forthcoming). Another source of bias comes from modern society's reliance on mass media communications, which can inundate large portions of the public with common flows of information that may be used to formulate responses to opinion questions (see Converse 1962; Zaller 1992a). Economic pressures that force rival news organizations to produce similar coverage – often written directly from wire service reports or influenced by the standards of pack journalism – create a homogenous news environment that makes this more likely than ever before. These various sources of bias can produce correlated errors in individual opinions, which when aggregated, produce skewed noise distributions.

Together, these considerations suggest that error or noise in respondent opinions will often be systematic rather than random, and that even random error is more likely to be either normally distributed or skewed to one side of the range of responses than to be uniformly distributed. Moreover, because this error can be influenced by so many factors, the shape of the noise distribution for any given survey measure can be in practice nearly impossible to predict.

Error Cancels Out

The claim that random errors cancel out when aggregated together is made so often and so casually in electoral and collective opinion studies that it is considered almost a truism of the field. As Page and Shapiro (1992: 15) put it: "The simple process of adding together or averaging many individuals' survey responses...tends to cancel out the distorting

economic evaluations, where people with high levels of exposure to media and campaign communications tend to share biased perceptions of national economic conditions (Hetherington 1996); and in prospective economic evaluations, where voters tend to expect an optimistic economic future regardless of the actual state of the economy (Haller and Norpoth 1994). Levels of political knowledge can also bias judgments about the economy (Duch, Palmer, and Anderson 2000; Krause and Granato 1998; Weatherford 1983). For example, many knowledgeable voters seem more willing than ill-informed voters to discount factual knowledge about the economy in favor of inaccurate projections of future economic performance based on political cues and personal experience (Conover, Feldman, and Knight 1987). However, lack of knowledge about economic indicators tends to bias retrospective evaluations of economic performance, which come to be based more on recent personal experiences than current economic conditions (Conover, Feldman, and Knight 1986).

effects of random errors in the measurement of individuals' opinions. Similarly, statistical aggregation tends to eliminate the effects of real but effectively random (i.e., offsetting) opinion changes by individuals." But the statement "random error cancels out" hides a grave semantic problem, for the claim is at once both true and false.

The paradox of this statement is not apparent even when it is expressed more formally: saying that random error cancels out is the same as saying that the expected value of the random error term is equal to zero. But the paradox is there nonetheless: while it is true that the expected value of the sum of random errors is zero, this is not because these errors "cancel" out. The critical point obscured by common usage of the phrase is that in order for random errors to sum to zero, they must be scaled in standardized form with a mean of zero. *While the expected value of standardized random error is zero, the expected value of unstandardized random error is equal to the midpoint of the range of possible responses.* In other words, random errors do tend to counteract one another, but this tendency does not cause these errors to simply dry up and blow away. Random errors do not, strictly speaking, cancel out; they tend merely to balance out.[7] This means that even when these random errors are perfectly offsetting, they continue to influence the location of means and modes as well as the shape of marginal percentages. Because of this, as a general rule, the greater the proportion of noise to signal in an aggregation, the more the aggregate parameters should reflect the distribution of noise rather than of signal. The implications of this statement are examined in depth later; the important point for the moment is that even uniform random errors influence the shape of collective opinion.

THE INFORMATION-POOLING PROPERTIES
OF COLLECTIVE PREFERENCES

If errors aren't always perfectly random, and if even perfectly random errors fail to cancel out, how then can we account for the consistent patterns in collective opinion that point to the presence of emergent rationality? Simulation data presented later suggest that three factors can contribute to the *appearance* of collective rationality: the shape of the noise distribution, the ratio of signal to noise, and the number of categories into which

---

[7] In using *balance* rather than *cancel*, I am simply trading one word for another to describe (somewhat more accurately, I hope) a fundamental and well-established concept stemming from the laws of large numbers.

responses are aggregated. In light of these factors, the first two of which are generally unknown to pollsters and survey researchers, the usefulness of public opinion surveys as a line of communication from the informed public to political leaders depends on whether it is possible to identify a signal in the midst of noise.

Means, modes, and marginal percentages are the parameters most commonly used to describe aggregate opinion distributions.[8] Signals conveyed through aggregate means play an important role in work by Converse (1990), Stimson (1990, 1991), and Erikson, MacKuen, and Stimson (2002), and means are the primary measures of population true scores in classical test score theory. Converse and Stimson each suggest that the mean of the collective opinion should generally indicate the direction of the signal mean – that is, the mean of informed opinions only – relative to the midpoint of the response range. While the use of means to describe aggregate distributions is confined mostly to academic studies and professional reports, the use of modes – the category containing the largest number of respondents, whether a plurality or majority – is especially widespread in journalistic coverage of opinion surveys as well as in the interpretation of election outcomes. The third commonly used parameter to describe aggregations is the frequency distribution of responses, sometimes called marginal percentages or marginal frequencies. Incremental, over-time changes in marginal percentages are used in several important studies of collective opinion as the primary indicators of change in unobserved signal distributions (Page and Shapiro 1992; Russett 1990; Stimson 1991). Marginal percentages are also the most common parameters used to describe opinion data in news stories.

Determining which of the three parameters might best communicate informed signals requires a test of their relative accuracy. Page and Shapiro's model is typical of measurement error approaches that draw from classical test score theory, but I employ Converse's formulation to examine the collective rationality hypothesis because it is the only one that can be straightforwardly subjected to an empirical test. The difficulty in developing a test for the Page and Shapiro model is that the tenets of measurement-error models are entirely axiomatic. In their classic book on the subject, Lord and Novick are quite clear on this point (1968: pp. 24–30, *passim*).

---

[8] One statistic of potential interest, the median, is ignored here. While the importance of the median has a long history in the rational choice literature, its many undesirable statistical properties ensure that it is rarely used in empirical studies of public opinion (for a brief discussion of these properties, see Kirk 1990: 97). As the median is also rarely used in mass media descriptions of attitudinal data, it is excluded from this study.

Although Lord and Novick suggest some hypothetical ways that classical test score theory could be tested (such as repeated tests of the same measure to groups of amnesiacs), they conclude that there is no practical test of classical test score theory as commonly formulated: one merely accepts its assumptions and uses it, or one does not. Because the Page and Shapiro model is inherently axiomatic, it admits of no straightforward empirical test that could determine whether its tale of signal and noise actually obtains in any given collective preference.

Measurement-error approaches to collective information pooling suffer from a more profound limitation: some of the most important distributional assumptions inferred from classical test score theory fail to obtain when one moves from theoretical distributions to actual measures of opinion which rely on a fixed number of response categories. A key premise that seems to be overlooked by many who infer information-pooling properties from classical test score theory is that its theoretical model is built on hypothetical continua of responses either with no clear boundaries on either end (Achen 1975; Lord and Novick 1968) or with far more response options than are commonly presented to survey respondents, as in the hundred alternatives in Page and Shapiro's hypothetical MX missile example (Page and Shapiro 1992: 19–23; Shapiro 1998). In these unique contexts, the effect of error in responses is to flatten out the collective distribution without disturbing the mean of the distribution. An overlooked point is that variance can increase in these contexts without influencing the location of the mean precisely because the opinion distributions are essentially unbounded. Lack of attention to this point can distract one from appreciating that because actual measures of opinion are not infinite continua, "real world" distributions tend not to behave in this way. In the case of dichotomous questions, for example, the mean is inseparably related to the variance of the distribution: change the variance, and the mean will follow.[9]

This problem should occur to greater or lesser extent in most collective opinions.[10] For instance, the American National Election Study lacks an

---

[9] This is the essence of the well-known pq formula for variance in a dichotomous variable, where the mean is the proportion of cases with a value of 1 and the variance is the product of the proportions of the two categories. In such a case the mean fails to be an accurate indicator of group true scores.

[10] More precisely, the problem should occur in any response distribution with (1) more than two response categories but less than an infinite number of categories, (2) an asymmetrical distribution of true scores around the midpoint of the range of response categories, and (3) at least one response in either of the boundary categories.

eighth category to the right of "extremely conservative" in its seven-point ideology scale. If a person's true score is at the "extremely conservative" point, the person's error score can only push her opinion toward the center of the response categories. We might assume that those whose error should push responses into the hypothetical eighth category would continue to register an opinion in category seven. But this means that error is no longer distributed symmetrically among such respondents, and it implies that error will shift the mean of the collective distribution if the true scores of enough respondents are in one or both of these outer categories.

This problem can be illustrated by revisiting the MX missile example used by Page and Shapiro to illustrate the principles of collective rationality. Suppose a hypothetical survey asks whether respondents believe the United States should increase, decrease, or keep the current number of MX missiles to provide effective nuclear deterrence. In the first case, shown in Table 2.1, the population's true scores are distributed symmetrically, with 20% desiring fewer, 60% wanting the current number, and 20% preferring more. For simplicity's sake we can suppose that error causes a person's opinion to randomly distribute as much as one category to the left or right of her true score, and that the three possible outcomes of adding errors to true scores – shifting one category to the right of the true score, remaining in the same category as the true score, and shifting one category to the left of the true score – occur with equal probability. Applying this error formula to the symmetrical true score distribution, we find that of the 60% with true scores in the middle category, the introduction of error causes a third to shift to the fewer category, a third to remain in the middle category, and a third to shift to the more category. The same occurs for the true scores in the more and fewer categories, except that the boundaries imposed by the available response options limit

TABLE 2.1. *Adding error scores to true scores shifts both marginal percentages and means*

	How Many MX Missiles?				
	Fewer	Same	More	Total	Mean
Symmetrical true scores					
True scores only	20%	60	20	100%	2.00
True + error scores	33%	33	33	100%	2.00
Skewed true scores					
True scores only	60%	20	20	100%	1.60
True + error scores	47%	33	20	100%	1.73

sideways shifting to one direction only. As shown in Table 2.1, the resulting collective opinion that includes both true and error scores has equal percentages of respondents preferring fewer, the same, and more missiles. There is no indication from these noisy percentages that the status quo has a strong majority preference in true scores – it would appear to the contrary that the population has no collective preference at all. Lacking additional categories to represent more extreme alternatives – eliminating the nuclear arsenal altogether on the one end and perhaps building more missiles while at the same time funding a missile defense shield on the other – the responses that should be shifted to those categories remain submerged within the more and fewer categories, and this boundedness is entirely responsible for obscuring the signal in a wash of noise.

This first example further shows that adding error scores to true scores can shift marginal percentages quite dramatically without influencing the mean, which remains unchanged as measurement-error models predict it should. But the second example in Table 2.1 shows that adding random noise can also shift the mean when the distribution of true scores is not perfectly symmetrical around the midpoint of response categories. Looking at the changes in both means and marginal percentages, it does not seem at all clear in this second example that the mean of the collective opinion reflects the distribution of true scores much better than the marginals, which flatten considerably once error is added to the mix. Since we have the true scores laid out before us in this table, we might decide that the marginal percentages do a better job of telling us the true score distribution in the second example, but that the mean is the better choice in the first. However, if all we had to go on were the noisy means and marginal percentages, there would be no obvious way to tell which provided the clearer signal from unobserved true scores.

This example demonstrates that the expectations from classical test score theory, which undergird Page and Shapiro's collective rationality argument, can fail to obtain in the expected way. The problem comes from conceiving of classical test score theory in terms of a hypothetical continuum of responses, which obscures how parts of its logic might not translate to real-world distributions. Given these difficulties with measurement-error models of collective information pooling (for other problems with these models, see Luskin 1987: 871–3), a test of the Converse version of the collective rationality model seems more promising.

Besides being better suited to empirical analysis, the black-and-white model proposes a straightforward test: How accurately do means, modes, and marginal percentages from collective opinions (which include both signal and noise responses) represent their counterparts from the underlying distribution of "signal" responses provided by well-informed citizens? This test is, of course, a narrow one, and its applicability to real-world situations is limited by the strict assumptions regarding the utter randomness of nonattitudes, which even Converse himself describes as representing the extreme rather than typical case (Converse 2000). But the unrealistically stark dichotomy built into the Converse model – individual responses are either fully noise, in which case they distribute randomly across response options, or fully signal, in which case they do not – also makes it a best-case test for the purported benefits of aggregation. If collective rationality doesn't emerge under these favorable conditions, it is unlikely to surface at all. And even a limited test can shed important light on the information-pooling properties of collective opinion that have so far eluded empirical investigation: we can deduce that skewed noise will produce bias in collective preferences, but no one yet knows how large or important this bias might be.

Simulating the Aggregation Process in Collective Opinion

One reason why basic questions like these remain unanswered is that the limitations of available survey data make almost impossible a systematic study of the information-pooling properties of collective opinion. It is still relatively uncommon in opinion surveys for information about policy issues to be measured along with policy preferences. Even when political information is measured, knowledge tests can give a misleading impression of informed opinion. Most measures used to test political knowledge fail to account for people who use cognitive shortcuts when answering preference questions. These respondents can appear ill informed in knowledge tests even though they answer questions as if they were well informed. Knowledge tests discriminate on a relative rather than absolute basis: respondents may appear informed because they pass a knowledge test, but the test may be too easy, too hard, or even irrelevant for a given issue. Simple knowledge measures may fail to tap important dimensions of political information. The most common kind of information test – consisting of a single filter or trailer question for each issue – is highly susceptible to guessing. Multi-item information scales overcome this problem, but they can tie up valuable survey time and are rarely used. Alternative estimates of political knowledge such as item nonresponse rates are also unreliable. Levels of "don't know" and "no opinion" responses fluctuate not only because of the salience of an issue but also because of different probing methods used by survey organizations (Converse 1976; Smith 1978).[11]

Given the limitations of available survey data, simulated measures of opinion provide a more promising start for systematically analyzing the information-pooling capabilities of collective opinion. A wide variety of opinion distributions can be generated where the characteristics of signal and noise responses are determined in advance, thus allowing for a pure test of information effects without the need to correct for the vagaries of knowledge tests and the misleading or poor-quality information used by respondents to formulate opinions. And by providing absolute control over treatment conditions and test cases, a computer simulation can be comprehensive enough to suggest general conclusions about the information-pooling properties of collective opinion measures.

I used a computer program to generate a core set of more than a thousand unique signal distributions (details on the simulation procedure are found in Appendix B). To ensure comparability across conditions, the same set of signal distributions was used in each condition to test the effects of being aggregated into fewer response categories, different types of noise, and varying ratios of signal to noise. To test the effects of aggregating the same signals into fewer response categories, the set of signal distributions was generated into a six-category response scale that was subsequently collapsed into three- and two-category scales.[12] To test the impact of different types of noise, each of these sets of signal distributions was then immersed into three noise patterns – uniformly distributed across all response options, normally distributed around the midpoint of the response options, and skewed to one side of the response options. Finally, within each category and noise condition, each set of signal distributions was mixed with noise responses at three noise-to-signal ratios: 25% noise to 75% signal, even amounts of signal and noise, and 75%

---

[11] The quality of information available to the public is also a critical determinant of what constitutes informed opinion (Page and Shapiro 1992). On some issues, media organizations and politicians might convey misleading information that is picked up by attentive publics and used to construct survey responses. Responses based on available information may look quite different from responses based on complete information. While it might be possible theoretically to control for the effects of misleading information (by content-analyzing key sources of news, for example), such an undertaking would be impractical at best.

[12] Six categories were collapsed into a dichotomous scale by treating the first three categories as one option and the second three categories as a second option, and into a three-point scale by treating categories one and two as a first option, three and four as a middle option, and five and six as a third option.

TABLE 2.2. *Average percentage point difference between signal opinions and collective opinions*

Number of Response Categories	Uniform Noise			Normal Noise			Skewed Noise		
	25%	50%	75%	25%	50%	75%	25%	50%	75%
Two	5	9	14	5	9	14	6	11	16
Three	6	13	19	7	15	22	8	16	24
Six	10	20	30	12	24	36	12	25	37

Note: Each cell shows the mean difference among 1,036 unique distributions of collective opinion.

noise to 25% signal. In the end, Tables 2.2–2.4 each summarize findings from nearly 28,000 unique collective opinions: a thousand signal distributions times three levels of aggregation times three noise patterns times three levels of signal to noise.[13]

Marginal Percentages as Estimates of Informed Opinion

Table 2.2 shows the average percentage point difference between the marginals of the signal distribution and those of the collective distribution (which merely adds noise to the signal) in each of the test conditions. A score of 0 would indicate a perfect match between the two sets of marginal percentages, whereas a score of 100 would indicate that the signal and collective marginals are mirror opposites.[14] For example, the upper left cell of the table shows that when (1) noise is distributed uniformly across all response options, (2) noise responses make up 25% of total responses, and (3) the survey question has two possible response options, the

---

[13] A more detailed report on the simulation data discussed in the following paragraphs – which includes details on the efficiency and unbiasedness of each aggregate parameter – is available from the author on request.

[14] Since collective marginal percentages are determined in part by signal percentages, a score of 100 is technically impossible in this simulation. The scoring method used here follows the system used by Page and Shapiro (1992). It should be noted, however, that the raw sum of the absolute differences between sets of marginal percentages reaches a maximum of 200 percentage points. For instance, if one distribution is 100% in favor and 0% opposed, whereas a second distribution is 0% in favor and 100% opposed, the sum of their absolute differences is $|100 - 0| + |0 - 100| = 200$. This result holds regardless of the number of categories making up the marginal percentages. While a scale ranging from 0 to 200 would be more precise, dividing the raw value by two makes a more intuitive 100-point scale that compares directly with important empirical work on change in opinion marginals.

average difference between the marginal percentages of the collective opinion and those of the signal distribution is plus or minus 5 percentage points.

The impact of the three types of noise can be judged by comparing the average percentage point difference for any given level of noise and number of categories across each of the three noise conditions. In general, uniform noise produces a smaller distortion in collective marginal percentages than either normal or skewed noise, but the differences between noise conditions are not very substantial. For instance, the largest difference between noise distributions in Table 2.2 is across the six-category, 75% noise condition: uniform noise creates an average difference between signal and collective marginals of 30 percentage points, which is only 6 points less than that for normal noise and 7 points less than that for skewed noise.

Similar to type of noise, changing the number of categories into which opinion data are aggregated has a small but substantive influence on the accuracy of collective marginals. The effect of increasing the number of categories can be seen by comparing differences within a given column in Table 2.2. In the 25% uniform noise condition, for example, aggregating signal distributions into two categories creates an average difference of 5 percentage points between the signal and collective marginals, while aggregating them into six categories creates an average difference of 10 points. These differences reflect a general pattern in Table 2.2: aggregating signal distributions into fewer categories increases the accuracy of marginal percentages as estimates of signal distributions.

Compared with type of noise and number of categories, the ratio of signal to noise is a much more important influence on the accuracy of marginal percentages. Under each of the three types of noise, three columns give the average differences in marginal percentages when noisy respondents make up 25%, 50%, and 75% of the whole. The effect of signal strength can be read by comparing across these three columns within each type of noise. The patterns here are quite clear: as the proportion of noise to signal increases, collective marginals become increasingly less accurate reflections of signal marginals. For example, in the three-category, normal noise condition, there is an average difference of 7 percentage points between the collective and signal marginals when 25% of the collective distribution is made up of "noise" respondents. This average difference climbs to plus or minus 22 points when the noise level reaches 75%. These averages tell only part of the story, however, since the standard deviation for this 22-point average is 11 percentage points, which means that in 19 out of 20 cases the actual difference lies somewhere between 0 and 44 percentage points. In the 20th case, the difference is expected to be greater than 44 points, and the largest observed difference in this cell between collective percentages and signal percentages is 56 points.

These findings reveal that marginal percentages are much less likely to reflect "informed" signals than the collective opinion literature suggests. The worst estimates were made from the six-category, 75% skewed noise condition, in which collective marginal percentages missed the mark by an average of plus or minus 37 points. Even the very best estimates were unimpressive: the marginal percentages in collective opinion from two-category data with 25% uniform or normal noise were off the mark by an average of 5 percentage points in either direction. With a best-case margin of error of plus or minus 5 points, these simulated data suggest that even when approximate signal strengths and noise patterns can be estimated, collective marginal percentages are incapable of attaining the precision imputed to them in the collective opinion literature.

Means as Estimates of Informed Opinion

While the inaccuracy of collective marginal percentages may come as little surprise to some, it also turns out that the mean of the collective opinion distribution performs unevenly as an estimate of the signal mean. The top portion of Table 2.3 reports average differences between the collective and signal means. To make these differences comparable across the two- , three- , and six-category conditions, they were standardized by dividing the values of each difference by the standard deviation of the signal distribution. For example, the cell for the three-category, 75% normal noise condition shows that the mean of the collective opinion tends to lie plus or minus .36 standard deviations from the mean of the signal distribution. While reporting such averages makes for an easier comparison across conditions, it is important to point out that these average differences tell only part of the story: this .36 average difference between means has a standard deviation of .33, which indicates that 19 out of 20 collective means lie somewhere within plus or minus 1.02 standard deviations of the signal mean. The largest observed difference in this condition is 2.81 standard deviations. In addition to standardizing the differences between means, this table also combines the uniform and normal noise conditions since they produce identical results: the mean of both the uniform and normal noise distributions is by definition the midpoint of the response scale.

TABLE 2.3. *Average gaps between the means of signal opinions and collective opinions*

	Uniform or Normal Noise			Skewed Noise		
	25%	50%	75%	25%	50%	75%
Average gap between signal and collective means						
Two response categories	.12	.23	.35	.13	.27	.39
Three response categories	.12	.24	.36	.15	.29	.44
Six response categories	.12	.25	.37	.16	.32	.48
Percentage of cases with signal and collective means on opposite sides of the midpoint						
Two response categories	0	0	0	9	20	49
Three response categories	0	0	0	4	30	49
Six response categories	0	0	0	0	42	50

Note: Each cell in the "average gap" rows contains the average absolute differences between signal means and collective means for 1,036 unique distributions of collective opinion. The size of these gaps is standardized across conditions to represent standard deviations of the signal distribution.

The results in the top portion of Table 2.3 show that collective opinions with fewer response categories tend to have smaller gaps between signal means and collective means, but the impact of reducing the number of response categories is usually quite small. Skewed noise produces larger gaps between signal means and collective means than does uniform or normal noise, and the differences in the gaps produced by each type of noise grow more pronounced at increasingly higher levels of noise to signal. However, as was the case with marginal percentages, the most important influence on the size of differences between collective and signal means is the ratio of noise to signal. To take one example, the six-category, skewed noise condition has an average gap of .16 standard deviations when responses are 25% noise, which triples in size to an average gap of .48 standard deviations in the 75% noise condition. In fact, all of the differences from low to high levels of noise are multiplicative relationships: doubling and tripling the amount of noise doubles and triples the average amount of error in the collective mean.

To be sure, even gross error in estimating the *actual location* of the hidden signal mean can nonetheless infallibly reveal the *relative direction* of that mean from the midpoint of the response scale. Because uniform and normal noise is by definition centered around the midpoint of the response categories, the relative direction of the collective mean (relative to the midpoint) will always reveal the relative direction of the signal mean with perfect accuracy, regardless of how much noise is in the mix (Converse 1990; Erikson, MacKuen, and Stimson 2002; Stimson 1990). However, this relationship holds only for the unlikely cases in which noise is perfectly symmetrical.

When noise is distributed with less than perfect symmetry, the ratio of noise to signal – and to a lesser extent the number of response categories – determines how often collective means will misreport the relative direction of signal means. The lower portion of Table 2.3 shows that incorrect signals are given by the collective mean in up to 9% of cases when noise is set to 25% of responses. At this low level of noise, the location of the collective mean is almost completely determined by the signal mean. But at 50% noise, the collective and signal means are on opposite sides of the midpoint in anywhere from 20 to 42% of cases; and at 75% noise, the collective mean appears on the wrong side with the same probability that it appears on the correct side. At these higher noise-to-signal ratios, the signal mean loses its influence over the position of the collective mean. To properly interpret these numbers, it is important to point out that the maximum possible value in this lower part of the table is 50% of cases.[15] When incorrect signals are given half of the time, collective opinion no longer functions to signal the relative direction of informed opinion. The relative location of the collective mean becomes overdetermined by random responses, and the relative location of the signal mean becomes irrelevant. When noise is skewed, the accuracy of the collective mean as an estimator of the signal mean depends almost entirely on the ratio of signal to noise.

Once the strong distributional assumptions in collective rationality models are relaxed, the collective mean cannot be trusted to reveal either the actual location or the relative direction of the signal mean.

Modes as Estimates of Informed Opinion

The final statistic considered here is the mode of the collective opinion – the response category containing a plurality or majority of responses. Table 2.4 shows that the modal category in a collective opinion is consistent with the signal mode only when noise is uniformly distributed

---

[15] This is because signal means are symmetrically distributed around the midpoint – see the methodology appendix for details.

TABLE 2.4. *Percentage of cases with different signal modes and collective modes*

Number of Response Categories	Uniform Noise			Normal Noise			Skewed Noise		
	25%	50%	75%	25%	50%	75%	25%	50%	75%
Two	0	0	0	0	0	0	10	20	49
Three	0	0	0	7	20	64	5	21	37
Six	0	0	0	4	25	57	5	26	62

Note: Cases in which collective opinions or signal distributions lack modal categories are excluded from this table. Each cell shows the percentage of incorrect modes for 1,036 unique distributions of collective opinion in the two-category condition, 972 distributions in the three-category condition, and between 790 and 894 distributions in the six-category condition.

across all response categories. When noise is normally distributed, the mode of the collective opinion is consistently the same as the signal mode only when there are two response categories. When normal noise is present in three- or six-category data, the accuracy of the collective mode goes down as the percentage of noise goes up. At 75% normal noise, nearly two-thirds of plurality or majority preferences reflect the mode of the noise rather than that of the signal. Skewed noise produces similar results.[16] As noise levels climb above a quarter of responses, the modal category becomes an increasingly unreliable indicator of the signal's preferred response option. The trend is unmistakable: when most individual opinions are mainly noise, most collective preferences are merely noise. If the ratio of noise to signal and the shape of the noise distribution are unknown, as is typically the case, then these findings confirm that the relative position of the collective mode cannot be trusted to reveal the position of the underlying signal mode.

However, further analysis reveals that these inconsistencies are directly related to the percentage of responses in the modal category: the

[16] Notably, when it comes to the accuracy of modal preferences, normal noise throws the collective preference off just as much as skewed noise. The primary difference between the effects of normal and skewed noise is that the latter biases the location of collective modes in the two-category condition, while the former does not. One other notable difference between these two types of noise comes in the three-category, 75% noise conditions, where skewed noise is actually less of a problem than normal noise. The reason is that normal noise in the three-category condition concentrates in the middle category, while the concentration of skewed noise is split between the middle and one of the end categories.

inaccurate signals given by collective opinion within normal and skewed noise conditions almost always occur when the size of the collective mode is relatively small.[17] Without a single exception in 17,280 unique distributions of opinion, any single category of the collective opinion containing more than 60% of responses shared the position of the signal mode, regardless of signal strength, noise pattern, or number of categories in the response scale.[18] Thus, the modal category turns out to have superior information-pooling qualities to means and marginal percentages, but the signal is conveyed by the size of the mode rather than merely by its location.[19]

[17] In these simulation data, the number of response categories determines the threshold at which emergent information-pooling properties appear in collective modes. For example, simple majorities were always perfect indicators of signal modes in the six- and three-category conditions, regardless of noise pattern. With two-category data, however, supermajority preferences were needed to guarantee perfect estimation of the signal mode. The number of response categories also influences both the percentage of distributions that have modes and the relative number of distributions that exhibit majority or supermajority preferences. While between three-quarters and almost 9 in 10 collective distributions have modes when data are aggregated into six response categories, nearly all of the two-category collective distributions have modes. Furthermore, while only 5.7% of all the six-category collective distributions have modes that contain a majority or supermajority of responses, the frequency of large modes increases to 35.7% in the three-category data and 99.6% in the two-category data.

Of the three kinds of treatment conditions, signal strength was the most closely related to the accuracy of collective modes and the presence of majority or supermajority preferences. When 75% of a collective distribution was signal, almost all collective modes, regardless of size or noise condition, shared the same response category as the signal mode. Furthermore, a high proportion of modes at this level of signal strength were majorities or supermajorities. In contrast, reliability plummeted when signal strength dropped to 25%. At this level, collective modes tended to be smaller in size and much less accurate as indicators of signal modes: in the three-category condition, just more than a third of collective modes shared the same category as signal modes.

[18] In the same way, majority preferences always shared the same category as the mode of the signal distribution when noise was normally distributed. When noise was skewed, however, majority preferences were perfect indicators of signal modes only in distributions having three or more categories. In the two-category condition, skewed noise decreased the accuracy of the collective mode as the percentage of noise responses increased: 91% of majority opinions shared the location of signal modes at 25% skewed noise, but only 80% were accurate at 50% skewed noise, and just 51% were accurate at 75% skewed noise.

[19] Majority and supermajority preferences can so accurately reveal the presence of the signal mode because of the way noise is distributed in these simulated measures of opinion. Although the shape of noise is here modeled as being much more variable than is commonly assumed in the collective opinion literature, this simulation shows how robust majority and supermajority preferences can be in the presence of large numbers of ill-informed responses. This is because even when noise responses make up three-fourths of

WHITHER COLLECTIVE RATIONALITY?

This chapter challenges two common premises in the collective opinion literature, that ill-informed responses should distribute evenly across all response categories and that the error represented by these noise responses should cancel out when preferences are aggregated together in sufficient numbers. Because noise is unlikely to distribute uniformly in surveys of political opinion and because noise balances rather than cancels out, many of the information-pooling characteristics attributed to collective opinion fail to materialize. For instance, Converse (1990: 378) writes that "The quickest 'fix' for a poor signal-to-noise ratio is to aggregate your data." This conclusion was found to be incorrect in an extensive simulation of nearly 28,000 unique opinion distributions. Aggregating data can amplify a relatively weak signal, but the biasing influence of noise on aggregate parameters severely restricts the application of this principle, no matter how large the numbers involved. Walter Lippmann (1922: 249) may have been right when he observed that "You cannot take more political wisdom out of human beings than there is in them." Aggregation by itself is no fix.

Relaxing the assumptions of the collective rationality hypothesis severely diminishes the power of aggregate parameters to reflect informed signals. Marginal percentages at best provide blunt estimates of informed opinion and at worst may be less accurate than flipping a coin. The relative location of means and modes can reflect the direction of informed opinion but are easily biased by the distribution of ill-informed responses. When the ratio of signal to noise and the distribution of ill-informed responses are unknown, marginal percentages and the relative location of means and modes cannot be trusted to communicate underlying signals from informed opinion.

In clarifying precisely how much information pooling goes on in simulated measures of collective opinion, these findings help to refine and extend some conclusions about collective rationality even as they challenge

the collective distribution, no single category of the noise distribution contains more than half of total responses. For example, the largest percentage of noise in a single category occurs in the two-category, 75% skewed noise condition, where one category of skewed noise contains 65% of the noise distribution. Multiplying the proportion of noise by the marginal percentage of the two-category noise pattern leaves a noise distribution with 731 ill-informed respondents (48.7% of total responses) in one category and 394 (26.3% of total responses) in the other. Any majority preference therefore must be determined by the distribution of well-informed responses, which make up the remaining 25% of total responses.

others. First, despite the poor performance of these widely used aggregate parameters, supermajority preferences can be perfect indicators of plurality choices made by well-informed respondents. This is so because while marginal percentages, means, and the location of modal categories were all biased by noise in ways unanticipated by the collective rationality literature, supermajority preferences in collective opinions never appeared when the distribution of noise was more concentrated into a single response category than the distribution of signal opinions. Supermajority preferences therefore may be able to help compensate for the mass public's chronic inattention to politics, so long as the assumptions built into these computer-generated data also hold for patterns of signal and noise in surveyed collective opinions.

A similar conclusion has been suggested by Condorcet's jury theorem and its many extensions, which explain the information-pooling qualities of majority decisions in terms of individual probabilities for making correct choices. In contrast, the results presented here suggest that any emergent information-pooling properties of majority decisions are largely determined by the distribution of ill-informed opinion. This analysis confirms that the conclusions of the Condorcet Jury Theorem can be extended in theory to ordinal-level data with majority or supermajority preferences (Miller 1996). But it also shows that Condorcet's theorem may not apply very well to collective preferences on relatively obscure or highly controversial issues, where noise responses become skewed in some way. When noise was skewed, the accuracy of majority decisions depended on the relative size of the well-informed group providing a signal through collective opinion. This chapter shows that whether aggregation produces collective rationality depends not only on the lopsidedness and skew of the noise distribution relative to the signal distribution, but more importantly on the ratio of noise to signal.

Second, one of the most important pieces of evidence in support of the collective rationality hypothesis is the finding of over-time stability in collective preferences (Page and Shapiro 1992; although see Mayer 1993). Seeking a way to account for this stability, Page and Shapiro suggested the measurement-error model of collective rationality and the Condorcet Jury Theorem as two possible explanations. This chapter reveals that signals are unlikely to be reproduced accurately in collective opinions, especially when relaxing the strict assumption of perfectly offsetting errors. However, my argument thus far has neglected the clear patterns of over-time stability in collective opinion revealed in Page and Shapiro's study. How then can we account for this regularity in collective opinion?

One possibility is that given a moderate to high ratio of noise to signal, nearly all opinion distributions should tend to be fairly stable over time. This should hold regardless of how accurately the collective distribution represents the characteristics of the signal distribution, and it occurs because noise balances rather than cancels out. This perspective turns the collective rationality argument on its head by suggesting that the most stable collective opinions should be those made up of mostly noise. So long as the noise distribution is stable and proportionally large relative to the signal distribution, collective preferences are likely to remain stable even if the signal distribution were to shift over time from one end of the response scale to the other. Contrary to the expectations of the collective rationality literature, this study suggests that the least stable collective opinions should be those made up of mostly signal, if informed people are in fact changing their preferences in response to new information.

A point that may be missed by Page and Shapiro's (1992) readers is that their collective rationality model posits over-time stability as a function of the information environment in which people update their opinions, rather than of the aggregation process itself. Aggregation, in their model, functions primarily to describe how a population's "true" attitudes can be represented in a collective opinion even in the presence of widespread public apathy toward and ignorance about public affairs. In other words, they present the aggregation component of their collective rationality argument as a way to account for over-time stability in surveyed opinion rather than as a reason to expect this stability.[20] However, this chapter shows that when large groups of ill-informed respondents provide consistently random or nonrandom opinions, the opinions of well-informed respondents would have to fluctuate quite drastically to budge the collective preference. Stability over time in collective preferences can just

---

[20] In a similar way, Page and Shapiro (1992) use evidence of parallel publics to support their collective rationality argument even though such movement among subgroup populations is not predicted by the aggregation component of their model. Rather, Page and Shapiro interpret parallel movement in the opinions of subgroup populations as evidence of common interests (294–5), evidence of common ways of receiving and processing knowledge (288), and evidence that individual differences in exposure and acceptance of political knowledge "may not ordinarily play a large part in processes of collective opinion change" (316). More recently, Erikson, MacKuen, and Stimson (2002: 211–9) also find evidence of parallel publics in GSS data on social preferences.

The interested reader should also note that the primary focus of Page and Shapiro's argument is on the dynamics of change in collective opinion rather than the quality of representation afforded by collective opinion. They repeatedly draw attention to problems of elite manipulation that can produce stable but misinformed and therefore poor quality collective opinions (Page and Shapiro 1992; Shapiro 1998).

as properly be taken as a sign of collective ignorance as of collective rationality.[21]

While the simulated opinion distributions used in this study were designed to mimic those found in the empirical world, the validity of conclusions drawn from these data depends entirely on how well they resemble actual patterns in collective opinion. Two assumptions in the model are especially important to the external validity of these findings. First, if the mean of the skewed noise pattern were moved closer to the midpoint of the response scale, the ability of aggregate parameters to estimate informed opinion would improve. Likewise, if noise can be even more skewed than the pattern used in this simulation, then aggregate parameters should be even more biased than those reported here.[22] Second, if fewer than a quarter of respondents were assigned to the signal distribution, the performance of marginal percentages, means, and modes as estimators of informed opinion would decline precipitously. Below some minimum threshold of signal strength, majority and plurality choices should lose their information-pooling qualities, but it is unclear what this implies for generalizing from these simulated data to surveyed collective preferences. As Converse long has pointed out (1964, 2000), his black-and-white model represents the extreme rather than general case. His original analysis determined that the question most affected by nonattitudes (on housing and electrical power) had about 20% signal and 80% noise responses, which corresponds roughly to the noisiest collective opinions considered here.[23] The simulation reported in this chapter was designed merely to test the expectations of collective rationality models.

[21] By no means am I suggesting that aggregation is *necessarily* ineffective at pooling information. This chapter shows to the contrary that under certain conditions, collective opinion does seem to have emergent properties like those described in the collective rationality literature. My point is merely that collective rationality models are no panacea for the public's low levels of political knowledge.

[22] In addition, if the distribution of signal means in the real world is more dispersed than assumed in this simulation (see Appendix B for details), the shape and relative size of noise distributions would have a much more negative impact on the reliability of aggregate parameters than this simulation suggests.

[23] Neuman (1986: Chapter 8) concludes that a "three publics" model seems a better fit than the black-and-white approach, and suggests that around 5% of the mass public is chronically attentive to public affairs, another 20% of the mass public is chronically apathetic, and the remaining three-quarters represent a group that is only occasionally concerned with politics. In this view, the percentage of signal in any question might range from less than 10% to as much as 80% of responses. In contrast, Delli Carpini and Keeter (1996) conclude that most people are moderately informed about politics, which suggests that ratios of noise to signal might tend to be quite low in responses to the typical survey question.

Aside from showing how these expectations often go unmet, this chapter sheds little light on how big a problem this might be in surveyed opinion.

The next chapter explores this question with empirical evidence that clarifies how the dynamics of aggregation work in actual rather than hypothetical survey results. In contrast to the expectations of collective rationality arguments, ill-informed opinion is often highly skewed relative to well-informed opinion. Of greater consequence, people who tend to be knowledgeable about politics also tend to share common demographic characteristics and, potentially, distinctive political interests.

3

Who Speaks for the People?

The power of the aggregation process to gather individually noisy opinions into a coherent and rational collectivity is held by many to be the reason why low knowledge levels should be of little consequence to the proper functioning of democracy and, more narrowly, to the validity of opinion surveys. Yet while the idea of collective rationality is widely acknowledged in the collective opinion literature, the test of this idea provided in Chapter 2 suggests that aggregation alone has rather limited knowledge-pooling properties. Moreover, while much of the recent work on the dynamics of collective opinion has offered descriptive analysis of trends in collective opinion, very little of this macro-level work has explored the micro-level behavior giving rise to collective preferences. In this chapter I develop a model of collective information effects built on micro-level theories of human cognition. I argue that aggregating individual opinions together may often fail to generate collective opinions that are representative of the populations whose views they are supposed to capture. In contrast to collective rationality models of information effects, I propose a theory of collective information effects in which something approximating collective rationality is but one possible outcome of the aggregation process.

Using a wide range of data from the 1988, 1992, and 1996 American National Election Studies, I show that the people who answer survey questions tend to be better educated, more affluent, middle-aged, white, and male than those who are included in the survey sample but fail to answer questions. I argue that this demographic bias among opinion givers is largely due to the link between opinionation and political knowledge: people who are ill-informed tend to give "don't know" and "no opinion" responses more frequently than well-informed respondents. And contrary to the predictions of collective rationality models, the aggregate opinions of ill-informed respondents are usually more one-sided than those of the well informed. Far from appearing "noisy" in the sense of randomly distributed, the opinions of poorly informed respondents tend to be more consistent with one another than are those of well-informed respondents. These two important differences – that opinion givers come disproportionately from certain demographic groups and that the mix of preferences expressed by informed respondents tends to be more evenly distributed than that of ill-informed ones – suggest that collective policy preferences must tend to reflect the voices and views of some kinds of respondents more than others.

The focus of what I call the depletion-convergence model is on the quality of representation afforded by collective policy preferences. Much attention has been focused on the desirable characteristics of majority rule, largely because it seems a fairer and more robust method relative to others for weighing individual preferences (Mueller 1989; Riker 1982). But individuals can also be categorized as members of groups, and at this level of analysis it turns out that the impact of groups on collective opinion can be quite different from that of individuals. Whereas the "one person, one vote" standard is a primary justification for majority decision rules, this chapter shows that even when this standard is respected, the collective distribution of group opinions can give some groups a disproportionate influence over the collective preference. Moreover, in contrast to the predictions of the collective rationality argument, it is often the least informed members of a population that exert this disproportionate influence. In short, the "invisible hand" of aggregation is not neutral with respect to persons.

THE IMPORTANCE OF POLITICAL KNOWLEDGE
TO POLICY PREFERENCES

To the extent that political knowledge makes any substantive difference to opinions expressed in surveys or registered in voting booths, the aggregate distributions of opinions held by politically knowledgeable people ought to look different from those of politically ignorant people.[1] This expectation has been confirmed in several studies (e.g., Althaus 1996; Bartels

---

[1] If the views of well-informed and ill-informed people were not different, then there would be little reason for concern over the low levels of political knowledge in mass publics.

1990, 1996; Converse 1964; Delli Carpini and Keeter 1996; Key 1961; Neuman 1986). While many explanations for such differences have been given over the years,[2] two are of particular importance for interpreting collective policy preferences.

First, factual knowledge about political processes, actors, and institutions is widely thought to be important to opinion formation and expression because it can help people arrive at better quality opinions than they might hold if they lacked this knowledge.[3] Our ability to form preferences consistent with our political predispositions is often mediated by the quality and quantity of political information we can bring to bear on an issue. The importance of knowledge to the formation of policy preferences stems from the way that values are connected to attitudes through beliefs: beliefs about the state of the world, cause-and-effect processes, what government is currently doing, and the likely outcomes of government actions (Delli Carpini and Keeter 1996: Chapter 6; see also Downs 1957: 79–80). One ill-informed person might believe that limiting the amount of foreign imports is the "correct" solution for loss of American manufacturing jobs to overseas competition, without knowing whether that policy is consistent with her predispositions (e.g., to "let each get ahead on his own") or whether it is the best way to address problems raised by the geographic migration of blue-collar jobs within an increasingly globalized economy. Another might support an auto insurance referendum that rolls back premiums by 20% because it serves his short-term financial interests (Lupia 1994), while someone with more perfect or complete information about the economics of the auto insurance industry could see that the referendum is diametrically opposed to that person's long-term financial interests (Kuklinski and Quirk 2000). Poor information quality might also prevent a person from distinguishing the effects of two different means to the same end, or even mistake the end itself, believing that legislative term limits should reduce the power of special interests when such limits might also exaggerate this power by reducing the average level of policy expertise among legislators.

---

[2] For example, these differences could result from the direct effects of political knowledge, which may lead informed respondents uniformly to become more conservative (Key 1961) or liberal (McClosky 1958) in their political attitudes. Such differences could also stem from the fact that politically sophisticated citizens have more highly constrained belief systems than unsophisticated and ill-informed citizens (Converse 1964, 1970; Lane 1962; Markus and Converse 1979; although see Achen 1975; Nie and Andersen 1974).

[3] This conclusion holds true for any number of different criteria for opinion quality (see Delli Carpini and Keeter 1996; Luskin 1987; Price and Neijens 1997; Zaller 1992a).

Because informed citizens are likely to have more accurate beliefs than citizens who are less knowledgeable about the issues,[4] they are more likely to form policy preferences in line with their political predispositions (Galston 2001). The policy preferences of people knowledgeable about politics tend to be more consonant with their political values than people who are poorly informed about politics (Converse and Pierce 1986; Judd and Downing 1990; Sinnott 2000; Zaller 1992a). For example, ideology is a better predictor of vote choice for people with higher levels of political knowledge than it is for people who are relatively less informed (Lockerbie 1991). Knowledgeable people who identify themselves as Democrats are more likely to express typically Democratic policy preferences than people who call themselves Democrats but have lower levels of political knowledge (Delli Carpini and Keeter 1996). Their voting is driven less by expectations about which candidate is likely to win and more by substantive considerations (Bartels 1988). In addition, the policy preferences of knowledgeable people are more likely to remain stable over time (Converse and Pierce 1986: Chapter 7; Delli Carpini and Keeter 1993, 1996; Feldman 1989), and they tend to correspond more closely to a recognizable liberal–conservative orientation than do the preferences of less knowledgeable citizens (Converse 1964; Delli Carpini and Keeter 1996; Lane 1962; Stimson 1975; although see Neuman 1986: Chapter 3). When changes in information about policies occur, the more knowledgeable respondents are likely to update their preferences so that they remain consistent with their predispositions (Zaller 1992a). In this way any differences in the opinion distributions of well- and ill-informed people could reflect the reduced levels of noise or error in the opinions of knowledgeable respondents.

There is also a second reason to expect differences between well- and ill-informed opinions that has received little attention in the collective rationality literature: informed people tend to share demographic

---

[4] It has also been suggested that "accurate" beliefs may at times do more to cloud the relationships between preferences and predispositions than to clarify them. For example, attempts at misleading the public may cause informed citizens to accept a version of events that suggests a particular course of governmental action. The Johnson Administration's use of the Gulf of Tonkin incidents to justify the U.S. entry into the Vietnam conflict is one example of this (Page and Shapiro 1992: 227–8). Moreover, mass media organizations may selectively frame issues in ways that reinforce governmental and industrial control over the content of political information available to citizens (Herman and Chomsky 1988; Parenti 1986). These concerns suggest that available information may be distorted in important ways. I use the term *accuracy* to refer to the actual state of affairs rather than to what elites happen to be saying about them.

characteristics that distinguish them from ill-informed people – demographic characteristics that may themselves be associated with particular needs, wants, and values. The Downsian cost/benefit view of information acquisition implies that knowledgeable people will tend to share some similar characteristics. They should be well educated because formal education is an efficient means of imparting knowledge and building the cognitive skills necessary to structure that knowledge in meaningful ways. Besides being educated, informed people should also tend to have higher incomes than ill-informed people. Affluent persons are more likely than others to acquire economic and political information through their daily activities. They may also be pressured by their social environments to keep up with current events (Katz and Lazarsfeld 1955). All of this reduces the opportunity costs of political information for persons of more comfortable means, and the economics of information acquisition suggest that knowledge of politics should be concentrated among those who are politically and socially advantaged, a finding that has been consistently supported in empirical studies (Bennett 1988; Delli Carpini and Keeter 1996; Luskin 1990; Neuman 1986; Sigelman and Yanarella 1986; Smith 1989; Verba, Burns, and Schlozman 1997).

Well-informed persons as a group may thus have different opinions not only because they are of better quality than those given by ill-informed persons, but also because they represent needs, wants, and values associated with the particular demographic characteristics common to politically knowledgeable people. For example, higher levels of education have a slight liberalizing effect on attitudes about social issues such as minority rights and abortion while higher levels of income are strongly related to conservative stances on economic and, particularly, domestic spending issues (Himmelstein and McRae 1988; Knoke 1979; Knoke, Raffalovich, and Erskine 1987; see also Althaus 1996). In this way well-informed people should tend to be more economically conservative and socially liberal than the ill informed, tendencies that may stem not from political knowledge itself but rather from the demographic traits that lead people to become knowledgeable in the first place.

The preceding discussion thus leaves us with one presumption and two problems. The presumption is that knowledgeable opinions are in some way better than ill-informed ones. While this view has its detractors (Edelman 1988; Yankelovich 1991), and while there is disagreement over the particular criteria that should be used to define quality (e.g., Kuklinski and Quirk 2001; Luskin 1987; Price and Neijens 1997), the general proposition that informed opinions are more desirable than ignorant ones can fairly be described as the consensus view among social scientists and political philosophers. The two problems are more controversial: how to distinguish the well-informed "signal" from the "noise" associated with ill-informed opinion, and how to know whether the collective opinion adequately represents the interests of all groups in a population.

Collective rationality models address the first problem by making strong assumptions about the distributional characteristics of ill-informed opinions. However, Chapter 2 showed that the information-pooling properties of collective opinion disappear rapidly as these assumptions are relaxed. Collective rationality models address the second problem in different ways even though the mechanisms they detail for expecting emergent properties of collective rationality are quite similar. Converse (1990) sees this as a potential concern, since in his model the only views represented in collective preferences are those articulated by well-informed respondents. "The troubling implication," Converse writes, "is that the representation system in spirit follows a 'one-person, one-vote' formula rather less than the letter of the law would suggest, and those poorly informed tend to suffer at least partial disenfranchisement as a result" (387). In this model, collective opinion should represent the interests of all members of a population only if, for any issue, the mix of preferences given by the well informed is roughly the same as that expressed by the ill informed, or if all members of a population have the same interests. The critical question thus becomes whether the preferences of well-informed respondents tend to be similar to those of ill-informed respondents. If this proves to be the case, then the overrepresentation of informed opinions should be of little concern (see Mansbridge 1996). But if the mix of views held by well-informed respondents tends to be different from that of ill-informed respondents, then collective preferences may at times fail to reflect proportionally the needs, wants, and values of all relevant demographic groups.

Page and Shapiro, in contrast, never address this problem directly in their argument. They recognize the importance of group-based differences in policy preferences, but perhaps because the emphasis of their book is on explaining changes in collective opinion over time rather than the makeup of collective opinion at one point in time, these differences in group opinion are not treated as problematic for interpreting collective opinion measures as if they represented all relevant interests in a population. On the contrary, Page and Shapiro present evidence that ordinary citizens possess "opinions consonant with their basic beliefs and values"

(388) and that "on many issues, most or all subgroups may have sufficiently similar interests (or a common concern for the collective public interest) so as to react to new events and changed circumstances in similar ways" (294–5).[5] Their conclusion that collective opinions have emergent properties of wisdom and rationality leans heavily on a presumption of common interests in the domain of public affairs.[6]

As was the case with Converse's model, if all citizens have the same interests or if the well informed represent adequately the mix of views held by the ill informed, then Page and Shapiro's model suggests that collective measures of opinion can represent all interests in a population. Yet there is a third criterion consistent with Page and Shapiro's argument that provides a much less stringent standard for representing all interests. If all of the assumptions in the Page and Shapiro model are valid (a view that I will challenge below), then so long as the people who give opinions are descriptively representative of the population they are supposed to represent, and to the extent that interests are reflected in "true attitudes," all interests in a population should be represented proportionally in measures of collective opinion. This conclusion should hold even if well-informed people do not share the mix of preferences held by ill-informed people, or if all citizens do not share the same interests. The reason why is that everyone in Page and Shapiro's model is presumed to have true attitudes about policies.[7] Well-informed people are presumed merely to have less error variance in their attitude reports. No matter how large or small the variance, the logic of Page and Shapiro's argument suggests that true attitudes ought to be revealed in the process of

---

[5] Erikson, MacKuen, and Stimson (2002: 211–9) also find individual-level evidence of "parallel publics" in trend data for policy mood.

[6] While much work has shown that the political opinions and behaviors of individuals are often inconsistent with simple calculations of self-interest (Finkel and Muller 1998; Kinder and Kiewiet 1981; Mansbridge 1990), it is quite another thing to conclude that the mass public shares common underlying interests. For one, contemporary political theorists typically regard the possession of knowledge as a prerequisite for identifying one's interests (Bartels 1990; Connolly 1993; Dahl 1989: 180–1; Delli Carpini and Keeter 1996; Lippmann 1955: 42; Mansbridge 1983: 24–6). Lacking such knowledge, it is difficult to ascertain the degree to which behaviors and attitude reports reflect underlying political interests (Bachrach 1975; DeLuca 1995). More generally, descriptive representation is a cornerstone of liberal theories of democracy precisely because these theories presume a competition among interests (Held 1987; Madison [1787] 1982; Pitkin 1967).

[7] Yet as Stanley Feldman (1989: 52) notes, "Given the low levels of political knowledge, interest, and involvement often found in the American public it would be odd if virtually everyone had specific opinions on matters of public policy that were perfectly stable over time."

aggregation when there is no systematic error in surveyed opinions. In this way, so long as the mix of people providing opinions accurately resembles the population from which a sample is drawn, the social distribution of political knowledge need not create representation problems in collective opinion.

PROBLEMS WITH THE DISTRIBUTIONAL ASSUMPTIONS OF COLLECTIVE RATIONALITY MODELS

In contrast to the optimistic conclusions of collective rationality models, I suggest that the low levels and uneven social distribution of political knowledge can create two potential sources of bias that undermine the quality of political representation in collective opinion measures: knowledgeable people are more likely to give opinions when asked, and they are more likely to base their opinions on a broader range of considerations than less knowledgeable people. The first source of bias affects the representation of voices in collective preferences. It undermines the likelihood that opinion givers will descriptively represent the population from which they are drawn because some kinds of people are better informed than others. The second source of bias affects the representation of interests in collective preferences. Groups that are more like-minded in their opinions have relatively greater influence over the shape of marginal percentages than groups with opinions that are more heterogeneous. As will be detailed later, the larger the group and the more lopsided its opinions, the more the group's preferences will be reflected in the collective opinion. Because the opinions of less knowledgeable respondents are often more similar to one another than those of more knowledgeable respondents, collective preferences often reflect the contours of ill-informed opinion more closely than any signal from the well informed.

Knowledgeable Respondents Give Opinions More Frequently

The first source of bias is that some kinds of people are more likely than others to answer "don't know" (DK) or "no opinion" (NO) to survey questions. For instance, DK/NO responses are more common among people with lower levels of education, income, perceived issue importance, interest in politics, cognitive ability, political efficacy, and political involvement (Althaus 1996; Converse 1976; Faulkenberry and Mason 1978; Francis and Busch 1975; Krosnick and Milburn 1990; Schuman and Presser 1981).[8] However, the strongest predictor of DK/NO responses is political knowledge: the more knowledgeable the respondent, the less likely she is to give a DK/NO response (Delli Carpini and Keeter 1996: Chapter 6; see also Zaller 1991). Moreover, when responding to questions that depend on factual knowledge for meaningful answers, ill-informed people are much more likely to give DK/NO responses than to guess wrongly (Schuman and Presser 1980).[9]

Because political knowledge is concentrated among demographic groups that tend to be politically advantaged, the people who opt out of collective opinions by giving DK/NO responses tend to come disproportionately from politically disadvantaged groups. One example of how political equality can be undermined in opinion surveys is given in Table 3.1. This table reports the differential rates of opinion giving,[10] averaged across three of the years in which the following question was asked in the American National Election Studies: "Some people have suggested placing new limits on foreign imports in order to protect American jobs. Others say that such limits would raise consumer prices and hurt American exports. Do you favor or oppose placing new limits on imports, or haven't you thought much about this?" Although there is some variation in DK/NO levels from year to year for this question, the averages are reported here to illustrate how chronic the inequalities can be in the demographic makeup of opinion givers.

The first column provides the mean percentage of DK/NO responses for each group across the three years this question was asked, and the second column indicates the percentage of respondents in the sample belonging to

---

[8] The reverse is also sometimes true. On highly obscure issues, respondents with higher levels of education are more willing to give DK/NO responses than respondents with lower levels of education, presumably because this latter group is swayed by social desirability effects to provide answers (Schuman and Presser 1980, 1981).

[9] For example, in one survey nine out of ten people correctly defined what a veto was. Those people were then asked "If the president vetoes a bill, can Congress override his veto?" Of those who did not provide a correct answer, five times as many respondents gave a DK response as an incorrect one (Delli Carpini and Keeter 1991: Table 1; see also Rapoport 1982). When asked which political party controls the Senate, almost twice as many respondents in the same survey gave a DK response as an incorrect one.

[10] By *opinion giving* I mean people who gave substantive responses to questions rather than answering "don't know," "no opinion," or being selected out of the pool of opinion givers with filtering questions. Respondents who volunteered idiosyncratic opinions in response to forced-choice questions rather than one of the standard response options were also counted as giving nonsubstantive opinions. While such opinions may be thoughtful and direct, the lack of commonality among these responses renders them largely uninterpretable to researchers.

TABLE 3.1. *Demographic differences in opinionation on the issue of limiting foreign imports*

	Mean % DK/NO	% of Sample	Mean % of Opinion Givers	Rep'n. Ratio	Index of Equality
Political knowledge					
Highest quartile	18.2	24.8	31.1	1.25	0.50
Lowest quartile	59.1	24.6	15.4	0.63	
Education					
College degree	23.0	24.5	29.0	1.18	0.62
No H.S. diploma	52.2	18.1	13.3	0.73	
Income					
Top quartile	24.0	28.8	33.3	1.16	0.69
Bottom quartile	47.4	24.1	19.3	0.80	
Race					
All others	32.5	87.9	90.9	1.03	0.73
Black	51.0	12.1	9.1	0.75	
Gender					
Male	24.1	44.9	52.2	1.16	0.75
Female	43.4	55.1	47.8	0.87	
Party identification					
Republican	30.4	39.1	41.7	1.07	0.83
Independent	42.1	11.4	10.1	0.89	
Democrat	36.5	49.4	48.1	0.97	

Source: Pooled data from the 1988, 1992, and 1996 American National Election Studies.

each group. The third column shows the percentage of respondents from each group giving substantive opinions. For example, an average of 18% of respondents from the highest knowledge quartile gave nonsubstantive responses when asked about limiting foreign imports, compared with an average of 59% DK/NO responses among those in the lowest knowledge quartile. The second column shows that each of these groups represents almost exactly a quarter of respondents in the pooled sample. But because of their different rates of opinionation on this issue, column three shows that the most knowledgeable respondents are numerically overrepresented in the pool of opinion givers, while the least knowledgeable are severely underrepresented. Of people who gave substantive opinions on this issue, 31% came from respondents in the highest knowledge quartile, while only 15% came from those in the lowest.

The fourth and fifth columns report two statistical measures of political equality developed by Steven Rosenstone and John Mark Hansen (1993) for the analysis of inequalities in political participation: the representation ratio and the equality index.[11] In the context of opinion surveys, the representation ratio is the percentage of opinion givers who come from a particular group divided by that group's percentage of respondents in the sample as a whole. It compares the number of opinions a group *actually* contributes to the number of opinions it *ought to* contribute to a collective preference, if all groups had the same opinionation rate. Underrepresented groups will have ratios taking values less than one, and overrepresented groups will have ratios greater than one. While the representation ratio is a measure of relative over- or underrepresentation for a specific group of respondents (such as people with grade-school educations), the equality index is a global measure of equality for a particular demographic variable (such as education level). The equality index for any demographic variable divides the representation ratio of the most underrepresented subgroup by that of the most overrepresented subgroup. For example, the equality index for education level is calculated by dividing the representation ratio of people with less than a high-school education by that of people with college educations.

The representation ratios for these groups indicate the substantive impact of differences in DK/NO rates. The higher opinionation rate of the most knowledgeable respondents caused them to be overrepresented among opinion givers to the extent that each of their opinions had 1.25 the weight it should have had ($31.1 \div 24.8 = 1.25$) if respondents at all levels of knowledge gave opinions at the same rate. In contrast, the lower opinionation rate of the least knowledgeable respondents meant that their share of substantive opinions was less than two-thirds the share they should have had ($15.4 \div 24.6 = .63$) if the rate of opinion giving was equal across knowledge quartiles. Another way of comparing these differences is given by the equality index scores in the last column. The equality index score for political knowledge is .50 ($.63 \div 1.25 = .50$), which means that the opinions of the lowest quartile carried only half the weight of opinions from the highest quartile, when they should have carried equal weight. Put another way, unequal DK/NO rates give knowledgeable respondents the equivalent of two opinions for every one given by ill-informed respondents.

---

[11] These measures have properties that make them more desirable than traditional measures of inequality such as the Gini Coefficient. For a discussion of these properties and a comparison of these statistics to alternative measures, see Rosenstone and Hansen 1993: 291–6.

Some might view this kind of inequality as all for the better, since siphoning off ignorant respondents should raise the average knowledge level of people who actually give opinions. But this tendency looks less benign when we recognize that political knowledge is distributed unequally among social groups that may have competing interests regarding a policy, as seems the case with the issue of limiting foreign imports. Table 3.1 shows that the affluent, the educated, whites, men, and Republicans are all overrepresented to various degrees in the ranks of opinion givers on the issue of limiting foreign imports. Not only are they overrepresented numerically, but each of these groups was also more opposed to restricting imports than the underrepresented groups. In these data only 52% of college graduates favored restrictions on imports, compared with 72% of high school dropouts, and only 58% of the most affluent respondents favored restrictions, compared with 78% of the least affluent respondents. Likewise, support for restrictions ran 79% for blacks, 73% for women, and around 71% for independents and Democrats; but only 65% for whites, 59% for men, and 60% for Republicans. These consistent differences suggest that higher levels of support would be registered in this question if all groups gave opinions at the same rate, although of course we have no direct way of knowing whether the opinions of those providing DK/NO responses might have differed from those giving substantive responses.

In their study of inequality in political participation, Rosenstone and Hansen (1993) present comparable inequality measures for education, income, and racial differences in a variety of political activities. While the demographic makeup of voters is known to be quite different from that of the adult population as a whole (Verba, Schlozman, and Brady 1995; Wolfinger and Rosenstone 1980), Table 3.1 shows that the demographic makeup of people who gave opinions on the foreign import question was just as skewed as the inequalities among voters reported by Rosenstone and Hansen (pp. 237, 244). For example, the analysis of voting behavior reported by Rosenstone and Hansen assigns an equality index score of .67 for differences in electoral participation among education levels, .60 among income levels, and .88 for differences between blacks and whites. Table 3.1 shows that inequalities among opinion givers for the foreign import question were only slightly better in the case of income, but slightly worse in the case of education and race. Although opinion surveys are designed to ensure that the "one person, one vote" standard is not violated (Gallup and Rae 1940; Verba 1996), this example shows that even the most well-executed academic survey can produce levels of inequality that exceed those found among voters in presidential elections.

A broader perspective on the substantive impact of these tendencies is given in Figure 3.1, which shows the distribution of equality index scores for 15 demographic variables. To detail how index of equality scores are distributed in these questions, this figure presents them in the form of box plots. Each box plot shows the index of equality scores calculated from 235 opinion questions in the 1988, 1992, and 1996 American National Election Studies, which include all the policy questions from these studies ($n = 172$), all of the questions measuring approval of Congress, the president, and presidential policies ($n = 16$), as well as all of the questions asking respondents to report politically relevant values or make value judgments of one kind or another ($n = 47$).[12] The box represents the interquartile range (that is, the distance from the 25th percentile to the 75th percentile) containing the middle 50% of cases, with the median case marked as a vertical line within the box. "Whiskers" extending from both ends of the box mark the location of the first equality index score that is less than or equal to the distance of 1.5 times the interquartile range from the edge of the box. Most of the scores will be found within the boundaries marked by the whiskers.

To ease interpretation of these box plots, a vertical line runs through Figure 3.1 at the point where index of equality scores take a value of one, indicating perfect equality. In the education category, for instance, points to the left of this vertical line represent questions in which people with less than a high school education are underrepresented relative to college graduates, while points to the right of the line represent cases where high school dropouts are overrepresented relative to people with college degrees. Figure 3.1 confirms previous findings that DK/NO responses are more consistently related to political knowledge than the other demographic characteristics: the largest inequalities tend to be found among people with different levels of political knowledge.[13] In part because they

---

[12] A complete list of these questions is available upon request from the author.

[13] Regressing the item nonresponse rate for individual respondents on political knowledge and 25 demographic variables (a description of these is given in Chapter 4) confirms the findings of Delli Carpini and Keeter (1996: Chapter 6) that political knowledge is the most significant predictor of opinion giving even after controlling for a variety of demographic variables. When predicting nonresponse rates for all 5,564 respondents while controlling for a range of demographic characteristics, political knowledge had by far the largest beta coefficient (beta $= -.409, p < .001$), followed far behind in magnitude by the next most important predictor, partisanship (for Democrats, beta $= -.173, p < .001$; for Republicans, beta $= -.136, p < .001$).

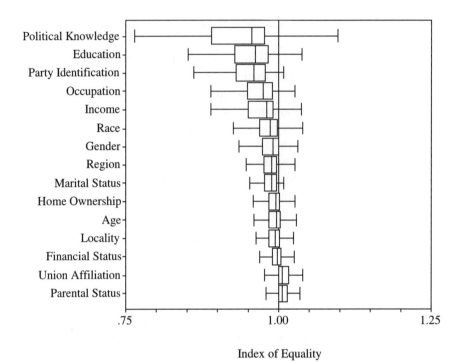

Index of Equality

FIGURE 3.1. The prevalence of demographic inequalities among opinion givers

are better informed, people who are better educated and more affluent tend to give opinions more frequently than people who have little formal schooling or who are relatively poor. Whites tend to give opinions more frequently than blacks, men more than women, and political partisans more than independents. While other influences besides political knowledge affect rates of opinion giving (Krosnick and Milburn 1990), the differences between groups closely follow the social distribution of political knowledge shown in Table 1.2. In 13 of 15 demographic categories, the mean index of equality score is less than 1.0. The two exceptions are union affiliation and parental status. Although union members and parents with children at home tend to be less knowledgeable about politics than people unaffiliated with unions and those without dependent children, these types of people are chronically overrepresented in the ranks of opinion givers.[14]

---

[14] A likely explanation for these patterns is that parents and union members probably have higher levels of motivation to answer these questions. See discussion of motivation later in this chapter and in Chapter 5.

Although the highest levels of inequality are seen when dividing respondents by levels of political knowledge, the mean equality index score for political knowledge is a fairly egalitarian .91 across the 235 questions, suggesting that inequalities among opinion givers tend to be modest in size.[15] However, the average equality scores obscure how severe demographic misrepresentation can get in survey results that are designed and expected to be profoundly egalitarian. The lowest observed index of equality score was .11 for political knowledge (meaning that each opinion from the highest knowledge quartile counted as much as 10 opinions from the lowest quartile), .29 for education, .45 for occupation, .48 for income, .58 for gender, .62 for region of the country, .63 for race, and .64 for partisan identification.[16] Despite the tendency for average inequalities among demographic groups to be relatively small, in any given question these differences can cause the group of opinion givers to take on demographic characteristics quite unlike those of the population they are supposed to represent.

The important point is not just that opinion givers may be drawn disproportionately from certain demographic groups, but rather that the skewed demographic makeup of opinion givers may also bias the mix of needs, wants, and values communicated through collective preferences.[17]

---

[15] Indeed, the average respondent from the highest knowledge quartile gave opinions in 96% of all 235 questions, compared to only 87% for the average respondent from the lowest knowledge quartile.

[16] It is also important to point out that index of equality scores are sensitive to the number of categories used in the calculation: given the same level of inequality, comparing two groups by dividing the demographic characteristic at the midpoint will yield equality index scores closer to 1.0 than if demographic characteristics are compared among groups at the extreme ends of the distribution. Although many demographic traits have equality scores that tend to cluster near the 1.0 mark, most of the categories are dichotomies (the categories used to construct the index of equality scores for each demographic trait are given in Table 1.2), so that apparently small inequalities can involve large numbers of people. For instance, a .95 equality index score can be obtained for occupation (which has six categories) when the pool of opinion givers contains 10 fewer homemakers than it ought to. The same index score for political knowledge (four categories) would require 25 DK/NO responses from the lowest knowledge quartile, and would require 50 women to be "missing" from the pool of opinion givers to produce a similar level of gender inequality.

[17] Underlying this expectation is the idea that subjective needs, wants, and values can be closely linked to demographic characteristics (Verba, Schlozman, and Brady 1995). This idea is at the core of descriptive representation and hardly needs elaboration: if preferences were unrelated to demographic traits, the demographic makeup of electorates, legislatures, and interest-group donors would be irrelevant. But as has been shown time and time again, vote choices and policy preferences are often mediated by demographic traits such as age, income, race, and gender, as well as by long-term orientations such as

Since the potential for this sort of misrepresentation seems likely to increase as the gaps in opinionation rates between groups grow larger, it becomes important to identify whether certain types of survey questions are more likely than others to be associated with differential rates of opinion giving. Doing so separately for each demographic characteristic would try the patience of even the most interested reader, but fortunately the degree of inequality among a wide range of demographic groups is usefully summarized by both the relative rate of DK/NO responses[18] and by the equality index scores for political knowledge.[19] The higher the rate of DK/NO responses in a question and the lower the equality index score for political knowledge, the more likely it is that blacks, women, the poor, the less educated, political independents, southerners, single people, renters, and people in rural areas are numerically underrepresented relative to whites, men, the affluent, college graduates, Republicans, people from western states, married people, home owners, and city dwellers.

partisanship that are largely influenced by demographic traits (Berelson, Lazarsfeld, and McPhee 1954; Campbell, Converse et al. 1960; Lazarsfeld, Berelson, and Gaudet 1948; Nie, Verba, and Petrocik 1979). To the extent that unequal levels of political knowledge bias the demographic makeup of opinion givers, it becomes increasingly unlikely that the resulting collective preferences should represent all relevant interests in proportion to their distribution in society.

[18] The correlation between the percentage of respondents giving DK/NO responses in a question and the equality index score for that question is $-.91$ for political knowledge; between $-.78$ and $-.86$ for education, occupation, income, gender, age, and partisanship; between $-.56$ and $-.69$ for home ownership, marital status, and region of the country; and $-.44$ for locality and $-.34$ for race.

[19] A principal components analysis of the equality index scores for all 15 demographic categories produced four factors, the first of which (eigenvalue = 8.68) accounted for 58% of explained variance in the scores. Oblimin rotation revealed that this factor produced large positive loadings for all demographic categories except financial status (no significant loading), parental status (no significant loading), and union membership (negatively loaded on this factor). Since item nonresponse in all of these demographic categories is most strongly predicted by political knowledge, this first factor appears to represent the direct impact of political knowledge. Three more minor factors (eigenvalues = 1.77, 1.27, and 1.03, respectively) were also extracted, interpreted as representing community involvement (large positive loading for parental status equality; large negative loading for home ownership equality), an urban/rural dimension (large positive loading for locality; moderate negative loadings for race and marital status equality), and a socioeconomic status dimension (large positive loading for financial status equality; moderate positive loadings for education, income, race, and occupational equality; moderate negative loading for union status equality). Together, these four factors accounted for 85% of explained variance in equality index scores, and the four factors were only somewhat correlated with one another: the political knowledge factor was correlated at the .22 level with the socioeconomic status factor, but somewhat negatively correlated with the community involvement factor ($r = -.14$) and the urban/rural factor ($r = -.09$).

Figure 3.2 presents the topical distribution of equality index scores for political knowledge. Most of the question categories in Figure 3.2 are self-explanatory (for the number of questions in each category, see Table 3.2), but a few deserve special mention. While most readers will be familiar with congressional and presidential approval questions, a third "presidential policy" category contains questions measuring approval for the president's handling of the economy, foreign relations, the 1990–1 Gulf Crisis, the environment, and health care policy. Fiscal questions address general issues regarding government spending and taxation.[20] The foreign policy category includes all questions about military defense, the use of military force abroad, economic sanctions, arms agreements, and whether the United States should become more involved in solving problems around the world. Governance issues deal with the size and scope of the federal government, the manner by which legislators should be elected, and government regulation of the economy.

Figure 3.2 shows that question categories in which respondents report values or make value judgments (i.e., "equality," "morality," and "other value" questions) lie toward the lower part of the figure, which means they tend to be more egalitarian than approval or policy questions. In the average value question, 95% of respondents from the lowest knowledge quartile and 99% of those from the highest quartile gave opinions, which translates into an average equality index score of .96 across the three categories of value questions. By contrast, the average approval question had 88% of the least knowledgeable versus 99% of the most knowledgeable giving opinions, resulting in an equality index score of .89 across the three categories of approval questions. While presidential and policy approval questions had relatively middling levels of inequality, congressional approval questions substantially undercut equality among respondents from the different knowledge quartiles.

Three patterns are apparent in this figure. First, knowledgeable respondents are numerically overrepresented on average in every question category, although in many cases the degree of misrepresentation is so small as to be of little consequence. Nonetheless, this suggests that when

---

[20] In light of the general population's low levels of knowledge about government spending (for example, in 1996 fewer than a third of respondents correctly perceived that the federal deficit had declined in size over the previous four years), questions on whether spending should be increased or decreased for particular programs or policy domains are used here as measures of approval or disapproval for programs or policies named in the question. In this way, questions on whether high levels of defense spending should be maintained fall into the "foreign policy" rather than the "fiscal" category.

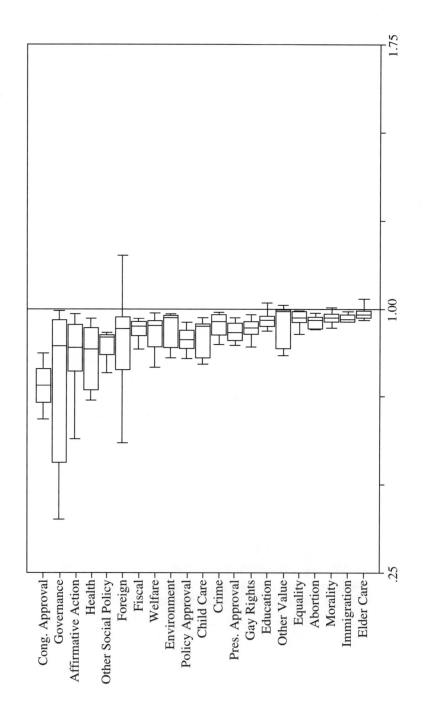

Index of Equality among Knowledge Quartiles

FIGURE 3.2. Inequalities among well- and ill-informed respondents, by question category

numerical misrepresentation occurs, added weight is almost invariably given to the opinions of knowledgeable respondents. Curiously, the primary exception to this rule is in foreign policy questions, where the ill informed are at least occasionally overrepresented relative to the well informed. Second, while individual questions like those reported in Table 3.1 can be highly unrepresentative, the typical imbalance tends to be more modest in size across question categories, just as it was across demographic groups. An example of a modest imbalance is given by the questions on environmental policy: while 99% of highly knowledgeable respondents on average gave opinions to questions about environmental policy, just 92% of respondents from the lowest knowledge quartile gave opinions to such questions. Knowledgeable respondents are overrepresented among opinion givers in these questions, but the mean equality index score of .93 for the environmental policy category suggests that the degree of misrepresentation in this case is not as great as might be found in other channels of public opinion expression, like voting in elections or financial donations to political campaigns (Rosenstone and Hansen 1993; Verba and Nie 1972; Verba, Schlozman, and Brady 1995; Wolfinger and Rosenstone 1980). Of course, some question categories are less representative than others. In approval questions on Congress, for example, nearly all knowledgeable respondents gave opinions compared with only three quarters of ill-informed respondents, resulting in a mean equality index score of .78.

The third observation is that differences in opinionation rates across question categories seem related to a topic's complexity and likely familiarity to respondents. Question categories with the largest differences between groups, such as health policy, approval of Congress, and governance issues like economic regulation all deal with topics far removed from the experiences of daily life for most people. In contrast, those categories with the smallest average differences tend to deal with topics that are "easy" for citizens to answer (Carmines and Stimson 1980) because they have long been on the political agenda (e.g., abortion and Social Security assistance to elderly people), and deal with symbolic ends rather than programmatic means to those ends (e.g., morality, equality, gay rights). These patterns are consistent with prior research on opinionation, which tends to find that topics perceived to be more personally relevant to respondents, such as moral issues, have higher rates of opinion giving than more unfamiliar and complex issues like foreign affairs and economic policy (Althaus 1996; Converse 1976). While Figure 3.2 contains some exceptions to this rule of thumb – for instance, there are small differences in opinionation on the topic of immigration but fairly large differences on the "easier" topic of affirmative action – the general patterns seem consistent with the notion that less familiar and more nuanced topics elicit higher nonopinionation rates and larger inequalities among groups.

In short, because knowledgeable people tend to come from different demographic groups than the ill-informed, their policy preferences may sometimes reflect different needs, wants, and values. When informed respondents are overrepresented in the pool of opinion givers, collective opinions give disproportionate numerical weight to the voices of socially advantaged groups.

Well-Informed Opinion Often Disperses More Evenly than Ill-Informed Opinion

The second source of bias affecting collective preferences comes from the tendency for knowledgeable respondents to more efficiently and accurately connect their political predispositions with the preferences they express in surveys. This can lead knowledgeable respondents to draw from a broader range of considerations than respondents who appear poorly informed about national politics. The same dynamic can also lead less informed respondents to deduce their policy preferences heuristically, and a heavy reliance on heuristic processing can cause their preferences to be quite similar to one another. This possibility is suggested by information-processing models of the survey response that have been developed by social psychologists (Chaiken 1980; Chaiken, Liberman, and Eagly 1989; Fiske and Taylor 1991; Krosnick 1991; Krosnick and Fabrigar forthcoming; McGuire 1969; Petty and Cacioppo 1986; Zaller 1992a; Zaller and Feldman 1992). Although never spelled out in this literature, the distributional expectations of these models are exactly opposite those of collective rationality models.

Information-processing models of the survey response suggest that opinions expressed in surveys may be less a noisy measure of "true" opinions than of the sometimes conflicting mix of considerations that happen to be available to respondents at the time they answer a question. As a result, the opinions of ill-informed respondents may not disperse as randomly across response categories as measurement-error models expect. This is because responses to survey questions can be strongly influenced by social cues such as the perceived credibility of the speaker (Taylor and Fiske 1978), the particular considerations that happen to be at the "top of the head" when a person expresses an opinion (McGuire 1969; Zaller 1992a), and respondent motivation to engage in a thorough retrieval of relevant information stored in memory before answering a question (Chaiken 1980; Chaiken, Liberman, and Eagly 1989; Krosnick 1991; Krosnick and Fabrigar forthcoming; Petty and Cacioppo 1986). These tendencies (among other reasons, see Kuklinski and Quirk 2000) should produce systematic rather than random errors in surveyed opinions.

The reasons for these dynamics can be illustrated with reference to the heuristic-systematic model of information processing (Chaiken 1980; Chaiken, Liberman, and Eagly 1989), which has emerged as a leading example of "dual process" models in social psychology. The heuristic-systematic model describes two dominant information processing strategies people use to form valid judgments in persuasive settings.[21] Systematic processing, which requires a great deal of cognitive effort, occurs when message recipients consider all available informational content in the message, analyze this content in detail, integrate other relevant considerations, and evaluate the message in a comprehensive manner. Heuristic processing occurs when message recipients consider only the informational content that allows them to use rules of thumb, schemata, or other inferential shortcuts to arrive at judgments. Because heuristic processing merely activates latent decision rules that people already possess, this mode requires minimal cognitive effort and can occur without the user being aware of it.

Reliance on one processing mode relative to the other, according to this model, ultimately depends on a combination of ability, motivation, and opportunity (Chaiken 1980; Chaiken, Liberman, and Eagly 1989). Cognitive ability determines which modes are available for use. At a minimum, people must have already developed a set of inferential rules before heuristic processing can occur, and the types of available rules determine the application of this processing mode. Systematic processing demands a higher degree of cognitive ability than some people may possess. Ability is a prerequisite, but the model suggests that motivation is equally important in determining which strategy people will use. Those engaging in an evaluative task and motivated by the subject matter to expend cognitive effort will use systematic processing alone or in combination with

[21] The heuristic-systematic model is functionally similar to Petty and Cacioppo's (1986) elaboration likelihood model, differing primarily in terminology. For a comparison of these models, see Chaiken and Eagly 1993: Chapter 7.

heuristic processing; those lacking this motivation will default to heuristic processing if they can. This is where opportunity comes in. If people are able and motivated and the message contains relatively unambiguous knowledge, they should be willing to process systematically. If unable or unmotivated to use systematic processing, people should adopt heuristic strategies to evaluate a message, particularly if the message contains heuristic cues. If no cues are available and a person lacks the motivation to engage in systematic processing, then even persons able to evaluate a message may refrain from doing so.

Information-processing models also suggest that guessing is unlikely to result in a random distribution of opinions across response categories. Instead, guesses are likely to be prompted by salient cues in the question itself, in the order of survey questions, and by frequent or recent exposure to apparently relevant information (Iyengar 1990; Price and Tewksbury 1997). In other words, if ill-informed people are motivated to answer a question but lack accessible attitudes, they should be more likely to deduce their opinions based on cues in the question as well as recent or salient pieces of knowledge than to mentally flip a coin and answer randomly. Because use of these heuristic cues and considerations introduces systematic error in attitude reports, the opinions of ill-informed respondents – who are likely to be influenced by a relatively small number of considerations, often the same ones – may become less dispersed than those of knowledgeable or sophisticated respondents. To the extent that this occurs, the aggregation mechanisms proposed by collective rationality models will fail to reflect either true attitudes or informed signals.

Table 3.2 reports three tests of relative dispersion for the 235 questions from the 1988, 1992, and 1996 American National Election Studies.[22] The first determines whether, for each question, the opinions of the lowest knowledge quartile were more evenly dispersed across response categories than those of the highest knowledge quartile, as predicted by the collective rationality hypothesis. The second details, for each question, the average percentage point difference in opinions between the least and most knowledgeable respondents. The third measure notes, for each question, when the collective preferences of the least and most knowledgeable respondents differed from one another, as when a majority of the least informed respondents prefer one policy option while a majority of the most informed respondents prefer another.

---

[22] For details on these tests, see Appendix B.

TABLE 3.2. *Opinion distributions among the highest and lowest knowledge quartiles*

Question Topic	Percentage of Questions where Lowest Quartile Is More Evenly Distributed	Average Percentage Point Difference between Lowest and Highest Quartiles	Percentage of Questions where Lowest and Highest Quartiles Have Different Modal Preferences	N =
Welfare	80.0	18.0 (9.1)	53.3	15
Foreign	70.0	13.6 (9.0)	26.7	30
Congressional approval	66.7	17.0 (11.6)	66.7	3
Other social policy	66.7	21.2 (5.8)	33.3	3
Affirmative action	64.7	11.1 (6.6)	23.5	17
Pres'l policy approval	55.6	11.9 (9.2)	33.3	9
Other value	55.6	13.9 (12.8)	44.4	9
Presidential approval	50.0	6.7 (7.6)	0.0	4
Fiscal	50.0	23.1 (12.7)	16.7	12
Gay rights	50.0	7.5 (7.3)	16.7	6
Equality	47.8	14.4 (6.7)	30.4	23
Education	45.5	11.5 (7.7)	18.2	11
Morality	40.0	14.1 (5.6)	33.3	15
Crime/Social unrest	35.7	10.2 (6.3)	7.1	14
Immigration	33.3	10.3 (5.3)	16.7	6
Governance	27.3	23.5 (12.9)	54.5	22
Abortion	16.7	18.1 (7.8)	33.3	6
Environmental	16.7	17.2 (3.9)	16.7	12
Health	16.7	12.0 (8.3)	33.3	6
Child care	0.0	10.3 (6.5)	0.0	5
Elder care	0.0	26.2 (13.1)	57.1	7
TOTAL ALL QUESTIONS	45.5	15.2 (9.8)	30.6	235

Note: In the middle column, standard deviations are in parentheses.
Source: Pooled data from the 1988, 1992, and 1996 American National Election Studies.

The first column of Table 3.2 shows, contrary to the collective rationality hypothesis, that well-informed opinions tend to distribute more evenly across response categories than ill-informed opinions. The aggregate opinions of the lowest knowledge quartile were more evenly dispersed than those of the highest quartile in only 46% of all questions. While this is close to what might be expected if evenness resulted from nothing more than chance, the trend across question categories reveals that this pattern is hardly random. Only in the domains of welfare policy, foreign policy, congressional approval, other social policy, and affirmative action do the least-informed respondents consistently distribute more evenly than the most well-informed ones. For example, in 70% foreign policy questions (21 out of 30) the highest knowledge quartile had a more lopsided distribution of opinion relative to the lowest quartile. There was rough parity among groups in the case of presidential approval, fiscal policy, education, gay rights, and value questions, with a slight tendency for the ill-informed to distribute less evenly. But in stark contrast to the predictions of collective rationality models, ill-informed respondents tended to be more like-minded than the most knowledgeable respondents in two-thirds of the questions about morality, crime, and immigration; three-quarters of the questions about governance issues; 8 out of 10 questions on the environment, abortion, and health policy; and in every question dealing with child care and care of the elderly. In only 5 of 21 question categories (welfare, foreign policy, congressional approval, presidential policy approval, and affirmative action) did the least informed consistently distribute as evenly across response options as collective rationality models predict they should.

Not only did well-informed responses tend to distribute more evenly across response categories, but the second column in Table 3.2 shows that the average percentage point differences between the aggregate opinions of the highest and lowest knowledge quartiles tended to be substantial. In this column, a 10-point difference would result if the highest knowledge quartile was 70% in favor of a policy and the lowest was 60% in favor. The average difference across all issues was 15 percentage points, with differences tending to be greatest in policy questions (mean = 15.8, s.d. = 10.2), somewhat smaller in value questions (mean = 14.2, s.d. = 7.7) and smaller still in those dealing with approval questions (mean = 11.6, s.d. = 9.3). The smallest average differences were found for presidential approval questions, which averaged slightly less than 7 points, while the largest point differences tended to appear in questions on fiscal policy, governance policy, abortion, care of the elderly, and welfare.[23] It is the exception rather than the rule for the best and least informed to provide similar opinions in response to survey questions.

The third column in Table 3.2 shows that differences between groups are so great that the modal preference of the lowest knowledge quartile is different from that of the highest knowledge quartile in nearly a third of survey questions. Some categories were especially prone to severe differences in the opinions of ill- and well-informed respondents: in more than half of the questions on congressional approval, governance issues, care of the elderly, and welfare policy, more-knowledgeable respondents expressed different collective preferences than their less-knowledgeable counterparts.

Contrary to the predictions of collective rationality models, ill-informed opinion is usually less evenly dispersed than well-informed opinion. Taken together, these findings also show that differences in opinion between knowledge quartiles are usually far from trivial. However, unlike inequalities brought about by uneven rates of DK/NO responses, differences in opinions given by the well and ill informed seem less clearly related to the "easiness" of the survey question. For example, in Figure 3.2 congressional approval and governance issues comprised the two question categories with the highest average levels of inequality among the ill and well informed. The first column of Table 3.2, by contrast, shows that while the opinions of the lowest knowledge quartile tend to be more evenly dispersed than those of the highest in congressional approval questions, they tend to be much more lopsided than those of the highest knowledge quartile in governance questions. In fact, index of equality scores for political knowledge are statistically unrelated to the relative lopsidedness of ill- to well-informed opinion ($r = .04$, $p = .59$).[24] Although it might appear that these distributional tendencies follow no obvious pattern across topical categories, the next two chapters help explain when and why ill-informed opinion tends to distribute in ways unlike well-informed opinion.

---

[23] More than a quarter of individual questions had differences in the opinions of ill- and well-informed respondents of greater than 20 points. Among individual questions, the largest observed difference in opinion between the highest and lowest knowledge quartiles was 47.1 points for a question on whether the deficit should be increased to allow more spending on domestic programs.

[24] Moreover, the rank order of categories in the first column of Table 3.2 and in Figure 3.2 are only modestly related to one another (Spearman's $\rho = .41$, $p = .07$).

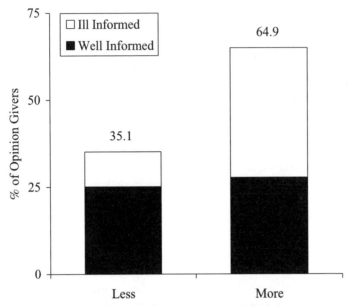

FIGURE 3.3. Dispersion effect in opinion on the size of government. "Which is closer [to your own opinion]: one, the less government the better; or two, there are more things that government should be doing?"

From a measurement-error standpoint, these patterns are as puzzling as they are unexpected. Yet they are entirely consistent with information-processing models of the survey response. The findings in Table 3.2 challenge the expectation of information-pooling properties in collective opinion laid out in collective rationality models. The important point is not merely that knowledgeable people often have different preferences than ill-informed people, but that the nature of these differences can cause the preferences of some groups to be amplified disproportionately in a question's marginal percentages. Figure 3.3 provides one example of how differences in group opinion can influence the shape of the marginal percentages. This figure shows responses to a question from the 1992 American National Election Study on the scope of government activity.[25] Responses to this question are shown divided into two groups: the "well

[25] The question read, "Next, I am going to ask you to choose which of two statements I read comes closer to your own opinion. You might agree to some extent with both, but we want to know which one is closer to your views: one, the less government the better; or two, there are more things that government should be doing?"

informed" from the top two knowledge quartiles ($N = 1,136$) and the "ill informed" from the bottom two quartiles ($N = 1,016$). Pretend for a moment that the marginal percentages are the only data available for this question. Looking only at the marginals (shown above each of the columns), there appears to be a sizeable majority opinion on this issue: 65% favor more government. But when responses are disaggregated by knowledge level, this collective preference can be seen to depend entirely on the lopsided distribution of ill-informed opinion. For some reason, the most knowledgeable opinion givers are almost evenly divided on this issue. Only 52% of well-informed respondents favor more government, compared with 79% of ill-informed opinion givers. The effect of these differences is striking: because well-informed responses almost perfectly balance one another out, the collective preference is determined by the less dispersed responses of ill-informed opinion givers.

Some readers may question this conclusion, noting correctly that each of the two groups exerts about the same pull on the marginals: the 65% favoring more government falls almost exactly between the 79% of ill-informed and 52% of well-informed responses in this category. Yet because of the way survey data are commonly interpreted, equal pull does not translate into equal influence. By *pull* I mean merely the ability to draw the collective marginals toward the shape of a group's opinion. By *influence* I mean the ability to create what appears to be a collective preference. Whichever group is less dispersed – in the dichotomous case, the group that has a greater percentage of responses in one category – pulls the marginals away from a tie. The more dispersed group pulls the marginals toward a tie, but also makes itself a platform (so to speak) for amplifying the less dispersed responses of the other group. Another way of looking at Figure 3.3 is to say that about half of the respondents were responsible for the appearance of a nearly two-thirds majority.

This example illustrates what I call a *dispersion effect*. Dispersion effects occur when a collective preference is disproportionately influenced by a group of opinion givers because their responses are relatively more concentrated into one or more response categories than those of other opinion givers. The more evenly dispersed a group's opinions across response categories, the more these responses balance out and leave the direction of the marginal percentages to be determined by groups with more one-sided opinions.[26]

---

[26] In an earlier study (Althaus 1996), I used the term *informed minority* to describe distributional characteristics which amplified the preferences of well-informed demographic

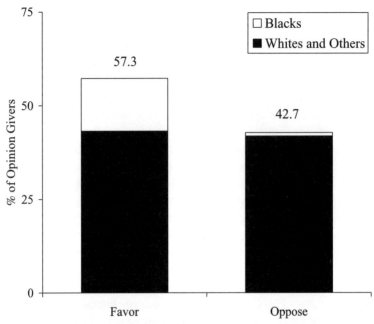

FIGURE 3.4. Dispersion effect in opinion on affirmative action. "Should the government in Washington see to it that black people get fair treatment in jobs or is this not the federal government's business?"

In extreme cases, a relatively small group of respondents can create a dispersion effect that significantly influences the shape of a collective preference. The theoretical possibility that a cohesive minority could overdetermine collective outcomes has been raised elsewhere (e.g., Davis, Hinich, and Ordeshook 1970; Miller 1986), but the logic behind this assertion is somewhat counterintuitive and bears illustration. One example of such a case is shown in Figure 3.4. This figure shows the aggregate patterns of responses to a question from the 1988 ANES that reads "Should the government in Washington see to it that black people get fair treatment in jobs or is this not the federal governments [sic] business?" The marginal percentages for this question showed that 57% of the public favored government intervention on behalf of African Americans. But the appearance of a collective preference on this issue is somewhat misleading, for it stems from a dispersion effect caused by the near-unanimous views of

groups. Here I use *dispersion effects* in place of the more restrictive *informed minority*, since, as will be shown later, characteristics of group opinion often amplify the preferences of ill-informed groups.

African-American respondents. Blacks were 94% in favor of government guarantees while whites, at 50.1% in favor, were almost perfectly divided between options. Despite the fact that African Americans made up only 12% of the sample, the one-sided distribution of their aggregate responses was entirely responsible for the appearance of a collective preference on this issue.

This example illustrates that small groups of people with similar opinions can wield more power over the appearance of a collective preference than large groups of people with mixed opinions. This example also suggests that dispersion effects among relatively less-informed groups may have little to do with the social distribution of political knowledge. African Americans tend as a group to be slightly less informed about national politics than whites, as noted in Chapter 1. They also have obvious interests at stake in this particular survey question, and it is unlikely that their lopsided opinions are merely an artifact of low knowledge levels or heuristic processing strategies. Likewise, there is no obvious way to conclude whether the lower knowledge levels or the unique demographic characteristics of ill-informed opinion givers are responsible for the dispersion effect in Figure 3.3. Less knowledgeable people tend to be socially and politically disadvantaged relative to more knowledgeable people, and preferring more government to less might be a sensible response to power inequalities arising from this state of affairs.

In the end, we can conclude from Figures 3.3 and 3.4 only that political knowledge probably has some kind of relationship with the lopsidedness of group opinions, without being able to specify what that relationship might be. The tendency for political knowledge to produce such confounding effects – diminishing the effective size of ill-informed groups while enhancing their influence over collective preferences – means that survey data alone can tell us little about the overall effects of political knowledge on opinion giving. We require some means of sorting out the unique influence of political knowledge from the influence of demographic differences and other characteristics that distinguish the ill informed from knowledgeable citizens. Such a method will be detailed and applied to these data in Chapter 4.

Taken together, the findings from this section imply that collective opinion must often reflect the preferences of ill-informed respondents more than those of well-informed ones.[27] Collective opinion may at times

[27] The opposite conclusion was suggested in an earlier study of information effects (Althaus 1996), which concluded that well-informed rather than ill-informed demographic groups

appear rational in the sense described by Page and Shapiro, but this result seems neither inevitable nor even likely. At best, collective rationality models describe the dynamics of collective opinion only part of the time. In the 1988, 1992, and 1996 American National Election Studies, ill-informed respondents were more likely to provide a "signal" than knowledgeable ones. Because of this tendency, dispersion effects should regularly amplify the preferences of ill-informed rather than well-informed demographic groups in the marginals of policy questions. Collective rationality models, as presently articulated, fail to anticipate or explain this important regularity in collective opinion. What is needed is a way to describe collective opinion that accounts for these various patterns and that can be used to predict the effects of differences in political knowledge levels on representation and political equality in collective preferences.

THE DEPLETION-CONVERGENCE MODEL
OF INFORMATION EFFECTS

The concern of the preceding section has been to identify aggregation effects that influence the quality of representation in measures of collective opinion. I conclude that decision rules like majority or plurality choices can guarantee equality of influence at the individual level, as exemplified in the "one person, one vote" standard, while nonetheless allowing groups to influence collective preferences out of proportion to the number of their members (for related observations, see Beitz 1989; Davis, Hinich, and Ordeshook 1970). Equality can be respected among persons while inequality reigns among groups because power to influence collective preferences resides in the shared distributional tendencies of individual opinions.

The two primary mediators of aggregation effects in collective preferences are group size and group unanimity. The size of one group relative to that of other groups determines pull, the power of numerical weight, and the variance of one group's opinion relative to that of other groups determines influence, the power of like-mindedness. Their roles can be

should generally be advantaged by dispersion effects. These conflicting conclusions can be resolved by taking two limitations of the earlier study into account. First, the earlier study used income as a necessary but indirect proxy for knowledge. The different conclusions reported here may be due in part to the use of different grouping variables. Second, the earlier study, building directly on collective rationality models, tested only for dispersion effects that favored well-informed groups. The tests presented here allow for effects in the other direction as well, and thus avoid the overly restrictive view of information effects suggested by measurement-error approaches.

summarized in two general rules:

1. The smaller the group, the less pull it has in determining the size and direction of the collective preference.
2. The more unanimous the group's opinion, the more influence the group has in determining the size and direction of the collective preference.

The first rule reflects basic common sense: the smaller the group, the less power it must have over the collective preference. The second rule, that dispersion effects in group opinions create a different kind of power over the shape of collective opinions, is in many ways the more important of the two precisely because it seems to defy common sense. The dispersion of group opinion across response categories can be seen as a resource for amplifying or squelching the preferences of one group relative to those of others contributing to the collective preference. The more concentrated or lopsided is a group's opinion relative to others, the more influence it has in drawing the collective opinion toward its preferred alternative. Likewise, the more conflicted or dispersed a group's respondents are, the less influence the group has over the collective preference. Dispersion effects are governed by a simple rule of thumb: for any number of equal-sized groups of respondents, the group that is more like-minded in its opinions has relatively greater influence over the shape of the collective preference. For groups of unequal size, the extent of any one group's influence on the collective preference is also dependent on the number of respondents it contains.

Power inequalities stemming from dispersion effects should be ubiquitous in collective preferences. The only time dispersion effects should fail to allocate power disproportionately is when all relevant groups have identical preferences on an issue, or when their preferences exactly counterbalance one another, as when one group is 60% opposed and another group is 60% in favor. In all other cases, the relative dispersion of group opinions will cause the preferences of some groups to be amplified disproportionately in collective opinions. No matter how closely we guard political equality at the individual level, disproportionate power among groups will be the inevitable result.

These two rules governing the representational dynamics of collective preferences allow us to identify two important mechanisms by which the micro-level distribution of political knowledge can create macro-level information effects. The tendency of micro-level information effects is to drain ill-informed respondents from the pool of opinion givers and to cause the substantive opinions given by the remaining ill-informed respondents to distribute systematically rather than randomly. These two tendencies form the basis of what can be called the *depletion-convergence model* of information effects. In this model, the twofold impact of micro-level information effects on macro-level opinion is to shrink the effective size of ill-informed groups (depletion) and to link the opinions of ill-informed people together by causing them to organize around heuristic cues or frames of reference generated by the survey instrument, or around common pieces of knowledge that have been recently or frequently activated in the minds of respondents by news reports or other common sources of knowledge (convergence).[28]

In short, this model describes how the social distribution of political knowledge can mediate aggregation effects in collective preferences. Unlike collective rationality models, which presume fairly predictable information effects since a deficit of political knowledge is held to consistently randomize individual opinions, the depletion-convergence model suggests that collective information effects should tend to vary in magnitude and substantive impact. Moreover, this model can be used to predict when information effects should occur in measures of collective opinion and when they should not. To avoid "predictive" tautologies ("the dearth of knowledge will have an effect on opinions when knowledge is important to forming opinions"), the elements of this model can be integrated with the rich micro-level theoretical and empirical literature associated with information processing theories of human cognition. Dual-process theories like the heuristic-systematic model and the elaboration-likelihood model postulate prior knowledge to be a component of cognitive ability (Chaiken 1980; Chaiken, Liberman, and Eagly 1989; Petty and Cacioppo 1986). Dual-process models thereby assign knowledge an important role in determining the mix of processing strategies people will use to answer survey questions. In the domain of politics, reliance on and choice among available heuristic shortcuts and processing strategies as well as the accuracy of beliefs about the world, are all held to be influenced by levels of general political knowledge (see also Mondak 1994b; Sniderman, Brody, and Tetlock 1991).

---

[28] For a good example of how the responses given by ill-informed respondents can be affected by adjacent but unrelated questions, see Sinnott 2000. Regarding how the recency and frequency with which knowledge is carried in news reports contribute to accessibility effects, see Price and Tewksbury 1997.

Because cognitive ability is modeled in part as a function of prior knowledge, the social distribution of political knowledge is expected to produce two effects in measures of collective opinion that should vary in magnitude with the importance of cognitive ability to opinion formation and expression. First, to the extent that higher levels of cognitive ability are required to render valid judgments about the object of a survey question, the people who give substantive opinions should become increasingly unrepresentative of the population from which they are drawn. Groups with higher levels of cognitive ability should be overrepresented in the collective opinion, and groups with lower levels of cognitive ability should be underrepresented. Second, to the extent that high levels of cognitive ability are required to render valid judgments about the object of a survey question, frames of reference, heuristic cues, and other considerations made relevant by the survey instrument should have an increasingly greater impact on the aggregate distributions of lower-ability respondents.

It is important to point out that while the model developed here predicts convergence behavior to occur among ill-informed respondents, such behavior could plausibly take many forms in the aggregate. Convergence behavior may lead to less dispersion in a group's collective opinion, but the same behavior can also cause a group's opinion to become more dispersed. For example, suppose we divided ill-informed respondents randomly into two groups and posed a slightly different question to each group. Asked whether they support widget controls, the first group shows 80% approval. The second group is asked the same question but is also told that a well-known politician opposes the policy, and the addition of this cue drops the support level down to 60%. Such a pattern is entirely consistent with the prediction of convergence, only in this case the cue in the second question leads opinion givers to become more dispersed than those presented with the first question. As convergence can be thought of as a systematic deviation in individual opinions brought about by cue-taking behavior, the directional influence of convergence behavior depends on the distribution of uncued opinion in the same group. Sometimes we can observe the impact of convergence behavior directly, as with a split-ballot test, but in most cases we will have no clear counterfactual measure of what a group's opinion might look like in the absence of convergence behavior. Only to the degree that uncued and completely uninformed opinions are random in nature can we be certain that convergence behavior will exaggerate the lopsidedness of ill-informed opinions. With these caveats in mind, the findings in this chapter nonetheless support the expectation that convergence behavior should tend to increase the lopsidedness of ill-informed opinion.[29]

Political knowledge should thus operate through cognitive ability to reduce the effective size of ill-informed groups and increase the unanimity of opinions among ill-informed people. This is not to say that the distributional expectations of collective rationality models should always fail to materialize. Something approaching the appearance of collective rationality may well obtain in measures of aggregate opinion. The point emphasized by the depletion-convergence model is that the distributional expectations of collective rationality models are merely one possible outcome of aggregating individual opinions together: collective ignorance may be just as likely to result. The outcome depends on the relative shape and size of group opinion distributions. The greater the importance of cognitive ability to opinion formation or expression, the less likely a collective opinion should be to take on the distributional assumptions posited by collective rationality models unless ill-informed respondents are otherwise motivated to process their opinions systematically.

CONCLUSION

Although the egalitarian tendencies of opinion surveys have been touted since the method's earliest days (Gallup and Rae 1940), opinion surveys can suffer from representation problems similar to those observed in elections. These findings suggest a sobering conclusion: collective preferences should often fail to represent accurately the range of voices and interests in a society.

Collective opinion may at times appear rational, but this result is neither inevitable nor even likely. Ensuring that a sample descriptively represents a population does not guarantee that the people who give opinions will accurately reflect the demographic makeup of that population. Knowledgeable respondents – who tend to be more affluent, educated,

---

[29] Other potential influences that bear on patterns of convergence behavior are the goals or motivations of respondents who answer questions. Opinion convergence among respondents whose primary goal is judgmental accuracy, which is often presumed in dual-process theories to be the typical motive (Chen and Chaiken 1999; Petty and Wegener 1999), may take a different form than among respondents who are just like them but whose primary goal is defending established attitudes. It is also possible, for any given topic, that the most knowledgeable respondents might have different processing goals than the least knowledgeable respondents. In either case, the conflation of motives and expressed opinions would tend to obscure the unique contribution of convergence behavior to the lopsidedness of group opinions.

male, white, and partisan than ill-informed respondents – usually are overrepresented in the ranks of opinion givers. As a result, the voices of relatively knowledgeable demographic groups may carry a disproportionate weight in surveyed opinion measures. And because the dispersion of one group's opinion relative to others is a resource for communicating group preferences through marginal percentages, groups with relatively lopsided distributions of opinion will tend to hold a disproportionate influence over the shape of collective preferences. As a result, the preferences of the least knowledgeable opinion givers – made up disproportionately of the less educated, the less affluent, blacks, women, and political independents – are often amplified in collective preferences because ill-informed people tend to give similar responses to survey questions.

While it is clear that the social distribution of political knowledge influences the quality of representation in collective opinions, sorting out its unique influence poses a difficult problem. The challenge lies in determining for any particular case how much of the dispersion in group opinions and the levels of "don't know" or "no opinion" responses are uniquely due to levels of political knowledge. If political knowledge were randomly distributed across all relevant groups in society, the answer would be simple: any difference in opinion among the various knowledge quartiles could reasonably be attributed to differences in knowledge. But since knowledge levels are related to demographic characteristics, the unique influence of knowledge is harder to pinpoint. What is the unique influence of political knowledge on the kinds of misrepresentation detailed here, and what might collective preferences look like if everyone were as well informed as the most knowledgeable respondents? Chapter 4 provides the missing piece of the puzzle. Correcting for the low levels and uneven social distribution of political knowledge often causes collective preferences to change in significant ways.

PART II

INFORMATION EFFECTS IN COLLECTIVE PREFERENCES

4

The Impact of Information Effects

Ever since Marx suggested that workers were imbued with a "false consciousness" that distracted them from their material interests, students of politics have grappled unsuccessfully with the question of how to tell when people's opinions might be at odds with their interests. Some, like Marx and Edmund Burke before him, argue that political interests are objective and can be identified for any group of people without regard to their stated preferences (Balbus 1971; Bay 1965; Lukes 1974).[1] Others, like Rousseau and, in some accounts, the early utilitarians (Cutler 1999; Minar 1960; although see Pitkin 1967: Chapter 9), claim that interests are subjective and thus inseparable from the expressed wishes of individuals speaking for themselves. Much of the theoretical rationale behind citizen referenda and modern opinion polling can be traced back to this subjective view of interests (Minar 1960).

But in light of inherent problems with each of these definitions,[2] recent work has focused instead on interests as "fully informed" or "enlightened" preferences (Bartels 1990; Connolly 1972, 1993; Dahl 1989: 180–1; Delli Carpini and Keeter 1996; Lippmann 1955: 42; Mansbridge 1983: 24–6). In this perspective, as Jane Mansbridge (1983) puts it, interests are revealed in "the preferences that people would have if their information were perfect, including the knowledge they would have in

---

[1] Leo Bogart (1967) summarizes the Marxian view of interests and opinions in this way: "Opinions that deviate from those appropriate to one's class are irrational; those unrelated to class interest are irrelevant" (334).

[2] For overviews of these problems and the controversies surrounding various definitions of political interests, see Balbus 1971; Bartels 1990; Connolly 1972, 1993; Mansbridge 1983; Pitkin 1967: Chapters 8 and 9.

retrospect if they had a chance to live out the consequences of each choice before actually making a decision" (25). By equating interests with hypothetical fully informed preferences, this perspective provides a useful approach for inferring when the preferences expressed by individuals may be at odds with their interests.

Connolly, Dahl, Mansbridge, and other theorists who find merit in the enlightened preferences ideal have themselves made no attempt to specify this standard at a level of detail that would allow an obvious test for the quality of actual preferences. To the contrary, Connolly (1993: 76) argues explicitly against such an endeavor: "To promise more, to offer to 'translate' these issues into a series of neat hypotheses amenable to precise and impersonal testing is inevitably to corrupt the enterprise undertaken. The outcome would join surface precision to profound obscurity." Some empirical work that attempts to apply this or related standards to actual preferences has at times appeared to take up just the enterprise that Connolly warns against (e.g., Bartels 1996; Delli Carpini and Keeter 1996; Lau and Redlawsk 1997), but these efforts have usually been made with little effort to explicitly justify the normative freighting that such studies presume to shoulder.

While the positive identification of political interests lies well beyond the scope of this (and perhaps any) study, and while the theorists advancing enlightened preference standards identify them as ideals rather than something that can be achieved in any existing society, this approach may nonetheless help clarify when surveyed opinion *might* reveal something like enlightened interests. "Since it is inevitable that no choice will ever be *fully* informed in this way," writes Connolly (1993: 69), "we must say that the most informed choice available to one in a particular context constitutes a judgment in serious pursuit of one's real interests" (emphasis in original). When matching preferences with interests, theories of enlightened preferences suggest the more information, the better.[3] The gap between expressed preferences and enlightened interests should narrow as a person's store of relevant knowledge becomes increasingly perfect and complete.

---

[3] It follows (and is often mentioned in this literature) that people should tend to acquire relevant information through the course of experience in such a way that their judgments made at later points in time should tend to be closer to the "enlightened preferences" ideal than their judgments at earlier points in time. "The privileged choice," writes Connolly (1993: 65), "is one made after the fact, so to speak, rather than before it."

The difficulty lies in sorting out the best among several possible ways of operationalizing this definition of interests: When might the subjective preferences that people express in surveys or voting be consistent with their fully informed preferences? Two traditional approaches have been used to explore what collective opinion might look like if opinion givers were relatively better informed than the general public usually is. The first is to purge ill-informed respondents from among the ranks of opinion givers through the use of filtering questions. For example, Bishop, Oldendick, and Tuchfarber (1983) found that the unfiltered form of domestic policy questions tended to produce response patterns in which a majority favored liberal stances such as government intervention in economic affairs. But when filters were added, DK responses increased by 27% to 48% and the marginals consistently reversed so that, of the remaining respondents, a majority favored more conservative stances such as private sector approaches to economic problems. While this is a particularly blunt method for estimating informed preferences – it ignores completely how individual opinions might change with more political knowledge – filter questions are nevertheless widely used by survey organizations to isolate an "informed" public opinion.

The second approach is to manipulate the amount and quality of information available to people who express preferences of various kinds. Experimental methods for assessing the role of information in preference formation have been used to isolate the unique impact of political knowledge on various kinds of judgments (e.g., Fiske, Lau, and Smith 1990), inform members of a treatment group about some issue and then compare their judgments about the issue to members of a control group given no information (e.g., Kuklinski, Quirk et al. 1998), and to explore what fully informed collective preferences might look like (Lau and Redlawsk 1997, 2001; Price and Neijens 1998). To date, the most ambitious use of such methods to simulate fully informed policy preferences has been James Fishkin's experiments with deliberative opinion polls. Deliberative polls bring a random sample of ordinary citizens to a central location where they are provided with detailed policy information and an environment in which to discuss issues (Fishkin 1991, 1995; Fishkin and Luskin 1999). In this way, argues Fishkin (1995: 171), "the deliberative poll can be thought of as an actual sample from a hypothetical society – the deliberative and engaged society we do not have." The impact of deliberation can be observed by comparing the opinions of participants before and after being immersed in a deliberative environment that exposes them to relevant information about political issues (e.g., Fishkin and Luskin 1999; Gastil and Dillard 1999).

Yet neither question filters nor experimentation provides a satisfactory measure of fully informed collective preferences. Encouraging high levels of "don't know" responses may be a good strategy for isolating people who are opinionated and better informed, but it does so at a price. Those who tend to be filtered away will come predominantly from certain demographic groups whose subjective needs, wants, and values may not be adequately represented by the remaining opinion givers. By encouraging even greater numbers of "don't know" and "no opinion" responses, the use of filter questions inevitably exaggerates the patterns of demographic misrepresentation discussed in Chapter 3. In contrast, we should expect a sample of opinion givers from a fully informed public to closely mirror the demographic makeup of that public because survey respondents with uniformly high levels of political knowledge should be less likely to exhibit the differential patterns of "don't know" responses that are so common in collective preferences.

A more compelling portrait of an informed public would consider what collective opinion might look like if *everyone* were as well informed as the most well-informed people. Experimental methods are in some ways better suited than filter questions to providing such a portrait, but using experimentation to simulate the views of a fully informed public has several important shortcomings. It is possible in an experimental setting to provide people who are normally oblivious to the political world with information that they can use to formulate preferences. But such settings are unable to equip ill-informed subjects with other important traits normally associated with being well informed: the cognitive styles and information processing strategies characteristic of politically knowledgeable people (Fiske, Lau, and Smith 1990; Judd and Downing 1990; Krosnick and Milburn 1990; McGraw and Pinney 1990; Popkin and Dimock 2000; Sniderman, Brody, and Tetlock 1991), the knowledge stored in long-term memory that affects how new information is perceived and used to update attitudes (Delli Carpini and Keeter 1996; Krosnick and Milburn 1990; Zaller 1992a), and the confidence, developed through experience, that one is able to understand complicated political issues and events (Krosnick and Milburn 1990).[4] Well-informed respondents also tend to base their opinions on different grounds than ill-informed respondents (McGraw and Pinney 1990). For example, knowledgeable respondents

---

[4] For a recent review of the literature documenting these differences, see Price 1999.

are more likely to use their own preferences on domestic issues to evaluate presidential performance (Delli Carpini and Keeter 1996). For the least knowledgeable respondents, presidential approval ratings are unrelated to opinions on domestic issues. Lacking these traits and resources, it is reasonable to question the causes and substantive meaning of any opinion change among normally ill-informed people. Simply providing ill-informed respondents with more information ignores the centrality of these various linkages between knowledge and opinion.

Typical experimental settings also fail to duplicate the social contexts in which political information is acquired and used to form preferences. As John Dewey (1927: 158) put it, "Knowledge is a function of association and communication; it depends upon tradition, upon tools and methods socially transmitted, developed, and sanctioned" (see also Delli Carpini and Keeter 1996; Wildavsky 1987). Political information is commonly filtered through interpersonal networks that influence the way this information is used to construct opinions (Berelson, Lazarsfeld, and McPhee 1954; Huckfeldt, Beck et al. 1995; Lazarsfeld, Berelson, and Gaudet 1948). Given the importance of these interpersonal networks, the process of removing people from their usual social settings, sitting them down in a laboratory and encouraging them to read position papers – as was done in Fishkin's National Issues Convention – seems a very artificial way of informing them. A more realistic way would take into account the social construction of needs, wants, and values and the cultural transmission of political knowledge. It would seem that while experimental methods are especially useful in differentiating informed from ignorant people, they are less suited to predicting the sorts of policies a fully informed public might prefer.

Three dynamics must be accounted for in any successful attempt at estimating the preferences of a fully informed public. First, increasing levels of information should cause more respondents to give opinions: the more uniformly high the levels of political knowledge in a population, the more accurately should the pool of opinion givers represent the demographic characteristics of the population from which they are drawn. Second, increasing levels of information should affect the kinds of processing strategies, heuristic shortcuts, and cognitive styles that respondents use in forming preferences, as well as the quality of inferences drawn from this information. These first and second dynamics represent the main effects of information. Third, the social construction of needs, wants, and values suggests that increasing levels of information may cause people with different demographic characteristics to arrive at different policy preferences. This dynamic represents the potential interaction effects between information and demographic characteristics.

SIMULATING FULLY INFORMED OPINION

Where filter questions and experimental methods fall short, a third way of simulating fully informed preferences offers promise. Independently pioneered in work by Michael Delli Carpini and Scott Keeter (1996: Chapter 6) and by Larry Bartels (1996), this approach uses multivariate regression to simulate how individual opinions might change if opinion givers were better informed about politics. Unlike filter questions and experimental methods, this approach is explicitly premised on the enlightened preferences concept and on the social construction of political interests. In this approach, estimates of fully informed opinions are generated by assigning the distribution of preferences held by the more highly informed members of a given demographic group to all members of that group, simultaneously taking into account the influence of a wide range of demographic variables. For example, if well-informed respondents who come from union families express different policy preferences than the ill-informed respondents from union families, this method assigns the mix of fully informed preferences to all respondents who come from union families. But instead of considering only the bivariate relationship between union membership and policy preferences, this method looks at union respondents who are women, from a certain income level, live in eastern states, are married, own homes, are of a certain age, and so on. If relatively better-informed people sharing all these characteristics have different preferences from their less-informed counterparts, the method identifies the relationship between knowledge and each characteristic in a way that suggests what people's preferences might be if they were more knowledgeable about politics.

Fully informed preferences were simulated for each of the 235 questions from the 1988, 1992, and 1996 American National Election Studies analyzed in Chapter 3, using a logistic regression (logit) model for dichotomous questions and an ordered logit model for trichotomous questions.[5]

---

[5] All survey questions not originally coded with two or three response options were recoded for this analysis into dichotomous or trichotomous distributions, as appropriate. Nondichotomous categorical variables were recoded into dichotomies, with the category of interest taking a value of one and all other categories taking values of zero. Further detail about the coding of individual questions is available from the author upon request.

The process of simulating fully informed preferences – as detailed in Appendix B – proceeds in four steps. In the first step, surveyed preferences are regressed on a scale of political knowledge, a variety of demographic characteristics, and a set of variables representing the interactions between knowledge and each of the demographic characteristics. By estimating the actual relationships between preferences and each of the predictor variables, this step provides a set of regression coefficients that will be used to simulate each person's fully informed preference. These coefficients jointly model the probability that a particular individual will choose each of the response alternatives in a particular survey question (e.g., decreasing spending, keeping spending the same, or increasing spending on military defense). Step two involves changing each respondent's score on the political knowledge scale to the highest possible value. In the 1992 ANES, for example, the highest possible value on the information scale was 23 points, and in this step all respondents in the 1992 study were assigned a knowledge score of 23. In the third step, each respondent's predicted fully informed preference is calculated by plugging the coefficient values obtained from step one into each respondent's actual demographic characteristics, substituting only the new values of the altered knowledge variable and interaction terms. This step produces, for each individual, a new set of probabilities for each response alternative that simulate the preference each person might report if she or he were more knowledgeable about politics. The final step aggregates all of the individual fully informed preferences together, including those of people who originally gave "don't know" and "no opinion" responses, by taking the mean of the individual probabilities for each of the alternative responses. These average probabilities, which represent collective preferences controlling for individual differences in political knowledge levels, are then compared to the actual percentage of respondents in each category of the survey results to reveal the impact of information effects.

The end result of this four-step transformation is for knowledge levels to become uniformly high across demographic groups and for all respondents to give opinions. In essence, the simulation is a sophisticated way of weighting the preferences of highly knowledgeable opinion givers who have a certain combination of demographic characteristics by the number of respondents who share those characteristics. However, since the simulation method does this by modeling the relative rather than absolute impact of knowledge on preferences within any given demographic group, these estimates do not require any members of a demographic group to actually achieve perfect scores on the political knowledge scale.

This is indeed fortunate, since this highest level of sophistication was observed in little more than 1% of respondents in the ANES data used here, and this tiny group has noticeably less demographic diversity than would be required for such an exercise. Rather, it is the degree of dissimilarity (if any) in the preferences expressed by relatively more and less knowledgeable people with a particular demographic profile that is used to estimate fully informed preferences for all people sharing that profile.

Using only the observed differences between well- and ill-informed respondents, this method imputes to all respondents the information processing strategies and cognitive styles employed by well-informed people. It also allows political knowledge to interact with demographic characteristics in ways that may move preferences in one direction for some groups and in the opposite direction for other groups. This flexibility allows the model to accurately reflect the social diversity of needs, wants, and values. Of course, increasing levels of information may lead instead to greater consensus of opinion across groups, and the simulation method leaves that possibility open as well. Most important, this method is not predisposed to finding any information effects at all: if well- and ill-informed respondents give essentially the same mix of preferences, then the shape of the resulting fully informed preference will be the same as the actual one (Bartels 1996: 208–9).

The simulated preferences produced by this transformation are only hypothetical. These fully informed preferences tell us not how people would *really* think if they knew more about politics, but only the extent to which different outcomes are produced when slight changes are introduced to a mathematical model that attempts to capture (in an extremely simplistic way) how political knowledge influences the relationships between demographic characteristics and preferences expressed in opinion surveys. As there is no obvious way to tell whether these simulated fully informed preferences have any relationship to the opinions that people would actually give if they were to become better informed about politics, the differences between surveyed and fully informed preferences are properly interpreted as indicating the relative importance of political knowledge to expressed opinions. In other words, a large difference between surveyed and fully informed opinion suggests only that the preference is heavily influenced by a person's level of political knowledge, while a small difference suggests that political knowledge has little bearing on responses to a particular survey question.

In this context, *fully informed* should be understood narrowly to mean *achieving a perfect score on a particular test of factual political knowledge.*

As there is no agreement on what political information is useful, let alone essential, for forming quality opinions (Kuklinski, Quirk et al. 1998), the term "fully informed" inevitably rings hollow. Because no knowledge scale can capture all or even the most relevant political information (Graber 1994, 2001; Popkin 1991), I use the term *fully informed* relative to a given scale rather than in a more absolute sense. I prefer this term to merely *informed*, which lacks precision, and *enlightened preference*, which suggests that informed people do indeed have a better grasp of their interests. While this may at times be true, and while it may be tempting to assume this for purposes of comparing fully informed simulations to actual survey data, there are many other reasons why informed people might express a different mix of preferences than ill-informed people. (The next two chapters explore these reasons at the individual and collective levels, respectively.) Most essentially, it is important to distinguish between what I call *fully informed* preferences and what political theorists label *enlightened* preferences. Although these terms are sometimes used interchangeably (e.g., Bartels 1990; Delli Carpini and Keeter 1996), the latter seems most appropriate as an ideal normative standard rather than as something that can be measured or estimated empirically.

The information measures used in this study are based on those constructed and tested by Delli Carpini and Keeter (1993, 1996). These indices, which are detailed in Appendix A, are primarily additive measures of correct answers to factual knowledge questions, where a correct answer is assigned a value of 1 and an incorrect response or no answer is given a value of 0.[6] Demographic variables used in the simulation account for the effects of education, income, age, partisanship, race, gender, marital status, occupation, religious affiliation, union membership, homeowner status, parental status, financial status, region, and type of community. These

---

[6] While this division of responses into "correct" and "incorrect/no answer" categories is standard in the literature, recent work has detailed how "guesses," DK/NO answers, and incorrect responses can be distinctive measures of political knowledge holding (Mondak 2000, 2001; Nadeau and Niemi 1995). In particular, this work suggests that allowing people to give DK/NO responses to factual knowledge items, and then collapsing those responses with "partially correct" answers, as is done here, can conflate the measurement of political knowledge with that of personality characteristics predisposing people to guess or abstain from guessing. In the present context, the likely effect of such contamination is to attenuate the apparent relationship between political knowledge and surveyed preferences (Mondak 2000: 80). Unfortunately, limitations imposed by the modeling approach and data used here preclude estimating a more precise measure of knowledge holding. In this light, it is likely that the simulation results presented below represent a conservative estimate of information effects: a more fine-tuned approach to modeling information holding might reveal larger information effects than those reported here.

characteristics represent all the available demographic variables that tend to be relatively stable features of a respondent's makeup and that might be expected to have some bearing on policy preferences. Excluded from this analysis were attitudinal variables that might be determined by or confounded with levels of political information.[7]

Four measures are used in this analysis to assess the differences between surveyed and fully informed opinions, two for assessing aggregate-level effects and two for assessing individual-level effects. (Additional details on the construction of these variables are included in Appendix B.) *Collective information effects* are measured as the absolute percentage-point difference between the actual marginal percentages from a survey question and those simulated for a fully informed public. This variable captures the substantive impact of micro-level information effects on the shape of collective opinion. Questions in which simulated collective opinion has a different preference ordering than surveyed opinion were coded

---

[7] The resulting mix of demographic variables is quite similar to that used by Bartels (1996) and by Delli Carpini and Keeter (1996). The one significant departure from the demographic characteristics considered by Bartels and Delli Carpini and Keeter is my inclusion of party identification variables. Party identification is a relatively stable trait, which puts it on par with the other demographic variables included in this analysis. More important, partisanship is a widely used cueing mechanism and information shortcut for issue positions (Campbell, Converse et al. 1960; Page 1978; Rahn 1993; Rahn and Cramer 1996). To the extent that party identification serves as a heuristic shortcut, excluding it from the analysis could exaggerate the apparent importance of factual information to policy preferences.

However, the need to control for partisanship is complicated by the fact that party identification is positively correlated with political knowledge, since political independents tend to be less knowledgeable than partisans. Regressing political knowledge on dummy variables for Republican and Democratic partisans (including leaners) produced positive coefficients for both party variables, but accounted for only between 6% and 8% of variance in knowledge levels. Thus, including partisanship controls should reduce the apparent size of information effects produced by the simulation method.

To estimate the substantive impact of this modeling choice, I re-ran the simulations without party identification variables for a subset of questions from the 1992 ANES. These "reduced form" models produced estimates of collective information effects that were essentially identical to the simulation results reported later. Among the questions analyzed in this way, 57.8% ($n = 26$) of the simulations that included controls for partisanship produced smaller estimates of information effects than the simulations that omitted party identification variables, hardly an improvement over chance. Moreover, the mean difference between those results with partisan controls and the measures of fully informed opinion without such controls was only two-thirds of a percentage point. Controlling for party identification therefore seems to have little influence on the size or direction of information effects in these data. Nonetheless, the great theoretical importance attributed to partisanship as an information shortcut justified the decision to retain these controls in the simulation results reported later.

as having *inconsistent collective preferences*. Three possible collective preferences were considered: a majority in favor of an option, a plurality in favor of an option, and a tie between options. Any case where the collective preference in surveyed opinion was different from that in the simulated marginals was coded as a change in preference order. For trichotomous data, a change in opinion was also coded when a majority opinion in survey data was downgraded to a plurality opinion in the simulation and vice versa.

A second set of measures is also needed to capture shifts in individual opinions, since controlling for unequal knowledge levels might leave the marginal percentages quite stable even though a substantial number of respondents change opinions in offsetting directions. Because such offsetting changes are likely to be missed by looking only at changes in a question's marginals, the amount of individual-level churn underlying any changes in collective preferences is assessed in two ways for those respondents who provided substantive responses in the survey data. *Individual-level information effects* are measured for each survey respondent as the absolute difference between the person's opinion probabilities from the survey data and fully informed opinion probabilities derived from the simulation method (cf. Bartels 1996). Individual-level effects are large when the simulation produces large shifts in a person's opinion probabilities, and small when such corrections make little difference in the probability of selecting one response alternative over another. To ease comparisons with collective-level information effects, these probabilities are translated into percentage-point differences between surveyed and fully informed opinions. These absolute differences are then averaged across all respondents who provided substantive answers to a given survey question to render the average individual-level information effect for a particular question. Individuals with different preference orderings in their surveyed and simulated opinions were coded as having *inconsistent individual-level preferences*. To construct this variable, the response category with the largest predicted probability was counted as the respondent's opinion. Respondents were coded as having inconsistent preferences if their predicted opinions calculated from the survey data were different from their predicted opinions derived from the simulation. While not as precise as measuring the change in probabilities for favoring various options, since it does not distinguish a small change (in the dichotomous case) of .49 to .51 from a large change of .30 to .70, this indicator nevertheless captures an important dynamic that underlies changes in the shape of collective preferences. Because the changes of interest at the individual level involve the difference between surveyed and simulated opinions, all respondents giving DK/NO answers in the survey data were therefore excluded from these measures of individual-level information effects.

INFORMATION EFFECTS IN COLLECTIVE PREFERENCES

The appropriate test for the significance of information effects in the regression models used here is the likelihood ratio test (Bartels 1996: 209).[8] This test was found to be significant at the $p < .01$ level in 76.6% of the 235 questions and at the $p < .05$ level in 84.3%. In other words, models that take information effects into account tend to provide a substantially better fit to the data than models that assume no information effects. Information effects in surveyed preferences appear to be the norm rather than the exception.

Before discussing the general findings from these simulations, it will be helpful to first take a close look at a few examples that demonstrate how unequal levels of political knowledge can bias collective preferences. These examples are issues that involve potential conflicts among the needs, wants, and values of men and women, the affluent and the poor, and political partisans. As such, they illustrate how between-group inequalities in political knowledge can significantly influence the apparent meaning of surveyed opinion.

Information Effects in Attitudes toward Abortion Rights

The first example comes from a question in the 1992 ANES that asked respondents to identify which of four statements came closest to their views on abortion. Respondents were divided into those who agreed that "by law, a woman should always be able to obtain an abortion as a matter of personal choice" and those who favored at least some restrictions on the availability of abortion. Figure 4.1 provides a detailed comparison of

---

[8] Similar to the F-test used to compare improvement of fit in ordinary least squares equations, the likelihood ratio test compares the log likelihoods of an unrestricted logit model, which includes all the variables, and a restricted logit model lacking the information and interaction terms to determine the significance of the differences between them. For example, the ending -2 log likelihood of the unrestricted equation in Table B.1 of Appendix B is 2314.6, while that of the restricted equation without interaction terms (not shown) is 2405.0. The result is a χ^2 value of 90.4 with $m = 25$ degrees of freedom, where m is equal to the number of parameters in the restricted model. This value is significant at the $p < .001$ level, so the null hypothesis of no information effects can be safely rejected.

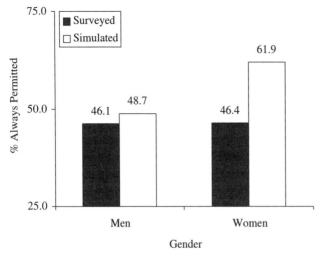

Total Sample	% Always Permitted	% At Least Some Restrictions
Surveyed Marginals	46.2%	53.8
Simulated Marginals	55.7%	44.3

FIGURE 4.1. Surveyed and fully informed opinion on abortion rights

the actual marginal percentages for this question and those simulated for a public with uniformly high levels of political knowledge. In the actual marginals, a slight majority said they favored at least some restrictions on abortion rights. Yet the fully informed collective preference reverses this balance, so that a slight majority favors making sure that abortion is always permitted by law. The only difference between these two measures is that the latter controls for the uneven social distribution of political knowledge.

Even more interesting than the substantive shift in the collective preference are the underlying dynamics of change among male and female respondents. Figure 4.1 shows that the direction of change from surveyed to simulated opinion is the same for both groups: controlling for information asymmetries led to increased support among both men and women for abortion rights. But the magnitude of this change was much smaller for men than for women. Collective opinion among male respondents shifted less than 3 percentage points, compared with 16 points among females. Further analysis revealed that this smaller change among males was due in part to a ceiling effect from their higher average information scores and to the weaker relationship for males between political information levels and support for abortion rights.

Another reason for the smaller shift was that individual-level information effects were more randomized among men than among women. The average individual-level information effect among men was 9.9 percentage points (s.d. = 11.01), while that among women was 19.0 points (s.d. = 18.27).[9] This smaller information effect among men meant that fewer males who came down on one side or another of this issue in the survey data changed their opinions in the simulated data, going from support for restrictions to support for unlimited abortion rights or vice versa. While 30% of female opinion givers ($n = 313$) changed their views in the simulated data, only 16% of male respondents ($n = 147$) were found to do so. Furthermore, the collective opinion among men shifted only a few points despite the nearly 10-point average gap among male respondents, which demonstrates that most of this individual-level change occurred in offsetting directions. In contrast, the 16-point collective information effect was nearly as large as the average individual-level effect among women: correcting for information effects almost always resulted in a pro-choice shift at the individual level among female respondents.

After assigning all respondents equally high knowledge levels, the group preference of fully informed men (i.e., support for restrictions) remained unchanged from that of surveyed opinion. Thus the 9-point swing in collective opinion came mostly from changes in the opinions of female respondents. As shown in Figure 4.1, group opinion among women shifted 16 percentage points in a pro-choice direction once information levels were raised and standardized. This resulted in a reversal of majority opinion among female respondents: whereas 54% of women said they *favored* some restrictions on abortion rights in the survey data, 62% of women said they *opposed* such restrictions in the simulated data.

These findings suggest that the information imbalances between men and women suppress the magnitude of pro-choice opinion revealed in opinion surveys. The fully informed majority preference of women on the issue of abortion rights is opposed to that of men, while their actual majority preference is the same as that of men.

---

[9] *T*-testing confirms that these differences among men and women are statistically significant, $t(1951) = -13.15$, $p < .001$.

Information Effects in Attitudes toward Economic Policy

The second example is a question from the 1996 ANES that reads "I am going to ask you to choose which of two statements I read comes closer to your own opinion. You might agree to some extent with both, but we want to know which one is closer to your views. One, we need a strong government to handle today's complex economic problems; or two, the free market can handle these problems without government being involved." When we turn to the distribution of surveyed preferences displayed in Figure 4.2, we find what appears to be a sharp division of opinion among income quartiles. The most affluent respondents are evenly split on this issue, with 49% preferring governmental control of free markets. In contrast, the poorest respondents are strongly opposed to free market solutions, with only 28% supporting free market solutions

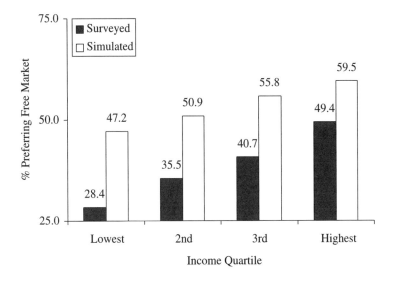

Total Sample	% Strong Government	% Free Market
Surveyed Marginals	61.7%	38.3
Simulated Marginals	46.8%	53.2

FIGURE 4.2. Surveyed and fully informed opinion on free market solutions to economic problems

and nearly three-quarters preferring government intervention in the economy. As wage laborers and working-class people are potentially more at risk with deregulation of the economy and have potentially more to gain with the imposition of protectionist trade policies, this division of opinion seems quite understandable. Regardless of the cause of these differences, the more lopsided opinions of lower income quartiles overlaying the evenly split opinions of affluent respondents create a dispersion effect that draws the shape of the collective opinion toward their preferred alternative. In what appears to be a strong majority opinion, 62% of all respondents in the survey data support strong government intervention in the economy, whereas only 38% prefer free market solutions.

Correcting for uneven levels of political knowledge results in a 15-point shift from surveyed to simulated marginals, so that only 47% of fully informed respondents favor strong government over free market solutions to economic problems. As a result, the collective preference shifts from support for government intervention to a split between options that slightly favors free market solutions. Controlling for information imbalances in the simulated measures also produces a preference change within three of the four income quartiles. In the surveyed opinion data, a majority of respondents in every quartile prefer government intervention in the economy (although in the case of the highest income group, this is a very thin majority). In contrast, fully informed opinion within the top three quartiles prefers free market solutions, while that for the lowest quartile retains a slight preference for government intervention. The direction of change is consistent across quartiles, and as expected, the largest change comes in the lowest quartile. With a 19-point shift in group opinion after controlling for information effects, the poorest group of respondents go from being strongly supportive of government intervention in surveyed opinion to being almost evenly split on this issue. A total of 25% of opinion givers from this quartile ($n = 86$) were found to change their views in the simulated data, and their average individual-level effect was 20.8 percentage points (s.d. = 20.5). These findings indicate that individual-level information effects tended to move opinions in similar directions for this group. The highest income quartile showed the smallest change in its group opinion, with a 10-point difference between surveyed and fully informed opinion. Only 12% of respondents from this quartile changed opinions as a result of raising information levels, and the average individual-level effect for this group was 12.1 percentage points (s.d. = 14.3), confirming that individual-level opinion changes in this group also tended to occur in similar directions.[10] As respondents from higher income quartiles tend to be better informed on average, this smaller amount of change comes as no surprise.[11] Whereas dispersion effects in surveyed opinion for this question privilege the views of less affluent respondents, they give a slight advantage to the opinions of more affluent groups in the simulated data. Yet because the differences in group preferences are much smaller in the fully informed data, with a 12-point difference between the opinions of the highest and lowest income quartiles compared to a 21-point difference in the survey data, the impact of differences in group dispersion is diminished in the simulated data.

Simulating the fully informed opinions of individual respondents reveals that the class-based stratification of opinion on federal economic policy in the survey data is exaggerated by differences in political knowledge among income groups. Correcting for information effects reduces the differences in opinions among income quartiles. Fully informed respondents become much more supportive of free market solutions, and this is particularly so among the least affluent respondents. It remains unclear whether this pattern of change reflects a shift from "pocketbook" to "sociotropic" evaluations of economic issues (Kinder and Kiewiet 1981), increased awareness of similar political interests, or merely different perceptions about the state of the economy and the relationship between federal policy and national economic performance. Perhaps the answer lies in some combination of these possibilities. The important finding is that the concentration of political knowledge among higher income groups appears to have made the public seem more accepting of government regulation of the economy than it might have been if more respondents had been better informed.

---

[10] Analysis of variance testing confirmed that differences in the size of individual-level effects among the four income quartiles were statistically significant, $F(3, 1378) = 13.5$, $p < .001$.

[11] This is not to say that the opinions of the highest quartile are unlikely to change very much in simulated measures because of ceiling effects. For instance, a question asked in the 1988 ANES on the issue of balancing the federal budget (Figure 4.3) showed a strong majority of all respondents – 69% – unwilling to have their taxes raised to reduce the deficit. Controlling for information effects created a preference reversal in the simulated marginals so that 52% of fully informed respondents were willing to have their taxes raised. It also resulted in preference changes for the three highest income quartiles, and even the highest income quartile had about a 20–point change between surveyed and fully informed opinion.

Information Effects in Attitudes toward Reducing the Federal Budget Deficit

Differences in the knowledge levels of respondents who identify with the major political parties can also have a bearing on the substantive meaning of collective opinions. Take, for example, a question from the 1988 ANES that reads "In order to reduce the size of the federal budget deficit are you willing or not willing to pay more in federal taxes?" The desire to lower federal taxes has been a staple of the Republican Party platform for years. Furthermore, at the time of this survey it was an issue that had been recently brought to the public's attention by important tax reduction packages in 1981 and 1986 as well as the continued growth of the federal budget deficit over the Reagan years. In this context, we might expect Democrats and Republicans to differ in their responses to this question. But the actual willingness of these groups to pay more in taxes for deficit reduction tells a different story.

Figure 4.3 shows that in the survey data just over two-thirds of respondents from both of these groups said they were unwilling to raise taxes. Among pure independents, resistance increased to nearly 8 in 10 being unwilling to raise taxes for deficit reduction. The disdainful response across the political spectrum to the idea of trading a lower deficit for higher taxes creates a collective opinion in which 69% say they are unwilling to have their taxes raised, an apparently clear collective preference on this issue. Yet the validity of this preference is called into question when we identify and correct for the information inequalities among partisan groups that give rise to it. Standardizing knowledge levels in the simulation produces a 21-point drop in the percentage of respondents unwilling to pay higher taxes. Whereas the survey data has a strong majority opposed to raising taxes, simulated fully informed opinion exhibits a slight majority in favor of raising taxes.

Artificially raising knowledge levels makes each of the three groups more receptive to paying down the deficit with higher taxes. Yet even fully informed independents and Republicans are still unwilling as groups to pay higher taxes for this purpose. It is the Democratic respondents whose opinions change most dramatically on this issue, from two-thirds unwilling to pay in the survey data to two-thirds willing to pay in the simulated data, a shift of 30 points in the marginals of this group's opinion. Moreover, 58% of Democratic opinion givers ($n = 437$) changed their opinions after correcting for information effects, compared to only 29% of Republican opinion givers ($n = 191$) and 21% of independents ($n = 37$).

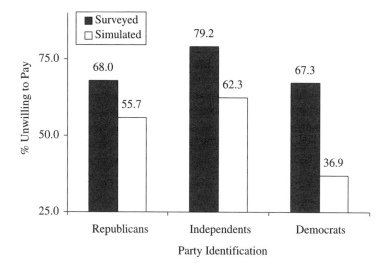

Total Sample	% Unwilling to Pay More	% Willing to Pay More
Surveyed Marginals	68.9%	31.1
Simulated Marginals	47.6%	52.4

FIGURE 4.3. Surveyed and fully informed opinion on increasing taxes to reduce the deficit

Individual-level information effects followed a similar pattern, averaging 30.5 points for Democrats (s.d. = 18.7), 14.8 points for Republicans (s.d. = 11.8), and 18.8 points for independents (s.d. = 14.4).[12] It comes as no surprise that Democratic opinion should be more affected than Republican opinion by standardizing knowledge levels, because Democrats are somewhat less knowledgeable as a group than Republicans. It is perhaps more interesting that the group opinion of independents should change by only 17 points (with nearly all individual-level effects leading independents to greater levels of support for paying higher taxes) given that they are so much less informed than either Democrats or Republicans. The impact of information effects is not necessarily largest for the least informed. As we shall also see in the next example, this finding suggests that political

---

[12] Analysis of variance testing confirmed these differences to be statistically significant, $F(2, 1600) = 183.9$, $p < .001$.

knowledge may interact with environmental and psychological factors in complex ways.

Information Effects in Preferences for More or Less Government

Chapter 3 illustrated the influence of dispersion effects on collective preferences with the results of a question from the 1992 ANES that read "Next, I am going to ask you to choose which of two statements I read comes closer to your own opinion. You might agree to some extent with both, but we want to know which one is closer to your views. One, the less government the better; or two, there are more things that government should be doing?" Turning to the marginal percentages from the survey data in Figure 4.4, we see that 65% of respondents preferred more government, while 35% preferred less. Correcting for information effects produced a simulated opinion that was evenly split between options, with 49%

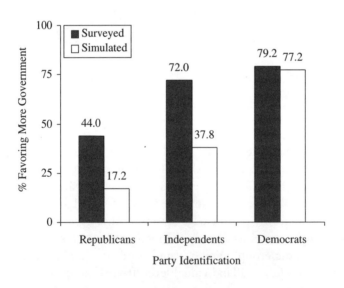

Total Sample	% More Government	% Less Government
Surveyed Marginals	64.9%	35.1
Simulated Marginals	49.3%	50.7

FIGURE 4.4. Surveyed and fully informed opinion on favoring more government

favoring more government and 51% favoring less. This fully informed collective preference turns out to be remarkably like the distribution of well-informed opinion on this issue in the survey data (see Figure 3.1 in Chapter 3. This finding clarifies that, in this case, lower levels of political knowledge rather than the demographic characteristics of less knowledgeable people were responsible for the lopsided distribution of ill-informed opinion in responses to this question.

In contrast to the previous example, changes in partisan opinion after correcting for information effects are less pronounced for Democrats than for Republicans and independents. Fully 79% of Democratic partisans said that they favored more rather than less government, and this group's fully informed opinion drops only a few points to 77%. Most of the difference between the surveyed and simulated marginals for this question came from changes in opinion among Republican partisans and independents. While 44% of Republicans and 72% of independents said in the survey data that they favored more government, levels of support for this option dropped 27 percentage points among Republicans and 34 points among independents when controlling for information inequalities. The resulting distribution of fully informed opinion among partisan groups more closely resembles the official positions of their parties than does their surveyed opinion. This does not arise merely because Democrats have more randomized information effects than other people: individual-level effects in this question averaged 7.4 points for Democrats (s.d. = 7.8), 27.7 points for Republicans (s.d. = 22.2), and 33.6 points for independents (s.d. = 20.9).[13] Taking information effects into account reveals a more coherent and plausible pattern of partisan opinion on an issue of major importance to the parties. In this case, the low levels and unequal distribution of political knowledge suppresses the diversity of opinion on this issue in a way that favors the Democrats.

GENERAL PATTERNS OF INFORMATION EFFECTS IN
COLLECTIVE PREFERENCES

The four examples just described illustrate how group differences in political knowledge can affect how accurately each group's fully informed needs, wants, and values are communicated through the marginals of

---

[13] Analysis of variance testing confirmed these individual-level differences among partisan groups to be statistically significant, $F(2, 1883) = 418.9, p < .001$.

survey questions. Correcting for differences in knowledge levels led in each case to a simulated collective preference quite different from that in the survey data. In the case of deficit reduction, government regulation of the economy, and especially abortion rights, differences between surveyed and simulated opinion were due largely to changes in the mix of preferences among relatively ill-informed groups. In the case of favoring more or less government, differences between surveyed and fully informed collective preferences were concentrated among Republicans, who tend on average to be better informed than Democrats. Many of these groups – women in the first example, poorer people in the second, Democrats in the third, and Republicans in the fourth – could also be seen as having distinctive political interests in the topic at hand, interests that seem to be more clearly articulated once information levels are raised and standardized for the entire sample.

These examples raise several questions about the influence of information effects on collective preferences. We might wonder whether the process of aggregating individually noisy opinions tends to produce collective opinions that bear a close semblance to the collective opinions that might be produced by a hypothetical population of fully informed citizens. While the four examples dealt with fairly large information effects, it is possible, in a manner consistent with the collective rationality hypothesis, that the typical effect of micro-level information disparities is to produce offsetting changes in individual opinions. If so, then even questions in which sizeable numbers of respondents are predicted to change their opinions with more complete information might nonetheless remain reasonable indicators of a population's fully informed views. Second, there may be some kinds of issues or opinion questions that are relatively immune to information effects, as well as some kinds of topics that are especially prone to them. Therefore we might wonder which types of issues are most influenced by such effects, when they occur. Third, we will want to know whether there are regular patterns to the consequences of information effects. Are there consistent differences between surveyed and fully informed opinions that suggest distinctive kinds of political bias in collective preferences, bias that stems directly from the uneven social distribution of political knowledge? Fourth, the preceding examples illustrate that the size of information effects can sometimes be relatively small for less-informed demographic groups, despite the fact that political knowledge tends to be concentrated among the politically advantaged. Are information effects consistently smaller for better informed demographic groups, so that the voices of the politically advantaged are more clearly articulated through collective preferences? It is to these questions that we now turn in examining the general findings from the simulation data.[14]

Does Collective Rationality Work?

Chapter 3 showed that the aggregate opinions of well- and ill-informed people often fail to meet the distributional assumptions of collective rationality arguments: ill-informed opinion is typically more lopsided than well-informed opinion, which means that collective preferences are often influenced disproportionately by the views of less knowledgeable opinion givers. However, the ill informed are also more likely to give DK/NO responses, which means that the numerical influence of ill-informed opinion over collective preferences may tend to be diminished. It is also possible that despite their lower levels of knowledge, the ill informed might use heuristic shortcuts or on-line processing in ways that produce knowledgeable responses. If this is the case, then the findings from Chapter 3 might only appear to undermine collective rationality arguments. The proper test of the collective rationality hypothesis is therefore to determine whether information effects at the individual level tend to occur in offsetting directions.

Because the collective information effect in any survey result is simply the average of all the individual information effects for that question, to the extent that errors occur in offsetting directions, the collective effect should tend to be smaller than the average absolute individual effect.[15] The degree to which individual effects balance one another out when aggregated can be seen in the relative difference in the size of the average individual effect and the collective effect for a given survey question. If collective rationality works, we might see large informational biases in individual responses, but when aggregated, these should produce relatively small collective effects. The top chart in Figure 4.5 illustrates such a pattern with hypothetical data. Values for the average individual-level information effect in each question are ranged along the vertical axis,

---

[14] Simulation results for the full set of individual questions are available from the author upon request.

[15] Because individual effects are calculated only for respondents who give substantive opinions in the survey data, while collective effects also include the fully informed opinions of respondents who give DK/NO responses, it is theoretically possible that collective effects could be larger than individual effects if a sizeable number of DK/NO respondents have roughly similar fully informed opinions. However, as will be detailed below and in the next chapter, this is almost never the case.

while values for a question's collective information effect are distributed along the horizontal axis. In this chart, the collective information effect remains small no matter how large the average individual-level effect, a pattern consistent with the collective rationality hypothesis. Individual effects may be quite substantial, but so long as they occur in offsetting directions, they will produce negligible collective effects (as we saw with

a. Mostly random information effects in individual responses
    (**hypothetical data**, $r = .02$)

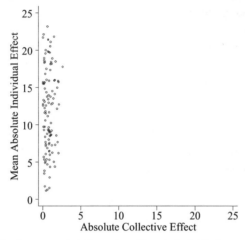

b. Mostly systematic information effects in individual responses
    (**hypothetical data**, $r = .99$)

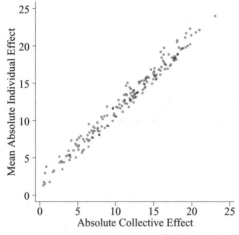

FIGURE 4.5. The potential impact of individual-level information effects on the size of collective-level information effects

male opinions on abortion rights in Figure 4.1). In such a case, the size of individual and collective effects are statistically unrelated to one another, and the surveyed collective preference is never far from the value of the simulated collective preference. However, if information effects at the individual level tend to produce systematic errors in opinions, we should tend to see mostly systematic informational biases in individual responses. The bottom chart illustrates this alternative possibility, in which the size of individual and collective effects are almost perfectly correlated. In these hypothetical data, the collective effect in each question is almost always as large as the average individual effect, which can only happen when information effects consistently push individual opinions in the same direction (as we saw with women in the case of abortion rights in Figure 4.1).

The actual relationship between individual and collective information effects is shown in Figure 4.6. If micro-level information effects were perfectly offsetting, their net result would produce the same collective preference as found in surveyed opinion. Such is not the typical case. Although there are several questions that exhibit the characteristics of collective rationality processes – large effects at the individual level but small effects in collective opinion – this chart makes clear that collective

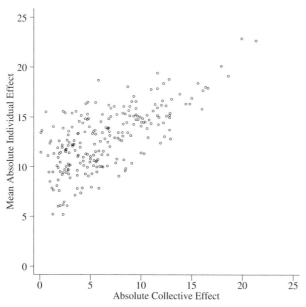

FIGURE 4.6. Actual relationship between the size of individual and collective information effects ($r = .69$)

rationality outcomes are the exception rather than the rule. Across all 235 questions, the average individual-level effect is 12.8 percentage points (s.d. = 3.1), while the average difference between surveyed and fully informed collective opinion is 6.5 percentage points (s.d. = 4.2). Under the metric of this variable, a score of 5 indicates a 5-point shift in the marginals of one of the response options, as when collective opinion changes from 50% to 55% in favor.

The correlation between the size of individual and collective effects is a healthy .69, which suggests that while the gaps between surveyed and simulated opinions at the individual and collective levels are positively related, they are not identical and are properly treated as distinctive indicators of information effects. The strength of this relationship also demonstrates numerically what the chart shows visually: individual-level information effects tend to occur in systematic rather than random directions. Aggregation alone cannot redeem an ill-informed public.

The Topical Distribution of Information Effects

Collective rationality may not work as a general model of aggregation effects, but the results thus far suggest that the typical information effect in collective opinion seems to be rather small and perhaps of minor consequence. If so, then the bottom line emerging from the collective rationality hypothesis could be correct – an uneven distribution of political knowledge might not matter much in the aggregate – even when the precise mechanisms underlying this expectation are not usually responsible for this result. However, the size of the typical information effect gives a somewhat misleading picture, because the distribution of point differences is skewed toward the low end of the scale. Fully 48% of the 235 questions had a collective information effect of between 0 and 5 percentage points, 34% differed between 6 and 10 points, 14% had differences of between 11 and 15 points, and 4% differed by more than 15 points. In the more than half of observations where nontrivial changes were observed – that is, changes of magnitudes greater than 5 percentage points – the differences between surveyed and fully informed opinion averaged 9.3 points. When collective opinion changed by more than a few points, it tended to shift quite dramatically.

The key question thus becomes whether these larger and more systematic information effects tend to be clustered in certain types of survey questions. Table 4.1 displays the average individual- and collective-level percentage point differences between surveyed and simulated opinion for

TABLE 4.1. *The average size of collective- and individual-level information effects by question category*

Mostly Random Information Effects			Mostly Systematic Information Effects		
	C	I		C	I
Pres'l policy approval	3.5	10.5	Other social policy	6.3	10.0
Child care	4.1	11.1	Equality	7.2	12.1
Affirmative action	4.3	12.9	Other value	7.2	11.2
Gay rights	4.3	12.3	Environmental	7.3	13.9
Welfare	4.7	14.1	Presidential approval	7.3	11.3
Education	5.0	11.2	Governance	8.4	14.8
Health	5.0	13.8	Abortion	9.2	14.6
Crime/Social unrest	5.4	12.5	Elder care	9.6	12.8
Foreign policy	5.6	12.1	Cong'l approval	10.2	15.4
Immigration	5.6	11.7	Fiscal	11.9	15.7
Morality	6.3	12.2			

Note: For each category, values in the C column indicate the average percentage-point size of collective information effects, while values in the I column indicate the average percentage-point size of individual-level information effects. The number of questions in each category is reported in Table 3.2.

each of the question categories. In this table, question categories in which the average collective bias is less than twice the average individual bias are counted as exhibiting "mostly random" biases. All others are counted as exhibiting "mostly systematic" biases. Within these groupings, question categories are listed in ascending order of average collective bias.

Question categories exhibiting mostly random information effects tend to be closer to the collective rationality ideal because these effects balance one another out in the aggregate. Approval questions dealing with aspects of presidential policy were least influenced by collective information effects, with surveyed opinion differing from fully informed opinion by less than 4 percentage points on average. Relatively small average effects were also found among questions dealing with affirmative action, child care, gay rights, and welfare. The largest average change in marginal percentages was found in questions dealing with fiscal issues, which shifted by nearly 12 percentage points on average after correcting for unequal levels of knowledge. Other topics found to have consistently large differences between surveyed and simulated opinion include approval of Congress, abortion, and questions addressing government programs to care for senior citizens.

Intuitively, it might seem that the size of collective differences between surveyed and simulated opinion should be smaller for "easy" question topics that are symbolic, involve policy ends rather than means, and have been on the public agenda for a long time (Carmines and Stimson 1980). Yet this expectation finds little support in the simulation results. Abortion is as "easy" an issue as one can find, and the quintessential "hard" issue is foreign policy, yet information effects are smaller at both the individual and collective levels for foreign policy than for abortion questions. Likewise, if information effects were driven only by the difficulty of the question, asking people simply to report their values should produce smaller information effects than asking people to report policy preferences. But this also is not the case. Taken together, questions dealing with values (i.e., equality, morality, and other value questions) had among the largest average collective information effects at 6.9 percentage points (s.d. = 4.1), while approval questions (i.e., those encompassing congressional, presidential, and presidential policy approval) had the smallest average collective difference between surveyed and simulated opinion measures at 5.7 points (s.d. = 4.1). The remaining categories of policy questions fell in the middle, with a mean absolute difference of 6.4 points (s.d. = 4.2).

The "easy" versus "hard" distinction can be tested directly on subsets of questions. Five of the foreign policy questions explicitly asked respondents their opinions on the appropriate goals for U.S. foreign policy.[16] A comparison of the mean percentage point differences between surveyed and fully informed opinion for these five relative to the other foreign policy questions showed that these "easier" questions had collective information effects that averaged two points smaller than the other questions, though these differences failed to attain conventional levels of statistical significance, $t(28) = 1.43$, one-tailed $p = .08$. Yet many apparently "easy" questions have large information effects, while apparently "hard" questions have small ones. For example, questions in 1992 and 1996 that asked, "A law has been proposed that would limit members of Congress to no more than 12 years of service in that office. Do you favor or oppose such a law?" Despite the complexities of this issue, the newness of the topic (at least in 1992), and the extended controversy among political observers about the desirability of term limits, these questions produced collective differences of only 1 and 2 percentage points between surveyed and simulated opinion. In contrast, questions on presidential approval, arguably among the "easier" questions in the National Election Studies

---

[16] These "easy" questions, all from the 1992 ANES, are v5940, v5941, v5942, v5943, and v5944.

since the president is the most visible and frequently discussed politician in the United States, produced average collective information effects of 7 points. Likewise, the apparently "easy" question of whether government should provide fewer or more services produced differences between surveyed and fully informed opinion of 7 points in 1988, 7 points in 1992, and 12 points in 1996. It would appear that although some "easy" issues are more resistant to information effects than others, there is no clear pattern in the simulation results to suggest that "hard" issues produce larger effects than "easy" ones.

One reason for this is that while individual-level information effects tend to be more similar in size across questions (s.d. = 3.1) than collective information effects (s.d. = 4.2), these effects are more randomized at the individual level in certain question categories. Take, for example, the issues of welfare and abortion, which should both be "easy" issues. Questions dealing with welfare have one of the highest average percentages of individual preference change after correcting for unequal levels of political knowledge – a 14.1 point mean individual information effect and 22.7% inconsistent individual preferences, on average. Nonetheless, the percentage point differences between surveyed and fully informed opinion in these questions were among the smallest of all question categories, averaging 4.7 points. In this set of questions, the macro-level impact of information effects was minimized because micro-level changes in opinion tended to occur in offsetting directions, along the lines suggested by the collective rationality hypothesis. The other extreme is illustrated by abortion questions, which also have relatively large individual-level information effects – 24% inconsistent preferences, on average, with a 15-point average gap between a person's surveyed and simulated preferences. Yet because these changes tended to move in similar directions, they produced one of the larger average deviations of 9.2 points in the marginals of abortion questions. Both abortion and welfare may be "easy" issues, but the gaps between surveyed and simulated collective preferences are smaller in the latter because welfare questions, for reasons not yet made clear, have more randomized information biases.[17]

---

[17] Another way to assess the amount of churn from offsetting individual effects that might be reducing the size of collective information effects is given by the average percentage of opinion givers who preferred one option in the survey data, but whose fully informed opinions were predicted to favor a different option for that same question. Across all 235 questions, 18.7% of respondents in an average question were found to change opinions after a statistical correction was made for uneven levels of political knowledge, but the standard deviation of 8.9 indicates that levels of inconsistency vary greatly across

These findings confirm that correcting for information asymmetries can lead to substantial shifts in collective opinion, but changes of equal size may not be equally meaningful. A 10-point change from 80% to 90% in favor of a policy is in some ways less important than a change from 45% to 55% support: the former merely reinforces the majority opinion, while the latter indicates a substantive change in majority opinion. The relative importance of the differences between surveyed and fully informed opinion can thus be clarified by noting when they cause collective preferences to change.

Controlling for uneven levels of political knowledge caused collective preferences in surveyed opinion to differ from fully informed collective preferences in 28.1% of the 235 questions. Changes in collective preferences occurred most frequently in value questions (34.0%), but were also common in policy (26.7%) and approval questions (25.0%). Figure 4.7 displays the percentage of questions in each topical category where the preference order of fully informed opinion is different from the order of preferences in surveyed opinion. Preference changes are most frequent in questions dealing with abortion, congressional approval, and governance policy, and least frequent in presidential approval, gay rights, and crime policy questions. The small number of questions in many of these categories makes it difficult to draw many firm conclusions about differences between specific topics, but the important point is that controlling for the effects of information on individual responses often results in new collective preferences. Shifts in collective preferences large enough to change what appears to be majority or plurality consensus on an issue occur quite frequently in these data.

This finding contrasts somewhat with the findings of Bartels (1996), who studied information effects in presidential voting. Although Bartels found information effects in vote choices that are comparable to the patterns examined here, in every election he studied, correcting the popular vote totals for the presence of information effects would have resulted in the same outcome as was historically the case.[18] In contrast, the collective

---

questions. In only 17% of questions did fewer than one in ten respondents change opinions, while in 5% of questions more than a third of respondents had inconsistent preferences. Levels of inconsistency were lowest for approval questions ($n = 16$), with an average of 14.6% changed preferences. Value questions ($n = 47$) had an average of 16.9% changed opinions, while questions about government policy ($n = 172$) had the highest levels of opinion inconsistency, with 19.6% of opinion givers changing their preferences in the typical policy question.

[18] Calculated from Table 2 of Bartels 1996 and popular vote totals from the *Statistical Abstract of the United States*. Correcting actual popular vote totals with the estimated aggregate deviations from fully informed voting reported in Table 2 of Bartels 1996 has

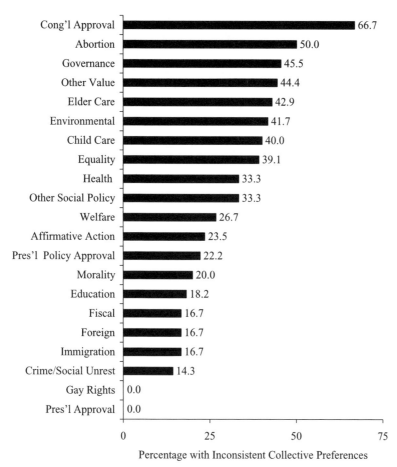

FIGURE 4.7. Percentage of questions with different surveyed and fully informed collective preferences

ordering of policy preferences seems to be much more sensitive to information effects than aggregate vote choices.

Collective information effects may be small, on average, but they often have a profound impact on the apparent meaning of the mass public's collective preferences. In 10 of the 21 question categories considered here, at least a third of the collective preferences registered in survey results

the following results: Nixon wins by 59.0% instead of 60.7% in 1972, Carter wins by 51.5% instead of 50.1% in 1976, Reagan wins by 56.3% instead of by 50.7% in 1980 and 53.9% instead of 58.8% in 1984, Bush wins by 56.4% instead of by 53.4% in 1988, and Clinton wins by 45.2% instead of 43.0% in 1992.

were artifacts of citizens' confusion about public affairs. Moreover, the types of questions thus affected are not easy to pick out of a line-up. They are typical. They deal with some of the most long-lived and foundational political controversies in American society. The scope and power of the federal government relative to lower levels of government was a controversial topic among the framers of the American constitution, and it remains an essential touchstone dividing Republicans from Democrats and conservatives from liberals. Yet collective preferences indicating the people's wishes regarding these issues are among the worst offenders of all the questions considered here: correcting for information effects changes collective preferences in nearly half of governance questions. If we want to take survey results as reflecting something like the voice of a people, or a step further as signaling the will of a nation, these are uncomfortable tidings. A people's collective voice may not be capricious, but neither is it reliable for conveying what the people might really want from government.

Reinterpreting Collective Preferences

How might the messages carried by collective opinions change if a people's voice were more resonant with its fully informed preferences? My interpretation of what simulated opinion looks like relative to surveyed opinion is given in Table 4.2. Turning first to approval questions, the general pattern is for fully informed opinion to give lower levels of approval toward Congress, the president, and the president's handling of specific policy domains. For example, Ronald Reagan's approval rating in 1988 dropped from 68% to 60% after correcting for information effects, George Bush's 1992 rating dropped from 43% to 33%, and Bill Clinton's 1996 rating dropped from 68% to 63%. Approval of Congress fell from 60% to 51% in 1988, from 31% to 18% in 1992, and from 49% to 40% in 1996. The only substantive exception to this pattern is a single question from 1992 on George Bush's handling of foreign relations, where approval rose from 62% to 75% after correcting for information effects. It would seem that the boost to approval ratings provided by the uneven distribution of political knowledge is quite similar to the incumbency advantage in presidential (Bartels 1996) and congressional voting (Althaus 2001) brought about by information effects.

The patterns of change among policy questions are more subtle and complex, but three general trends stand out in these data. First, fully informed opinion on foreign policy issues is relatively more interventionist

TABLE 4.2. *Qualitative differences between surveyed and fully informed collective preferences*

Question Type	Fully Informed Opinion Relative to Surveyed Opinion
Approval	
Congressional	Less approving
Presidential	Less approving
Presidential policy	Less approving
Policy	
Abortion	More pro-choice
Affirmative action	More supportive of the principle of affirmative action, less supportive of specific types of remedial solutions
Child care	More supportive of parental leave
Crime/Social unrest	Less supportive of increasing spending to reduce crime, drugs, and homelessness, but less supportive of punitive solutions to crime
Education	Less supportive of prayer in schools
Elder care	Less supportive of expanding Social Security and Medicare
Environmental	Less supportive of doing more to protect environment
Fiscal	Less supportive of cutting taxes; more willing to cut domestic programs and pay higher taxes to reduce federal budget deficit; less supportive of raising taxes to fund domestic programs
Foreign	More interventionist in general, more dovish concerning military
Gay rights	More progressive
Health	More supportive of free market solutions to health insurance problems
Immigration	More progressive
Governance	More libertarian
Other social policy	More supportive of increased spending on space and science research
Welfare	More supportive of decreasing spending on welfare
Value	
Equality	More supportive of equal rights, but not at all costs; less likely to see unequal opportunities as the source of many social problems
Morality	Less supportive of adjusting morals to accommodate changing society, attaches less importance to being tolerant of other people's different moral standards, less supportive of position that newer lifestyles are contributing to social breakdown
Other value	No clear pattern

than surveyed opinion but slightly more dovish when it comes to the use and maintenance of military power. For example, while 29% of respondents in 1988 agreed that the United States should stay out of problems in other parts of the world, the level of agreement dropped to just 18% of fully informed responses. Likewise, in 1992 agreement on this question dropped from 26% in surveyed opinion to 14% in simulated opinion, and in 1996 dropped from 27% to 16%. Yet fully informed opinion also tends to be more dovish than surveyed opinion when it comes to the use of military force. For example, a question from the 1988 ANES asked, "Do you favor or oppose using American military forces in the Middle East to protect oil shipments?" While 64% of surveyed responses favored military deployment, support dropped to 57% of fully informed responses. Fully informed opinion is more in favor of having a strong military but less in favor of using military force to solve problems. When asked in 1988, "Which do you think is the better way for us to keep peace – by having a very strong military so other countries won't attack us, or by working out our disagreements at the bargaining table?", support for having a strong military rose from 26% in surveyed opinion to 33% in simulated opinion. Yet two questions later, when asked whether "The U.S. should maintain its position as the world's most powerful nation even if it means going to the brink of war," the percentage disagreeing with this statement rose from 37% in surveyed opinion to 43% in simulated opinion.

The second pattern among policy questions is for fully informed opinion to hold more progressive attitudes on a wide variety of social policy topics, particularly on those framed as legal issues. For example, simulated opinion was consistently more pro-choice on abortion than surveyed opinion (e.g., with 39% of fully informed respondents opposed to parental notification laws, compared with just 25% in surveyed opinion), more supportive of gay rights (e.g., 40% of fully informed responses favor allowing gay couples to adopt children, compared with just 28% of surveyed responses), and less supportive of prayer in schools (e.g., only 24% support in fully informed opinion for some kind of spoken prayer in schools, compared with 32% in surveyed opinion). This tendency toward more progressive opinions after controlling for information effects was also common among questions dealing with immigration, education, crime, and child care policy. The two exceptions are welfare policy, where fully informed opinion favored decreasing spending or holding spending to current levels rather than increasing spending, and affirmative action, where fully informed opinion tended to be somewhat less progressive on specific programs aimed at giving preferential treatment to African Americans. At the same time, simulated opinion was slightly more progressive than surveyed opinion on the general need for government to guarantee equal opportunities and fair treatment to blacks.

The third pattern in policy questions is for simulated opinion to be more ideologically conservative on the scope and applications of government power. In particular, fully informed opinion tends to be fiscally conservative when it comes to expanding domestic programs, to prefer free market solutions over government intervention to solve policy problems, to be less supportive of additional governmental intervention to protect the environment, and to prefer a smaller and less powerful federal government. Simulated opinion on fiscal issues tends to be more willing than surveyed opinion to pay for deficit reduction and to see the deficit as a major concern (e.g., 80% calling it a "very serious" problem in simulated 1988 data, compared with only 63% in the survey data). At the same time, fully informed opinion tends to be less willing to raise taxes to pay for expanding domestic programs (from 59% opposed in surveyed 1992 data to 77% opposed in simulated data) or to increase spending on a variety of governmental programs and services. For example, when asked in 1996 whether government should provide fewer or more services in areas such as health and education, 50% of fully informed responses preferred that the government provide fewer services and reduce spending, compared with 38% of surveyed responses. In general, however, fully informed opinion is more supportive than surveyed opinion of the status quo when it comes to government spending, rather than being supportive of cuts in funding. There were two notable exceptions to the tendency for fully informed opinion to oppose increased levels of federal spending. While 35% of respondents agreed that "The government ought to cut taxes even if it means putting off some important things that need to be done," agreement dropped to 22% when controlling for information effects. Likewise, only 30% of surveyed respondents in the 1992 ANES said that they would be willing "to pay more in taxes so that the government could spend more on the services you favor," but simulated support for more government spending rose to 46% among fully informed respondents.

Related to this is the tendency for simulated opinion to favor free market solutions more than surveyed opinion. When asked to agree with one of two statements ("One, we need a strong government to handle today's complex economic problems; or two, the free market can handle these problems without government being involved"), support for free market solutions in 1992 ran 38% in fully informed opinion, compared with 27% in surveyed opinion. In 1996, support for free market solutions increased to 53% in simulated opinion, compared with 38% in surveyed opinion. In a complementary fashion, fully informed opinion is more opposed to limits on foreign imports than surveyed opinion. In 1988, for example, surveyed opinion supported limits on imports by 66%, a level of support that dropped to 57% in simulated opinion.

When it comes to governance policy issues, the simulations reveal that fully informed opinion is relatively more opposed than surveyed opinion to the idea of "big government." While 63% of surveyed opinion givers in 1988 agreed that "the government is getting too powerful," the level of agreement rose to 71% among fully informed respondents. Likewise, in 1996, 55% of surveyed respondents agreed that "there are more things that government should be doing," compared with only 35% of fully informed respondents (see also Figure 4.4). In simulated opinion, nearly two-thirds of respondents preferred instead the statement "the less government the better." At the same time, this libertarian tendency in fully informed opinion is not focused solely on the power held by the federal government. In response to a series of questions from 1996 asking whether national, state, or local government should be responsible for various policy concerns, simulated opinion was more supportive of having national government handle environmental problems and welfare issues. Only on the topic of crime was simulated opinion more inclined than surveyed opinion to prefer that national government be less involved than state or local government.

Unlike approval and policy questions, the patterns of change among value questions are somewhat less clear cut. Among the value questions dealing with equality and civil rights, simulated opinion tended to be more egalitarian than surveyed opinion. For example, while 40% of surveyed respondents in 1988 disagreed with the statement, "We have gone too far in pushing equal rights in this country," disagreement rose to 52% among fully informed respondents. Responses to the same question in 1992 were 40% disagreeing in surveyed opinion and 51% in fully informed opinion, while in 1996 disagreement ran 32% in surveyed opinion and 41% in simulated opinion. This pattern of greater support for equal rights in fully informed opinion was evident in nearly all the equality questions save two. Levels of agreement to the question, "If people were treated more equally in this country we would have many fewer problems," ran, depending on the year, 4 to 7 percentage points lower in simulated opinion than in surveyed opinion. And the percentage agreeing that "our society should do whatever is necessary to make sure that everyone has an equal opportunity to succeed" was 1 to 6 points lower, depending on the year, among fully informed responses compared to surveyed responses.

Among the value questions dealing with issues of morality, fully informed opinion tended to be less progressive than surveyed opinion. In 1988, agreement to the statement, "The world is always changing and we should adjust our view of moral behavior to those changes," ran 49% in surveyed opinion but only 39% in fully informed opinion. In 1992, levels of agreement in surveyed opinion ran 53%, compared with 37% in simulated opinion, and in 1996 ran 37% in surveyed opinion while dropping to 27% of fully informed responses. In a similar way, fully informed opinion tended to be less concerned about tolerance of different moral standards than surveyed opinion. Agreement among fully informed respondents with the statement, "We should be more tolerant of people who choose to live according to their own moral standards, even if they are very different from our own," ran 7 points lower than surveyed opinion in 1992 and 8 points lower in 1996. At the same time, fully informed respondents were somewhat less likely than surveyed respondents to agree that "the newer lifestyles are contributing to the breakdown of our society," with agreement running between 3 and 6 points lower in simulated opinion, depending on the year.

The general patterns arising from these simulation data are for surveyed opinion to appear relatively more approving of presidents and Congress than it might be if all citizens were equally well informed, more hawkish and isolationist on foreign policy, more conservative on social and environmental issues, and more libertarian on governance issues. Surveyed opinion also seems less supportive of equal rights and more progressive on morality issues than it might be if the political knowledge levels of all respondents were raised and standardized. These findings point to a general conclusion: information effects produce consistent patterns of ideological bias in collective opinions across a range of issues.[19]

[19] It is interesting to note that these general tendencies toward regular types of ideological bias were also found when a subset of the simulations were re-estimated using years of education in place of the factual knowledge scales and when they were re-estimated using only statistically significant variable clusters. Furthermore, these general patterns of differences between surveyed and fully informed opinion tend to be consistent with results from other simulation methods (Althaus 1996; Delli Carpini and Keeter 1996:

The Demographic Distribution of Information Effects

While the preceding analysis of aggregate-level data shows that information effects often influence the structure and direction of collective preferences, it is nonetheless possible that these macro-level patterns of bias do not systematically privilege the voices of particular demographic groups. As we saw with the example in Figure 4.4, correcting for unequal levels of political knowledge sometimes has unexpected effects, and it is not the case that the opinions of the ill-informed change consistently to a more moderate position in response to such a correction. Rather, there seems to be a complex set of interactions between issues and demographic traits that may be understandable in hindsight but difficult to predict. This raises the possibility that the chronically underinformed demographic groups might often be able to compensate for their relative deficit of knowledge.

Up to this point in the chapter we have examined the size of information effects averaged across questions, but identifying the demographic correlates of information effects requires an examination of such effects across individuals. Such an analysis also requires a slightly different measure of individual-level information effects than those used earlier. The earlier measures of individual-level effects were derived by averaging *for each question* the information effects from all individuals who provided substantive answers. To identify the demographic correlates of information effects, it becomes necessary to average *for each person* the value of their information effects across all questions to which they provided substantive responses. The average information effect for particular individuals can then be compared across different types of people to reveal which demographic characteristics are associated with larger or smaller information effects.

Table 4.3 confirms that the voices of relatively less knowledgeable demographic groups tend consistently to be distorted by larger information

Chapter 6; Kuklinski, Quirk et al. 2000), the broad patterns of opinion change among participants in deliberative polls in the United States (Fishkin and Luskin 1999), and the results of question filter experiments (Bishop, Oldendick, and Tuchfarber 1983). They are also consistent with previous studies comparing differences between well- and ill-informed survey respondents on a variety of policy issues (e.g., Althaus 1996; Key 1961: 331–41; Neuman 1986: Chapter 3; Popkin and Dimock 1999). Additional research on information effects in collective preferences has demonstrated that deliberative polling and the simulation method used here can produce essentially similar results (Sturgis 2003).

effects than the voices of relatively more knowledgeable groups. Between-group differences in the values of individual-level gaps between surveyed and simulated opinions show that the magnitude of information effects closely follows the social distribution of political knowledge (see Table 1.2).

Overall, micro-level information effects altered individual opinion probabilities by an average of 13.1 points (s.d. = 7.7) and produced inconsistent preferences between an individual's surveyed and fully informed opinions in an average of 18.9% of questions (s.d. = 11.9). As Table 4.3 details, between-group differences on both measures of micro-level information effects are statistically significant for all of the demographic characteristics save the relationship between inconsistent preferences and financial status.[20] Moreover, the patterns of differences consistently favor demographic groups that are socially and politically advantaged. The average individual-level effect among high-school dropouts is twice the size of that among the college educated; and the average effect among the poorest respondents is nearly one and a half times the size of that found among the most affluent respondents. The opinions reported by Republicans are more immune to information effects than those reported by Democrats, as are the views of men, whites, middle-aged people, those living in western states and residents of cities and suburbs relative to the opinions of women, blacks, younger and older people, and those living in southern states or rural areas. While many of the differences among other demographic groups are substantively small, the patterns in Table 4.3 present a consistent picture: the collective preferences of groups with relatively higher levels of political knowledge appear consistently closer to the fully informed ideal than do the aggregate opinions of groups with relatively lower levels of political knowledge.

Not only do larger information effects tend to be clustered in certain types of questions, they also tend to be concentrated in certain types of

---

[20] Although used as a demographic variable in the preceding analysis, religious affiliation is excluded from this table. There are no significant differences in political knowledge levels among Protestants, Catholics, those with other religious preferences, and those with no religious affiliation. As a consequence, there are no significant differences in either measure of micro-level information effects among these groups. While these findings could indicate a rough equality of knowledge across religious affiliations, this traditional way of operationalizing religious affiliation using American National Election Studies data has been shown to obscure many important differences among religious traditions (Leege and Kellstedt 1993), and thus it is equally likely that these null findings result from poor operationalization in the grouping variable.

TABLE 4.3. *Group differences in information effects*

	Average Individual Point Change from Surveyed to Fully Informed Opinion		Average Individual Percentage of Inconsistent Preferences		$N =$
Educational attainment					
College degree	8.2 (6.1)	$F_{(2, 5007)} = 619.11$ $p < .001$	11.6 (9.5)	$F_{(2, 5007)} = 518.49$ $p < .001$	1237
High school diploma	13.5 (7.0)		19.6 (11.1)		2902
Less than high school education	18.9 (7.8)		26.8 (11.5)		871
Income					
Highest quartile	9.7 (6.5)	$F_{(3, 5006)} = 230.67$ $p < .001$	14.1 (10.3)	$F_{(3, 5006)} = 173.76$ $p < .001$	1220
High middle quartile	11.7 (7.1)		17.0 (11.3)		1234
Low middle quartile	14.0 (7.4)		20.3 (11.5)		1288
Lowest quartile	16.9 (7.9)		23.9 (12.1)		1268
Occupation					
Executive/Professional	9.0 (6.5)	$F_{(5, 5004)} = 106.81$ $p < .001$	12.8 (10.2)	$F_{(5, 5004)} = 92.13$ $p < .001$	1050
Technical/Sales	12.0 (7.5)		17.6 (11.5)		465
Clerical	13.7 (6.8)		19.7 (11.0)		501
Retired	13.1 (7.2)		19.3 (11.6)		767
Homemaker	16.3 (8.3)		22.4 (12.2)		454
Other	14.9 (7.7)		21.6 (11.8)		1773
Party Identification					
Republican (including leaners)	11.9 (8.3)	$F_{(2, 5007)} = 111.31$ $p < .001$	17.1 (12.4)	$F_{(2, 5007)} = 116.33$ $p < .001$	1971
Independent	17.3 (7.7)		25.6 (11.6)		561
Democrat (including leaners)	13.1 (6.8)		18.9 (10.9)		2478
Age					
17–34	14.3 (7.8)	$F_{(2, 5007)} = 38.89$ $p < .001$	20.4 (11.7)	$F_{(2, 5007)} = 29.68$ $p < .001$	1551
35–54	12.0 (7.5)		17.4 (11.7)		1940
55 and older	13.3 (7.7)		19.3 (12.0)		1519
Marital status					
Currently married	12.3 (7.5)	$t_{(5008)} = 8.61$ $p < .001$	17.8 (11.6)	$t_{(5008)} = 7.64$ $p < .001$	2803
Currently not married	14.2 (7.8)		20.3 (12.1)		2207

					N
Homeowner status					
Owner	12.4 (7.5)	$t(5008) = 8.68$, $p < .001$	18.1 (11.6)	$t(5008) = 6.75$, $p < .001$	1714
Renter	14.4 (7.9)		20.5 (12.2)		3296
Current financial status					
Worse off than last year	13.5 (7.6)	$t(5008) = -2.35$, $p = .019$	19.3 (11.8)	$t(5008) = -1.38$, $p = .167$	1513
Same or better off than last year	12.9 (7.7)		18.8 (11.9)		3497
Parental status					
Parent of minor child	13.6 (7.8)	$t(5008) = -3.22$, $p = .001$	19.5 (11.7)	$t(5008) = -2.81$, $p = .005$	1883
All others	12.8 (7.7)		18.5 (12.0)		3127
Union affiliation					
Union household	12.6 (6.6)	$t(5008) = 2.31$, $p = .021$	18.0 (10.7)	$t(5008) = 2.42$, $p = .016$	894
Non-union household	13.2 (7.9)		19.1 (12.1)		4116
Race					
All others	12.7 (7.6)	$t(5008) = -9.84$, $p < .001$	18.7 (11.9)	$t(5008) = -2.71$, $p = .007$	4417
Black	16.0 (7.9)		20.1 (11.5)		593
Gender					
Male	11.1 (7.4)	$t(5008) = -16.81$, $p < .001$	16.6 (11.8)	$t(5008) = -12.84$, $p < .001$	2274
Female	14.7 (7.5)		20.8 (11.6)		2736
Region					
East	12.4 (7.4)	$F(3, 5006) = 36.44$, $p < .001$	17.8 (11.6)	$F(3, 5006) = 31.60$, $p < .001$	872
Midwest	12.9 (7.4)		18.8 (11.8)		1358
South	14.5 (8.2)		20.8 (12.2)		1802
West	11.5 (7.1)		16.5 (11.1)		978
Locality					
Urban	12.3 (7.4)	$F(2, 5007) = 47.16$, $p < .001$	17.3 (11.5)	$F(2, 5007) = 53.83$, $p < .001$	1958
Suburban	12.7 (7.6)		18.5 (11.8)		1651
Rural	14.8 (8.0)		21.6 (12.2)		1401

Note: Standard deviations are in parentheses.

Source: Pooled data from the 1988, 1992 and 1996 American National Election Studies.

respondents. The quality of representation afforded to groups whose voices are distorted by information effects thus suffers a twofold blow in opinion surveys. Socially and politically disadvantaged groups become numerically underrepresented in the ranks of opinion givers due to depletion, and the substantive opinions given by members of these groups tend to be farther from their own fully informed mark than those given by members of more privileged groups. At the same time, since information effects tend to increase the lopsidedness of ill-informed opinion, these socially and politically disadvantaged groups are often responsible for distorting the shape of collective preferences, thus reducing the likelihood that survey results will represent the collective interests of all citizens. Those who stand most to gain from an accurate rendering of collective preferences, because they are otherwise marginalized from more direct forms of political involvement, seem precisely those who stand most in the way of realizing this goal.

FULLY INFORMED OPINION AND ENLIGHTENED PREFERENCES

Thinking of political interests in terms of enlightened preferences opens the possibility that simulating the mass public's fully informed opinions may indeed provide rough estimates of the preferences the public would come to adopt were it better informed. But there is an obvious problem with interpreting simulations of fully informed opinions in these cases as revealing enlightened interests. The most knowledgeable members of various demographic groups – on whose preferences the fully informed collective opinions are based – may simply be mistaken in their views. It is one thing to say that knowledgeable respondents are more likely than ill-informed ones to express policy preferences consistent with their political predispositions. It is quite another to claim that knowledgeable respondents are more in touch with their political interests than poorly informed people.

Estimating anyone's fully informed opinion is fraught with challenges: the items used to measure political knowledge may fail to capture important aspects of the information used by citizens to construct preferences, and it remains unclear whether simulations, experimental methods, or some other technique might provide more valid estimates of such opinions under different conditions. But even though the concept of enlightened preferences has been put forward by philosophers as a normative standard rather than something that could actually be attained by a person or population, it is at least possible that the opinions given by people who are more fully informed than others – relative to a given scale of political knowledge – could approximate something like enlightened preferences. In such a case, simulations of fully informed opinion might represent something more than a statistical curiosity. They might tell us something useful about what people really want from government.

Determining whether estimates of fully informed collective preferences are laden with the sort of "recommending force" that James Fishkin (1995: 162) claims for deliberative polls would require surmounting some imposing objections. First, although the enlightened preferences standard has been invoked by many as a means for evaluating the quality of collective preferences (e.g., Althaus 1998; Bartels 1990, 1996; Delli Carpini and Keeter 1996; Page and Shapiro 1992), it is important to point out that the enlightened preferences literature has been focused almost exclusively on defining individual-level interests. The political philosophers associated with the enlightened preferences standard have yet to detail a parallel realm of aggregate-level interests which could serve as a basis for evaluating the quality of collective preferences (although see Dahl 1989). A second problem is that the simulation results themselves suggest no obvious criteria for determining when they might reveal (or validate the presence of) enlightened interests. Some people may be inclined to accept fully informed opinion as enlightened when it conforms to their own values or ideas about "correct" policy. Others may be inclined to disagree, and with good reason. Because different people see interests in different ways, the simulation results – when taken in isolation – are ultimately unconvincing. Moreover, since the concept of enlightened preferences represents an ideal that cannot be achieved in the real world, there is no compelling reason to suppose that any method could estimate such preferences.

In addition, several potential limitations of the simulation method also suggest that fully informed opinion should not be used to divine a public's enlightened preferences.

The Simulation Model May Have Specification Errors

The simulation method presumes that the demographic variables used to identify significant group differences in opinion (1) actually perform that function, and (2) capture the most important group characteristics related to policy preferences. This is certainly a tall order, and specification error in the simulation model – especially in the form of omitted variables – is a real possibility. For example, Protestants represent such a diverse array of theological and political views that a dummy variable for "Protestant" affiliation may not represent an easily specifiable group of policy preferences (Leege and Kellstedt 1993). Hence using a single dummy variable to represent Protestant opinion provides only the roughest measure of differences between persons of various religious traditions (i.e., "Catholic," "other," and "none"). Nevertheless, the large number of parameters to be estimated in such simulations require economy in variable selection, and thus dummy variables provide necessary albeit error-prone measures of the demographic features of interest in a population.[21]

Measures of Political Information May Be Inadequate

Since the simulation method depends so heavily on statistically transforming respondents' levels of political knowledge, the validity and reliability of the factual knowledge indices becomes critical. Because the content and length of these indices varies slightly from year to year, random error due to minor differences in the knowledge scales may cause fully informed opinion to shift erratically over time. Furthermore, while the scales used here have been extensively tested and are backed by solid empirical research, they represent just one of many ways to conceive of political sophistication (Graber 1994, 2001; Lupia and McCubbins 1998; Luskin 1987). Although political knowledge generally has been considered unidimensional (Delli Carpini and Keeter 1996), there may be important exceptions to this rule that introduce error into simulations of fully informed preferences on certain issues (Gilens 2001; Mondak 2000). Moreover, there is no universal standard with which to identify the information rich: the scales used here may overestimate levels of

---

[21] Likewise, Delli Carpini and Keeter (1996: 248–51) have shown that beliefs about the Bible interact with the relationship between political knowledge and support for gay rights issues. Among people who believe that the Bible is not the word of God, high levels of political knowledge are strongly related to support for gay rights. In contrast, political knowledge has almost no relationship with opinions on gay rights among people who believe the Bible is literally the word of God. This suggests that omitting a variable that captures beliefs about the Bible may introduce specification error into the simulation results: people who oppose gay rights on religious grounds inadvertently may be assigned the wrong fully informed preferences. Nevertheless, some of this relationship is captured in the religious preference variables, and while refining the selection of variables may improve the fit of simulation models to the data, there is little evidence to suggest that doing so should significantly influence the shape of fully informed collective opinion.

issue-specific knowledge in some circumstances and underestimate them in others.

Knowledgeable Members May Misrepresent Group Interests

It is likely that in addition to these random perturbations, there also may be systematic error introduced into measures of fully informed opinion by assumptions underlying the simulation method. One possibility is that the preferences of the most informed people may be influenced by the narrow range of policy options that happen to be covered by news organizations. If they were exposed to a broader discussion of issues, policies, and outcomes than typically is carried in mainstream news accounts, the preferences of these knowledgeable respondents might shift in important ways. In such a case, the simulation results might tell less about enlightened interests than about the sorts of preferences more people might have if they paid close attention to the elite opinions carried by mass media.

A second problem is that, for various and inscrutable reasons, some people from every walk of life choose to become more informed than others in spite of the costs involved. Variations in ability, motivation, and opportunity account for some of these differences (Delli Carpini and Keeter 1996). Others are harder to pin down: perhaps some people just enjoy politics more than others, or perhaps they are afflicted with a genetic urge to read civics textbooks. The problem is that the preferences of the most informed members of any demographic group might be influenced by their *reasons for* and the *process of* becoming informed in a costly information environment. In other words, these same people might hold different views were they to come to their policy opinions in a fully informed world where knowledge was cheap and policy consequences obvious.

Third, systematic bias may also be introduced by selection errors in the simulation method. The simulation assumes that the opinions of the relatively more knowledgeable persons in each of various demographic categories indicate the "correct" views, against which all other opinions of similar people should be judged. It is easy to see where this assumption might prove untenable. The husband of a union worker might resent union organizers for taxing his wife's time and money, but be identified as representing union interests because he is knowledgeable and married to a union member. It can only be hoped that selection errors are randomized, but the data provide no way of knowing for certain. While multivariate regression should control for some of these extraneous influences, it is likely that informed respondents differ in subtle but consistent ways from their less knowledgeable counterparts.[22]

Finally, some scholars have argued that political interests are discovered in the process of participating in politics and in shaping collective decisions that affect one's own life (Bachrach 1975; Barber 1984; Christiano 1990; DeLuca 1995; Miller 1992). By this line of reasoning, the opinions of knowledgeable people may be a poor surrogate for the latent interests of the ill informed for the simple reason that those interests can only be articulated by the ill informed themselves. If some people are currently unable to articulate their informed preferences, it may be inappropriate to simulate fully informed opinion by imputing to all citizens the preferences of the few who (presumably) can, no matter how congruent their enlightened views are likely to be.

These many considerations make clear that simulations controlling for the uneven social distribution of political knowledge should not be treated casually as measures of enlightened preferences. The possibility of error introduced by inadequate models and data easily trumps the potential warrant that the simulation results might have as estimates of enlightened interests. At the same time, it is possible that simulated opinion might reveal something like enlightened interests under certain conditions.[23] To gain a clearer appreciation for the conditions under which these simulations might tell us something useful about what the people want from government, Chapters 5 and 6 examine the structure, causes, and dynamics of information effects.

---

[22] For example, citizen activists tend to be much more knowledgeable about politics than their uninvolved neighbors (Verba et al. 1995: 500–6). Activists from lower income and minority groups also tend to have different opinions about welfare and government assistance to minorities than the people whose interests they seek to represent (Verba et al. 1995: 213–5, 239–41). Likewise, politically knowledgeable respondents are much more amenable to being interviewed in surveys than those poorly informed about politics (Brehm 1993: 61–4). It is quite possible that some of these differences are due to factors other than the interaction between knowledge and social characteristics.

[23] If information effects are caused primarily by social processes, such as uneven rates of knowledge diffusion among different segments of the mass public, then fully informed opinion might be able to predict what surveyed opinion will look like at a future point in time. Such a tendency would suggest that simulated opinion could provide a better indicator of political interests, narrowly defined, than surveyed opinion. Of course, information effects also might be the macro-level manifestation of micro-level psychological factors such as chronic inattentiveness in some segments of the population or stable differences in values and political orientations that are related to knowledge levels. If psychological rather than social processes give rise to information effects, then measures of fully informed opinion should have little predictive power for anticipating changes in surveyed opinion. These possibilities are explored in Chapter 6.

CONCLUSION

Correcting for the low levels and uneven social distribution of political knowledge can cause the apparent meaning of collective preferences to change in significant ways. The effects of information asymmetries on collective opinion are both larger and more common than suggested by previous work: controlling for information effects produces an average change of nearly 7 percentage points in question marginals and reveals that one in four survey questions might have a different collective preference if all respondents were equally well informed about politics. All of this suggests that the aggregation of surveyed preferences often produces a measure of collective opinion that is substantively different from collective opinion based on fully informed preferences. Information effects tend to be frequent, often large, and usually significant. Political knowledge matters.

The findings in this chapter challenge two widely held views about the nature of collective opinion. First, while many respondents may use heuristics, on-line processing, and information shortcuts to arrive at the political opinions they express in surveys, these substitutes for political knowledge do not necessarily help ill-informed people express policy preferences similar to those of well-informed people. If they did, surveyed opinion across the board should closely resemble fully informed opinion. While the precise impact of information shortcuts is obscured in these data, it is clear that their use by poorly informed citizens often fails to make up for a lack of political knowledge. Second, the process of aggregating opinions together does not necessarily produce collective preferences that are similar to what they might look like if everyone were equally well informed. This finding runs counter to an extensive body of work – discussed in previous chapters – which suggests that aggregating opinions should be a relatively efficient means for pooling information. Most of this work is grounded either in Condorcet's jury theorem or in measurement-error approaches to collective opinion. While these two theoretical viewpoints provide useful insights into the dynamics of collective opinion, both predict that the aggregation of individual preferences should create a better-informed collective preference. The simulation results presented in this chapter show that this prediction is often wrong.

It remains unclear how much of the differences between surveyed and simulated opinion are due to uneven rates of opinion giving and how much are due to differences in opinion between well- and ill-informed respondents. Understanding the relative contributions of these two sources of bias, as well as the reasons why information effects produce distortions in collective preferences, may help opinion researchers determine how to construct and administer surveys in ways that compensate for such effects. This topic is the focus of Chapter 5, which examines the components of the depletion-convergence model to clarify how representation problems arise in collective opinion.

5

The Structure and Causes of Information Effects

Simulating the opinions of a hypothetical fully informed public reveals that surveyed opinion is influenced in significant ways by the low levels and uneven social distribution of political knowledge. But Chapter 4 has left us with something of a mystery. Each individual making up the collective has a fixed amount of political knowledge at the time they express their opinions in surveys. If the size of information effects were merely determined by these fixed levels of political knowledge, such effects should be approximately the same size across questions and within individuals. Yet they are not. Individual-level effects are larger for some topics, smaller for others. They are more randomized in some questions, so that they bias the collective preference hardly at all, and more systematically distributed in others. Information effects also have consistent patterns of directional impact for certain types of questions. When controlling for information asymmetries, collective opinions become less approving of presidents and Congress, less hawkish and isolationist on foreign policy, less conservative on social and equal rights issues, and more conservative on governance, environmental, and morality issues. If levels of general political knowledge are constant within individuals, then variance in the size and direction of information effects must arise from something else besides knowledge, or something that works in conjunction with knowledge, or something that conditions the impact of knowledge.

Some of this variance may be attributed directly to the topical domains of different questions, which cover issues more and less familiar to the typical survey respondent. Some may arise from the survey instrument itself, if question wording and order effects tend to bias the opinions of less knowledgeable respondents to a greater degree than those of more knowledgeable opinion givers. Differences in the size of gaps between surveyed and simulated opinion may also be rooted less in how much information people carry around with them than in how well people use the limited amount of information they do have. It is possible that the ill informed are better able to employ heuristic shortcuts or other forms of "low information rationality" (Popkin 1991) when answering certain types of questions, or that their attitude structures are more consonant with those of the well informed in some topical domains than others. Variance in the size of information effects may also indicate that the specific questions included in general knowledge scales have less relevance for particular topics posed in survey questions or for particular contexts in which citizens are asked to make judgments. "Civics test" scales of political knowledge have been forcefully criticized in recent years on precisely these grounds (Erikson, MacKuen, and Stimson 2002; Graber 1994, 2001; Lodge, McGraw, and Stroh 1989; Lodge, Steenbergen, and Brau 1995; Lupia and McCubbins 1998; Popkin 1991). While this criticism falls short as a blanket indictment – the findings from the previous chapter show that "civics test" knowledge clearly affects the responses people give in opinion surveys – it seems likely that levels of general political knowledge may be more relevant to some kinds of opinions than others. Finally, since political knowledge is often used to predict chronic exposure to public affairs information in the news media (Price and Zaller 1993; Zaller 1992a, 1996), variance in the size of information effects may be related to the intensity of news coverage given to different political topics. Information effects might be smaller on some issues because news coverage about those issues has reached even the most inattentive citizens, while larger information effects might reflect the more typical situation where knowledge about an issue remains concentrated in a small group of highly attentive citizens.

Solving this mystery requires first that we examine the structural components of information effects to clarify the mechanisms by which these effects are produced in collective preferences. To what extent are the gaps between surveyed and fully informed opinion produced by dispersion effects, and to what extent by the lack of demographic correspondence between survey samples and the group of people who give opinions? Understanding how information effects work can provide insight into the ways they might be remedied. If the skewed demographics of opinion givers is the main problem, information effects might be corrected by encouraging more respondents to give opinions. If the main cause lies in the tendency of well- and ill-informed opinion givers to express different preferences, then information effects might be lessened by asking questions in ways that encourage ill-informed people to engage in systematic more than heuristic processing of information. Determining the primary mechanism by which knowledge asymmetries are translated into information effects may also make it possible to estimate the influence of information effects without conducting a complicated, individual-level simulation. If the only way to detect and measure information effects is to use the sort of simulation method described in Chapter 4, then information effects are likely to remain undetected: few consumers of polling data have the computing resources, technical expertise, or access to the individual-level data needed to run such simulations. But if the general impact of information effects can be predicted from the sort of crosstabular data that might be reported in a newspaper article, then politicians, journalists, and ordinary citizens could have a powerful means at their disposal to differentiate between unstable "mass opinion" and high-quality "public judgment" (Yankelovich 1991).

This chapter begins by assessing the relative contributions made by depletion and convergence behavior to information effects. The findings presented below reveal that collective information effects are caused primarily by the different mix of preferences expressed by knowledgeable relative to poorly informed opinion givers. The extent of this influence makes it possible to estimate the direction of fully informed opinion relative to surveyed opinion using only observable characteristics of the opinion distribution. The chapter then examines some of the psychological and environmental factors that can influence the quality and distributional characteristics of survey responses. This analysis reveals that the impact of political knowledge on opinion is conditioned by a complex array of influences. The challenges are many that face ill-informed citizens in matching preferences to interests, but those who are motivated to do so can overcome the typical effects of limited knowledge. Environmental factors turn out to play an important role in moderating the impact of political knowledge on surveyed opinion, which suggests that the keys to addressing the problem of information effects may lie in the ways that governmental institutions, leaders, and journalists prioritize, confront, and publicize political issues.

THE STRUCTURAL COMPONENTS OF INFORMATION EFFECTS

The depletion-convergence model discussed in Chapter 3 proposes two mechanisms for producing information effects in collective preferences.

First, knowledgeable people tend to give opinions more frequently than those who know little about the political world, which means that the social distribution of political knowledge affects which voices get represented in the ranks of opinion givers. Second, people who are well informed about politics are better able to form opinions consistent with their political predispositions, which means that opinion givers who are ill informed may be mistaken about their needs, wants, and values: they might give opinions that they wouldn't give if they were more knowledgeable about politics. We now turn to examine whether and how each of these mechanisms contributes to the size of information effects.

The Relative Impact of Convergence and Depletion

The *convergence hypothesis* suggests that information effects in collective preferences should be especially large when the opinions of ill-informed respondents are substantially more or less lopsided than those of more knowledgeable respondents, but only when this relative lopsidedness stems from low or uneven levels of political knowledge rather than from underlying demographic differences between well- and ill-informed opinion givers. The size of collective information effects should be equally large regardless of whether the well- or ill-informed are more lopsided, since correcting for information asymmetries should tend to move ill-informed opinion in the direction of well-informed opinion, regardless of which group is more lopsided to begin with.[1] However, the analysis in Chapter 2 showed that the response category selected by the largest number of respondents should represent the fully informed collective preference when the most knowledgeable respondents are also the most lopsided in their opinions. It follows that changes in collective preferences should be more likely to occur when the distribution of ill-informed opinion is more lopsided than that of well-informed opinion.

Figure 5.1 displays the size of collective and individual-level information effects by the relative lopsidedness of the preferences expressed by well- and ill-informed opinion givers. This measure of relative dispersion is obtained for each survey question by subtracting the lopsidedness score of the bottom knowledge quartile from the lopsidedness score of the top knowledge quartile (see Appendix B for details). Questions are

---

[1] The exception to this tendency is when the difference between well- and ill-informed opinion is due to demographic differences between groups rather than to differences in knowledge levels.

a. Size of point change in collective opinions

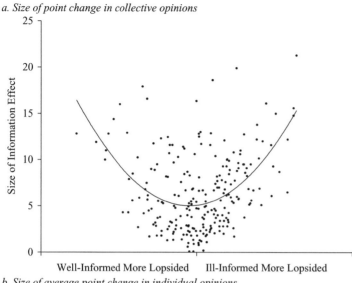

Well-Informed More Lopsided   Ill-Informed More Lopsided

b. Size of average point change in individual opinions

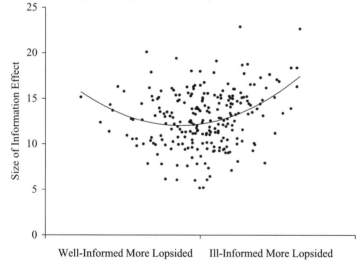

Well-Informed More Lopsided   Ill-Informed More Lopsided

FIGURE 5.1. Size of information effects by relative lopsidedness of well- and ill-informed opinion givers

then ordered in the graphs from left to right on the value of this variable, with points on the left representing questions in which the surveyed opinions of the most knowledgeable quartile are substantially more lopsided than those of the least knowledgeable quartile, points in the middle indicating parity in relative dispersion, and points on the right side representing questions in which the opinions of the least informed are increasingly more lopsided than those of the most informed. As expected, the size of information effects tends to be similar at both extremes. Dividing the questions into thirds, we find that gaps between surveyed and simulated collective opinions in the third of questions in which well-informed opinion is more lopsided average 6.7 percentage points, compared with 4.9 points for the middle third and 7.9 points for the third in which ill-informed opinion is relatively more lopsided. Average gaps for individual opinions follow a similar course, with information effects of 12.6 points for the third of questions in which the most knowledgeable opinion givers have the most lopsided opinions, compared with 12.1 points for the middle third and 13.8 points for the third in which the least knowledgeable opinion givers have the most lopsided opinions.[2]

The unexpected pattern revealed in this figure has to do with the middling questions. Questions with roughly the same degree of dispersion between high and low knowledge groups can be expected to have relatively smaller information effects, since these are often questions where the two groups are expressing a similar mix of opinions. But Figure 5.1 also shows that among this middle group of questions, information effects are relatively smaller for collective opinions than they are for individual opinions – the pattern is more curvilinear in the top graph than in the bottom one. Recall that gaps in collective preferences should become smaller than average gaps in individual preferences when information effects push individual opinions in offsetting directions. This figure reveals that individual-level effects tend to be more random in the middling questions where dispersion effects among knowledge quartiles are relatively less consequential. Questions with the same degree of lopsidedness in well- and ill-informed opinion also tend to produce offsetting information effects at the individual level, which reduce the size of the collective information effect. The significance of and reason for this pattern will become clear presently.

As expected, the ordering of collective preferences also tends to be more stable when the most informed opinions are relatively more lopsided than the least informed opinions. Information effects changed the

---

[2] Analysis of variance tests confirm that these differences are statistically significant at conventional levels, $F(2, 232) = 11.5$, $p < .001$ for collective opinions, and $F(2, 232) = 6.0$, $p < .01$ for individual opinions. Scheffé contrast tests confirm in each case that the means of the two extreme groups are significantly different from that of the middle group but are not significantly different from each other.

order of collective preferences in only 19% of questions where the well informed were more lopsided in their opinions, compared with 28% in the middle third and 37% in the third of questions where the ill informed were more lopsided in their opinions.[3] By this measure, something like collective rationality is more likely to obtain when the preferences of the least-informed opinion givers are more dispersed across response options, but only when we look for it in majority and plurality preferences.

Taken together, these relationships provide strong support for the convergence hypothesis. Dispersion effects that bias the shape of collective preferences do not arise merely because well- and ill-informed people tend to have different levels of socioeconomic status or demographic characteristics. Rather, they tend to be produced by low levels and an uneven social distribution of political knowledge.

The second mechanism by which information effects might come about is group depletion. The *depletion hypothesis* suggests that because the people who give "don't know" and "no opinion" answers tend to share not only low levels of knowledge but also similar demographic characteristics, survey questions with higher levels of DK/NO responses should tend to misrepresent the fully informed preferences of all citizens. If group depletion uniquely influences the size of information effects, then a second relationship should also be observed: as less knowledgeable respondents are drained away from the pool of opinion givers, the average size of individual-level information effects among the remaining opinion givers should diminish. This should occur because the remaining opinion givers will be relatively better informed as a whole than they would be if everyone were giving opinions. If group depletion increases the size of information effects in collective opinions while diminishing them among the individuals who actually give opinions, then we can conclude that the exclusion of ill-informed respondents is contributing to information effects in collective preferences.

A second possibility – contrary to the first – is that draining ill-informed respondents from the pool of opinion givers improves the representational quality of collective preferences. This might occur because removing the least knowledgeable citizens from the ranks of opinion givers should exclude the very people most likely to engage in convergence behavior

---

[3] Analysis of variance tests confirm that these differences are statistically significant at conventional levels, $F(2, 232) = 3.3$, $p < .05$. Scheffé contrast tests confirm that the mean of the two extreme groups are significantly different from that of the middle group, and a polynomial contrast test confirms the linearity of differences across groups.

contributing to information effects. Indeed, encouraging such depletion with "don't know" prompts and filter questions has long been an accepted practice in the survey research literature for just this reason. If removing ill-informed respondents from the ranks of opinion givers improves the quality of collective preferences, we should find higher levels of group depletion associated with smaller information effects in collective opinions and smaller average information effects for the remaining individuals who provide substantive responses.

However, the actual relationships between group depletion and the size of information effects are consistent with neither of these expectations. If the depletion hypothesis is correct, the size of collective information effects should be positively related to the percentage of DK/NO responses and negatively related to the equality index measures. The opposite should hold if collective information effects are diminished when ill-informed respondents are removed from the ranks of opinion givers. The first column of Table 5.1 reveals a striking pattern: none of the correlations for

TABLE 5.1. *Correlations between size of information effects and measures of group depletion*

	Size of Point Change in Collective Opinions	Size of Average Point Change in Individual Opinions
% DK/NO responses	−.08	.13[†]
Knowledge equality index	.03	−.19**
Education equality index	−.01	−.22**
Partisan equality index	.04	−.23**
Occupation equality index	−.00	−.22**
Income equality index	−.02	−.24**
Racial equality index	−.05	−.17**
Gender equality index	.01	−.15*
Region equality index	.01	−.14*
Marital status equality index	.01	−.15*
Home ownership equality index	−.04	−.04
Age equality index	.03	−.12[†]
Locality equality index	−.03	−.15*
Financial status equality index	−.01	−.19**
Union equality index	.08	.13**
Parental equality index	−.03	−.06
N =	235	235

[†]$p < .10$
*$p < .05$
**$p < .01$

collective-level information effects is even marginally significant, and there are about as many positive and negative relationships as would be predicted by chance. Regardless of how it is measured, the degree of demographic misrepresentation among opinion givers turns out to be unrelated to the size of information effects in collective preferences.

Previous attempts to estimate the effects of group depletion (e.g., Althaus 1996) suggest a similar conclusion. Higher numbers of respondents give DK/NO responses when explicitly encouraged to do so either with filtering questions ("Do you have an opinion on X or not?") or by providing them with legitimate excuses for giving such answers ("... or haven't you thought much about this?"). However, no clear evidence has yet emerged from experiments with filter questions and DK/NO prompts that encouraging DK/NO responses in these ways changes the results of opinion surveys in consistent ways (for a review, see Krosnick and Fabrigar 1997: 152–8). Some of the more recent attempts to estimate group depletion biases have simulated the impact of group depletion on aggregate-level biases in collective preferences.[4] Correcting for the tendency of certain types of people to opt out of the ranks of opinion givers through the use of an impressive battery of sophisticated methods – bivariate probit and Heckman selection models as well as heteroskedastic probit models – this research (Berinsky 1999, 2000, 2002) demonstrates that selection bias often occurs in survey questions dealing with racial issues: certain types of respondents give DK/NO answers because they are uncomfortable with expressing their true opposition to black candidates, school integration, and affirmative action policies. However, this work also confirms that the aggregate consequences of group depletion are usually quite small, biasing collective preferences by only 2 or 3 percentage points at most.[5]

---

[4] For estimates of group depletion biases in survey samples rather than individual questions, see Brehm 1993.

[5] One of the exceptions to this tendency comes in a question on school integration from the 1992 American National Election Studies (Berinsky 1999), where correcting for group depletion in surveyed opinion lowers support for school integration by nearly 14 percentage points. My analysis of the same question offers an alternative interpretation of this finding. The filter question preceding the school integration question prompted more than a third of respondents to offer a DK/NO response, a very high level of item nonresponse by ANES standards. It nonetheless seems implausible that selection bias alone could be responsible for such a large drop in estimated support for school integration, since reducing levels of surveyed support from 49% to 36% requires the unlikely assumption that 810 of the 812 "missing" respondents would have opposed integration in a question where the people who gave opinions were divided almost evenly on the issue. More important, modeling selection bias without accounting for information effects captures

Although it appears that depletion itself has almost no unique influence over the size of collective information effects, the reasons why this is so reveal a more complicated story. First, the rate of nonopinionation in American National Election Studies questions is relatively low compared to commercial and media polls, averaging just 6.3% of respondents across the 235 questions studied here.[6] In the 1992 ANES, for instance, this worked out to an average of 152 "don't knows" out of 2,255 total respondents. Such small average numbers of DK/NO responses should tend to diminish the potential impact of group depletion in these data. Second, demographic misrepresentation tends to be lower in questions that address topics in which competing group interests are likely to be at stake. For example, among abortion questions the lowest equality index score for gender is .98, compared with a low of .58 for other policy questions. More generally, if we separate the policy questions into two groups – those dealing with foreign, fiscal, environmental, and governance policy on the one hand, and those dealing with social policy issues on the other – we find that equality index scores tend to be higher among the social policy questions than among the other policy questions. Equality index scores for race, gender, and income have respective averages of .99, .98, and .96 for the social policy questions, compared with averages of .94, .94, and .93 for the other policy questions, a pattern that holds generally for all of the equality index categories.[7] This suggests that the higher DK/NO levels tend to be found in questions on which politically disadvantaged groups are less likely to have competing interests. When this is the case, patterns of group depletion are less likely to mute politically distinctive voices.

These two factors may limit the impact of group depletion, but they should not eliminate it altogether. If demographic misrepresentation

---

only half of the action, since a primary cause of item nonresponse is a lack of substantive knowledge (Delli Carpini and Keeter 1996). Controlling simultaneously for selection bias and information effects with the simulation method used here reveals a smaller 8-point decline in support for integration, with selection bias alone lowering support by less than 1 percentage point after first controlling for information effects.

[6] In part the low levels of DK/NO responses are due to the topical selection of questions asked in the ANES, which tend to be about issues that are somewhat familiar to many because they have long been on the political agenda. In addition, respondents in the ANES are also rarely encouraged to provide DK/NO responses. In the 235 questions analyzed here, only 12% prompted respondents to provide DK/NO answers with such phrases like "or haven't you thought much about this?" and fewer than 3% used filter questions to reduce numbers of opinion givers. The ANES also has conducted its surveys using face-to-face interviews, which tend to have lower rates of DK/NO responses compared to surveys conducted by telephone (Holbrook, Green, and Krosnick 2003).

[7] T-tests confirm that each of these differences is significant at the $p < .01$ level.

among opinion givers is related at all to the size of information effects in collective preferences, we should be able to detect this relationship, however small it may be.[8] Yet the first column in Table 5.1 suggests it is not there to be found. The reason is that questions with higher DK/NO levels also tend to be questions with larger individual-level information effects that occur in offsetting directions.

Shifting ill-informed respondents out of the ranks of opinion givers should produce smaller individual-level gaps between surveyed and simulated opinions among the remaining respondents, but the second column in Table 5.1 shows the opposite to be the case. In general, the greater the level of demographic inequality, the larger the individual-level information effects among the people who give substantive answers, even though these remaining respondents tend collectively to be better informed than the whole. If these larger individual-level gaps between surveyed and simulated opinions occurred in systematic directions, they would produce larger gaps in collective preferences. They do not because information effects in questions with higher levels of DK/NO responses tend to produce randomized errors.[9]

---

[8] A more sensitive test for depletion effects is to separate the amount of change in collective opinion brought about by imputing full knowledge to people who gave substantive opinions in the survey data from the amount of change brought about by adding in the predicted opinions of people who gave "don't know" and "no opinion" responses in the survey data. Counting only those respondents who originally gave substantive opinions, the average gap between surveyed and fully informed collective opinions was 6.6 percentage points. When the simulated opinions of the missing respondents are included in the calculation, the average gap shrinks slightly to 6.5 percentage points. While small, the difference between these measures is statistically significant, $t(234) = 3.19$, $p < .01$. These findings suggest that while factoring in the predicted preferences of DK/NO respondents tends to reduce the size of information effects in collective preferences, the resulting change tends not to be substantive. The average difference in the estimates of fully informed opinion produced by these two ways of calculating information effects amounted to less than a quarter of a percentage point per survey question. Indeed, only two of 235 questions shifted more than 3 points when the predicted opinions of respondents who actually gave "don't know" responses were factored in along with the rest, and the largest observed difference was only 5.4 points.

[9] One measure of the randomness in individual errors is given by subtracting for each question the size of the information effect in collective opinion from the size of the average individual-level information effect. Questions in which large individual-level effects produce small collective effects will take higher values, indicating randomized errors, while questions in which the size of effects at both levels are roughly the same will take lower values, a sign that information effects shift opinions in a uniform direction. The correlation between this randomness measure and the percentage of DK/NO responses is .24 ($p < .001$), indicating that higher DK/NO levels are positively associated with randomized biases brought about by information effects.

Not only do questions with high levels of group depletion tend to have more randomized information effects, but the surveyed opinions of both the most and least knowledgeable opinion givers in such questions are also more randomly distributed across response options. If group depletion tends to shift out of collective preferences those ill-informed people most likely to engage in convergence behavior, we should find DK/NO rates to be statistically related to the lopsidedness of ill-informed opinion but unrelated to the lopsidedness of well-informed opinion. It turns out, however, that the correlation between DK/NO rates and the lopsidedness of ill-informed opinion ($-.32$, $p < .001$) is just as strong as that with the lopsidedness of well-informed opinion ($-.34$, $p < .001$). The surveyed opinions of both groups tend to disperse more evenly across response categories in questions with higher DK/NO levels.

That surveyed opinions in questions with high levels of item nonresponse should become more evenly dispersed and that individual-level information effects should become larger but also more offsetting suggest that something about the questions themselves is producing all three tendencies. One likely suspect is the degree of cognitive ability required to answer these questions. Question categories with high levels of demographic inequality tend to deal with issues like foreign policy and governmental control of the economy that are both complex and remote from the daily concerns of ordinary citizens (see Figure 3.2, Chapter 3). While the size of collective information effects for "easy" issues (Carmines and Stimson 1980) revealed in Chapter 4 were not consistently smaller than for "hard" issues, "harder" issues do tend to have higher levels of item nonresponse, as has been noted in previous research (Converse 1976; Francis and Busch 1975; Krosnick 1999b: 556–9; Krosnick and Milburn 1990; Rapoport 1982). The cognitive demands of the survey questions are likely to be implicated in these patterns, but it is important to point out that DK/NO levels are not merely functions of question difficulty, and that the multifaceted and subtle relationships between cognitive ability and the survey response can take many forms (Krosnick 1991; Krosnick and Fabrigar forthcoming; Tourangeau, Rips, and Rasinski 2000). Levels of item nonresponse are, at best, only a rough and imperfect indicator of the cognitive demands placed on survey respondents.

The analysis thus far has clarified that while the tendency for opinion givers to come from certain demographic groups may be a cause for concern on normative grounds, the biases in surveyed opinion brought about by information effects seem unrelated to the numerical underrepresentation of politically disadvantaged groups. They seem unrelated because so few respondents tend to give DK/NO answers in ANES data, DK/NO levels tend to be lower in questions where group interests are likely to conflict, and the simulation method allocates DK/NO responses into substantive opinions based on the response patterns of people who actually gave substantive responses. The larger and more randomized individual-level information effects among opinion givers in questions with high DK/NO levels dissipate the potential impact that imputing missing opinions might have.

This evidence against the depletion hypothesis is offered with an important qualification, for it rests on an assumption about the nature of DK/NO responses that, while plausible, has only weak empirical warrant: the notion that people who withhold substantive responses in the actual data would provide the same mix of fully informed preferences as people who resemble them demographically and who actually give opinions in the first place. While used here as a convenient way to treat DK/NO responses as substantive data, the assumption of response homogeneity within demographic groups is more axiomatic than it is empirically grounded. While not arbitrary, this assumption is nonetheless based entirely on circumstantial evidence. For example, nonvoters have about the same mix of policy preferences as those who turn out to vote in presidential elections (Verba, Schlozman, and Brady 1995: 204–6; Wolfinger and Rosenstone 1980: Chapter 6; although see Bennett and Resnick 1990). Likewise, correcting survey data for nonresponse error usually has little effect on substantive results (Berinsky 2000; Brehm 1993; Keeter, Miller et al. 2000). Schuman and Presser (1981: 126–8) conclude that filter questions make no appreciable difference in the shape of question marginals, despite the fact that they sharply increase rates of item nonresponse. And Bishop, Oldendick, and Tuchfarber (1983) find that filter questions designed to increase the number of DK/NO responses affect the shape of question marginals in only half of cases. Yet is important to be clear that while researchers have used a variety of methods to reinterpret "don't know" responses as substantive answers (e.g., Berinsky 1999; Berinsky 2000; Feick 1989) or to correct for nonresponse bias (Brehm 1993), there seems to be no simple method for estimating the error introduced into survey data by respondents who provide nonsubstantive answers (Lin and Schaeffer 1995).

The status of the depletion hypothesis therefore remains open to question despite the disconfirming evidence presented here. The firmest conclusion that can be drawn at the moment is that high DK/NO levels resulting from the cognitive difficulty of survey questions make it hard to estimate what fully informed opinions might look like. Chapter 6 offers a different test of the depletion hypotheses using longitudinal data, and the results of that analysis confirm that group depletion has important consequences for the quality of representation afforded by collective preferences.

Identifying Collective Preferences with Large Information Effects

Since differences between ill- and well-informed opinion are so strongly related to the size of information effects while levels of DK/NO responses are not, it should be possible to estimate the magnitude of gaps between surveyed and simulated opinion without resorting to a detailed statistical simulation. The percentage point difference between the highest and lowest knowledge quartiles turns out to be closely related to the size of information effects estimated by simulation. The difference in opinion between the least and most knowledgeable respondents has a correlation of .72 ($p < .001$) with the size of information effects in collective opinion, and of .54 ($p < .001$) with the average size of individual-level information effects.[10]

Dispersion effects among ill-informed respondents influence collective opinion the way they do because the mix of preferences expressed by well-informed opinion givers tends to resemble the simulated opinions that a fully informed public might have. For example, in the abortion question discussed in Figure 4.1 in Chapter 4, only 32% of respondents in the lowest knowledge quartile favored unrestricted access to abortion services, compared with 53% of those in the highest knowledge quartile. The collective preference in surveyed opinion was 46% favoring unrestricted access, which shifted to 56% support in simulated opinion after correcting for information effects. The direction of the effect and a rough approximation of fully informed opinion were both telegraphed by the relative distribution of well- and ill-informed opinion. More generally, across the 235 questions under study, the average absolute difference between the actual marginal percentages of the highest knowledge quartile and the simulated marginals of fully informed collective opinion was only 4.0 percentage points (s.d. = 2.6); by contrast, the average difference in

---

[10] In addition, the lopsidedness of the highest knowledge quartile's opinion is negatively correlated with the size of information effects (at the collective level, $r = -.14$, $p < .05$; at the individual level, $r = -.44$, $p < .001$), but the lopsidedness of the lowest knowledge quartile's opinion only predicts the size of information effects at the individual level ($r = -.22$, $p < .001$).

the marginals between simulated opinion and the mix of preferences held by the lowest knowledge quartile was 13.7 points (s.d. = 8.9).

However, while the opinions of the highest knowledge quartile tend to be closer to the mark than those of the least informed, they can also provide decidedly inaccurate estimates of what collective preferences might look like if purged of information effects. Given the size of the absolute mean difference between simulated collective opinion and the opinion of the most knowledgeable respondents, basing estimates of fully informed collective opinions on the percentage point values of well-informed opinion would require a 95% confidence interval of ±9.2 percentage points. The percentage point value of well-informed opinion taken in isolation therefore cannot serve as a reliable bellwether of fully informed collective opinion. Rather, it is the relative difference in opinion between the ill and well informed that marks questions biased by information asymmetries. The telltale sign of large information effects in collective preferences is a sizeable gap between ill- and well-informed opinion, which indicates both the relative direction and the approximate magnitude of such effects. Simulations may be required to render precise estimates of these effects, but their presence in collective preferences can readily be seen in the divergence of opinion between the well and ill informed.

WHAT CAUSES INFORMATION EFFECTS?

The analysis thus far still leaves us with a puzzle. Differences in the shape and distribution of group opinions account for most of the variance in information effects, but these differences do not seem to arise from depletion effects. They could, of course, represent the main effects of political knowledge, but this straightforward interpretation is complicated by the relationship between knowledge and demographic characteristics. Moreover, critics of the "civics test" approach to political knowledge certainly have a point about the limited usefulness of many particular bits of political information that survey researchers try to tease out of respondents. Even defenders of this approach justify their focus on a narrow range of political facts by noting that possession of these bits indicates retention of a much broader array of information as well as chronic attentiveness to public affairs (Delli Carpini and Keeter 1996; Luskin 1987; Price and Zaller 1993). The few bits measured in surveys may have a direct connection to some of the political topics posed to survey respondents, but certainly not all. Another likely explanation is that these differences of opinion reflect real and enduring divisions in the needs, wants, and values represented by various kinds of people. Given the demographic disparities between the most and least knowledgeable citizens, the social distribution of political interests must surely account for some part of these differences. However, as we have seen, correcting for imbalances in political knowledge often changes the substantive mix of opinions given by ill-informed respondents. This means that the disparity between the opinions of the most and least informed often flows from a deficit of knowledge rather than a divergence of interests. A third explanation is that these differences are in some way associated with the topical focus of survey questions, and Chapter 4 confirmed that the size of information effects varies considerably by question topic. But it is unclear why this should be so. What is needed to clarify each of these possibilities is a better understanding of how differences in knowledge give rise to differences of opinion.

The rest of this chapter examines four factors that may help account for the distributional differences between knowledge quartiles: question format and mode effects produced by the survey method itself; the attitude structures and information processing strategies used by people with varying levels of knowledge; the social distribution of policy-specific knowledge relative to general political knowledge; and variations in issue salience among well- and ill-informed respondents. The impact of these factors can be shaped by the information environments in which respondents construct, update, and change their opinions, as will be demonstrated in a case study of opinion toward gay rights. It is unclear which of these factors is most responsible for the differences between surveyed and fully informed opinions, and other variables associated with political knowledge also might be contributing to the appearance of information effects. Nonetheless, these four possibilities seem especially good starting points for understanding how and why information effects arise in collective preferences.

Question Format and Survey Mode Effects

The results of sample surveys are often interpreted as simply reflecting the mix of opinions that exist "out there" in a population. Seen from this perspective, surveys act as mirrors or spotlights that make public the normally private views held by a broad range of citizens on pressing matters of the day. However, an alternative perspective holds that surveys can create the very thing they appear to reveal (Blumer 1948; Ginsberg 1986; Weissberg 2002a, 2002b; see also Zaller 1992; Zaller and Feldman

1992). In the extreme version of this view, "public opinion does not exist" (Bourdieu 1979) independently of the survey instrument used to measure it. Critics of the survey enterprise sometimes draw attention to the potential for slight changes in the wording of questions to overdetermine responses (e.g., Schuman and Presser 1981), to race-of-interviewer effects (as when white respondents are more supportive of affirmative action policies when the questions are posed by African-American rather than white interviewers, e.g., Schuman and Converse 1971; Singer and Presser 1989), and to the differences obtained by open-ended questions that ask respondents to provide answers in their own words versus forced-choice questions that require respondents to pick an opinion from a small list of alternatives (e.g., Schuman and Scott 1987; Singer and Schuman 1988).

The survey research community has long been attentive to the possibility that survey results are conditioned in ways subtle and gross by the methods of sampling and asking questions. A sizeable literature has developed over the past 60 years to address concerns about the effects of question wording, order, and mode of administration. While earlier research aimed to provide practical guidance to pollsters by describing common question design and response problems (e.g., Payne 1951; Rugg and Cantril 1944), more recent work has offered new insights on these problems by clarifying the psychological processes giving rise to survey response effects (e.g., Schwarz and Sudman 1996; Tanur 1992; Tourangeau, Rips, and Rasinski 2000; Zaller 1992a; Zaller and Feldman 1992). An important finding from this work that bears on the present discussion is that ill-informed people can be more prone than others to a wide range of response effects (Narayan and Krosnick 1996; Krosnick 1991; Krosnick and Alwin 1987; Schuman and Presser 1981; although see Knäuper 1999). Because response effects introduce systematic errors into surveyed opinions, and because these errors are especially likely to bias the opinions of the ill informed, response effects should contribute to the magnitude of information effects in collective preferences.[11] Variations

---

[11] This expectation assumes that response effects among actual survey respondents would be reduced to an unknown extent in a simulated world of fully informed respondents. I assume not that respondents with high levels of political knowledge invariably engage in purely optimal systematic processing of the survey instrument, but merely that imputing higher levels of ability to all respondents should mitigate response effects brought about by heavy reliance on heuristic processing. It follows that variance in the size of information effects revealed by the simulations should be related to the amount of error in individual opinions produced by response effects in the survey data.

in the size of information effects across question topics thus could be produced merely by the presence or absence of format characteristics known to prejudice responses in survey questions. If the gaps between surveyed and simulated opinions are manifestations of question wording and order effects introduced by the survey questionnaires themselves, then the consistent patterns of ideological bias revealed in Chapter 4 could be meaningless artifacts of the survey process rather than meaningful evidence that information inequalities cause certain points of view to be systematically underrepresented.

A program of research by Jon Krosnick and colleagues (Alwin and Krosnick 1991; Krosnick 1991, 1999a, 1999b; Krosnick and Fabrigar 1997, forthcoming) has shown that many question wording and order effects arise from *satisficing* behavior: strategic responses to the cognitive demands placed on survey respondents with lower levels of cognitive ability or motivation.[12] Lacking the ability or motivation to engage in systematic processing of the survey response, these respondents become inclined to choose the first acceptable response they are offered (weak satisficing) or even to disengage from thoughtful responses altogether by carelessly choosing any answer that *appears* to be an acceptable choice (strong satisficing). The effects of satisficing range from biases in retrieving information from long-term memory to selecting answers randomly or responding with "don't know" answers merely to avoid effortful processing of the survey question. Rather than suggesting that respondents who satisfice are mistaken about their opinions, favoring a policy, for instance, when with greater knowledge they might oppose it, this literature suggests that opinion convergence may also result from relatively mindless responses to the attributes of survey questions rather than to the topics of these questions. Since as much as 40% of the variance in attitude measures is due to systematic error introduced by the survey instrument itself (Cote and Buckley 1987), identifying features of survey questions that contribute to information effects might help survey researchers design

---

[12] Several other dual-process models have been developed to explain the survey response process (e.g., Cannel, Miller, and Oksenberg 1981; Tourangeau, Rips, and Rasinski 2000). Unlike most models of the survey response which typically focus on psychological processes alone (e.g., Zaller 1992a; Zaller and Feldman 1992), Krosnick's satisficing theory (adapted from Simon 1957) makes specific predictions about the impact of question attributes and respondent characteristics on the likelihood for systematic processing ("optimizing," in the parlance of Krosnick's model) in a way that can account for a variety of well-documented response effects. The power of the model lies in its potential for explaining a wide range of disparate and seemingly inconsistent findings on response effects dating back to the beginning of the 20th century.

questions that minimize the gaps between surveyed and fully informed opinion.

The satisficing literature identifies several attributes of survey questions that can be expected to produce opinion convergence among ill-informed respondents:

- *Questions phrased in the form of assertions.* There exists a well-documented tendency for respondents to answer in the affirmative any question that uses yes/no, agree/disagree, willing/not willing, and favor/oppose response options.[13] Acquiescence bias can be seen to result from satisficing, where less able or motivated respondents search first for reasons to agree with an assertion, responding with "disagree" only in the absence of such reasons (Krosnick 1991).
- *Rating scales containing a middle position.* An easy way to answer questions about policy issues is to select the middle point in the response scale, which might indicate favoring the status quo or merely neutrality on the issue (Krosnick 1991). Since questions with middle options are less reliable than those without them (Alwin and Krosnick 1991), it would seem that many respondents select the middle point as a strategy for coping with the cognitive demands of the survey interview rather than as an accurate report of underlying attitudes.
- *Series of sequential questions using the same response scale.* To make a survey more efficient by reducing the time it takes to read and answer questions, survey designers often group together several questions sharing the same response scale. Yet when faced with such a question series, less motivated respondents often select the same point on the scale to answer all the questions, a tendency known as "response set" or "scale nondifferentiation."[14]

---

[13] This tendency is thought to result from a habit of being insufficiently critical of generalizations or from social deference toward the survey interviewer (Schuman and Presser 1981). Schuman and Presser found that the tendency to acquiesce was common to all classes of respondents, but was relatively more predictable among the less educated.

[14] Such behavior can be quite common: one out of ten respondents in the 1980 General Social Surveys rated all of the objects in a 13-item question series using the same point on the rating scale, and the answers of over 40% of respondents showed substantial evidence of nondifferentiation (Krosnick and Alwin 1988). Yet the interpretation of such findings is sometimes open to question. For instance, the reliability of individual items located later in a scale series can be higher than that of items placed toward the beginning of a series (Knowles and Byers 1996), suggesting that respondents either learn how to more reliably map their opinions onto the scale with subsequent questions or that respondent fatigue or disinterest increases scale nondifferentiation.

- *Question order*. Because motivation to engage in systematic processing should decline over the course of an interview as respondent fatigue increases, the relative location of a question within the survey instrument should be related to the prevalence of response effects. Satisficing behavior should be more common for questions appearing later in the survey (Krosnick 1991).
- *Mode of administering the survey*. Satisficing behavior is expected to produce different consequences in face-to-face and telephone surveys due to the different memory processes that come into play when response options are presented visually or verbally (Holbrook, Green, and Krosnick 2003; Krosnick 1991). The confounding effects of a variety of factors as well as the lack of comparability across studies have resulted in few general conclusions about data quality associated with mode effects (Groves 1989: Chapter 11; Krosnick and Fabrigar forthcoming), but it seems reasonable to expect that the decreased social presence of the interviewer in a telephone survey should lessen respondent motivation to engage in systematic processing.[15]

Consistent with previous findings on question format effects (for reviews of these findings, see Alwin and Krosnick 1991; Krosnick 1991, 1999a, 1999b; Krosnick and Fabrigar 1997, forthcoming), Table 5.2 shows that the percentage of DK/NO responses is lower in questions phrased in the form of assertions,[16] questions with ordinal scales containing a middle response option, and questions that are part of a series

---

[15] Put another way, while a desire to please the interviewer or to avoid appearing disinterested in a socially important topic should not differ between respondents in telephone and face-to-face interviews, the physical presence of the interviewer in a face-to-face setting allows respondents to monitor the nonverbal feedback from interviewers in addition to the verbal feedback common to both modes of survey administration. Given this increased social presence, respondents may be more motivated in face-to-face interviews to give opinions and engage in systematic processing. Yet while the added motivation provided by face-to-face interviews could lead to optimizing behavior, it might also lead to biased processing by encouraging low-ability or unmotivated respondents to lean heavily on heuristic cues, to engage in biased information retrieval, to be especially prone to social desirability effects, or to give opinions on topics for which they possess no attitudes. For example, one study found that the accuracy of reporting past voting behavior was greater in telephone than in face-to-face interviews, with the increased social presence of in-person interviews leading to greater misreporting of voting when the respondent had not in fact voted (Rogers 1989).

[16] The assertion variable was coded 1 for all questions using agree/disagree, willing/not willing, favor/oppose, for/against, or approve/disapprove formats, and 0 otherwise.

TABLE 5.2. *Impact of question format and survey mode on depletion, dispersion, and size of information effects*

	Depletion	Dispersion		Information Effects	
	Average % DK/NO Responses	Average Lopsidedness of Lowest Quartile	Average Lopsidedness of Highest Quartile	Average Point Change in Collective Opinions	Average Point Change in Individual Opinions
Question format					
Worded as assertion (n = 98)	4.21[a]	23.19	24.39[a]	6.68	12.39
Not worded as assertion (n = 137)	7.76[a]	23.01	20.24[a]	6.36	13.12
Middle option (n = 142)	4.05[a]	27.44[a]	25.53[a]	6.36	12.90
No middle option (n = 93)	9.68[a]	16.43[a]	16.54[a]	6.69	12.69
Question in series (n = 136)	2.10[a]	29.91[a]	26.19[a]	6.68	12.74
Question not in series (n = 99)	9.32[a]	18.12[a]	18.90[a]	6.35	12.87
From 1st half of survey (n = 86)	5.85	19.95[a]	18.97[a]	5.98	12.48
From 2nd half of survey (n = 149)	6.52	24.90[a]	23.71[a]	6.79	13.01
Mode of administration					
Face-to-face (n = 51)	4.99	23.84	23.00	7.09	13.85
Telephone (n = 51)	4.89	24.22	22.36	7.09	12.92

[a] t-value for differences within column pairs $p < .05$.

Note: Mode of administration differences based on split sample comparison in the 1996 ANES post-election study. All other differences based on the full set of 235 questions from the 1988, 1992, and 1996 ANES.

sharing the same response scale,[17] since these format characteristics make it easy for respondents to give substantive responses with little cognitive effort. Similarly, item nonresponse rates are slightly higher for questions appearing later in a survey,[18] since respondent fatigue should be higher at the time such questions are asked. This much is in line with expectations.

However, while satisficing is expected to be more common among respondents with lower ability and motivation levels, it turns out that these question characteristics influence the lopsidedness of group opinions to similar degrees in both the highest and lowest knowledge quartiles. In each case, question formats known to produce satisficing behavior significantly increase the lopsidedness of group opinions. While such patterns are consistent with the predictions of the satisficing literature, the novel finding here is that the effect of these question formats is so similar among the most and least able respondents. And in the case of questions worded as assertions, respondents in the highest knowledge quartile appear to satisfice more than those in the lowest.

Because both groups are affected in similar ways, none of these question attributes has a consistent or significant impact on the size of information effects, despite the fact that they are notorious in the literature for reducing the quality of survey responses. Information effects should become smaller to the extent that respondents across levels of political knowledge reliably satisfice when presented with such questions, because this form of satisficing should reduce differences in opinion among the well and ill informed. Although none of the problematic question formats produce significantly smaller gaps between surveyed and fully informed opinion, differences in the size of individual-level information effects for all but questions with middle options are consistent with this account. This illustrates that smaller information effects should not be taken as prima facie evidence of

[17] A series is defined as three or more adjacent questions that share the same response scale. For the 1988 and 1992 data, this attribute was coded from copies of the actual survey instruments presented to respondents (available on the ANES CD-ROM), whereas for the 1996 data this attribute was coded from the ANES codebook.

[18] This variable was constructed by arranging sequentially every question stem (labeled with a letter and a number in the ANES codebook) within each wave of the ANES data and numbering them from 1 to n, with n representing the last question in the survey instrument. The identifying letter and number combination for each question was obtained from the questionnaires archived on the ANES CD-ROM for the 1988 and 1992 data, and from the codebooks for the 1996 data. For each wave, the sequential number of each question was divided by the total number of questions in the wave, to produce a variable ranging from approximately 0 to 1, with lower scores representing items that appeared relatively early in the questionnaire and higher scores representing later questions.

improved validity or representational quality, since they may result just as easily from reliable errors generated by the way a question is worded.

Table 5.2 also reports findings on mode effects arising from a split-sample experiment conducted in the post-election wave of the 1996 ANES.[19] While all respondents answered the same questions, half were interviewed in person at their places of residence, while the other half were interviewed over the telephone. As can be seen in this table, mode of interview had no significant effects on group depletion, the lopsidedness of well- or ill-informed opinion, or the size of information effects.

A vast number of possible question format and mode effects is documented in the literature, but most are difficult to test with ANES data, since doing so requires that split-ballot tests or survey experiments be built into questionnaires. However, the small number of problematic question design features that can be tested with these data have no substantive impact on the size of information effects. This is largely because they tend to affect rates of DK/NO responses, which are themselves unrelated to the size of information effects, and because they tend to produce the same response effects in the opinions of both ill- and well-informed respondents. While limitations in the available data preclude testing for a broader range of question format effects, the few tests that can be conducted suggest that the consistent patterns of ideological bias brought about by information effects are not merely artifacts of the survey instrument.

Differences in Attitude Structures and Information-Processing Strategies

Information effects in collective preferences might also arise from differences in heuristic strategies and attitude structures common to well- and ill-informed respondents. Knowledgeable respondents tend to have more highly developed and constrained attitude structures than ill-informed respondents (Converse 1964; Delli Carpini and Keeter 1996; Lockerbie 1991), which may make them less prone to question wording and

---

[19] Because the American National Election Studies data are typically obtained with face-to-face interviews, mode of interview effects could not be tested in the full set of questions. But a split-sample experiment conducted in the post-election wave of the 1996 ANES provides an opportunity to assess the influence of mode effects. In this wave, respondents were randomly assigned to receive face-to-face ($n = 776$) or telephone interviews ($n = 752$). A total of 51 policy and value questions were asked in the post-election wave, and for each question separate measures of information effects were calculated for the group of respondents in the face-to-face condition and for the group in the telephone condition. This resulted in a total of 102 collective opinions.

order effects (Kinder and Sanders 1990; Krosnick 1991; Yankelovich 1991; Zaller 1992a). They also tend to rely on different heuristic shortcuts than ill-informed people, which can cause them to structure their attitudes in ways unlike less knowledgeable respondents or to construct different opinions from the same attitude structures (Chaiken and Maheswaran 1994; Conover, Feldman, and Knight 1987; Duch, Palmer, and Anderson 2000; Lau and Redlawsk 2001; Sniderman, Brody, and Tetlock 1991). For example, two similar questions about American financial support of the Nicaraguan Contras were posed to a national sample in 1989. The first asked simply "Would you like to see aid to the Contras in Nicaragua increased, decreased, or kept about the same?" The second version identified the Contras as anti-communist guerrillas and presented pro and con views on the issue before leading into the first question. Politically attentive respondents understood both versions of the question in terms of anti-communism, but inattentive respondents answered the second question as if it were measuring their feelings about anti-communism and the first as if it were asking about their views on government spending (Zaller 1992b). Ill-informed respondents reasoned from a similar basis as the well informed only when prompted by the anti-communist cue in the second question.

Question wording effects that evoke different attitude structures for evaluating the same stimulus object can occasionally produce large differences between the opinions of the well and ill informed. A widely noted and curious example of these effects hinges on whether "welfare" or "aid to poor people" is used to describe government assistance to the poor (Rasinski 1989; Smith 1987). A direct test of this wording effect was conducted in the 1996 ANES. Respondents were first presented with the following question: "Should federal spending on welfare programs be increased, decreased, or kept about the same?" Later in the interview, respondents were asked this question again, except that the term "poor people" was used in place of "welfare programs." This small change in wording produced dramatic effects in collective opinions: 58% wanted to decrease spending on welfare programs, but only 13% wanted to decrease spending on poor people.

This crucial difference in terms also produces a larger information effect in one of the questions. Differences of opinion are of a similar magnitude in surveyed opinion for both questions: 65% of respondents from the highest knowledge quartile versus just 44% of those from the lowest wanted to decrease spending on welfare, while 22% from the highest quartile and only 4% from the lowest wanted to decrease spending on poor people. However, the modal preference for both quartiles is the same in the welfare question – pluralities in both groups preferred to decrease welfare spending – but different in the poor people question, where 47% of the highest quartile preferred to keep spending about the same, but 63% of the lowest preferred to increase spending. Dispersion effects therefore gave additional influence to well-informed opinion in the welfare question but to ill-informed opinion in the poor people question. As a consequence, correcting for information effects makes more of a difference in one than the other. While the percentage wanting to decrease spending goes up in simulated opinion for both questions, the increase is smaller for welfare (6 points) than for poor people (12 points). After correcting for information effects, the percentage wanting to increase spending in simulated opinion remains the same for the welfare question, but goes down by 13 points in the poor people question.[20]

The poor people question has a larger gap between surveyed and simulated preferences because a dispersion effect in surveyed opinion advantaged the views of ill-informed respondents. But what explains why the views of the ill-informed were more lopsided in one question than the other? Responses to social spending questions are marked by a high degree of ambivalence – most Americans can list as many reasons for supporting as for opposing welfare (Zaller and Feldman 1992) – and it may be that less knowledgeable respondents gravitated toward similar (and simpler) decision rules for resolving this ambivalence. In social spending questions such as these, support increases when recipients of spending are perceived as especially deserving of help (Appelbaum 2001; Cook and Barrett 1992; Nelson and Kinder 1996) and when questions focus on specific programs rather than general categories of programs (Jacoby 2000).[21] Spending on poor people seems somewhat more specific than spending on welfare programs, and poor people elicit more positive

---

[20] That the welfare version of this question produces smaller information effects does not mean that it produces opinions which are generally "better" or more worthy of consideration than the poor people question. From a question design standpoint it has several undesirable properties: it activates primarily negative evaluations of social spending (Smith 1987), and it is vague – as Cook and Barrett (1992: 221) point out, "no program called 'welfare' actually exists." From the perspective of political representation, the only sense in which the welfare version is "better" is that the uneven social distribution of political knowledge makes less of a difference for people who answer it.

[21] Preferences on welfare spending in the United States are also strongly influenced by attitudes toward African Americans, so much so that welfare gives all appearances of being a racial code word (Gilens 1999). However, the magnitude of this association appears to be the same for both versions of the question considered here (Smith 1987).

TABLE 5.3. *Attitude structure of support for increased spending on welfare programs and poor people*

	Lowest Knowledge Quartile		Highest Knowledge Quartile	
	Welfare Programs	Poor People	Welfare Programs	Poor People
Feelings toward poor people	.11	.18**	−.06	.20**
Feelings toward people on welfare	.30**	.03	.17**	−.09
Concern for social equality	−.02	.21**	.24**	.31**
Gov't should ensure a good standard of living	.07	.13*	.39**	.38**
$R^2 =$	.13	.14	.41	.39
$N =$	313	313	337	336

*$p < .05$
**$p < .01$
Note: Cells contain standardized OLS (beta) coefficients.
Source: 1996 American National Election Studies.

feelings than people on welfare: in the 1996 ANES, the average feeling thermometer score for poor people was 70 out of 100, compared to a tepid 51 for people on welfare. It is therefore tempting to conclude that information effects in these questions take the shape they do merely because the ill informed lean more heavily than the well informed on a "desert" heuristic (Sniderman, Brody, and Tetlock 1991) when deducing their spending preferences. However, the data reveal a more complicated story.

The attitudes of ill-informed people toward welfare spending do seem to reflect a simple desert heuristic, but their attitudes toward spending on poor people have a more complex structure (Table 5.3). Feelings toward welfare recipients are the only significant predictor of support for increased welfare spending among the least knowledgeable respondents. In contrast, spending preferences for poor people among these respondents are significantly influenced by their feelings toward poor people, concern for social equality, and opinions on governmental responsibility for taking care of the poor.[22] These attitudes are also significant predictors

[22] Feeling thermometer scores were used to represent feelings toward poor people (v961035) and people on welfare (v961036). A scale of egalitarianism was constructed by averaging v961229[reversed], v961230, v961231[reversed], v961232, v961233, and v961234[reversed]. Attitudes toward governmental responsibility for jobs and a good standard of living was constructed from the standard seven-point item (v960483), which was reverse-coded so that higher values reflected higher levels of governmental responsibility.

among respondents from the highest knowledge quartile, who apply the same attitude structure to both questions, differing only in whether feelings toward poor people or welfare recipients are brought to bear when answering each question.

It is not clear why such slight wording changes should produce such different attitude structures among the least informed, but it is notable that even though the poor people question prompts ill-informed respondents to think about spending in basically the same way that well-informed people do, this change results paradoxically in larger information effects. The reason for this is that well- and ill-informed respondents shared essentially the same feelings toward welfare recipients and the same levels of concern for social equality, but the least knowledgeable felt more positively toward poor people (with a mean thermometer score of 74) than the most knowledgeable (who have a mean score of 67), and they also were more likely to hold government responsible for helping the poor (with a mean of 3.8 for the lowest quartile, compared with 2.9 for the highest).[23] Because feelings toward welfare recipients are unrelated to levels of political knowledge, this simple attitude structure produces opinions that are similar to those of the well informed. In this case, it would appear that the desert heuristic does indeed compensate to some degree for lower levels of political knowledge. But because the ill informed have more positive feelings toward poor people and also stronger beliefs that government should do more to help the poor, their reliance on these attitudes in the poor people question drives their opinions away from those of well-informed respondents.

Wording effects such as these can result from convergence behavior that inclines ill-informed respondents to draw from different attitude structures or information processing strategies than the well informed. This example illustrates how the composition of attitude structures can moderate the appearance of information effects, even in questions about the same topic. Information effects can appear not only when questions prime the ill informed to draw from different considerations than the well informed (as will be illustrated in the gay rights examples later in this chapter), but also, as this example shows, when questions lead both groups to draw from the same mix of considerations. Patterns in the

---

[23] Mean differences in feeling thermometer scores for poor people are significantly different among the highest and lowest knowledge quartiles, $t(758) = 5.33, p < .001$, as are mean differences in support for government-guaranteed standards of living, $t(692) = 6.36$, $p < .001$. Differences between quartiles for the other two variables are not statistically significant.

size and direction of information effects might therefore follow patterns of divergence in attitude structures and heuristic strategies across levels of political knowledge. In such cases, controlling for information effects imputes to all respondents not knowledge itself but rather the attitude structures of knowledgeable people.

The Social Distribution of Policy-Specific Knowledge

Information effects might arise not from a lack of general political knowledge per se, but rather from a lack of policy-specific knowledge relevant to the particular question at hand. If levels of general political knowledge reflect merely the propensity for an individual to possess policy-specific knowledge on a wide range of issues, then the actual social distribution of policy-specific knowledge may help explain why information effects are large in some collective preferences but small in others. Researchers have demonstrated that policy-specific knowledge can influence attitudes independently from general political knowledge (Gilens 2001; McGraw and Pinney 1990). Using a simulation method similar to the one employed here, Gilens found that a lack of policy-specific knowledge generated unique information effects between two and six times as large as the information effects produced by low levels of general political knowledge.

This finding raises the possibility that the size of information effects produced by low levels of general political knowledge might be moderated by the social distribution of policy-specific knowledge, which sometimes is spread much more evenly across social strata than general political knowledge. Possessing policy-specific knowledge should tend to reduce the size of information effects in relevant survey questions even among people who have lower levels of general political knowledge. The Gilens study provides some suggestive evidence on this point. Gilens found that half of Americans knew in 1988 that the unemployment rate had declined over the previous eight years, and information effects produced by general political knowledge were almost nonexistent in a question about whether government should increase spending to help the unemployed. Only one in five respondents knew that federal efforts to protect the environment had declined over that time period, and fairly large information effects were found in collective preferences about the need for additional spending on environmental protection.

This work also suggests that the social distribution of policy-specific knowledge can be only part of the story. The Gilens study shows that fully 75% of Americans knew in 1988 that the deficit had been rising, yet information effects in collective opinions about paying down the deficit averaged a stratospheric 18 percentage points. My analysis of similar data from eight years later shows far fewer knew that the deficit had been falling – just 29% of Americans got this question right in 1996 – yet information effects in collective opinions about fiscal issues averaged around 9 percentage points, roughly half the size of information effects about fiscal issues in 1988. The Gilens study also concludes that the effects of policy-specific information depend on the possession of general political knowledge. Table 4 of that study suggests that policy-specific knowledge alone compensated for low levels of general knowledge in only one or two of seven questions studied. However, it is possible that these conclusions might hold only for collective information effects, since individual-level effects were not analyzed in the Gilens study. A check on these findings is provided by individual-level data from the 1996 American National Election Studies, which contains a relatively larger number of policy-specific information items that can be related directly to a larger number of opinion questions than had been available in the 1988 data examined by Gilens.

Rather than replicating the sophisticated, multistage simulation method employed by Gilens, a similar perspective is provided by comparing information effects among people who lack policy-specific knowledge to those for people who possess it, while controlling for levels of general political knowledge.[24] Four policy domains can be studied in this way: abortion rights, spending on military defense, competing priorities in governmental budgeting, and the amount of government effort that should be devoted to various aspects of environmental protection. Among the available measures of policy-specific knowledge, 29% of respondents knew

---

[24] For the analysis presented in this section, correct answers to each policy-specific knowledge question were removed from the standard scale of political knowledge used elsewhere in this book for 1996 data. Thus, correct answers to the candidates' stands on abortion were subtracted from general political knowledge when assessing the unique impact of both kinds of knowledge on abortion attitudes, leaving all other knowledge items (including those about defense spending, the deficit, and environmental positions taken by the parties) in the general political knowledge scale. For assessing the impact of policy-specific knowledge on defense spending preferences, correct placements of the two parties on defense spending were subtracted from the general knowledge scale for the defense spending comparison, leaving all other knowledge items (including those about the candidates' abortion stances, the deficit, and environmental positions taken by the parties) in the measure of general political knowledge. Such comparisons allow a simple test of the relative impact of policy-specific knowledge versus general political knowledge.

the federal budget deficit had declined over the previous four years, 58% could correctly place President Bill Clinton as relatively more prochoice on abortion rights than candidate Bob Dole, 49% could correctly place the Republican Party as favoring larger increases in defense spending than the Democratic Party, 52% correctly placed Clinton as favoring stronger environmental protections than Dole, and 49% correctly did the same for the Democratic Party relative to the Republican Party (43% got both of these environmental stance questions correct).[25] None of these questions provide an especially good test of policy-specific knowledge for, as Gilens (2001: 388–9) points out, all single-item measures are susceptible to guessing. Indeed, the percentages correct in each case are very close to what we would expect by chance: the deficit question has three possible answers, so a third of guessers should get it right, while the other knowledge items are scored as correct when candidates or parties are placed in correct relative position to one another, which means that about half should get these right by guessing. Nonetheless, these questions are the best available in ANES data, so they will have to do.

The 1996 ANES fares much better when it comes to providing opinion questions related to the policy-specific knowledge items. Although only one abortion rights question and one defense spending question are included, a set of six questions presented tradeoffs between pairs of alternatives to clarify respondent preferences about priorities in governmental budgeting.[26] Respondents were also asked to specify whether more, less,

---

[25] The correlations between each of these items and all the other items making up the scale of general political knowledge were as follows: .22 for knowledge of the deficit, .50 for knowledge of the candidates' abortion stances, .50 for knowledge of the parties' relative stances on increasing defense spending, and .55 for answering both environmental knowledge questions correctly.

[26] Respondents were asked whether they would change levels of domestic spending, taxes paid by ordinary people, or the size of the federal budget deficit in order to support their preferred policy outcomes (more spending, lower taxes, or lower deficits). The series of questions was presented as follows: "Each year the government in Washington has to make decisions about taxes, spending, and the deficit. We'd like to know your opinions about what the government should do about the budget. Do you favor an increase in the federal budget deficit in order to increase spending on domestic programs like Medicare, education, and highways? (Yes, favor; No, don't favor) Do you favor cuts in spending on domestic programs like Medicare, education, and highways in order to cut the taxes paid by ordinary Americans? (Yes, favor; No, don't favor) Do you favor an increase in the federal budget deficit in order to cut the taxes paid by ordinary Americans? (Yes, favor; No, don't favor.)" After five intervening questions, respondents were again asked: "Here are a few more questions about what the government should do about the budget. Do you favor increases in the taxes paid by ordinary Americans in order to increase spending on domestic programs like Medicare, education, and highways? (Yes, favor; No, don't

or the same governmental effort should be expended in seven different forms of environmental protection.[27] Not only does each set of questions correspond directly to a policy-specific knowledge item, but the deficit item should be at least indirectly relevant for the questions dealing with defense spending and environmental policy as well: both deal with activities of the federal government (the deficit question reveals knowledge about the federal government), and the defense question deals with levels of government spending.

Table 5.4 reveals that, after controlling for levels of general political knowledge, individual-level information effects were generally smaller among respondents in possession of relevant policy-specific knowledge. Moreover, these information effects did not tend to be significantly smaller for people with policy-specific knowledge that was clearly unrelated to the questions being answered. For example, correct knowledge of candidate stances on abortion was associated with smaller information effects in the abortion question, but not for any of the other questions. There are also a few exceptions to the rule: knowing where the parties stood on defense spending was related to smaller information effects in the defense spending question, the abortion question, and one of the environmental questions. It also predicted larger effects in one of the fiscal questions. A small amount of overlap like this is expected, since the logic behind a general measure of political knowledge is that people who know something about one aspect of politics should also know things about other aspects of politics. However, the general pattern in Table 5.4 is clear-cut: policy-specific knowledge exerts a consistent and independent influence on the size of information effects produced by uneven levels of general political knowledge. Even in cases where more than one type of policy-specific knowledge is shown to significantly influence the size of information effects, the correlations for the more directly relevant knowledge item are always larger than for the more distantly related item.

favor) Do you favor cuts in spending on domestic programs like Medicare, education, and highways in order to cut the federal budget deficit? (Yes, favor; No, don't favor) Do you favor increases in taxes paid by ordinary Americans in order to cut the federal budget deficit? (Yes, favor; No, don't favor)."

[27] The environmental questions appeared in a series that was worded as follows: "Now I am going to ask you what you think of the government's current activities in various areas of environmental policy. In each case, just tell me whether you think the government should put less, the same amount, or more effort into that area than it does now. Do you think the government should put less, the same amount, or more effort into <reducing air pollution>?" The same stem was used for each question, which differed only in the target activity mentioned (the full list of these activities is shown in Table 5.4).

TABLE 5.4. *Partial correlations between correct answers to policy-specific knowledge items and the size of information effects in individual opinions, controlling for general political knowledge*

Policy Domain	Know Candidate Stances on Abortion	Know Party Stances on Defense Spending	Know Federal Deficit went Down	Know Party and Candidate Stances on Environment
Abortion				
Abortion always allowed	−.09**	−.06*	.07*	−.01
Foreign policy				
Increase/decrease defense spending	.03	−.08**	−.02	−.02
Fiscal policy				
Raise deficit to raise spending	−.03	.03	.01	.02
Raise deficit to cut taxes	.04	−.03	−.10**	−.01
Cut spending to cut taxes	.02	.05	−.13**	−.11**
Cut spending to cut deficit	−.02	.07**	−.14**	−.10**
Raise taxes to raise spending	−.01	.03	−.07**	.03
Raise taxes to cut deficit	−.05	.01	.05*	.05
Environmental policy				
Improving and protecting the environment	−.01	.01	−.09**	−.13**
Reducing air pollution	−.00	.04	−.10**	−.15**
Managing natural resources	.00	.02	−.12**	−.13**
Cleaning up lakes and parks	.04	−.05*	−.05	−.13**
Cleaning up hazardous or toxic waste	−.04	.02	−.11**	−.12**
Reducing solid waste and garbage	−.02	.01	−.05*	−.09*
Addressing global warming	−.01	.02	−.09**	−.13**

*p < .05
**p < .01
Note: Columns contain partial correlation coefficients between policy-specific knowledge and the size of individual-level information effects for each opinion question, controlling for the impact of all other items making up the 1996 knowledge scale.
Source: 1996 American National Election Studies.

While useful for their statistical clarity, the partial correlations reported in this table are less helpful for conveying the substantive impact of policy-specific knowledge. A better sense is given by examining the estimated mean size of information effects among people with different levels of policy-specific knowledge, while correcting for (by holding constant) the impact of general political knowledge.[28] The average individual-level information effect in abortion questions was estimated to be 14.3 percentage points among people who could correctly identify Clinton as more pro-choice than Dole, compared with 16.6 points among people who could not. The average gap between surveyed and simulated opinion on defense spending likewise ran 15.5 points among people who correctly placed the parties on defense spending, compared with 17.7 points for others, and across the six fiscal questions ran 13.3 points among people who knew that the federal budget deficit had declined under President Clinton, compared with 14.8 points for others. The average individual-level information effect across the seven environmental questions ran 8.9 percentage points among people who correctly placed both the candidates and the parties on relative concerns about environmental protection, 11.8 points among those who correctly placed either the candidates or the parties on

---

[28] Univariate analysis of variance tests for all the relationships reported in this paragraph (using general political knowledge as a covariate) were significant at conventional levels. For the abortion question, $F(1, 1395) = 11.9$, $p < .01$ for the unique effects of policy-specific knowledge, and $F(1, 1395) = 763.9$, $p < .001$ for the unique effects of general political knowledge. The uncorrected group means were 10.5 points among people with correct knowledge about candidates' abortion stances, compared to 22.0 points among those lacking policy-specific knowledge. For the defense spending question, $F(1, 1219) = 8.7$, $p < .01$ for the unique effects of policy-specific knowledge, and $F(1, 1219) = 399.6$, $p < .001$ for the unique effects of general political knowledge. The uncorrected group means were 12.4 points among people with correct knowledge about the parties' defense spending positions, compared to 21.6 points among those lacking policy-specific knowledge. For the fiscal policy questions, where information effects from all six questions are averaged together, $F(1, 1302) = 17.2$, $p < .001$ for the unique effects of policy-specific knowledge, and $F(1, 1302) = 2,445.6$, $p < .001$ for the unique effects of general political knowledge. The uncorrected group means were 10.4 points among people with correct knowledge about the federal budget deficit, compared to 16.0 points among those lacking policy-specific knowledge. For the seven environmental policy questions, where information effects from all questions are averaged together, $F(2, 1285) = 46.7$, $p < .001$ for the unique effects of policy-specific knowledge, and $F(2, 1285) = 369.4$, $p < .001$ for the unique effects of general political knowledge. The uncorrected group means were 5.0 points among people with correct knowledge about the federal budget deficit, 10.6 points among those who correctly placed either the candidates or the parties on relative concerns about environmental protection, and 18.2 points among those lacking policy-specific knowledge.

relative concerns about environmental protection, and 15.5 points among those lacking policy-specific knowledge.

Another pattern worth noting in Table 5.4 is the varying impact of policy-specific knowledge on information effects in relevant questions. For example, the independent effect of deficit knowledge is greater for the two fiscal questions mentioning spending cuts than for the other fiscal questions. These are also the only fiscal questions in which the size of information effects is related to knowledge about environmental stances taken by the parties and candidates. Knowing party and candidate environmental stances has fairly uniform associations with information effects in all the environmental questions, but knowing the deficit went down has a less consistent impact on information effects for these questions. The impact of policy-specific knowledge may therefore depend on whether and how people associate that knowledge with the attitudes they report in opinion surveys.

These findings confirm that information effects can arise from deficits in policy-specific knowledge, general political knowledge, or both. As a consequence, information effects in collective preferences can vary in size depending on the social distribution of policy-specific information. When relevant policy-specific knowledge is available even to respondents who appear ill-informed on scales of general political knowledge, differences in general knowledge will matter less to the shape of collective preferences.

The Relative Salience of Political Issues

Information effects are also related to differences between more- and less-knowledgeable citizens in the salience of political issues. *Issue salience*, as I use it here, is meant broadly as a catchall term to encompass a variety of related concepts, such as issue involvement (Verba, Schlozman, and Brady 1995), the perceived importance, novelty, or personal relevance of issues, or simply that some issues come more readily to mind than others (Higgins 1996).

The more salient an issue or topic, the more motivated a respondent should be to answer a survey question about that topic using systematic processing (Krosnick and Fabrigar forthcoming). Evidence supporting this conclusion is widespread in the literature. Questions dealing with topics having high salience to respondents tend to have lower levels of DK/NO responses than questions on less salient topics (Converse 1976; Francis and Busch 1975; Krosnick 1999b: 556–9; Krosnick and Milburn 1990; Rapoport 1982). In addition, the less salient the topic of a question, the more random the responses to those questions tend to be over time. For instance, over-time correlations among foreign policy items tend to be substantially lower than for domestic policy items, which is often interpreted as reflecting the relative salience of these topical domains (Achen 1975; Converse 1964; Converse and Markus 1979; Feldman 1989). Moreover, this pattern is generally consistent with the average magnitude of information effects discussed in Chapter 4. Among the least stable responses are those to questions regarding taxes (Feldman 1989), a tendency reflected in the high average point difference in the fiscal category used in the present study (see Table 4.1). Among the most stable responses are those to social issues, which also tend to have the smallest information effects.

When issue salience is relatively high among even the least knowledgeable people, information effects should tend to be small. This may be because the perceived importance of an issue leads people to acquire domain-specific information, which enhances their ability to answer questions about the issue, or because issue salience motivates people to answer questions more systematically than they would otherwise. ANES data contain a variety of questions that ask directly or indirectly about the salience of issues and public affairs. Since the 1996 data are especially rich in such measures, they provide a good test of the relationships between political knowledge, issue salience, and the size of information effects.

People with higher levels of political knowledge tend to perceive a broader range of issues as important, to attach greater levels of importance to issues, and to be more interested in public affairs (Delli Carpini and Keeter 1996; Luskin 1990; Neuman 1986). These relationships are illustrated with correlations in the first column of Table 5.5. Knowledgeable people report higher levels of "average issue salience," which is a measure of perceived importance across the five issues in which issue importance was directly measured in the 1996 ANES.[29] They tend to mention a greater number of issues than the ill informed when prompted to name important national problems, and they tend to perceive a larger number of important differences between the national parties than less knowledgeable respondents. They report higher levels of interest in public affairs than the ill informed, and they consistently report higher levels of interest in election campaigns at all levels.

While political knowledge is not the same as salience, the two constructs are positively related to one another. All of the salience measures

---

[29] These measures of issue importance address the provision of government services, defense spending, affirmative action, abortion, and environmental protection.

TABLE 5.5. *Individual-level correlations between political knowledge, salience measures, and information effects*

	(1)	(2)	(3)	(4)	(5)	(6)	(7)	(8)	(9)
(1) Political knowledge index	1.00								
(2) Average issue salience	.17**	1.00							
(3) Number of important national problems	.29**	.21**	1.00						
(4) Number of differences between national parties	.47**	.15**	.23**	1.00					
(5) Interest in public affairs	.44**	.25**	.15**	.26**	1.00				
(6) Interest in political campaigns	.39**	.27**	.15**	.19**	.56**	1.00			
(7) Interest in presidential election	.28**	.23**	.06	.21**	.35**	.35**	1.00		
(8) Interest in U.S. house election	.30**	.31**	.08*	.20**	.47**	.47**	.43**	1.00	
(9) Average point change in individual opinions	−.93**	−.15**	−.21**	−.42**	−.40**	−.36**	−.29**	−.27**	1.00
Average point change in individual opinions, *lowest knowledge quartile only*	. . .	−.04	−.02	−.12†	−.10†	−.09†	−.23**	−.07	1.00

†*p* < .10
*p < .05
**p < .01
Source: 1996 American National Election Studies.

are positively correlated with each other as well as with political knowledge, and a factor analysis suggests that they represent different facets of a single underlying construct.[30] Nonetheless, while the general trend between knowledge and salience is unmistakable, it is also important to note that none of these correlations is especially large. Political knowledge and issue salience are related but only modestly so, which means that salience can moderate the size of information effects independently from levels of political knowledge. The last two rows of Table 5.5 show that the opinions of people with higher levels of salience have smaller average information effects.[31] This relationship holds even after controlling for levels of political knowledge by testing for salience effects among the least knowledgeable quartile, although the impact of salience for this group is much more limited than it is among all respondents taken together.

The same tendency can be observed in questions about topics that should be more salient to some kinds of respondents than others. A good example of this comes in differences between respondents from union and non-union families for a question asking whether foreign imports should be limited in order to protect American jobs.[32] Individual-level information effects were significantly smaller among respondents from union households in each of the three years this question was asked, despite the fact that union respondents were slightly less knowledgeable on average compared to non-union respondents.[33] At the group level,

---

[30] Principal components analysis of the seven salience measures returns two factors, which oblimin rotation shows to be only slightly correlated ($r = .19$). The first factor consists of significant positive loadings for average issue salience, interest in public affairs, and the three measures of campaign interest; whereas the second has positive loadings for the number of important national problems and differences between parties mentioned by respondents. This second factor may well represent nothing more than propensity toward talkativeness, since these two salience measures are counts of problems and differences volunteered by respondents under prompting from the survey interviewer. A two-factor solution is still returned when political knowledge is entered along with the salience measures. In this expanded model, however, political knowledge has positive and similarly large loads on both factors.

[31] The measure of individual-level information effects used in this table is each respondent's average percentage-point gap between surveyed and simulated opinion across all questions answered.

[32] The exact wording of this question is "Some people have suggested placing new limits on foreign imports in order to protect American jobs. Others say that such limits would raise consumer prices and hurt American exports. Do you favor or oppose placing new limits on imports, or haven't you thought much about this?"

[33] Among the group of respondents from union families, who stood to be directly affected by limits on foreign imports, the average individual-level information effect was 12 points in 1988, 12 points in 1992, and 7 points in 1996. Among non-union respondents, the

however, a somewhat different picture emerged. Union respondents had a 2-point gap between their surveyed and fully informed collective opinion in 1988, a gap of 9 points in 1992, and a gap of 6 points in 1996. Among non-union respondents, the difference between surveyed and simulated collective opinions was 11 points in 1988, 6 points in 1992, and 5 points in 1996. Even though the individual-level information effects were smaller for union respondents in each of these years, the direction of these effects tended to be fairly random in 1988 but more systematic in 1992 and 1996. At the collective level, union opinion in the latter years had larger collective-level information effects than non-union opinion while at the same time having smaller individual-level effects. The underlying reason for this change is unclear, although it could arise from changing attitude structures, rising levels of domain-specific knowledge, changes in the salience of this issue, or shifts in cultural or historical dimensions of the foreign imports issue. To get a better purchase on such possibilities, it becomes important to consider how political issues are constructed, discussed, and connected to one another in the flows of information reaching citizens through mass media and interpersonal networks.

ENVIRONMENTAL INFLUENCES ON ATTITUDE STRUCTURES, POLICY-SPECIFIC KNOWLEDGE, AND ISSUE SALIENCE

Information effects can arise when well- and ill-informed citizens possess different attitude structures, amounts of policy-specific knowledge, or levels of issue salience. But what can explain these divergences? Less knowledgeable citizens were shown to think about welfare programs quite unlike the way their more knowledgeable counterparts did, to be less aware of an important development in the country's fiscal health, and to be less concerned about specific issues and public affairs in general. The most likely source of these differences is the information environments in which people come to form their policy preferences.

Since well-informed people tend to pay more attention to mass media communications about public affairs than other people (e.g., Price and Zaller 1993; Zaller 1992a), subtle biases in the way news is constructed or framed may be especially likely to influence the policy preferences

average individual-level gap between surveyed and simulated opinions was 18 percentage points in 1988, 14 points in 1992, and 14 in 1996. These differences were all significant: $t(1108) = 4.84, p < .001$ for 1988, $t(1395) = 2.00, p < .05$ for 1992, and $t(774) = 6.49$, $p < .001$ for 1996.

adopted by knowledgeable respondents (Krosnick and Brannon 1993), even though the framing of issues and events in the media also influences the preferences of ill-informed people (Converse 1962; Krosnick and Kinder 1990; Miller and Krosnick 1996). Knowledgeable citizens are more directly exposed than less attentive people to the opinions of political elites, whose views tend to dominate political news coverage (Bennett 1990; Bennett and Manheim 1993; Epstein 1973; Gans 1979; Sigal 1973; Tuchman 1978). From this perspective, the direction of fully informed opinion relative to surveyed opinion shown in Table 4.2 might reflect the contours of elite political debate in the late 1980s and early 1990s when these surveys were in the field. It may be that simulated opinion is less isolationist when it comes to foreign affairs because mainstream news outlets, at least according to some accounts, emphasize internationalist approaches to foreign policy (Herman and Chomsky 1988; Parenti 1986). Likewise, the tendency for fully informed opinion on governance issues to favor a more libertarian approach to economic regulation might reflect a pro-business economic agenda in news coverage (Bagdikian 1990; Danielian and Page 1994; Herman and Chomsky 1988; Parenti 1986). The shifts in simulated opinion toward more progressive stances on many domestic policy topics might reflect a liberal tilt to news dealing with social issues (Lichter, Rothman, and Lichter 1986; Rothman and Lichter 1987).

Framing, agenda-setting, and priming effects may thereby contribute to the pattern of differences between actual and fully informed opinion, although the influence of these effects on policy preferences is certain to be blunted by the fact that citizens play an active role in negotiating the meaning of the news they see and read (Neuman, Just, and Crigler 1992). People are clearly not passive receptacles of the information communicated by mass media: the "hypodermic needle" view of media effects has long been discredited (Klapper 1960). But the issues and perspectives communicated through news coverage can influence policy preferences by directing attention temporarily toward certain issues or by framing issues in particular ways (Iyengar 1991). When this happens, politically attentive citizens will tend to evaluate politicians, policies, and institutions in light of the relevant issues and frames given prominent attention in news discourse.

The reverse may also be true: the difference in opinion between knowledge quartiles might reflect sources of political information used more heavily by the ill informed. Biases in the attitudes of ill-informed people could stem from the local opinion environments of those not directly exposed to elite communications. For example, attitudes and voting decisions tend to be mediated by the norms and values esteemed by an individual's immediate social environment (Berelson, Lazarsfeld, and McPhee 1954; Lazarsfeld, Berelson, and Gaudet 1948; Noelle-Neumann 1984). These micro-level social environments can have a substantial impact on macro-level opinion. Politically knowledgeable citizens are more likely to engage in political discussions than other people, a process that exposes them to a range of socially communicated opinions and information which may influence their own political preferences (Bennett, Flickinger, and Rhine 2000; Huckfeldt, Beck et al. 1995; MacKuen 1990). Because ill-informed people are less likely to engage in political conversations (Eliasoph 1998), they can be insulated against the macro-level flows of information that might challenge their opinions. In this perspective, some of the differences between surveyed and fully informed collective opinion can be seen as resulting from biases in the information environments of the ill informed.

Subtle distortions in the "marketplace of ideas" should contribute to differences between well- and ill-informed opinion, but it is unclear whether these differences arise from biases in the political information used by knowledgeable citizens to form their preferences, or from biases in the political information available to ill-informed respondents. From either genesis, the upshot is that differences between well- and ill-informed opinion are, in the final analysis, products of history and culture rather than of psychology, arising from changes in the definitions of social problems, the social contexts in which those problems appear, the evolution of political discourse about those problems, and the manner in which they are confronted or ignored by political institutions.[34]

An illustration of such dynamics is provided by the issue of workplace discrimination against homosexuals, which grew in importance as an item on the American news agenda through the mid-1980s and early 1990s. Figure 5.2 displays the annual number of broadcast news stories about gay rights issues appearing on ABC, CBS, and NBC nightly news broadcasts between 1980 and 1996.[35] Coverage of this topic grew

---

[34] For a similar perspective focusing on the utility of heuristics, see Sniderman 2000 and Jackman and Sniderman 2002. For reviews of the literature detailing the importance of history and culture to the formation of public opinion, see Kinder 1998; Kinder and Sears 1985; Mayer 1993; and Page and Shapiro 1992.

[35] These data were obtained from keyword searches conducted on the *Vanderbilt Television News Abstracts*, which are available at tvnews.vanderbilt.edu. The search term used for this analysis was "(gay or homosexual or lesbian) and (rights or right or discrimination

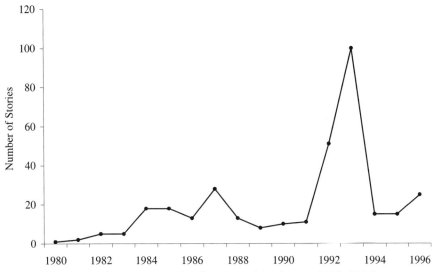

FIGURE 5.2. Broadcast news stories about gay rights issues, 1980–1996

slowly through the early 1980s as the developing AIDS crisis drew attention to the issue of mandatory testing for the HIV virus. Coverage during this early period tended to focus on legal battles over anti-sodomy laws and privacy rights in the workplace, rather than employment discrimination (which would become a dominant angle in later years). For example, only 7 of 28 stories about gay rights issues aired during 1987 explicitly focused on concerns about workplace discrimination, although the subtext of many other stories dealing with privacy issues hinted that AIDS testing potentially could be used as a means of discrimination. Job discrimination did not become a primary focus of gay rights coverage until 1992, when the campaign activities of Bill Clinton and others brought this issue to the front burner of public attention. The peak level of news coverage came in 1993, a year when gays in the military became a top issue for the new Clinton administration, and when the issue of gay rights was taken up in numerous city ordinances and referenda campaigns, notably in Oregon

or discriminate or adopt or marriage or military or armed or army or navy or force)." A search of Vanderbilt holdings revealed that abstractors routinely use such terms as "homosexual rights," "gay rights," and "gays in the military" as headlines for abstract entries about gay rights issues. As a consequence of this choice of headline terms – which supplement the textual content of the abstracts themselves – keyword searches on these terms should accurately turn up the population of relevant stories that are primarily about these topics (Althaus, Edy, and Phalen 2002). Subsequently, search results were culled for false hits involving stories irrelevant to gay rights issues.

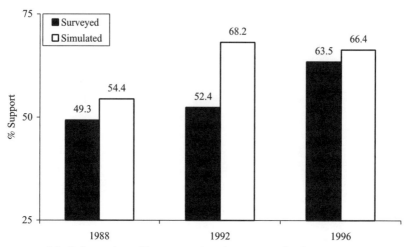

FIGURE 5.3. Information effects over time in support for laws protecting gays from job discrimination, among respondents in lowest knowledge quartile

and Colorado. Following the intense period of coverage in 1992 and 1993, levels of news attention to this issue fell back to more typical levels through 1996.

The American National Election Studies asked about gay rights in 1988, 1992, and 1996 with the question, "Do you favor or oppose laws to protect homosexuals against job discrimination?" Support for such laws in surveyed opinion rose steadily from 54% in 1988 to 60% in 1992 and 64% in 1996. This question never had large information effects in collective opinion – levels of fully informed support for gay rights protections ran 57% in 1988 and 65% in both 1992 and 1996 – but the dynamics of information effects for this question tracked changes in the news agenda quite closely. This trend is particularly evident in the opinions of respondents from the lowest knowledge quartile for each of these years, a group of particular interest because its members are less likely than other people to follow the news (Price and Zaller 1993; Zaller 1992a). Figure 5.3 shows that the group opinions of the least knowledgeable quartile had modest information effects in 1988 and 1996, but a 16-point gap between surveyed and simulated opinions in 1992.

The most plausible explanation for the emergence and disappearance of this large information effect was the sudden increase in news attention to gay rights in 1992. Because they are chronically inattentive to the news, less knowledgeable people are slower than others to update their preferences in light of new information (Zaller 1992a). When news attention shifts to focus on a particular topic, the rapidity of this change can create a temporary disjuncture between the opinions of the least and most informed citizens. A large percentage-point difference between actual and fully informed opinion thus may indicate the presence of a knowledge gap (Tichenor, Donohue, and Olien 1970) caused by uneven rates of information diffusion among various segments of society.

In the case of discrimination against gays, the apparent impact of knowledge gaps is visible not only across time but also across different types of opinions registered at a single point in time. In addition to its question about workplace discrimination, the 1992 ANES also asked about military service ("Do you think homosexuals should be allowed to serve in the United States Armed Forces or don't you think so?") and adoption rights ("Do you think gay or lesbian couples, in other words, homosexual couples, should be legally permitted to adopt children?"). Of the 51 gay rights stories in 1992, network news programs aired none about adoptions by homosexuals (in fact, only one such story could be found between 1980 and 1992), 15 about workplace rights, and 27 about the military, focusing mainly on highly publicized cases of a sailor who was beaten to death by fellow crewmembers and the discharge of a gay noncommissioned officer from the Navy. This disparity in news attention is reflected in the size of gaps between the surveyed and simulated opinions of respondents from the lowest knowledge quartile: a 20.1 percentage point gap for the adoption question, a 15.8 point gap for the job discrimination question, and an 8.1 point gap for the gays in the military question.[36] Figure 5.4 shows that while all three questions deal with gay rights, surveyed opinion among the least knowledgeable citizens more closely resembled fully informed opinion on the aspects of gay rights that received more prominent attention in the news.

It is notable that once news attention to this topic receded after 1993, attitudes toward gay rights did not revert to their pre-1992 levels (see Figure 5.3). Instead, support for legal protections in surveyed opinion rose by more than 10 points among the least informed, a change that was telegraphed in advance by the direction and distance of simulated opinion relative to surveyed opinion. A large gap between surveyed and simulated opinion in 1992 accurately predicted a large shift in surveyed opinion in 1996, which moved in the direction indicated by

---

[36] Information effects for collective opinions including all respondents ran 12.2 points for the adoption question, 5.4 points for the job discrimination question, and 2.9 points for the gays in the military question.

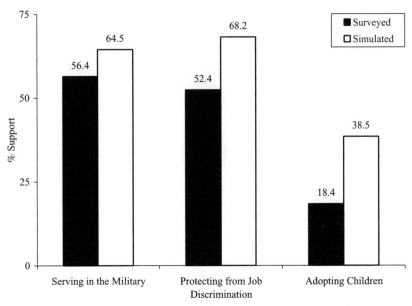

FIGURE 5.4. Information effects in 1992 support for gay rights, among
respondents in the lowest knowledge quartile

fully informed opinion in 1992. The same foreshadowing can be seen in
the 1988 comparison, where a small gap between surveyed and simulated opinion predicts a relatively small increase in surveyed support for
1992.

These patterns can be interpreted as arising from different rates of information diffusion among the least and most knowledgeable citizens.
The most informed updated their opinions quickly in 1992, while the
least informed took much longer to update their views in response to a
changed information environment. Any of three mechanisms could have
brought about the observed changes. First, news coverage could have
moderated information effects by providing domain-specific information
about gay rights issues, thereby enhancing the ability of respondents
to answer these questions. Second, news coverage could have increased
the salience of these issues without influencing levels of domain-specific
knowledge, thereby increasing respondent motivation to provide systematic rather than heuristic responses to the questions. Or, third, news coverage could have influenced the attitude structure of the least informed
respondents, to bring their attitudes more in line with the structure of
their more knowledgeable counterparts.

TABLE 5.6. *Attitude structure of support for laws protecting gays from job discrimination, by knowledge quartile*

	Lowest Knowledge Quartile			Highest Knowledge Quartile		
	1988	1992	1996	1988	1992	1996
Feelings toward homosexuals	.44**	.38**	.31**	.46**	.36**	.29**
Concern for social equality	.02	.15**	.21**	.24**	.22**	.32**
Tolerance for newer morals/lifestyles	.02	−.06	.13**	.12**	.25**	.23**
$R^2 =$	.20	.18	.19	.46	.47	.50
$N =$	294	424	363	380	562	343

*$p < .05$
**$p < .01$
Note: Cells contain standardized OLS (beta) coefficients.
Source: 1988, 1992, and 1996 American National Election Studies.

Although ANES surveys contain no questions that could be used to test the first two possibilities, they do allow for a test of the third. Support for laws to prevent job discrimination against homosexuals can be modeled as a function of positive feelings toward gays as a group, concern for social equality, and tolerance for newer morals and lifestyles.[37] Table 5.6 shows that although the trend over time among both groups is for feelings toward gays to become a somewhat less important predictor of support, and for egalitarianism and tolerance to become somewhat more important, the difference for the most informed is one of degree while that for the least informed is one of a kind. The attitudes of respondents from the highest knowledge quartile were consistently structured over the three years, with each of the three variables serving as a significant predictor of opinions toward gay rights. The opinions of the least knowledgeable respondents in 1988 were primarily reflections of feelings toward homosexuals as a group. Attitudes toward gay rights among the least informed became

[37] This model produces significant coefficients for all three variables in each time period, and consistently accounts for nearly a third of variance in responses to the job discrimination question. For the 1996 ANES data, feeling thermometer scores were used to represent feelings toward gays (v961042). A scale of egalitarianism was constructed by averaging v961229[reversed], v961230, v961231[reversed], v961232, v961233, and v961234[reversed]. A scale of tolerance for newer lifestyles was constructed by averaging v961247, v961248[reversed], v961249, and v961250[reversed]. The same questions from the 1988 and 1992 data were used to form comparable scales.

more rooted in concern for social equality in 1992 and tolerance of newer lifestyles in 1996, by which time the attitude structures of both groups were basically identical.

Seen from this perspective, the trend in surveyed opinion toward higher levels of support over time arises because the attitude structures of well- and ill-informed respondents grow more similar to one another. Feelings toward homosexuals figure prominently in the attitude structures of both groups, with more knowledgeable respondents having more positive feelings toward gays. The average feeling thermometer scores toward gays rose for both groups over this period (out of a possible 100 points, from 24 to 29 to 35 points for the lowest knowledge quartile, and from 34 to 43 to 44 points for the highest quartile), but the most knowledgeable respondents remained 10 points warmer toward gays in 1988, 14 points warmer in 1992, and 8 points warmer in 1996.

Given the increasingly positive feelings toward gays over time, we might expect that surveyed support in 1992 should be higher than it actually was, falling about midway between the earlier and later values. The reason it is not has to do with the importance of egalitarian attitudes for both groups: in 1992 the lowest quartile was significantly less concerned about social equality than the highest quartile, but in 1996 the lowest quartile was relatively more concerned about social equality. The significant impact of concern for social equality thus lowered support for gay rights in 1992 but raised support in 1996 by more closely joining the opinions of both groups on this issue. Adding tolerance as a significant variable in 1996 also diminished the difference between groups in surveyed opinion, since ill-informed respondents in that year tended to be more accepting of newer lifestyles than the well informed.[38]

The connection between attitude structures and information effects is now apparent: by 1996, ill-informed respondents thought about gay rights in essentially the same way as well-informed respondents did, but in 1988 and especially 1992 differences in attitudes and attitude structures led the ill informed to be less supportive than the well informed of laws protecting homosexual workers from discrimination.

Dissimilar attitude structures also help explain differences in the size of information effects across the three gay rights questions from 1992.

---

[38] Mean differences in feeling thermometer scores for gays are significant among the highest and lowest knowledge quartiles, all $ts > 4.2$, all $ps < .001$. Mean differences in egalitarianism are significant for 1992, $t(1071) = -8.64$, $p < .001$, but not significant for 1996, $t(759) = 1.35$, $p = .18$. Mean differences in tolerance are marginally significant for 1996, $t(773) = -1.96$, $p = .05$, with the lowest quartile being slightly more tolerant ($M = 2.61$) than the highest ($M = 2.50$).

TABLE 5.7. *Attitude structure for 1992 gay rights questions, by knowledge quartile*

	Lowest Knowledge Quartile			Highest Knowledge Quartile		
	Military	Jobs	Adopt	Military	Jobs	Adopt
Feelings toward homosexuals	.48**	.38**	.41**	.42**	.36**	.34**
Concern for social equality	.05	.15**	.01	.11**	.22**	.08**
Tolerance for newer morals/lifestyles	−.06	−.06	.16**	.32**	.25**	.40**
$R^2 =$	.23	.18	.23	.51	.47	.48
$N =$	418	424	428	555	562	557

*$p < .05$
**$p < .01$
Note: Cells contain standardized OLS (beta) coefficients.
Source: 1992 American National Election Studies.

Table 5.7 shows that while the most knowledgeable respondents applied essentially the same attitude structure to opinions about gay rights regardless of context, the least knowledgeable respondents drew from different mixes of attitudes when thinking about gay rights in terms of military service, job discrimination, and adoption rights. For both groups, feelings about homosexuals as a group were significant predictors of attitudes toward gay rights, especially in the case of military service. However, the gap between surveyed and simulated opinion was relatively larger for the jobs question because egalitarianism was added as a significant predictor of opinions among the least informed. As discussed earlier, bringing concerns for social equality into the mix drove the views of ill- and well-informed respondents further apart than when the least informed considered only their feelings toward gays. Finally, opinions on adoption rights among the least informed primarily reflected feelings toward gays, but among the most informed primarily reflected tolerance for newer lifestyles. Tolerance was also a significant predictor of support for adoption rights among the ill informed, but although the two groups had essentially the same level of tolerance,[39] the opinions of the well informed were so much more constrained by tolerance attitudes that their opinions became relatively more supportive than those of the ill-informed. Underlying attitude structures cannot completely explain the differences between opinions

[39] Mean differences in tolerance are not significant for 1992, $t(1073) = -0.31, p = .75$.

on this question and the others – Figure 5.4 shows that overall levels of support are dramatically lower in this question than for the other two, even in fully informed opinion – but they do clarify one route through which news coverage can create and resolve information effects in collective preferences. Levels of general political knowledge remain stable over time, but this knowledge can become a less important determinant of attitude structures when news coverage directs public attention toward particular issues.

To the extent that news coverage is responsible for changes in attitude structures, in this case it would seem to have had a twofold effect: priming the application of equality and tolerance concerns in opinions on gay rights issues, and leading people to evaluate homosexuals as a group more favorably over time. Studies of news content from the 1992–1993 period suggest that gay rights supporters tended to frame their arguments in terms of civil rights (Dion 2000), which would be consistent with the heightened importance attached to equality concerns among ill-informed respondents beginning in 1992. At the same time, news content tended to construct discourse about the issue that subtly privileged the existing ban on gays in the military (Meyers 1994; Steele 1997), although some observers noted that media coverage during this period tended to portray the gay rights movement as more mainstream and broad-based than it otherwise appeared to be (Shepard 1993). If news coverage was not overly one-sided on this issue, then we must look for something other than the tone of news to explain the rise of positive feelings toward gays over this period.

The most likely alternative is that the issue of gay rights was being covered at all. The mere act of covering an issue tends to legitimize the cause being covered, as Lazarsfeld and Merton (1948) pointed out so long ago. The degree of legitimation conferred to the gay rights issue was likely heightened in 1992 and 1993 by the fact that it was for the first time being taken up aggressively and conspicuously by mainstream political institutions. When issues once marginalized become thus transformed into topics of legitimate social controversy, reporting about those issues is likely to become more balanced toward and less suspicious of what had formerly been "deviant" perspectives or groups (Hallin 1986). Seen in this light, the direction of change in Americans' feelings about homosexuals may be less telling than the fact that this change represented a thaw in what had been extremely negative impressions. The American population's mean score on the relevant feeling thermometer jumped from 29 in 1988 to 37 in 1992 before climbing more gradually to 40 by 1996, but even at the end of this period the mean score remained well below the lukewarm 50 mark. It is not that the American public became more admiring of gays, but that it became less hostile toward them. This change was quite likely ushered in by the sudden surge of news attention given to this issue in the early 1990s.

CONCLUSION

Information effects in collective preferences are caused primarily by people who express different opinions in surveys than they otherwise might in a hypothetical world populated by fully informed citizens. Convergence behavior at the individual level produces information effects in collective preferences, but group depletion caused by uneven rates of opinion giving appears to make a negligible contribution to the gaps between surveyed and simulated collective opinions. In other words, correcting for asymmetries in political knowledge had its nearly full effect through changing the views of opinion givers who were poorly informed. As a consequence, the rough magnitude of information effects in any collective preference can be assessed by looking for differences in surveyed opinion between the least and most knowledgeable respondents. When these groups have essentially the same distributions of opinion, one can be reasonably confident that any information effects are similarly small. Large differences between the well and ill informed indicate the presence of substantial information effects, and the likely direction of fully informed opinion is given by the direction of knowledgeable relative to poorly informed opinion. While not as precise as simulation results, the opinions of the most knowledgeable respondents also tend to more closely match fully informed collective preferences than the opinions of the least knowledgeable respondents.

Information effects are not merely artifacts of the survey process itself.[40] More important, the relationship between knowledge and opinion quality is neither constant nor inevitable, even among the ill informed.

---

[40] Future research on the determinants of dispersion effects and opinion convergence may want to explore more nuanced features of the survey instrument that could lead to information effects. Recent work has identified subtle elements of syntax and word choice in survey questions that tend to produce response errors (e.g., Schwarz and Sudman 1996), and a careful analysis of such factors might reveal a stronger relationship between question format and information effects. In particular, features of the question that increase task difficulty at different stages of the question answering process might be associated with different influences on the opinions of ill-informed respondents (Lessler and Forsyth 1996).

Information effects are not merely a function of cognitive ability. This is welcome news, because it confirms that collective preferences can represent something like fully informed opinions without submitting the masses to weekly doses of *Time* and *Newsweek*. Rather, information effects vary in size and duration. They do so because the relationship between knowledge and opinion quality is ultimately conditioned by the changing political environment in which citizens develop and refine their preferences. The political environment influences the social diffusion of domain-specific knowledge across populations, so that under the right conditions even those who inhabit the lowest percentiles of general political knowledge can be relatively informed on particular issues like the budget deficit. The political environment primes people to evaluate issues using some attitudes rather than others, and when the attitudes thus primed are themselves unaffected by knowledge gaps, smaller information effects result. The political environment encourages citizens to update their preferences in response to new developments, and it influences the perceived salience of issues in ways that can motivate the ill informed to render more thoughtful judgments than they might otherwise produce for the anonymous interviewer calling from far away.

As a consequence, information effects may tend to be smaller for issues that receive prominent media attention and larger for issues that remain out of the public spotlight (see Shamir and Shamir 1997). This relationship between news coverage and the size of information effects suggests that the social distribution of issue salience may be a key motivating factor that conditions the impact of cognitive ability. The size of information effects goes down as levels of salience and interest in politics go up. Issue salience seems to act as an accelerant in conjunction with political knowledge: when relatively high among those with low levels of general political knowledge, issue salience can mitigate the relative imbalance of knowledge and minimize information effects. But when an issue is only salient among the most politically knowledgeable citizens, the social imbalances in political information are likely to have an exaggerated influence in collective policy preferences.

The gaps between surveyed and fully informed opinion are often substantial, and this chapter has helped to clarify how and why these gaps come about. Yet the weight of evidence presented here leaves much to be desired. The many examples from this chapter illustrate how different mechanisms can regulate the size and direction of information effects, but these examples do not tell us whether these mechanisms are typical. A clearer picture would be provided by tracking the development of information effects over long periods of time and across a wide range of issues. If information and perceptions tend to diffuse within groups and across populations over time, as seems to have been the case in the gay rights example, then information effects may tend to dissipate over time. If this occurs on a regular basis, then simulated opinion measured at one point in time might be a reliable predictor of future changes in surveyed opinion, since social diffusion processes should operate by passing the views of highly informed and attentive citizens outward to the less aware. Moreover, to the extent that environmental changes in issue salience affect the development of gaps between surveyed and simulated opinion, we should find that information effects decline in size as popular attention becomes temporarily focused on public affairs. In either of these cases, to the extent that differences between surveyed and simulated opinion at one point in time predict later changes in surveyed opinion, estimates of fully informed opinion may be useful to consumers of survey data as a way to determine when surveyed opinion might approach the ideal of enlightened opinion. Chapter 6 explores these possibilities and also sheds additional light on the environmental factors that influence the appearance and disappearance of information effects over time.

6

The Temporal Dynamics of Information Effects

Referring to information effects as a source of bias in collective opinion implies that the method for simulating fully informed preferences might estimate the opinions a public would indeed come to have if it were more knowledgeable about politics. If information effects are caused primarily by social processes, such as uneven rates of knowledge diffusion among different segments of the mass public, then fully informed opinion might be able to predict what surveyed opinion will look like at a future point in time. Of course, information effects also could be the macro-level manifestation of micro-level psychological factors such as chronic inattentiveness in some segments of the population or stable differences in values and political orientations that are related to knowledge levels. If psychological rather than social processes give rise to information effects, then measures of fully informed opinion should have little predictive power for anticipating changes in surveyed opinion.

Using time series data from the American National Election Studies, this chapter examines how information effects evolve over time. After detailing the ways that social and psychological processes can influence how information diffuses in large populations, the chapter traces changing levels of political knowledge and interest in politics over the 1980–1998 period. The rest of the chapter addresses several questions about how gaps between surveyed and fully informed collective preferences develop over time. Do information effects tend to resolve, remain stable, or grow in size? Once resolved, are information effects likely to reappear? Does surveyed opinion eventually come to resemble fully informed opinion, and under what conditions is this outcome likely to obtain? If it does not, what keeps surveyed opinion from eventually becoming more fully informed?

THE NATURE OF INFORMATION FLOWS IN LARGE POPULATIONS

Although some examples from Chapter 5 suggest that information effects might tend to diminish over time, the empirical literature on the nature of information flows in large populations offers good reason to expect that fission rather than fusion should mark the typical development of gaps between surveyed and fully informed collective opinions. Moreover, to the extent that psychological rather than social processes are responsible for information effects, the dynamic relationship between surveyed and fully informed opinions may tend to follow a cyclical rather than linear pattern over time, if the distance between these measures changes at all.

Social Factors Contributing to Information Effects

Study after study on the diffusion of news and technological innovations shows that *functional* information – information that people find useful for accomplishing various goals – tends to spread across populations over time, although a variety of moderating factors can limit the rate and degree of diffusion (Rogers 1995). Regarding information about politics, several early studies found that social networks organized around influential opinion leaders appeared to be a primary mechanism by which political knowledge was disseminated through populations (Berelson, Lazarsfeld, and McPhee 1954; Katz and Lazarsfeld 1955; Lazarsfeld, Berelson, and Gaudet 1948). This "two-step" flow model proposed that mass media communications directly influence a small population of attentive opinion leaders, who in turn distill and disseminate those communications through interpersonal contacts to a larger population of people relying on acquaintances rather than mass media as a primary source of political information. Subsequent research on the diffusion of political information has defined a much more complicated set of social and environmental factors regulating the flow of political information within and among interpersonal networks (e.g., Eliasoph 1998; Gamson 1992; Huckfeldt 2001; Huckfeldt, Beck et al. 1995; Huckfeldt and Sprague 1995; Kim, Wyatt, and Katz 1999; MacKuen 1990; Mondak 1995b; Mutz and Martin 2001; Wyatt, Katz, and Kim 2000). These more recent studies note the limited opportunities for most individuals to be exposed to conflicting sources of political information through their social networks, but also conclude that mass media coverage plays a critical role in exposing people to varied perspectives and in stimulating political conversations. These two conclusions leave intact the premise that information tends to become socially dispersed across populations, though they add that the degree of dispersion is likely to be moderated by the amount of media coverage given to an issue, and that new information is likely to be transmitted through a collectively diverse arrangement of internally homogenous social networks.

The politically functional information thus circulating through these social capillaries is unlikely to consist merely of discrete facts about political institutions or figures. Factual information is surely distributed in this way (Huckfeldt 2001), but since levels of general political knowledge tend to be relatively stable over time (Bennett 1988; Delli Carpini and Keeter 1991, 1996; Neuman 1986; Smith 1989), it would seem that these interpersonal networks must also be coursing with information of another sort. Among the likely alternatives identified by previous research are cues about the experiences, beliefs, attitudes, and values of other people (Huckfeldt and Sprague 1995; Mutz 1998; Noelle-Neumann 1984; Shamir and Shamir 2000); signals about the policy preferences of particular social groups (Kuklinski and Hurley 1994; Lippmann 1922; Lupia and McCubbins 1998; Zaller 1992a); "popular wisdom" about how other people make sense of politics using particular heuristics or analogies (Gamson 1992); the topical agenda of news media communications (Katz and Lazarsfeld 1955; Mondak 1995b); expectations about the future (Shamir and Shamir 2000); and perceptions of novelty or threat in the political environment (Marcus, Neuman, and MacKuen 2000). Although these other types of social information may not consist of political facts, they should nonetheless condition the appearance and structure of information effects. They could motivate people to investigate particular issues, thereby affecting levels of domain-specific knowledge without disturbing levels of general knowledge. Social information of this sort could also moderate perceptions of issue salience, influence the ways that people structure political attitudes, and encourage people to evaluate political matters more or less systematically than they otherwise might.

Over time, these processes of information diffusion should supply populations with a regular stream of new facts, popular perceptions, and cues. Yet a population's absolute level of functional political information should tend to equilibrate rather than grow ever higher with each generation, because no one has a bottomless mental reservoir into which this current of fresh data could be directed and contained. Instead of committing most new information to memory, individuals tend to form and update impressions on-line, discarding relevant information as soon as a summary judgment is revised (Fiske and Taylor 1991; Hastie and Park 1986).

When people do commit information to long-term memory, the new often displaces the old. Even if individuals tend to become relatively more knowledgeable over time, generational replacement ensures that much of this knowledge gain is lost collectively. Few of us have many incentives to retain outdated information about political matters. Information relevant to a political problem can be discarded when the problem is superceded by another, when it leads to the formation of social norms, or when it leads to the codification of laws (see Davison 1958). Moreover, knowledge acquired by populations, if indeed functional, will come to be stored in more enduring and efficient media than the fragile vessel of human memory conveyed by word of mouth. As Plato noted long ago, the ability to commit information to writing lessens the need to remember things.[1] Thus, while old information tends to be lost as new information is gained at the level of individuals, at the level of populations old information tends to ossify into a diverse array of culturally relevant and broadly accessible forms.

Yet even as social diffusion processes should tend to constantly replenish a population's store of politically functional information, ample research has shown that because some groups tend to acquire new information more rapidly than others, information of this sort tends to become relatively more concentrated into certain segments of a population. In particular, higher socioeconomic status groups should tend to acquire relatively more political information than other segments of a population. This knowledge gap hypothesis was taken to provide "a fundamental explanation for the apparent failure of mass publicity to inform the public at large" (Tichenor, Donohue, and Olien 1970: 161). Tichenor and his colleagues observed that if media attention were focused on an issue for a sustained period of time, eventually knowledge gaps related

---

[1] In Section 275 of Plato's *Phaedrus*, Socrates relates the Egyptian god Ammon's reply to Theuth, upon being told that Theuth had invented writing to improve the memory of humanity: "You, who are the father of writing, have out of fondness for your offspring attributed to it quite the opposite of its real function. Those who acquire it will cease to exercise their memory and become forgetful; they will rely on writing to bring things to their remembrance by external signs instead of on their own internal resources. What you have discovered is a receipt for recollection, not for memory. And as for wisdom, your pupils will have the reputation for it without the reality: they will receive a quantity of information without proper instruction, and in consequence be thought very knowledgeable when they are for the most part quite ignorant. And because they are filled with the conceit of wisdom instead of real wisdom they will be a burden to society." This quote is from *Phaedrus and the Seventh and Eighth Letters*, Walter Hamilton, trans. New York: Penguin Books, 1973.

to that issue should disappear as information saturates even the least-educated segments in a population. But because media attention tends to shift to other topics well before all relevant information is fully disseminated in a population, knowledge gaps should tend to be chronic rather than temporary.[2]

Expectations about the longitudinal relationships between surveyed and fully informed opinion are complicated by the simultaneous tendency for information flows to (1) continually replenish politically functional information in a population and (2) increase the relative concentration of that information within certain segments of a population. The former tendency toward social diffusion suggests that gaps between surveyed and fully informed opinion on any issue should diminish over time if the overall amount of relevant information increases within a population, or if a fixed amount of relevant information becomes more diffused throughout a population. However, if new information is regularly communicated to a population over time, or if the nature of the issue or social context in which that issue is evaluated changes significantly over time, then information effects may grow as a result of these social diffusion processes. Likewise, if political knowledge tends to become more socially concentrated, as the knowledge gap literature suggests, gaps between surveyed and fully informed opinion might generally grow over time if they change at all.

Because processes of social diffusion and concentration each can be responsible for widening and sustaining gaps between surveyed and simulated opinion, clearer evidence for their relative priority in explaining collective information effects will be found in the ability of fully informed opinion to predict future values of surveyed opinion. If social diffusion is the key process underlying the development of information effects, we should see a time lag between measures of fully informed and surveyed opinion that makes simulated opinion a reasonable predictor of future

---

[2] In the original formulation of this hypothesis (Tichenor, Donohue, and Olien 1970), the key mechanism underlying the tendency for knowledge gaps to grow over time was thought to be the heightened cognitive ability of better-educated persons to process and integrate new information relative to less-educated persons. More recent studies (for a review, see Viswanath and Finnegan 1996) have expanded this account to highlight the importance of motivational variables in modifying the contribution of ability to the development of knowledge gaps (e.g., Genova and Greenberg 1979; Viswanath, Kahn et al. 1993). For example, one study of knowledge acquisition during the 1992 presidential campaign (Kwak 1999) found that levels of formal education were more closely related to levels of political knowledge among persons who expressed little interest in the campaign than among those who were very interested in the campaign.

changes in surveyed opinion.[3] In such a case, simulations of fully informed opinions could accurately anticipate a population's future preferences even if such simulations revealed the presence of large information effects at any given point in time. But to the extent that such effects are driven by knowledge gaps, we should find fully informed opinion to be an unreliable predictor of future changes in surveyed opinion.

Psychological Factors Contributing to Information Effects

Social factors should be central to the appearance and maintenance of information effects, but to the extent that individual-level psychological factors also drive the waxing and waning of such effects, they should tend to modify the impact of social processes in ways that are difficult to predict in advance or identify in hindsight. Two such factors are over-time changes in a population's levels of cognitive ability and motivation to process information. A third is whether information effects stem in part from conflicts in core beliefs or values.

A population's ability to process domain-specific political information can be influenced by gradual changes in a population's socioeconomic status, for example, or from sudden changes in the mass public's agenda of political problems. While the typical American was probably unable to even recognize anthrax as a potentially lethal disease in the summer of 2001, the bio-terror attacks against media and governmental institutions in October of that year suddenly raised the ability level of the entire American population to assess biological threats. One month following these attacks, surveys revealed that 90% of Americans had learned correctly that inhalation anthrax was more deadly than the cutaneous form of the disease (Prior 2002). In addition to long-term secular trends and short-term changes in the political environment, a population's ability levels can also vary with the topics on which survey respondents are asked to offer evaluations. As no individual is likely to be an expert on the full range of potential public affairs issues, and many important political topics like arms control or environmental policy are so arcane as to puzzle even the most knowledgeable among us, this latter possibility seems especially likely. While there is good reason to object to Schumpeter's ([1942] 1976) blanket charge that "the typical citizen drops down to a lower level

---

[3] A related set of expectations was developed in a paper by Renée Smith (1993), who found that changes in aggregate measures of presidential approval could be explained by time lags in the diffusion of economic information to different segments of the American public.

of mental performance as soon as he enters the political field" (262), it seems clear enough that the mass public is wanting for expertise on a wide variety of political issues.

Identifying a population's ability to answer a given survey question is no easy task. Chapter 5 showed that survey questions with higher levels of "don't know" and "no opinion" seem to place especially high cognitive demands on respondents. While imprecise, the average percentage of DK/NO responses for a given question topic can be used as a rough gauge for estimating the population's ability to process information about the topic. Chapter 5 also showed that information effects tend to be no larger in questions with high DK/NO levels than in questions with low levels of group depletion. However, there is good reason to expect that the development of information effects within a given question trend should be related to the degree of demographic congruence between opinion givers and the population they are supposed to represent. Knowledge gap processes should be especially likely to structure the flow of information relevant to questions that place higher cognitive demands on a population, while social diffusion processes should be more typical in questions that require less cognitive ability to answer. If these expectations are correct, then the size of information effects should grow over time in questions with higher DK/NO levels, and should lessen in questions with lower DK/NO levels. As noted earlier, stability in the size of such effects could be produced by either of these processes. Fully informed opinion also should better predict future changes in surveyed opinion for topics on which the typical citizen possesses a reasonable level of expertise or familiarity. This might come about because the most knowledgeable people will be especially competent in judging such matters, or because ill-informed people will be less likely to engage in convergence behavior when answering survey questions on such topics, or because the ill informed are more likely to update their views on such topics.

A second psychological factor likely to complicate the interpretation of longitudinal changes in the size of information effects is a population's level of motivation to process information about public affairs. The amount of politically functional information acquired by a population varies with the presence or absence of incentives for information-seeking, incentives that are structured at least in part by the larger social environment (Kuklinski, Quirk et al. 2001). In addition, the more motivated is an opinion giver to provide an accurate judgment, the more likely that person is to engage in a systematic search for relevant information stored in long-term memory. During times when the social environment motivates people to seek greater quantities of relevant information, increasing levels of information acquisition (or merely of motivation to process knowledge already held in long-term memory) should tend consistently to shrink the gaps between surveyed and fully informed opinion. In this way, elections, critical events, political crises, and other environmental factors that temporarily heighten the perceived salience of political issues should serve as shocks to a population's normal willingness to engage in systematic processing. Such temporary shocks could cause information effects to suddenly diminish or even disappear without affecting a population's level of general political knowledge.

Changes in a population's willingness to engage in effortful processing can produce odd trends in collective preferences. During the week following the Super Tuesday primaries in the 2000 presidential elections, 49% of American adults said they had yet to commit to a candidate. But the number of uncommitted voters increased substantially to 59% in the following week as public interest in the primary campaign declined (Vanishing Voter Project 2000b). Not only did the shifting information environment produce a higher percentage of uncommitted voters, but the percentage of Americans able to identify major policy positions held by Bush and Gore declined precipitously over the primary season. Immediately following the New Hampshire primary in early February, 24% of Americans could correctly identify George W. Bush's position on gun registration, but only 13% could do so by mid-April (Vanishing Voter Project 2000a).[4] Such short-term quirks of collective memory – whether caused by actual forgetting or simply lowered motivation to engage in systematic memory searches – could greatly complicate the interpretation of fully informed preferences.

In the context of collective preferences, gaps between surveyed and fully informed opinions should grow when the information environment provides fewer incentives to motivate people, because their judgments should come to be less rooted in systematic memory searches. Conversely, gaps between a population's surveyed and fully informed opinions should narrow during periods when public attention is especially focused on political issues. While the precise influences of individual-level memory processes

---

[4] In a similar way, Delli Carpini and Keeter (1996: 121) find evidence that the political climate of the 1960s increased the amount of factual political knowledge available to Americans in long-term memory. In contrast, they found that average levels of political knowledge were about nine percentage points lower in the 1970s than the 1960s, a difference they attribute to the political disengagement of the American public during the decade of Watergate and the end of the Vietnam War.

on collective preferences may be unclear in any given case, the ANES data allow for a simple test of what we might call the "intermittent attention" hypothesis. If motivation to process information is an important contributor to macro-level information effects, then the gaps between surveyed and fully informed opinions should tend to be smaller in presidential election years than in midterm election years, because public interest in campaigns is likely to be higher and the information environment relatively more focused on political matters. Moreover, the findings in Table 5.5 from Chapter 5 suggest that interest in presidential rather than congressional campaigns reduces the size of information effects among the least knowledgeable citizens. The intermittent attention hypothesis suggests that information effects should follow a sawtooth pattern in which gaps narrow during presidential election years and widen again during midterm election years. These regular fluctuations should also tend to reduce the predictive accuracy of fully informed opinion. This should be especially true for predictions made in midterm election years, when lower levels of motivation are likely to produce higher levels of convergence behavior.

A third psychological factor that could obscure the impact of social factors on information effects is the potential for such effects to stem from conflicting core beliefs or values that produce unstable opinions (Zaller 1992a; Zaller and Feldman 1992). Respondents who are internally conflicted or uncertain about their political preferences are less able to report consistent opinions than other respondents, and this diminished capacity should make it difficult to estimate what their fully informed opinions might be. Research by R. Michael Alvarez and John Brehm (1995, 1997, 1998, 2002) has distinguished between ambivalence, which is response instability due to internalized conflict; and uncertainty, which is instability caused by confusion about the objects being evaluated or the grounds for evaluating those objects. Alvarez and Brehm show that political knowledge reduces uncertainty by clarifying the relevant attributes of an object and the considerations most appropriate for evaluating the object. As a result, reducing levels of respondent uncertainty can produce two outcomes. In the typical situation, opinion stability is increased because knowledgeable people will become more aware of relevant considerations that should tend to reinforce a preference. But when dispelling the clouds of uncertainty reveals that policy or candidate preferences are ultimately rooted in irreconcilable considerations, response instability should increase. In such cases of ambivalence, higher levels of knowledge lead people to become more aware of conflicting values underlying their preferences, and this greater awareness further destabilizes their opinions.

Applying this logic to the evolution of collective policy preferences suggests that information effects arising from respondent uncertainty should diminish in size over time as relevant knowledge in a population increases or becomes more broadly diffused. But the same diffusion processes should not reduce information effects rooted in respondent ambivalence. Reducing uncertainty for opinions marked by widespread ambivalence may even increase the gaps between surveyed and fully informed opinion. To the extent that uncertainty is relatively lower among the well informed than the ill informed, simulated fully informed collective preferences marked by ambivalent responses may also be less stable over time than surveyed opinion.

Since the typical survey respondent seems remarkably able to generate considerations favoring both sides of most issues (Chong 1993; Craig, Kane, and Martinez 2002; Hochschild 1981; Schuman, Steeh et al. 1997; Zaller 1992a; Zaller and Feldman 1992), it can be difficult to tell whether the underlying cause of response instability is uncertainty or ambivalence. In the parlance of Alvarez and Brehm, ambivalence produces relatively more unstable responses among the well informed, while uncertainly increases response instability among the ill informed, but these patterns have been studied in too few issues to draw firm conclusions about the likely process involved in particular survey questions. However, the logic of Alvarez and Brehm's model suggests that ambivalence and uncertainty should be more prevalent causes of response instability in different types of questions. Policy questions should be relatively less likely to tap incommensurable core values that are similarly weighted and highly salient to ordinary citizens (Alvarez and Brehm 2002). Response instability in policy questions, they argue, is therefore more likely to be produced by respondent uncertainty than ambivalence. If this is the case, and to the extent that response instability is an important contributor to the gaps between ill- and well-informed opinion, we should tend to see a narrowing of information effects in policy questions over time. As a corollary, we should find that fully informed opinion reliably predicts future levels of surveyed opinion among questions dealing with public policy issues.

Compared with questions dealing with specific policy issues, more abstract value questions such as those asking people to agree or disagree whether "the country would be better off if we worried less about how equal people are" or "we should be more tolerant of people with different moral standards" seem to have a higher probability of eliciting conflicts in core values that are easily accessible and comparably weighted (Chong 1993; Hochschild 1981). If ambivalence is more likely to mark responses

TABLE 6.1. *Summary of expectations about the evolution of information effects over time*

	Expected Influence on Evolution of Gaps between Surveyed and Fully Informed Opinion	Expected Influence on Predictive Ability of Fully Informed Opinion
Social factors		
Diffusion of information across population	Narrow	Improve
Concentration of information within population	Enlarge	Diminish
Psychological factors		
Population's ability to engage in effortful processing	Narrow for topics with low average DK levels; enlarge for topics with high average DK levels	Improve for topics with low average DK levels; diminish for topics with high average DK levels
Population's motivation to engage in effortful processing	Narrow in presidential election years; enlarge in off-years	Diminish
Uncertainty and ambivalence as sources of response instability	Narrow for policy questions; enlarge for value questions	Improve for policy questions; diminish for value questions

to value questions, then to the extent that response instability contributes to macro-level information effects, the gaps between surveyed and fully informed opinion on value issues should fail to resolve over time. Moreover, we should find that fully informed opinion is a poorer predictor of changes in surveyed opinion among value questions than among policy questions.

As summarized in Table 6.1, the foregoing discussion suggests some plausible reasons why fully informed opinion could provide a reliable estimate of future changes in surveyed opinion. So long as functional political information relevant to an issue tends to diffuse across populations over time, and so long as this information tends to become less socially concentrated as time passes, simulations of fully informed opinion made at one point in time should anticipate the tendencies of surveyed opinion at later points in time. Yet, several other factors listed here should tend to limit the conditions or types of questions in which fully informed opinion might accurately predict future changes in surveyed opinion. Since the factors hypothesized to influence the evolution of information effects are themselves unobserved – we can only test whether the predicted relationships are found in the information effects data – it will be difficult to sort out the unique impact of these different factors. Nonetheless, taking them into account serves to broaden our expectations about the variety of forms that the longitudinal relationships between simulated and surveyed data might take.

Before analyzing how information effects evolve over time, it is important first to examine changes in the American population's levels of political knowledge and interest. Doing so will clarify whether changing gaps between surveyed and simulated opinions might reflect nothing more than rising or falling levels of general political knowledge. Charting evolving patterns of interest in politics will also clarify whether a population's motivation to process information tends to be stable or variable. If levels of motivation to process information about politics move with the electoral calendar, then this dynamic might cause populations to acquire more political knowledge or more thoroughly process the knowledge they already possess in high-motivation periods.

CHANGES IN POLITICAL KNOWLEDGE AND INTEREST OVER TIME

A wide range of research has suggested that the mass public's average levels of political knowledge and interest appear to be relatively stable over time (e.g., Delli Carpini and Keeter 1996; Neuman 1986; Smith 1989). However, much of the evidence for this conclusion comes from studies that compare knowledge levels at just two points in time (Bennett 1988, 1995b, 1996; Delli Carpini and Keeter 1991) and from studies that analyze individual-level variation in knowledge levels rather than aggregate change (Bennett 1989; S. E. Bennett 1993). In contrast, studies that compare knowledge at multiple points in time often find that while aggregate levels are usually stable, knowledge of particular facts rises and falls in response to changes in political interest and news attention (Bennett 1994; Delli Carpini and Keeter 1996; Smith 1989). Aggregate levels of knowledge can also rise in periods of high popular engagement in politics (Bennett 1989; Delli Carpini and Keeter 1996), such as during the 1960s in the United States. However, researchers have yet to test for systematic variations in aggregate political knowledge and interest levels between presidential and nonpresidential election years.

Since the availability of suitable knowledge questions is severely limited in ANES studies prior to 1980, the present analysis focuses on trends between 1980 and 1998. The specific questions suitable for use in knowledge scales vary from year to year (see Appendix A for details), but they cluster into three general categories: questions asking whether the Republicans or Democrats controlled the House and Senate before the current election, differences in issue positions staked out by the Republican and Democratic parties, and knowledge of national and international political leaders. The upper left chart in Figure 6.1 displays the average percentage of respondents providing correct answers to questions making up each of the three categories of factual knowledge.[5] Knowledge of party control of Congress and the names of political leaders rose over this period, while knowledge of party issue differences remained somewhat more stable, hovering around the 50% mark except for low periods in 1980 and 1990. Moreover, the percentage of correct responses to questions dealing with party control of Congress and the names of political leaders are noticeably higher in the presidential election years of 1980, 1984, 1988, 1992, and 1996. In contrast, no election-year differences are observed for aggregate knowledge of party issue differences.[6]

It is not surprising that knowledge levels have grown over the 1980–98 period, given the surge of mass partisanship (Bartels 2000; Hetherington 2001) and shifts in party control of government during this time, as well as the sexual scandal culminating in the impeachment crisis for President

---

[5] The specific questions in these categories change from year to year. These knowledge indices included a total of 10 different party difference questions producing 43 observations over time, two party control questions (one for the House, one for the Senate) producing 17 observations, and 17 open-ended questions asking for the political offices held by different political leaders, which produced 34 observations over time. See Appendix A for details on questions constituting the knowledge indices for this longitudinal analysis.

[6] T-tests using pooled observations for all of the ANES data from 1980 to 1998 confirm that differences in knowledge levels between on- and off-year surveys are significant for names of political leaders, $t(12,814) = -7.75, p < .001$, and party control of Congress, $t(17,790) = -11.17, p < .001$, but not statistically significant for knowledge of party issue differences, $t(17,790) = -0.73, p = .46$.

T-tests also confirm that knowledge levels in the early years of the series (1980–88) are significantly higher than those in the later years of the series (1990–98) for party control of Congress, $t(17,790) = -19.13, p < .001$, but not for party issue differences, $t(17,790) = -0.01, p = .99$. Since questions asking about knowledge of political leaders didn't appear until 1986, that trend was split between 1986–92 and 1994–98. This revealed a significant rise in levels of such knowledge, $t(12,814) = -14.87, p < .001$. Splitting the trend between 1986–90 and 1992–98 produced essentially the same results.

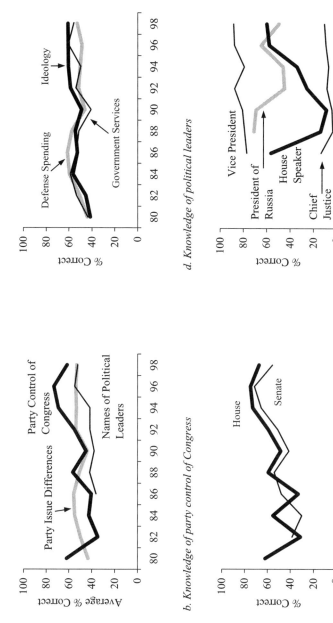

a. Aggregate trends by knowledge category

b. Knowledge of party control of Congress

c. Knowledge of party issue differences

d. Knowledge of political leaders

FIGURE 6.1. Changing levels of knowledge about political leaders, party differences, and party control of Congress, 1980–1998

Clinton that unfolded in 1998. However, some of this growth may be an artifact of the changing mix of knowledge questions in each category over time. To control for this possibility, the three remaining charts in Figure 6.1 detail the trends for the few questions within each category that were asked in the same form over the entire time period.

Levels of knowledge about party control of the House and Senate were quite similar after 1986, but in the early 1980s knowledge of House control fluctuated dramatically between on- and off-year elections. Knowledge of party differences regarding the provision of government services was higher in presidential election years, but was essentially the same in the 1990s as it was in the 1980s. Knowledge of party differences in ideology rose significantly over time, while knowledge of party differences in defense spending priorities was much lower in the 1990s than in the 1980s, when the Reagan defense buildup was a topic of substantial controversy between Democrats and Republicans (cf. Hetherington 2001). However, the mass public was no more accurate at identifying party differences in ideology and defense spending in presidential years than it was in years with only congressional elections at the top of the ballot.[7]

Over time, higher percentages of the mass public became able to identify the American vice president (George Bush in 1986, Dan Quayle in 1990, then Al Gore after 1992), the chief justice of the U.S. Supreme Court (William Rehnquist), and the speaker of the U.S. House of Representatives (Tip O'Neill in 1986, Jim Wright in 1988, Tom Foley from 1990 through 1994, and Newt Gingrich thereafter). While the increase in recognition of the vice president and chief justice was gradual and consistent over time, recognition of the House speaker dropped precipitously after Tip O'Neill was replaced by Jim Wright, then grew steadily over the Foley years before reaching record highs during the years in which Gingrich adeptly used the speaker's position to generate press coverage for the House majority's policy agenda. In contrast, the percentage correctly identifying the president of Russia declined over time as a less familiar Boris Yeltsin took over

---

[7] Party differences on government services were significantly higher in on- (mean = 54%) versus off-year surveys (mean = 50%), $t(17,790) = -5.52$, $p < .001$, but not for later versus earlier years (both means = 52%), $t(17,790) = 0.82$, $p = .82$. Party differences on ideology were significantly higher in later (mean = 57%) than earlier years (mean = 51%), $t(16,256) = -7.93$, $p < .001$, but not significantly different in on- versus off-year surveys (both means = 53%), $t(16,256) = -0.12$, $p = .99$. Party differences on defense spending were significantly lower in later (mean = 49%) than earlier years (mean = 55%), $t(14,714) = 7.50$, $p < .001$, but not significantly different in on- versus off-year survey (both means = 53%), $t(14,714) = 0.73$, $p = .46$.

the helm in 1991 from his highly visible predecessor, Michail Gorbachev.[8] Recognition of political leaders also varied by election cycle. Perhaps as a result of the shifting topical focus of American politics, Americans were less likely to recognize Chief Justice Rehnquist and the Speaker of the House in presidential election years, but more likely to correctly identify the vice president and the president of Russia.[9]

In short, year-to-year fluctuations in some kinds of political knowledge are associated with the heightened public attention given to national politics during presidential elections. Aggregate levels of certain types of political knowledge can also change more gradually, rising or falling in apparent response to changes in the issues and actors populating the political environment. But have *overall* levels of political knowledge grown over this time period, and is the mass public's command of factual information about politics *generally* higher in presidential election years? These questions are more difficult to answer, in part because few of the knowledge questions posed to ANES respondents are asked in identical form over more than a few consecutive studies (Bartels 1996; Delli Carpini and Keeter 1996; Smith 1989; Zaller 1992a). Aggregate trends in the small number of questions that retain the same wording over time (displayed in charts b, c, and d of Figure 6.1) could be artifacts of selection bias: such questions are likely to be a biased sample of all possible knowledge questions, since most such items are not repeated in identical form. And even if a much larger number of identical knowledge questions were available, the range of facts tapped in any given survey would still be quite small relative to the population of relevant bits of information.

However, the ANES data provide an alternate indicator of political knowledge that can be used to validate trends found in factual information

---

[8] *T*-tests revealed significantly higher levels of recognition in later years for the vice president (1986–90 mean = 79%, 1992–98 mean = 86%), $t(11,039) = -9.09$, $p < .001$, the chief justice (1986–90 mean = 7%, 1992–98 mean = 9%), $t(12,814) = -2.61$, $p < .01$, and the Speaker of the House (1986–90 mean = 28%, 1992–98 mean = 41%), $t(12,814) = -16.45$, $p < .001$. Recognition levels were lower in later years for the president of Russia, (1986–90 mean = 70%, 1992–98 mean = 51%), $t(10,638) = 19.81$, $p < .001$. These differences remain significant if the same comparison is made between 1986–92 and 1994–98.

[9] Knowledge levels were lower in presidential years for the chief justice (on-year mean = 7%, off-year mean = 9%), $t(12,814) = 3.60$, $p < .001$, and the Speaker of the House (on-year mean = 31%, off-year mean = 38%), $t(12,814) = 8.95$, $p < .001$. In contrast, knowledge levels were higher in presidential years for the U.S. vice president (on-year mean = 88%, off-year mean = 81%), $t(11,039) = -9.36$, $p < .001$, and the president of Russia, (on-year mean = 56%, off-year mean = 51%), $t(11,039) = -2.68$, $p < .01$.

scales: a five-point item recording the interviewer's subjective assessment of the respondent's knowledge of politics.[10] Although the interviewer's summary judgment is almost certainly influenced by the respondent's ability to supply correct answers to the factual items used to construct knowledge scales, this judgment should also draw upon the respondent's verbal and nonverbal behavior throughout the interview, and it may well render a more subtle assessment of respondent sophistication than would be apparent from looking only at correct answers to knowledge questions.[11]

Higher levels of political knowledge may enhance a population's ability to answer questions about public affairs, but the degree to which a population is motivated to answer such questions should also have a bearing on the size of information effects in collective preferences. While political scientists have written a good deal about change and stability in levels of political knowledge over time, much less attention has been given to aggregate changes in political interest over time. When interest in public affairs is studied directly, it tends to be subsumed as one of many indicators of political sophistication (e.g., Neuman 1986), or as a variable that affects (or is affected by) the acquisition of political knowledge (e.g., Bennett 1989; Delli Carpini and Keeter 1996; Luskin 1990). One study to directly examine changes in interest levels over time (Smith 1989) concluded that aggregate levels of interest in campaigns were quite stable between 1956 and 1980. However, this study examined data from presidential election years only. While the drop-off in voter turnout for congressional election years clearly suggests declining levels of interest in political campaigns, it is unclear whether interest in public affairs more

---

[10] This question, answered by the survey interviewer immediately following the interview, reads "Respondent's general level of information about politics and public affairs seemed: very high, fairly high, average, fairly low, very low." It was asked in identical form over the 1980–98 period, and in most presidential election years is found in both the pre-election and post-election waves (all nonpresidential-year ANES surveys are conducted after the election is over). To ensure continuity over time, only interviewer ratings from the post-election wave are used. The one exception is in 1988, when the pre-election interviewer rating is used because the question was not included in the post-election wave. In Figure 6.2, the "well informed" by this measure are respondents rated either very or fairly high in political knowledge, while those rated average are considered "moderately informed," and those rated as fairly or very low in political knowledge are considered "ill informed."

[11] Interviewer ratings discriminate well relative to factual knowledge scales (Zaller 1985), but correlations between these measures run between .57 and .68, demonstrating that the two are not synonymous (Delli Carpini and Keeter 1992, 1993; see also Luskin 1987).

generally is tied in a similar way to the electoral calendar, or whether there might be parallel trends in aggregate levels of interest and knowledge. Fortunately, measuring levels of political interest over time provides fewer methodological challenges, since identical questions were used in the 1980–98 period to assess respondent interest in public affairs[12] and in political campaigns.[13]

Changes in the social distribution of political knowledge and interest in politics follow cyclical as well as secular trends. The left-hand graphs in Figure 6.2 show that aggregate levels of political knowledge tended to be higher in presidential election years and also tended to rise over the 1980–98 period. These graphs show the percentage of the American population falling into each of three levels of political knowledge (see preceding footnotes for details). In 1980, for example, interviewer ratings of respondent knowledge categorized 29% of adults as ill-informed, 41% as moderately informed, and 30% as well informed. For that same year, 22% of adults provided correct answers to fewer than one-third of questions in a political knowledge scale, while 47% answered between one-third and two-thirds of these questions correctly, and 31% answered more than two-thirds of these questions correctly.[14] Mean levels of political knowledge are significantly higher in presidential than nonpresidential

---

[12] The question gauging interest in public affairs reads as follows: "Some people seem to follow what's going on in government and public affairs most of the time, whether there's an election going on or not. Others aren't that interested. Would you say you follow what's going on in government and public affairs most of the time, some of the time, only now and then, or hardly at all?" In Figure 6.2, respondents answering "most of the time" are considered "highly interested," those answering "some of the time" or "only now and then" are coded as "moderately interested," and those answering "hardly at all" are coded as "uninterested."

[13] The question measuring interest in political campaigns reads as follows: "Some people don't pay much attention to political campaigns. How about you? Would you say that you have been very much interested, somewhat interested, or not much interested in the political campaigns so far this year?" Respondents answering "very much" are considered "highly interested," those answering "somewhat" are coded as "moderately interested," and those answering "not much" are considered "uninterested."

[14] Due to the limited availability of suitable knowledge questions across the ANES surveys, the knowledge indices used here vary somewhat from year to year in depth and scope. To minimize the potential impact of election-specific items on the apparent knowledge levels of the public, items tapping knowledge about issue differences between presidential candidates were omitted from these scales. The resulting measures of political knowledge (which are detailed in Appendix A) are all reliable and primarily tap knowledge of differences between the parties as well as the identities of various public officials. In addition, the knowledge scales were all standardized to range between 0 and 1 to eliminate the possibility that differences in the number of scale items across years could influence the apparent size of information effects.

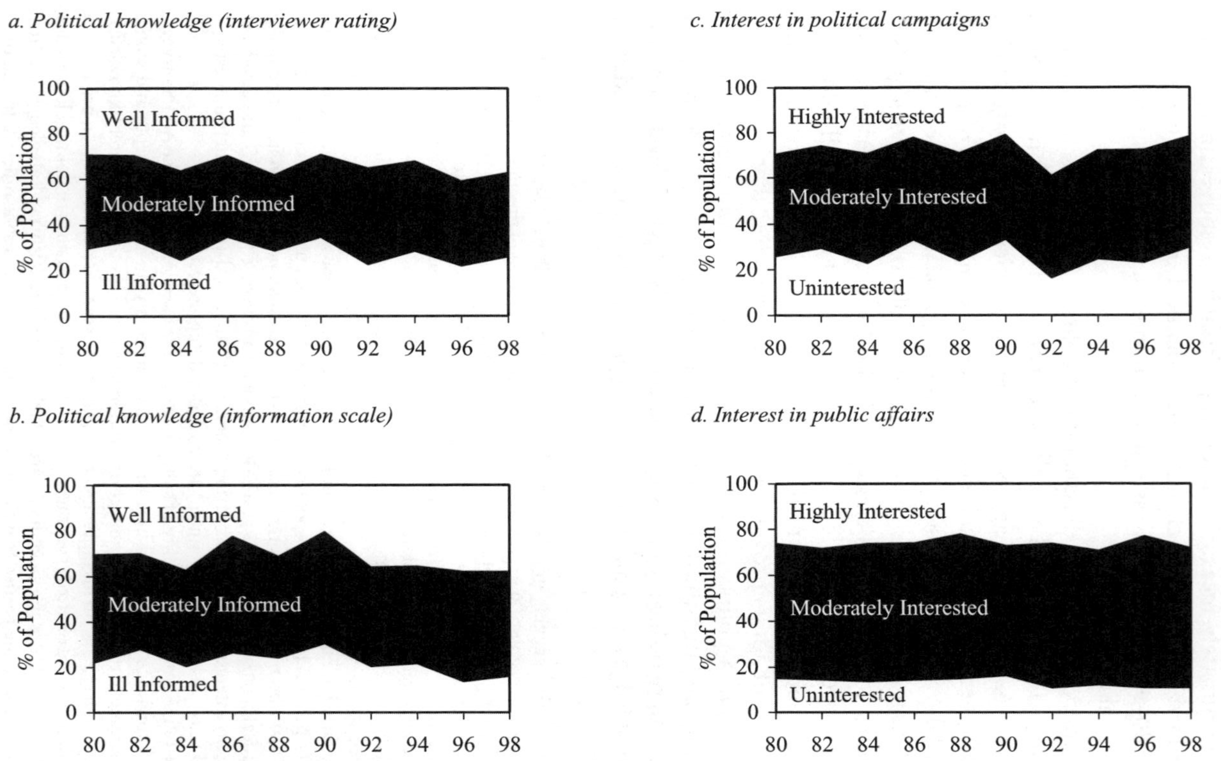

a. *Political knowledge (interviewer rating)*

b. *Political knowledge (information scale)*

c. *Interest in political campaigns*

d. *Interest in public affairs*

FIGURE 6.2. Changing social distribution of political knowledge, interest in campaigns, and interest in public affairs, 1980–1998

election years for both measures,[15] although the differences tend to be fairly small: over the entire time period, the average person answered 51% of factual knowledge questions correctly in off-year surveys and 55% correctly in on-year surveys. In addition to this cyclical trend, the American population's mean level of knowledge rose somewhat in both measures over time, with the average respondent answering 52% of knowledge questions correctly in the 1980–88 period and 54% correctly in the 1990–98 period.[16]

The right-hand graphs in Figure 6.2 reveal similar tendencies for interest in political campaigns but no cyclical pattern for interest in public affairs. The American population became slightly more interested in both campaigns and public affairs over the 1980–98 period.[17] And, as expected, the American population's mean levels of interest in political campaigns tend to be higher in presidential than nonpresidential election years. However, these changes do not have a spillover effect on levels of interest in public affairs, which vary hardly at all between election years.[18]

Levels of knowledge and interest in the campaigns are higher in presidential election years, and it seems likely that presidential campaigns are stimulating these cyclical changes. Yet it is unclear whether campaigns produce these patterns by raising levels of motivation or ability (or both at once). Higher levels of interest in the campaigns could lead people to become more informed about politics, but the increased availability of public affairs information produced by presidential campaigns could just as easily lead people to become more interested in the campaigns.

One clue to disentangling this puzzle is that knowledge levels are even higher in the pre-election wave of the ANES than the post-election wave: the average interviewer rating for respondent knowledge is 3.23 out of

---

[15] *T*-tests reveal significant between-year differences for both interviewer ratings (on-year $M = 3.21$, off-year $M = 3.00$), $t(17,686) = -12.95$, $p < .001$, and information indices (on-year $M = .55$, off-year $M = .51$), $t(17,790) = -10.75$, $p < .001$.

[16] *T*-tests reveal significant differences between these periods for both interviewer ratings (earlier $M = 3.04$, later $M = 3.17$), $t(17,686) = -7.67$, $p < .001$, and information indices (earlier $M = .52$, later $M = .54$), $t(17,790) = -5.12$, $p < .001$.

[17] *T*-tests reveal significant differences between earlier and later years for both interest in political campaigns (earlier $M = 3.00$, later $M = 3.06$), $t(17,693) = -2.99$, $p = .003$, and interest in public affairs (earlier $M = 2.73$, later $M = 2.79$), $t(17,431) = -3.97$, $p < .001$.

[18] *T*-tests reveal significant differences between election years for interest in political campaigns (on-year $M = 3.19$, off-year $M = 2.86$), $t(17,693) = -14.84$, $p < .001$, but not for interest in public affairs (on-year $M = 2.75$, off-year $M = 2.76$), $t(17,431) = 0.94$, $p = .35$.

5 points during the presidential election campaign, but only 3.14 after the election is over.[19] Given that the average off-year interviewer rating is only 3.00, it would appear that Americans are collectively most knowledgeable about politics during presidential election campaigns, less knowledgeable in the months immediately following presidential elections, and least informed in the months following off-year congressional elections. Examining the individuals whose political knowledge changes from one period to another can help clarify whether this pattern stems from shrinking levels of ability or interest in the campaign. The impact of the campaign itself should be clearest in changes from the pre- to post-election waves of the on-year surveys. If these changes are produced by shifting levels of cognitive ability, the cause is likely to be differences in the ease with which public affairs information can be accessed in working memory. The ongoing campaign could stimulate a wide range of political beliefs and attitudes in associative memory, making each of them more temporarily accessible when a respondent is called upon to answer political knowledge questions.[20] If, however, these changes are produced by shifting levels of interest in the campaign, then this interest is likely to influence knowledge levels by affecting a respondent's willingness to think more carefully or search memory more systematically for relevant bits of information before answering survey questions.

The relative impact of these two possible mechanisms should therefore be seen in the amount of time each respondent takes to answer survey questions. While no record is kept of how long respondents spend answering particular questions, interviewers do record the starting and ending times for each person's interview. If temporary changes in cognitive ability explain changing levels of political knowledge, then respondents who appear to become more or less informed after the election than they were before it should be answering questions at the same pace in the pre- as in the post-election interview. In such a case, respondents who appear to be less informed following the election would not be taking less time to consider relevant information. The relevant information would simply be coming less readily to mind after the campaign was over. But if a temporary loss of motivation to engage in effortful processing explains

---

[19] Paired samples T-tests reveal significant differences between pre- and post-election waves, $t(6,213) = 8.55, p < .001$.

[20] Campaign-initiated priming effects of this sort have been shown to affect the partisanship of less knowledgeable voters (Dimock 1998).

why some respondents appear less knowledgeable after the election, then we should find these people answering questions at a more rapid pace than they did before the election, just to get the interview over with more quickly (Krosnick 1991).

Comparing the mean interview durations among respondents whose apparent information levels changed between the pre- and post-election interviews suggests that these differences stem from changes in motivation rather than ability. Respondents who were rated less informed in the post-wave than they were in the pre-wave ($n = 1,658$) took significantly less time to complete their post-election interviews than they did to complete their pre-election interviews. Likewise, respondents who were rated as more knowledgeable after the election than before it ($n = 1,176$) took slightly longer to complete the post-election wave than they did to finish the pre-election wave, but this difference was not statistically significant.[21] People appear more knowledgeable in presidential election years not because they are smarter, but because they are more willing to use the smarts they already have.[22]

INFORMATION EFFECTS OVER TIME

If information effects arise merely from a popular deficit of general political knowledge, then findings from the previous section suggest that information effects should decline in size over the 1980–98 period. Information effects should also be smaller in presidential election years,

---

[21] Since the number of questions in ANES interviews varies both within and across years, interview lengths were standardized into z-scores for each wave, which gave every wave a mean interview length of 0 and standard deviation of 1. Paired-sample *T*-tests reveal that respondents who appeared less knowledgeable after the election than before it completed the post-election wave more quickly ($M = -.076$) than they did the pre-election wave ($M = -.004$), $t(1,657) = 3.38$, $p = .001$. In contrast, those who appeared more knowledgeable after the election than they did before it took relatively more time to complete the post-election wave ($M = .046$) than they did for the pre-election wave ($M = .005$), but this difference failed to achieve conventional levels of significance, $t(1,176) = -1.41, p = .16$.

[22] This finding is also consistent with recent work (Mondak 2000, 2001; Mondak and Davis 2001) that shows the standard design of factual knowledge questions makes citizens seem less knowledgeable than they actually are. Allowing DK answers to such questions discourages respondents from making informed, as opposed to random, guesses and leads personality factors to confound apparent levels of knowledge. In the present context, the stimulus of the presidential campaign appears to make survey respondents more willing to search available memory and venture informed guesses than they might otherwise be.

because people seem more motivated in those years to process information about political matters. Yet, the findings in Chapter 5 showed that changes in attitude structures, the social distribution of domain-specific knowledge, levels of issue salience, and features of the information environment can also influence the development of information effects. If these mechanisms play a more important role than general political knowledge, then changes in the size of information effects over this time period may follow unexpected patterns.

Testing these possibilities requires examining information effects in survey questions that were asked in identical form over a relatively long span of time. Many of the 235 cases analyzed in previous chapters represent questions that were asked in more than one year of the American National Election Studies, but a maximum of three data points spaced four years apart hardly provides an adequate basis for analyzing trends. To compensate for this limitation, I selected questions that appeared in the ANES between 1980 and 1998 and were repeated at least five times in consecutive surveys. These criteria identified one approval question, 15 policy questions, and 11 value questions with two-year lags between observations.[23]

Changes in the Size of Information Effects over Time

Rising levels of political knowledge and interest suggest that information effects should diminish somewhat in size over time, but Table 6.2 reveals a different pattern. In this table, trends for each of the 27 opinion questions were divided in half to test for differences in the size of information effects between the earlier and later years of each series.[24] Among all questions

---

[23] Due to the two-year lag between observations, presidential approval questions were not included in this analysis because no single U.S. president could serve long enough to produce five data points in ANES questions. Instead, approval of Congress is analyzed here. The topical categories used to organize policy questions in previous chapters were retained in this chapter, though in many cases a category is represented here by a single question (details are available from the author upon request). As appropriate, the response categories of each question were recoded into dichotomous (in the case of nominal data) or trichotomous variables (in the case of ordinal data, where the middle option in the original coding was retained as the middle category and the two tails of the response distribution were recoded into each of the remaining two categories).

[24] Each trend was divided into two stages, and the percentage point differences between surveyed and fully informed opinion were averaged within earlier and later years of the series. Question trends having an even number of data points across years were divided so that earlier and later years had the same number of observations. In cases of trends containing an odd number of time periods, the middle period was included

TABLE 6.2. *Mean point differences between surveyed and fully informed collective opinion, by position in time series*

Question Type	Earlier Years	Later Years	T =	N =
By topic				
Approval (congressional)	*10.46*	*15.76*	*−2.08**	*10*
Policy	*6.72*	*8.38*	*−2.12**	*113*
Abortion	8.98	11.34	−1.86[†]	9
Affirmative action	4.58	4.22	0.28	16
Child care	3.25	6.33	−1.81[†]	5
Crime/social unrest	4.90	5.67	−0.40	6
Education	7.52	8.15	−0.28	13
Elder care	10.04	18.33	−3.11*	7
Environmental	9.18	6.13	0.78	7
Foreign	7.57	10.19	−1.40[†]	18
Governance	9.08	10.03	−0.65	10
Health	2.88	11.40	−5.90**	5
Welfare	5.33	5.65	−0.21	17
Value	*8.01*	*7.43*	*0.55*	*81*
Equality	8.60	7.43	0.98	53
Morality	6.98	7.43	−0.21	28
By ability level				
High-depletion topics	6.40	8.59	−2.29*	81
Low-depletion topics	8.07	8.26	−0.22	123
TOTAL ALL QUESTIONS	7.42	8.39	−1.51[†]	204

[†]$p < .10$
*$p < .05$
**$p < .01$ (one-tailed)
Note: A negative sign on the *t*-statistic indicates a relationship consistent with the knowledge gap hypothesis, while a positive sign indicates a relationship consistent with social diffusion hypothesis.

taken as a whole, the last row shows that gaps between surveyed and fully informed opinion tended to increase over time, though this increase is only marginally significant and amounts to a difference of just one percentage point. The reason for this becomes apparent when questions are divided by topic: information effects increase significantly over time in policy and approval questions, but exhibit no significant differences over time in value questions. Differences are large enough to be significant in

in the earlier years category. A detailed listing of how each trend was coded, as well as of which questions were included in the categories listed here, is available from the author.

three of the individual question trends (congressional approval, elder care, and health policy) and marginally significant in another three (abortion, child care, and foreign policy). It is notable that every significant difference is a case where information effects grow over time. Moreover, the size of information effects is larger in later years for all but three of the individual question categories (affirmative action, environmental policy, and equality).

The impact of ability to engage in effortful processing is shown in Table 6.2 by sorting the questions according to their average percentages of DK/NO responses.[25] Question categories with higher average DK/NO levels indicate topics in which the mass public's ability to process information is relatively lower, while lower average DK/NO levels indicate higher ability topics. The mean differences in earlier and later years among low and high depletion topics clearly supports the ability hypothesis, as high depletion topics saw increasing gaps between surveyed and fully informed opinion over time, while low depletion topics had no significant over-time differences in the size of information effects.

The motivation hypothesis also finds clear support when differences in the size of information effects are compared by type of election year, as shown in Table 6.3. The last row shows that across all questions the average information effect was nearly 9 percentage points in midterm election years compared with 7 points in presidential election years. As in Table 6.2, differences are significantly smaller in presidential election years for policy and approval questions, but value questions had no significant differences between type of year. The impact of election-year factors was strong enough to produce significant differences in four of the individual question categories (abortion, crime/social unrest, education, and welfare policy) plus a marginally significant difference in two others (congressional approval and foreign policy questions), all of which showed substantially smaller information effects during presidential election years. In fact, only governance questions showed a slight but insignificant on-year increase in the size of information effects: all other question categories

---

[25] The median level of DK/NO responses across categories was 5.29%, and categories with average DK/NO levels above the median were classified as "high depletion," whereas those with lower levels were classified as "low depletion" topics. The high depletion category includes congressional approval (10.38 average DK/NO percentage), affirmative action (13.64), childcare (5.51), foreign (6.75), governance (13.99), health (7.11), and welfare policy (5.93). The low depletion category includes abortion (2.24 average DK/NO percentage), crime/social unrest (5.08), education (3.96), elder care (3.50), environmental policy (4.36), equality (1.81), and morality questions (1.79).

TABLE 6.3. *Mean point differences between surveyed and fully informed collective opinion, by election year*

Question Type	Midterm Election	Presidential Election	$T =$	$N =$
By topic				
Approval (congressional)	*15.52*	*10.70*	*1.81*†	*10*
Policy	*8.66*	*6.50*	*2.81***	*113*
Abortion	11.65	9.20	1.97*	9
Affirmative action	4.56	4.20	0.27	16
Child care	4.68	4.35	0.13	5
Crime/social unrest	7.00	3.57	3.54*	6
Education	10.72	5.32	3.46**	13
Elder care	14.98	12.55	0.55	7
Environmental	10.05	6.24	1.01	7
Foreign	10.38	7.68	1.44†	18
Governance	9.36	9.75	−0.26	10
Health	6.78	5.97	0.15	5
Welfare	7.26	3.89	2.61**	17
Value	*8.07*	*7.43*	*0.60*	*81*
Equality	8.59	7.59	0.83	53
Morality	7.28	7.02	0.12	28
By ability level				
High-depletion topics	8.45	6.53	1.98*	81
Low-depletion topics	8.98	7.40	1.87*	123
TOTAL ALL QUESTIONS	8.77	7.06	2.69**	204

†$p < .10$
*$p < .05$
** $p < .01$ (one-tailed)
Note: A positive sign on the *t*-statistic indicates a relationship consistent with the intermittent attention hypothesis.

had smaller gaps between surveyed and fully informed opinion during presidential election years, although many of these were not statistically significant.[26] Information effects in both high and low depletion topics

---

[26] Alternative interpretations of these findings could result from two possible artifacts of the methodology employed here, but no evidence of such contamination was found. First, it is possible that the reduced size of presidential-year information effects could result from sensitization brought about by respondent exposure to the pre-election interview wave (ANES studies in midterm election years only contain post-election interviews). In this scenario, information effects in questions from the post-election wave could be smaller if respondents were somehow prompted by the pre-election interview to engage in more effortful processing of post-election questions. A *t*-test of differences in the size of information effects between pre- and post-wave interviews during presidential election

are smaller in presidential election years. Although high depletion topics have smaller average effects in presidential years than low depletion
topics, this difference is not significant.[27]

Taken together, the findings in Tables 6.2 and 6.3 are more consistent with patterns predicted by the knowledge gap hypothesis than with
those predicted by the social diffusion hypothesis. Strong support is also
found for cognitive ability and motivation as factors that condition the
size of collective information effects, but the findings are contrary to those
predicted by the response instability hypothesis. Most important, information effects grew in size over a period marked by rising average levels of
general political knowledge and interest in the campaigns. This finding, in
conjunction with the cyclical pattern of growth and decay between types
of election years, suggests that a population's willingness to process information may be more foundational to the development of information
effects than its ability to recall facts about politics. Indeed, the American

years finds no support for this possibility. To the contrary, mean pre-wave collective
information effects average 6.04 percentage points compared to an average of 6.92 points
among post-wave questions, $t(233) = 1.61$, two-tailed $p = .11$. Approaching marginal
levels of significance, the substantive difference is opposite of that expected: it would
appear that any pre-wave sensitization artificially inflates the size of presidential-year
information effects, thus suppressing a potentially larger average difference between on-
and off-year effects.

A second potential artifact stems from the knowledge indices employed in the analysis, which tend to contain more items and different proportions of certain types of
knowledge questions in presidential election years (see Appendix A). In this scenario,
smaller presidential-year information effects could result from either of two sources: (1)
the knowledge scales in the on-year studies could somehow do a systematically better
job of tapping relevant knowledge, such that the between-year differences actually stem
from substantive differences in the knowledge scales themselves, or (2) the longer scales
used in presidential election years could be more reliable than the shorter off-year scales,
so that the between-year differences arise from a greater amount of measurement error in
the off-year knowledge scales. Regarding the first possibility, the knowledge scales were
designed to omit campaign-specific information about current candidates for office. All
knowledge scales were also standardized to vary between 0 and 1, in order to correct
for differences in information effects that might arise merely from differences in scale
length. As discussed earlier in this chapter, average knowledge levels are higher during
presidential years, but this change is registered in both knowledge indices and interviewer
ratings, thus diminishing the possibility that this tendency is merely an artifact of index
construction. Regarding the second possibility, an analysis of the Cronbach's alphas for
the knowledge indices used here reveals no significant differences in average reliability
between type of election year: the average alpha level was .828 in off-year and .816 in
on-year surveys, $t(9) = 0.57$, two-tailed $p = .57$.

[27] *T*-tests show that mean differences between high and low depletion topics are not significantly different in either presidential election years, $t(104) = -1.09$, $p = .29$, or midterm
election years, $t(96) = -0.51$, $p = .61$.

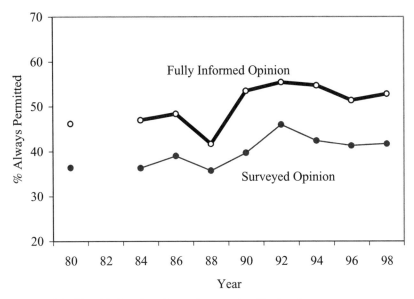

FIGURE 6.3. *Should abortion always be permitted by law?*

public's apparent ability level seems to vary with its motivation to process information about politics.

However, the relationships between surveyed and simulated opinions are more complicated than these tables suggest. Information effects sometimes grow over time because levels of surveyed opinion move away from stable levels of fully informed opinion, but sometimes because simulated preferences diverge from stable levels of surveyed opinion. The smaller information effects in presidential election years sometimes result when surveyed opinion shifts to appear more fully informed, but at other times when simulated opinion comes to more closely resemble surveyed opinion.

Three examples can serve to illustrate the complex associations between fully informed and surveyed opinion. The first shows levels of agreement in surveyed and fully informed opinion to the proposition, "By law, a woman should always be able to obtain an abortion as a matter of personal choice."[28] Figure 6.3 shows that the gap between surveyed

---

[28] The full question appearing in the ANES reads as follows: "There has been some discussion about abortion during recent years. Which one of the opinions on this page best agrees with your view?...(1) By law, abortion should never be permitted; (2) the law should permit abortion only in case of rape, incest or when the woman's life is in danger; (3) the law should permit abortion for reasons other than rape, incest or danger to

and simulated opinion on this issue is substantial – averaging 10.3 percentage points – and despite rising levels of support for abortion rights over time, this gap has remained relatively stable across the 18 years covered by these data.[29]

Yet when surveyed opinion on this issue shifts, it tends to move in the direction of fully informed opinion. The most revealing pattern in support for abortion rights occurs between 1988 and 1992. In 1988, majorities in both surveyed and simulated opinion favored at least some legal restrictions to abortion services. But support for unrestricted access in fully informed opinion rose 13 points between 1988 and 1990, and stabilized at around 55% thereafter. The catalyst for this abrupt change may have been the Supreme Court's 1989 *Webster v. Reproductive Health Services* decision, which allowed states to deny the use of public funds for abortion counseling and to restrict access to abortion services provided by public facilities and personnel. Public advocacy by both prolife and prochoice groups flared around the time of the decision, and the perceived threat to the status quo resulted in increased support in opinion polls for keeping abortion "legal as it is now" (Wlezien and Goggin 1993).

In contrast to the sudden shift in fully informed opinion following *Webster*, the change in surveyed opinion was in the same direction but at a much more gradual pace: 4 percentage points higher between 1988 and 1990, and another 6 points between 1990 and 1992. This lagged response in surveyed opinion may reflect a social diffusion process at work: it appears that it simply took longer for the threat *Webster* posed to abortion rights to be recognized as such by the mass public. While some research contends that conflicts in core beliefs about abortion should cause the opinions of knowledgeable respondents to be relatively less stable than those of ill-informed respondents (Alvarez and Brehm 1995, 2002), the trend line revealed in Figure 6.3 shows that, in the aggregate, fully informed responses are just as stable as surveyed opinion. This persistent gap between surveyed and fully informed opinion could be a collective manifestation of the individual-level ambivalence that this research has associated with abortion attitudes. Alternatively, it may be that the mass public has resolved its conflicting values on the issue of abortion (Yankelovich 1991:

the woman's life, but only after the need for the abortion has been clearly established; (4) by law, a woman should always be able to obtain an abortion as a matter of personal choice."

[29] It appears that the marginally smaller information effects in this question for earlier years (reported in Table 6.2) stems largely from the unusually small gap in 1988.

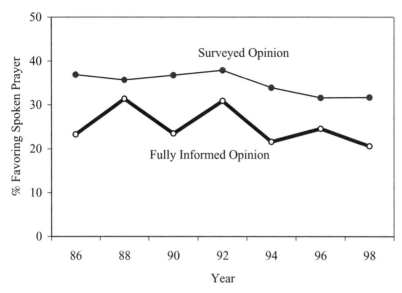

FIGURE 6.4. *Should the law permit prayer in public schools?*

26–8). If so, what appears to be a large and enduring information effect may instead result from principled differences of opinion between ill- and well-informed citizens, who may privilege different values when resolving internal ambiguity. For whatever reason, abortion attitudes present a case where information effects are persistent and unlikely to go away in the near future.

In other cases, fully informed opinion behaves quite erratically relative to surveyed opinion. This pattern is revealed in opinion toward prayer in schools (Figure 6.4). Perhaps because school prayer is such an easy issue to grasp, collective opinion on this issue has been remarkably stable since the early 1960s. While levels of public opposition remain low, support for prayer in schools has gradually declined in some questions from around 80% in the years following the Supreme Court's 1962 *Engle v. Vitale* ruling to just above 60% in the late 1980s (Page and Shapiro 1992: 113). Since 1986 the American National Election Studies have included a question on the topic, which asks, "Which of the following comes closest to your opinion on the issue of school prayer?...(1) By law, prayers should not be allowed in public schools; (2) the law should allow public schools to schedule time when children can pray silently if they want to; (3) the law should allow public schools to schedule time when children, as a group, can say a general prayer not tied to a particular religious faith;

(4) by law, public schools should schedule a time when all children would say a chosen Christian prayer." The percentages of opinion givers favoring some kind of spoken prayer (options three and four) are displayed in Figure 6.4.

After correcting for information effects, measures of simulated opinion become more opposed than surveyed opinion to the idea of spoken prayer in public schools. Yet while surveyed support for this issue holds steady at around 36%, levels of support in fully informed opinion are highly variable. Not only is simulated opinion less stable, but the gap between surveyed and fully informed opinion narrows considerably in presidential election years, particularly in 1988. The gap between these measures averages 6.1 percentage points in the three presidential election years, but doubles to 12.6 points in midterm election years. However, information effects are smaller in presidential election years not because surveyed opinion falls in line with simulated opinion, but because fully informed opinion climbs as much as nine points closer to the stable levels of surveyed opinion before falling back to off-year levels. This example illustrates that smaller information effects in presidential election years can result from changes in fully informed opinion just as much as from changes in surveyed opinion.

The reason behind this trend in simulated opinion is unclear. If the average person tends to be more interested and better informed in presidential election years, then the pattern in Figure 6.4 could result merely from cyclical changes in the makeup of knowledgeable and motivated citizens. People who are somewhat more favorable toward school prayer might also happen to become more interested or informed during presidential elections, and the result shifts fully informed opinion toward surveyed opinion. Alternatively, the narrowing gaps in presidential election years could be related in some way to the content of campaign communications. It seems plausible that the furor over the Pledge of Allegiance raised by George Bush in the 1988 election might have affected levels of support for school prayer, and similar explanations might be found for the other presidential election years. However, it would be strange for this to be the case without affecting levels of surveyed opinion. Whatever the cause or causes, the result is a measure of fully informed opinion that tends to converge toward surveyed opinion rather than the other way around.

Although simulated opinion sometimes is known to be more erratic than surveyed opinion, attitudes toward gender equality provide an example where fully informed opinion correctly anticipates more gradual

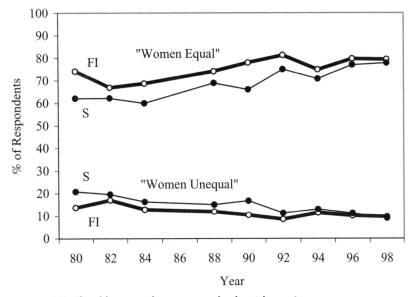

FIGURE 6.5. *Should women have an equal role with men?*

long-term shifts in surveyed opinion (Figure 6.5). The question from which this third example is drawn reads, "Recently there has been a lot of talk about women's rights. Some people feel that women should have an equal role with men in running business, industry, and government. Others feel that women's place is in the home. Where would you place yourself on this scale, or haven't you thought much about this?"[30] Opinion on this issue has risen steadily from 49% in the 1972 ANES (when the question was first asked) to even out at 62% in 1980 (Page and Shapiro 1992: 100). Figure 6.5 shows that surveyed support for women's rights rose again after 1984 to an all-time high of 78% in 1998.

Fully informed opinion was consistently more supportive of women's rights than surveyed opinion, and information effects in this question declined steadily in size over time because surveyed opinion came to be more in line with simulated opinion. Moreover, the gradual changes in surveyed opinion were consistently anticipated by rising levels of support in simulated opinion. In this case, fully informed opinion was remarkably prescient in predicting future changes in surveyed opinion.

---

[30] The first three responses were coded as favoring gender equality, while the last three were coded as opposing gender equality.

Predicting Future Levels of Surveyed Opinion from Estimates of Fully Informed Opinion

These examples illustrate that the findings reported in Tables 6.2 and 6.3 tell only part of the story. A more precise way of analyzing the longitudinal development of information effects is to test how accurately simulations of fully informed opinion predict future trends in surveyed opinion. Fully informed opinion at t_1 seems to do a good job of predicting levels of surveyed opinion two years later at t_2: the correlation between these measures is an impressive .90 and is two-tailed significant at the $p < .001$ level. Yet the apparent prescience of simulated opinion is put in proper context when the tables are turned: the correlation between fully informed opinion at t_2 and levels of surveyed opinion at t_1 is an equally impressive .87. The reason for this apparent symmetry is that when collective opinion changes over time, it tends to shift in small increments rather than all at once (Page and Shapiro 1992: 45). The strong associations among both sets of measures are largely due to the fact that the average change in surveyed opinion between t_1 and t_2 is only 4.5 percentage points, thus ensuring that any measure of opinion at t_1 is almost always a good predictor of opinion at t_2.

These results call for a sophisticated approach for determining the ability of fully informed opinion to predict changes in surveyed opinion. One of the most widely used methods for sorting out the reciprocal impact of two highly correlated variables over time is the Granger causality test (Granger 1969; Gujarati 1995).[31] Table 6.4 summarizes the results of these Granger tests. Each of the four columns represents a different model, such that one lag involves predictions from data two years prior, two lags involve predictions from data two and four years prior, and so on to four lags, which use all available data going back eight years to predict current values of the variables of interest. Because the Granger test is sensitive to the number of lags used (Gujarati 1995: 623), results from all four models are reported to clarify when test results are robust under different model specifications.

Examining first the breakdown of results by question topic, Table 6.4 shows that within the domain of policy questions, fully informed opinion Granger-predicts future values of surveyed opinion in three out of four models, although results in one of these models are of only marginal

---

[31] Appendix B includes a brief description of the statistical logic behind the Granger causality test.

TABLE 6.4. *Granger tests for predicting changes in surveyed opinion from measures of fully informed collective opinion*

Question Trend	One Lag	Two Lags	Three Lags	Four Lags
By topic				
Approval (congressional)	S n.r. FI (9)	S n.r. FI (8)	[a] (7)	[a] (6)
Policy	S ← FI† (159)	S ← FI** (134)	S ← FI** (109)	S*** ↔ FI*** (84)
Value	S n.r. FI (138)	S† → FI (114)	S* → FI (90)	S* → FI (68)
By ability level				
High-depletion topics	S n.r. FI (118)	S ← FI* (101)	S n.r. FI (84)	S*** ↔ FI*** (67)
Low-depletion topics	S n.r. FI (188)	S ← FI† (155)	S ← FI* (122)	S* ↔ FI** (91)
TOTAL ALL QUESTIONS	S n.r. FI (306)	S ← FI** (256)	S ← FI* (206)	S† ↔ FI*** (158)

†$p < .10$
*$p < .05$
**$p < .01$
*** $p < .001$ (two-tailed)

[a] No Granger test could be calculated for these relationships due to an insufficient number of cases.

Note: Numbers in parentheses are the number of cases used in the Granger test. Arrows indicate directional influence of Granger relationships, and "n.r." indicates no relationships in either direction. Significance tests are for the *F*-statistics associated with the lags of one variable, either surveyed opinion (S) or fully informed opinion (FI), predicting current values of the other. Each lag represents a two-year interval.

significance, with the fourth model suggesting a feedback relationship between surveyed and simulated opinion. In contrast, among value questions surveyed opinion tends to Granger-predict fully informed opinion, although results in one of the models are of only marginal significance, and the single-lag model suggests no relationship between these variables. Granger tests on surveyed and fully informed opinions regarding Congressional approval suggest that these measures are unrelated to one another in the short term.

While these patterns show clear differences in the predictive ability of simulated opinion across policy, value, and approval questions, Table 6.4 offers mixed evidence on the differences among questions with higher and lower average levels of DK/NO responses. Two of the four low depletion equations show that fully informed opinion Granger-predicts surveyed opinion, but so does one of the four high depletion equations. In addition, feedback effects are found in the four lag models for both high and low depletion topics. The findings from this test of predictive accuracy offer only limited support for the ability hypothesis: it would appear that simulated opinion predicts surveyed opinion nearly as well in questions with high levels of opinion depletion as in those with lower levels of depletion.

The combined results for all questions in the last row of Table 6.4 reveal that fully informed opinion Granger-predicts surveyed opinion in two of the four equations, and while there is a feedback relationship in the four-lag equation, it is based on the marginally significant influence of surveyed on simulated opinion. Under conventional significance levels, three of the four equations would indicate that simulated opinion Granger-predicts surveyed opinion. This conclusion is consistent with the workings of social diffusion processes, and appears to be at odds with the knowledge gap hypothesis. Of course, the specific workings of these conflicting dynamics are obscured in these data, and it may be that simulated opinion would be even more accurate if not for the tendency of knowledge to become socially concentrated. But taken together, the findings in Table 6.4 suggest that simulations of fully informed opinion can be quite prescient in predicting future trends in surveyed opinion. As predicted by the response instability hypothesis, simulated opinions are most accurate in the domain of policy questions, and least accurate in the domain of value questions.

It is important to keep in mind that while revealing in its statistical precision, the Granger test is designed only to indicate which of two variables is a relatively better predictor of the another, and does not reveal the specific degree of accuracy afforded by one or the other. Measures of fully informed opinion also might do a better job of predicting either stability or change in surveyed opinion, but the Granger test is indifferent to the reasons for predictive accuracy. Moreover, the Granger test allows no obvious check on the motivation hypothesis, since the influence of motivation should be found not in pitting one group of questions against another over the complete series of data points, but rather in the diminished predictive ability of fully informed opinion across all questions in every other year of the data series. Answering these questions requires a different approach to the data. Asking how well a series of lagged values predicts future trends in a dependent variable provides useful insights, but what we really want to know is how accurate the predictions of stability or change made by fully informed opinion at one point in time turn out to be at future points in time.

Conducting such an analysis requires taking two measures into account: any change in surveyed opinion from t_1 to t_{1+n}, and the proximity and relative direction of fully informed to surveyed opinion at t_1. Each of these parameters can be considered bounded by a confidence interval of plus or minus 3 percentage points, corresponding roughly to the confidence interval for point estimates made from the survey data. By this metric, each measure of fully informed opinion at t_1 can be said to predict either a change in surveyed opinion, if it lies more than 6 percentage points from surveyed opinion at t_1, or stability in levels of surveyed opinion, if it lies within 6 percentage points of surveyed opinion at t_1. We can say that fully informed opinion accurately predicts future values of surveyed opinion if (1) change is predicted and surveyed opinion at t_{1+n} has moved at least 6 percentage points in the relative direction of simulated opinion at t_1, or (2) stability is predicted and surveyed opinion at t_{1+n} has remained within 6 percentage points of its value at t_1. This way of calculating the accuracy of predictions made by simulated opinion for various future values of surveyed opinion can reveal not only whether fully informed opinion is a better predictor of short-term or long-term trends in surveyed opinion, but also whether simulated opinion is a better predictor of change or stability in surveyed opinion, and whether predictions made in high-motivation presidential election years are more accurate than predictions made in low-motivation midterm election years.

The accuracy of different types of fully informed predictions for future trends in surveyed opinion are broken out in Figure 6.6. In this figure, points on the solid lines represent the accuracy of predictions for stability in surveyed opinion, and points on the dashed lines detail the accuracy of predictions for specific directional changes in future levels of surveyed opinion.[32] The dotted horizontal line in each chart represents the accuracy rate expected by chance (i.e., 33.3%), as each future measure of surveyed opinion can move 6 or more percentage points in one direction from the t_1 value of surveyed opinion, 6 or more points in the other direction, or remain within 6 points of the t_1 value. The accuracy rate of cases where fully informed opinion predicted future stability in surveyed opinion is

---

[32] To count as an accurate prediction of change, surveyed opinion has to move at least 6 percentage points in the direction indicated by fully informed opinion at t_1. A substantial change in the opposite direction is counted as an inaccurate prediction. Accuracy rates at $t_{1+2\ years}$ are based on a total of 159 stability predictions and 147 change predictions. There are 138 stability predictions and 125 change predictions for $t_{1+4\ years}$, 114 stability and 101 change predictions at $t_{1+6\ years}$, and 93 stability and 76 change predictions for $t_{1+8\ years}$.

remarkably high. The upper left panel reveals that 77% of all stability predictions turned out to be correct two years after the predictions were made, a level that declines and stabilizes around 60% correct predictions at six and eight years following the prediction. In each case, the accuracy of these stability predictions made by simulations of fully informed opinion is significantly higher than expected by chance.

Yet, even as fully informed opinions are surprisingly accurate when predicting future stability in surveyed opinion, the simulations are equally remarkable in their dismal record of predicting future directional changes in surveyed opinion. In the remaining cases where fully informed opinion predicted a specific directional change in surveyed opinion, the upper left panel shows that only 17.7% of these predictions proved to be accurate at two years in the future, a rate that gradually improves to only 24% correct predictions at eight years. The best that can be said for a prediction of directional movement given by fully informed opinion is that, over time, it should eventually augur nearly as well as a draw among one long and two short straws. In the near term, however, change predictions are decidedly less accurate than would be expected by chance.[33]

Stability predictions for value questions are nearly always on the mark, with 88% accurate predictions at two years in the future and retaining a 77% accuracy rating at eight years out. The quality of stability predictions is reduced for policy questions, with accuracy rates dropping from 71% at two years to around 50% at six and eight years from the time of the prediction, but all remain significantly different from chance. Change

---

[33] It is important to point out that these accuracy rates would be quite different under less stringent assumptions about the distance that surveyed opinion needs to move to be counted as a "change." If we were to reduce the size of the confidence interval around these point estimates from plus or minus 3 percentage points to plus or minus 1 point, at two years in the future we would find the accuracy rate for stability predictions falling to 49% (n of stability predictions $= 61$) and the accuracy rate for predictions of directional change rising to 38% (n of change predictions $= 333$). Under such conditions, both types of predictions would be significant improvements over chance, $z = 2.63, p < .01$, and $z = 1.68, p < .05$, respectively. In a similar way, the significance levels for fully informed opinion in the Granger tests reported in Table 6.4 represent predictions made with no confidence intervals at all. These findings show that fully informed opinion is more likely to Granger-predict surveyed opinion (in 8 of 22 tests) than surveyed opinion is to Granger-predict simulated opinion (in 3 of 22 tests). Taken together, these findings suggest that the conditions imposed on the data reported in Figure 6.6 produce conservative estimates of the predictive accuracy of fully informed opinion. Nonetheless, convention dictates use of the larger confidence interval, and the robust nature of these more conservative estimates suggest that they provide a more appropriate measure of the potential that simulated opinions might accurately predict future levels of surveyed opinions.

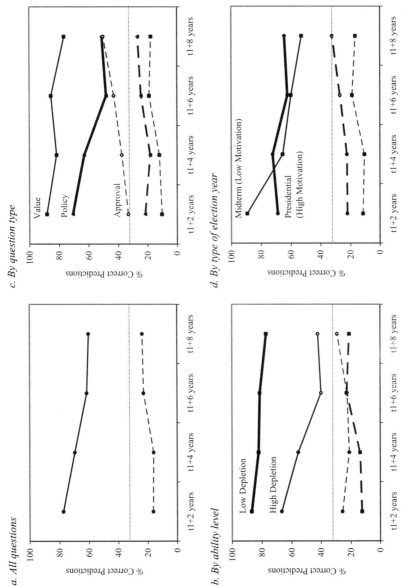

FIGURE 6.6. *Predicting future trends in surveyed opinion from t_1 measures of fully informed opinion, by type of prediction. Note:* Solid lines represent predictions of stability in future levels of surveyed opinion, and dashed lines represent predictions of specific directional changes in future levels of surveyed opinion. The dotted horizontal line in each frame represents the percentage of predictions that should be correct by chance. Shaded data points have Z-values that are significant at the two-tailed $p < .05$ level; open data points represent rates that are not statistically different from chance.

233

predictions are relatively more accurate for policy than for value questions, though all such predictions are less accurate than would be expected by chance. While changes predicted for congressional approval questions are more likely to come about over the long term,[34] none of these prediction rates is significantly different from chance due to the small number of observations making up each data point (see Table 6.4).

Motivation and ability to engage in effortful processing also appear in Figure 6.6 as determinants of predictive accuracy. At two years from the time of prediction, stability forecasts made in presidential election years were substantially less accurate than midterm forecasts. But beyond two years, stability predictions made in presidential years were slightly more accurate than midterm forecasts. Change predictions made in presidential election years were on average twice as accurate as change predictions estimated during midterm election years, but none of these rates were significantly greater than would be expected by chance. More pronounced differences are found when questions are grouped by the population's average ability levels. Stability predictions are much more accurate for low than for high depletion questions, with the latter declining to statistical insignificance at six years and beyond. Even eight years after predictions were made, surveyed opinion in low depletion questions remains within 6 percentage points of its original value in more than three of four cases where fully informed opinion predicts this result. Although the analysis in Chapter 5 showed that DK/NO levels were essentially unrelated to the size of gaps between actual and fully informed opinion, here we find that fully informed opinions in questions with relatively fewer DK/NO responses provide much more accurate stability forecasts than they do in questions with higher average levels of opinion depletion. High levels of demographic inequality among opinion givers may not influence the size of information effects, but they clearly reduce the likelihood that fully informed opinions tell us something useful about future trends in surveyed opinion.

Despite the poor performance of change predictions made from fully informed estimates, it would be premature to take this as evidence that simulated opinions are usually inaccurate when it comes to predicting changes in future levels of surveyed opinion. This is because the prevalence of incorrect change predictions stems not from cases where change occurs in the opposite direction of that predicted, but rather from cases where change in surveyed opinions fails to occur at all. Take, for example, the

---

[34] All of the predictions for the congressional approval questions are for change in one direction or another.

accuracy rate in predictions about specific directional changes discussed earlier. Two years after a specific directional change in surveyed opinion was predicted to occur, 16.3% of these predictions turned out to be correct (as reported in the upper left panel of Figure 6.6), another 14.3% involved cases where significant change occurred in the opposite direction, and the remaining 69.4% of cases were instances where levels of surveyed opinion had remained stable. Eight years after fully informed opinion predicted a specific directional change in surveyed opinion, 23.7% of these predictions turned out to be correct (as reported in the upper left panel of Figure 6.6), another 14.5% predicted change in one direction when it actually occurred in the other, and the remaining 61.8% of cases were instances where levels of surveyed opinion remained stable relative to the t_1 measure of surveyed opinion. At both two- and eight-year lags, when predictions of directional change made by fully informed opinion were incorrect, they were usually wrong because they predicted change that never occurred. Given the gradual levels of improvement in directional predictions with increasingly longer time lags, the accuracy of change predictions made by fully informed opinion may grow to be quite high beyond the eight-year window considered here.

Table 6.5 presents a summary of findings regarding the factors thought to influence the evolution of information effects. Limited support is found

TABLE 6.5. *Summary of findings on the evolution of information effects over time*

	Expected Influence on Evolution of Gaps between Surveyed and Fully Informed Opinion	Expected Influence on Predictive Ability of Fully Informed Opinion
Social factors		
Diffusion of knowledge across population	Not supported	Supported
Concentration of knowledge within population	Supported	Not supported
Psychological factors		
Population's ability to engage in effortful processing	Supported	Supported
Population's motivation to engage in effortful processing	Supported	Supported
Uncertainty and ambivalence as sources of response instability	Not supported	Supported

for the competing forces of social concentration and social diffusion of political information. The tendency for information effects to grow in size over time is better explained by the knowledge gap hypothesis, but if this tendency diminishes the predictive ability of simulated opinions, its influence is not strong enough to cancel the centrifugal forces of social diffusion apparent in the prediction findings. While information effects are often chronic, the success of stability predictions tells us that once resolved, they tend to stay resolved. In addition, the increasing accuracy of change predictions over time and the tendency for fully informed opinion to Granger-predict changes in surveyed opinion are consistent with the workings of social diffusion processes. However, as revealed in Figure 6.6, this latter finding may lean heavily on the success of stability rather than change predictions, and knowledge gaps among ill- and well-informed citizens could well account for the limited success of change predictions. In short, some evidence is found to support both hypotheses about the nature of information flows in large populations, but the unique contribution of each to the development of information effects remains unclear.

While the analysis produced mixed evidence for the two social factors, the expected macro-level manifestations of micro-level psychological factors received more consistent support. All of the tests showed that a population's ability and motivation to engage in effortful processing of political judgments influence the size of information effects and the predictive accuracy of fully informed opinion, though this pattern was more pronounced in some kinds of questions than in others. The gaps between surveyed and simulated opinion evolve in a sawtooth pattern predicted by the intermittent attention hypothesis, and also tended to grow over time in a manner consistent with the knowledge gap hypothesis. Information effects grow over time for question categories with high average levels of DK/NO responses, and although the gaps for questions with low DK/NO levels persist rather than shrink over time, the predictive accuracy of fully informed opinion is much higher in these latter questions than in those with high DK/NO levels. In the same way, predictions about future trends in surveyed opinion made from data gathered in presidential election years are much more accurate than those made from questions asked in midterm election years. Evidence supporting the impact of uncertainty and ambiguity as sources of response instability is most striking in the Granger tests, with limited support provided by the forecast accuracy tests. However, the expected influence of response instability was not observed in the evolution of information effects, which tended to grow in a manner more consistent with the knowledge gap hypothesis.

HOW ENLIGHTENED IS FULLY INFORMED OPINION?

To the extent that simulations of fully informed opinion resemble anything like enlightened preferences, it seems reasonable to expect that they should anticipate future trends in surveyed opinion so long as knowledge relevant to an issue has the tendency to become less socially concentrated as time passes. Instead of arguing blindly or resorting to an objective but contestable standard, this approach relies on the mass public's own future preferences as the standard for deciding when past estimates of fully informed opinion may have been consistent with the ideal of enlightened opinion. Can we conclude from the preceding analysis that statistical controls for the low levels and uneven social distribution of political knowledge produce collective preferences more proximate to a population's enlightened preferences than the opinions expressed by that population?

Simulated measures of fully informed opinion accurately predict when collective policy preferences will remain stable but are decidedly less precise when forecasting that surveyed opinion should change in significant ways, at least in the short term. While simulation results at times may be consistent with the ideal of enlightened preferences, these findings confirm that statistical simulations are unreliable indicators of political interests. Indeed, this chapter has presented a much more complicated picture than that envisioned by the political philosophers who deploy the enlightened preferences standard as a normative heuristic. Some of the problems arise from using an individual-level concept as a standard for collective preferences, but aside from Connolly's (1993) warning against translating the idea of enlightened preferences into testable forms, the preceding analysis calls into question its usefulness even as an idealized standard. The evolving gaps between surveyed and simulated opinion follow more complicated patterns than those anticipated by the enlightened preferences literature, and the current forms of the enlightened preferences ideal offer few guidelines for interpreting this complexity. If we are to successfully navigate the translation of this concept into empirical terms, we shall require a more refined definition of enlightened preferences. While statistically modeling a seemingly more informed citizenry can provide important insights into the relationship between opinions and political knowledge, the results of such an exercise should be accorded no greater normative status than the surveyed opinions from which they are derived.

CONCLUSION

Information effects in collective preferences tended either to grow or remain stable over the 1980–98 period, but once surveyed preferences came to resemble fully informed opinions, the gaps between these measures tended to remain small. Sometimes information effects diminished because fully informed opinion shifted to become more like surveyed opinion, but the Granger analysis shows that movement in simulated opinion tended to anticipate rather than follow movement in surveyed opinion, particularly in policy questions. The findings in this chapter underscore how hard it is to predict when information effects might emerge in surveyed preferences, and whether they will resolve in time. Yet, once the source of an information effect is identified – whether knowledge gaps, low levels of motivation, or ambiguous preferences, as discussed in this chapter; or attitude structures, low levels of issue salience, or lack of news coverage, as discussed in Chapter 5 – it may be possible to identify the likely course that such effects will follow.

Four implications from the findings in this chapter are especially important for understanding the nature and consequences of information effects. First, the size of information effects seems more sensitive to aggregate changes in motivation than in ability. Indeed, information effects grew over the 1980–98 period at the same time as the mass public's levels of general political knowledge were going up, suggesting that differences in opinion between ill- and well-informed citizens may often be rooted in factors other than cognitive ability. The cyclical rise and fall in the mass public's interest in and apparent levels of knowledge about politics, combined with regular drops in the size of information effects during presidential election years, underscore the key role played by environmental factors in moderating the importance of cognitive ability. These patterns confirm findings from Chapter 5, which showed that changing levels of issue salience and news attention can influence the size of information effects. They affirm that while the mass public is often distracted from and inattentive to public affairs, when roused to attention, the social distribution of political knowledge becomes less important to the shape of its collective preferences. Yet, these findings also reveal that the patterns and consequences of information effects detailed in Chapters 3 and 4 present a best-case scenario, since all of the findings reported in those chapters came from presidential election years.

Second, to the extent that environmental factors not only condition the impact of political knowledge on surveyed opinions but also influence the mass public's apparent levels of political knowledge, opinion quality may be more difficult to pin down with standard survey measures than is commonly supposed. Chapter 5 showed that respondent satisficing strategies for coping with the cognitive demands of the survey interview had a negligible influence on the size of information effects, primarily because such strategies produced similar patterns of convergence behavior in both the most- and least-informed respondents. However, the questions studied in Chapter 5 all came from presidential election years. This chapter reveals periodic fluctuations in information effects and apparent knowledge levels that could well be products of survey satisficing. If the quality of surveyed collective preferences depends on environmental factors to motivate respondents, then seasonal variation in response quality should be recognized as one of the many methodological problems facing survey researchers. Furthermore, to the extent that surveys produce collective preferences that appear more fully informed during presidential election years, the ability of polling methods to capture what the people collectively desire may depend on factors beyond the control of survey researchers. These findings warrant further research to explore whether other cyclical factors influence response behavior in public affairs questions.

Third, this chapter confirms that the development of information effects is influenced by uneven rates of opinion giving among survey respondents. Because rates of DK/NO responses go up in questions with higher levels of cognitive difficulty, the size of collective information effects is unaffected by levels of group depletion at any one point in time (Chapter 5). But since knowledge gaps are more likely to occur in topics with higher levels of cognitive difficulty, information effects in questions with higher levels of DK/NO responses tend to develop differently than they do in questions with lower levels of group depletion. Granger tests showed that estimates of fully informed collective preferences are more accurate in predicting future levels of surveyed opinion for questions with low average DK/NO levels than for questions with higher levels of depletion. Similarly, predictions of stability in future levels of surveyed opinion were strikingly accurate in low depletion questions, even out to eight years in the future. In contrast, stability forecasts made for questions with higher DK/NO levels rapidly declined in accuracy, becoming statistically indistinguishable from chance after four years. Questions with higher levels of group depletion may not have larger information effects in collective preferences, but the information effects they do have are likely to grow in size over time.

Fourth, surveyed opinion tends to remain stable in cases where information effects are small. Since the aggregate opinion of the most knowledgeable respondents tends to resemble fully informed collective preferences (as discussed in Chapter 5), a simple comparison of well- and ill-informed opinion on a given issue may provide a reliable barometer of future stability in the mass public's policy preferences. For the politician in a betting mood, the odds are good that the mass public's preferences will remain steady over the near term when there are few differences in the opinions of well- and ill-informed citizens. Sizeable differences between knowledgeable and poorly informed opinion can also indicate when collective preferences are likely to be unstable, although it may be difficult to anticipate how such instability will resolve itself. These findings suggest that political actors familiar with the structure and dynamics of information effects may come to see greater potential for leadership of public opinion than survey results might seem to indicate. To the extent that educating the public on important issues of the day speeds up the diffusion of relevant political knowledge, active leadership of public opinion could help to shorten the life of information effects.

With the findings of this and previous chapters in hand, we are now positioned to delve into larger theoretical questions that have been lurking in the background of this extended analysis. Opinion surveys can potentially provide a unique vehicle for identifying and communicating the voice of a people, but the presence of information effects calls into question the usefulness of opinion surveys in democratic politics. What do information effects tell us about the ability of collective preferences to represent a people's voice? And if information effects are common to collective preferences, what, if anything, can opinion surveys tell us about a people's interests? Answers to these questions demand a normative framework for evaluating quality in opinion surveys that moves beyond the shortcomings of the enlightened preferences standard and that clarifies the limitations of the opinion survey as a channel for political representation. It is to the development of such a framework that we now turn.

PART III

OPINION SURVEYS IN DEMOCRATIC POLITICS

7

Opinion Surveys and the Will of the People

Socrates: My good Crito, why should we care so much for what the majority think? The most reasonable people, to whom one should pay more attention, will believe that things were done as they were done.

Crito: You see, Socrates, that one must also pay attention to the opinion of the majority. Your present situation makes clear that the majority can inflict not the least but pretty well the greatest evils if one is slandered among them.

Socrates: Would that the majority could inflict the greatest evils, for they would then be capable of the greatest good, and that would be fine, but now they cannot do either. They cannot make a man either wise or foolish, but they inflict things haphazardly.

– Plato, *Crito*

Plato's *Crito* presents a jail-cell dialogue between Socrates and his friend, Crito, over the propriety of the death sentence handed down against Socrates by the citizens of Athens. He could flee into exile, as Crito urges, or stay and be executed. Both agree that the trial, carried out in front of 501 jurors chosen by lot, was conducted fairly. At issue is the quality of the verdict. Those citizens who were most knowledgeable about the circumstances leading up to the charges voted to exonerate Socrates. Crito and Socrates agree that if every juror were as well informed as the most knowledgeable jurors, Socrates surely would have been acquitted. Their disagreement is over the legitimacy of the jury's decision: Should Socrates disregard the unjust opinion of the ill-informed majority and live, or submit to it and die?

Crito explores the tension between truth, held by the few, and power, wielded by the many. This tension provides a fruitful analogy to the problems in democratic governance that are introduced by the low levels and uneven social distribution of political knowledge in mass publics. The previous chapters have shown that majority opinion does seem to "inflict things haphazardly": sometimes collective preferences resemble fully informed opinions, sometimes they do not. This unpredictability is at the root of the problem with measures of collective opinion, such as the results of opinion surveys. If one could determine whether the public's opinions were usually wrong or usually right, it would be a simple matter consistently to dismiss or legislate survey results. What to make of a public that manages to compensate for its lack of knowledge only part of the time, with no obvious way of determining when this might happen? Such is the dilemma facing political representatives in the era of the sample survey.

In her classic treatment of political representation, Hanna Pitkin (1967) distinguishes between representation as a quality of semblance, in the sense that a photograph "stands for" an actual person or numerical census data "stand for" the people of the United States, and representation as a form of substantive activity, as when a member of Congress "acts for" her constituents by voting on legislation in a way that is consistent with their interests. Opinion surveys provide for representation in both of these senses. In particular, we can think of surveys as a channel for political representation in at least two different occasions.[1] The first is when a political decision maker perceives or recognizes a random sample of individuals as standing for a larger population. Here, the focus is on the quality of descriptive representation afforded by opinion surveys and the degree to which political equality is respected by them. From this standpoint it becomes important to assess how accurately survey respondents embody the significant features of a population, whether the mix of opinions expressed by the sample is an accurate portrayal of the opinions that would be expressed by the population if all members were invited to speak for themselves, and the degree to which individuals in the sample contribute equally to the collective preference.

The second occasion for political representation is when a political decision maker takes the opinions of a sample into account when acting for

---

[1] In addition to these two occasions, it is also consistent with Pitkin's account that the mere act of conducting a survey is a form of representation, but this sense of the term will not concern us here.

a population. The concern here is with the quality of interest representation provided by surveys, and centers on two questions in particular: how accurately the opinions of survey respondents resemble the interests of a larger population, and how heavily those opinions are weighed by decision makers who act on behalf of a population. These concerns over the quality of interest representation lie at the heart of what Pitkin calls the mandate-independence controversy: whether representatives should act as delegates of their constituents, merely carrying out the expressed wishes of those who elected them, or rather serve as trustees by making decisions on behalf of constituents without regard to the expressed wishes of those represented. In the context of opinion surveys, this controversy translates into a disagreement about the normative status of survey results. Is it more appropriate to view survey results as representing the *active voice of the people*, a voice that delegates might heed and trustees ignore, or to view them merely as providing *information about the people*, information that might be useful even to trustees, but that should be granted no special normative status even by delegates?

The argument laid out below is that survey results are often less representative than they appear, primarily because survey researchers tend to conceive of representation in relatively narrow terms as standing for rather than as acting for those represented. Given this problem, I explore the complications that arise when survey results are used in the political process. I suggest in the following pages that it is inappropriate to think of survey results as the active voice of the people even when information effects are minimal or nonexistent. Yet it is also incorrect to view survey results as purely informational measures of what the public thinks. I conclude instead that the quality of interest representation afforded by survey results should guide their political uses.

OPINION SURVEYS AS A CHANNEL FOR DESCRIPTIVE REPRESENTATION

The legitimacy imputed to opinion surveys as expressions of the public voice rests on the perception that surveys are both scientific and representative. Survey practitioners have promoted this view of surveys since the method's earliest days (Gallup and Rae 1940). Not only do majorities of ordinary citizens and journalists believe that most polls are accurate measures of public opinion (Herbst 1993: 126–9), but variations of this view are also common among academics and survey practitioners. For example, Sidney Verba (1996) writes that "Surveys produce just what democracy is supposed to produce – equal representation of all citizens. The sample survey is rigorously egalitarian; it is designed so that each citizen has an equal chance to participate and an equal voice when participating."[2]

I argue that this common perspective on opinion polls is fundamentally mistaken. Opinion surveys never have been "rigorously egalitarian" except in the most formal sense of the term. To explain why, it is important to separate the two claims in Verba's definition: that surveys promote descriptive representation, in the sense that a survey sample accurately represents the quantifiable characteristics of a population, and that surveys promote political equality, in the sense that each person can provide only one opinion and all opinions are given the same weight. It is my position that this view of surveys is mistaken on three important points: that matching the demographic characteristics of a sample to that of a population is a sufficient definition of representation, that descriptive representation in a sample of respondents translates into descriptive representation in the group of people who give opinions, and that respecting political equality among individuals is sufficient to guarantee political equality in aggregate measures of opinion.

Descriptive Representation Is Only One Kind of Representation

When pollsters think about representation, it tends to be in descriptive terms. This perspective is neatly summed up in the famous words of John Adams: "A representative legislature should be an exact portrait, in miniature, of the people at large, as it should think, feel, reason and act like them."[3] One way of satisfying this requirement is to draw a random sample of "the people at large" (Swabey 1937). In what survey researchers call a "representative" sample, everyone in the target population has a theoretically equal chance of being chosen. Combined with the central limit theorem, which states that larger samples will tend better to reflect the actual distribution of traits in a target population, these two rules provide the basis for the claim that polls can accurately gauge the pulse of public sentiment (Brady and Orren 1992). The closer a sample

---

[2] James Fishkin (1995: 37) presents a similar view. Political equality, he states, "is served when those who participate are statistically representative of the entire citizenry and when the process of collective decision weighs their votes equally." Fishkin then goes on to say that "A properly conducted national random sample will be statistically representative of the entire country. In that sense, it embodies the condition of political equality" (44).

[3] Quoted in Sterne 1969: 73.

comes to being perfectly random, the more descriptively representative it should be.

Although this view of representation has a long history in democratic thought, it is but one of several definitions of representation that have been suggested over the years (Birch 1971, 1993). Pitkin notes that the root meaning of representation is "re-presentation": "the making present *in some sense* of something which is nevertheless *not* present literally or in fact" (Pitkin 1967: 8, emphasis in original). There are many senses in which representation can occur: a king can be said to represent the will of his subjects, a talent agent can be said to represent a movie star in formal negotiations, and former Senator Jesse Helms can be said to have represented the interests of tobacco producers even though they may have been physically located outside the state of North Carolina. The problem, as Pitkin (1967) points out, is that descriptive representation fails to satisfy these other important meanings of representation: "the representative sample is a misleading model for understanding political representation . . . because it is only a partial account of what it means to represent" (75). In Pitkin's other accounts of representation, individuals who are not descriptively representative of their constituents can nevertheless act "in the interests of the represented, in a manner responsive to them" (209). In surveys, those who give opinions do not necessarily act in the interests of those who answer "don't know" or "no opinion," nor are they responsive to them. Only to the extent that opinion givers speak in the interests of those who give nonsubstantive answers and those who are not polled at all, and only to the degree that opinion givers are responsive to these excluded persons, can the results of opinion surveys be considered representative in any but the narrowest sense of the term.

A Representative Sample Is No Guarantee that Survey Results Will Also Be Representative

A second problem with the view that surveys are "rigorously egalitarian" is the mistaken belief that survey *results* must be descriptively representative when a survey *sample* is descriptively representative. To focus solely on representation in the survey sample is to misunderstand the concept of descriptive representation, for it is rarely the full sample of respondents that gives substantive opinions. Chapter 3 showed that demographic groups already advantaged in the political process, such as males, whites, and those with higher levels of socioeconomic status, tend to be overrepresented in the ranks of opinion givers. Disadvantaged groups, in contrast, tend to be underrepresented among opinion givers due to higher rates of DK/NO responses.

At issue is whether giving DK/NO responses counts as a form of participation. If so, then there may be no reason to be concerned about the demographic makeup of opinion givers. One line of thought on this issue holds that giving respondents an opportunity to voice opinions satisfies the conditions of descriptive representation:

[T]he problem is not so much one of insuring that every citizen is politically active on every issue as it is one of insuring that all citizens have approximately equal opportunity to act, using "opportunity" in the realistic rather than the legalistic sense. If all citizens have an approximately equal opportunity to act, there is a high probability that those who do act will be roughly representative of those who do not. (Dahl and Lindblom 1953: 313)

In the typical case, all respondents in a survey sample are given an opportunity to present an opinion. The difficulty is in determining whether these opportunities are equal: Do abstainers voluntarily choose to withhold their participation, or are they unable to participate effectively because they lack necessary resources (see Verba 1996; Verba, Schlozman, and Brady 1995)?

Recent work has demonstrated that political information is a critical resource in the formation and expression of opinions in surveys (Delli Carpini and Keeter 1996). Two questions follow. The first is whether people rationally choose whether and how much to inform themselves. If the answer is yes, then differences in information levels may not be a normative problem: some people choose to inform themselves; some choose to do other things with their time. If people rationally decide to invest in political information, then the second question is whether the system of costs and benefits in which people make these rational decisions is normatively acceptable. If either one of these questions cannot be answered in the affirmative, then the skewed demographic makeup of opinion givers produces a representation problem, although the problem need not be significant or serious.

The answer to the first question is open to debate. The view associated with Anthony Downs (1957) that people rationally choose to invest in political information has been challenged on at least two fronts. First, it has been argued that some people, perhaps many, may be unable to inform themselves. This view, which dates back to the writings of Plato, can be found in work by Walter Lippmann (1922, 1925) and Joseph Schumpeter ([1942] 1976), among others. Lippmann argued that the ideal of the omnicompetent democratic citizen was a sham because our political opinions tend to be based on simplified mental pictures of the world derived from stereotypes, prejudice, and personal experience. With particular regard to ability, Lippmann pointed to the inherent limitations of symbolic language as a barrier to the accurate conveyance and interpretation of necessary facts (1922: Chapter 5). Schumpeter was even more blunt than Lippmann in asserting that "the typical citizen drops down to a lower level of mental performance as soon as he enters the political field. He argues and analyzes in a way which he would readily recognize as infantile within the sphere of his real interests. He becomes a primitive again" (262). The appropriate solution, in Schumpeter's view, was to define a "realist" model of democracy that depended on competition among elites rather than on the behaviors or attitudes of ordinary citizens.

A second criticism of the Downsian view comes from those who point out that a lack of opportunities can hinder people – who are otherwise able and willing – from developing or expressing informed opinions. In this view, individuals are not ultimately responsible for their lack of political engagement. For example, many people probably fail to become informed due to the absence of a social environment that encourages deliberation (Dewey 1927; Fishkin 1991, 1995; Jacobs and Shapiro 2000; although see Lupia and McCubbins 1998). Mass media messages may also divert people from reflecting on the structural causes of social problems and thus hinder activation of the public's latent political attitudes (Gamson 1992; Iyengar 1991). A third consideration consistent with this perspective emphasizes that modern democracies lack the socially inclusive political structures needed to foster critical thought (Bachrach 1975; DeLuca 1995; Habermas 1989). If want of opportunities is the problem, then political equality might be enhanced by removing the obstructions that hinder people from constructing and articulating opinions on political issues.

If many people are simply unable to generate informed opinions because of individual cognitive limitations, as Lippmann and Schumpeter suggest, then it is possible that no crisis of political equality exists. If such a pattern occurs on the grand scale that these authors also suggest, then democratic politics may be so inherently at odds with the ideal of political equality as to make the need for descriptive representation in collective preferences almost irrelevant. The second perspective suggests that barriers to political equality in opinion surveys may be problematic if opportunities to become informed can be provided at negligible social cost. In either of these cases, a lack of information cannot be said to result from choice alone.

The answer to the second question about rational ignorance is more straightforward. It has been pointed out that equal opportunity is sufficient to guarantee political equality only when the costs and benefits of participating are the same for all participants (Mansbridge 1983: 248–51). This, of course, is almost never the case. Critical resources that reduce the costs of political involvement are disbursed unevenly by civil institutions (Verba, Schlozman, and Brady 1995). The costs of participating in political life tend to rise in the absence of mobilization efforts, and these costs tend to fall heaviest on those who are already disadvantaged politically (Avey 1989; Kleppner 1982; Rosenstone and Hansen 1993). Studies of voting behavior suggest that the costs and benefits of electoral participation are shaped by legal and institutional barriers as well as by structural differences between political regimes (Avey 1989; Boyd 1989; Dalton 2002; Key 1950; Wolfinger, Glass, and Squire 1990; Wolfinger and Rosenstone 1980). In the same way, the costs of becoming informed are subsidized by a variety of factors, including the structure of media markets, the intensity of political campaigns, educational attainment, occupation, childhood socialization, interest in politics, trust in government, and sense of civic duty (Delli Carpini and Keeter 1996: Chapter 6). The movement toward direct democracy in large republics – such as the introduction of primary elections and referenda campaigns – may also differentially reduce or increase the incentives to become politically informed (Fishkin 1995: 23–5).

It thus appears that survey respondents are not provided, strictly speaking, with equal opportunities to express opinions. Other factors besides rational decisions may influence whether and how much a person becomes informed. While the normative status of the existing schedule of information costs is open to debate, it is certainly the case that information costs vary from person to person. In light of these complications, it cannot be said that survey results are representative (in a descriptive sense) if the pool of opinion givers is demographically biased.[4]

Whether this sort of misrepresentation is a problem depends in part on the standard by which one judges the responsibilities of citizens

---

[4] Of course, one need not rely on this line of reasoning to call the normative applicability of survey results into question. As Verba, Schlozman, and Brady (1995: 528) point out, "if the ultimate concern is equal governmental treatment of all, it is possible to treat as a red herring the issue of whether the underrepresentation of the disadvantaged in participatory input represents the exercise of free choice."

in democratic societies. While information costs vary from person to person, ill-informed citizens may nonetheless have a civic obligation to work harder than other people to attain a minimal level of political competence. Given the wide availability of nearly costless political information through broadcast services and social contacts, it may be that poorly informed citizens lack a reasonable excuse for their ignorance despite the special barriers they face in overcoming it. Seen in this light, the overrepresentation of certain groups in the ranks of opinion givers may not pose a problem worthy of concern.

While the nature of civic responsibility has a direct bearing on this issue, it is a topic much too broad to be dealt with adequately in these pages. But regardless of whether one sees citizens as having a duty to become informed, it is clear that the opportunities given survey respondents to express opinions are not equivalent. The weakness of the claim advanced by Verba and others is that it fails to appreciate the possibility of resource problems that affect who gives opinions in sample surveys. "Don't know" and "no opinion" responses do not necessarily represent participatory acts. Although surveys probably do tend to present a more representative portrait than most forms of nonelectoral participation, this appearance can be deceiving. The important issue is whether the group of actual opinion givers, rather than the sample of potential opinion givers, is statistically representative of a population. Survey researchers and pollsters are mistaken when they presume that accurate representation in the sample makes for representative expressions of collective opinion.

Equality at the Individual Level Is No Guarantee of Proportionality at the Group Level

It has been observed that persons are the standard units of analysis in democratic theory (Swabey 1937: 17). Concerns about political equality therefore have tended to focus on the relative weight given to individual votes or opinions, as in the famous "one person, one vote" rule.[5]

One might think that equality of influence at the individual level will always translate into proportionality of influence at the group level, but it does not. Dispersion effects – which occur when the collective opinion of one group is more lopsided than those of other groups – enhance

---

[5] Notable exceptions are in such cases as racial and gender equality, where the emphasis is often placed on aspects of equality among groups. Yet even these cases tend to fall back on the notion of equality among individuals to justify the need for equality among groups.

the influence of some groups over the shape of collective preferences in a way that dilutes the influence of other groups contributing to those preferences. The possibility that some group members may fail to give an opinion reinforces the potential for political inequality in the relative influence of group preferences. My primary concern in this study has been with that part of the larger set of dispersion effects which comes from group differences in political knowledge, but the ubiquitous presence of dispersion effects more generally is an issue that needs to be addressed in normative theories of aggregate decision making.

The problem is that the way votes and opinions are aggregated has a reciprocal influence on political equality. It is inappropriate to say that dispersion effects cause individual opinions to count unequally: each opinion is still an equal unit in the aggregation. But dispersion effects influence collective preferences nonetheless. Although each vote or opinion is equal in weight, the shared characteristics of these inputs can create power inequalities among groups when votes or opinions are aggregated together.[6] A similar situation exists in the case of gerrymandered legislative districts, which can be shaped to dilute artificially the strength of various demographic groups in a way that "simultaneously treat[s] voters both equally and unequally" (Beitz 1989: 8). In cases where all citizens have a common set of interests, this sort of power imbalance can be dismissed as irrelevant so long as all citizens act in accordance with those common interests (Mansbridge 1983, 1996). But in cases where citizens have competing interests, where interests are unclear, or where citizens unwittingly act against their interests, the disproportional influence of some groups over collective preferences is a potentially serious normative concern.

Despite claims that opinion surveys are representative and egalitarian, surveys can suffer from the same kinds of representation problems as other channels of public opinion. This is not to say that surveys tend to be as descriptively unrepresentative as other expressions of public opinion (for an analysis of these, see Rosenstone and Hansen 1993; Verba, Schlozman, and Brady 1995; Wolfinger and Rosenstone 1980). Opinion polls are still

---

[6] This is not to suggest that political equality is an irrelevant standard, although such problems point to inadequacies in traditional definitions of political equality as equal power over outcomes (Beitz 1989). My point is only that guaranteeing political equality for individuals does not ensure that the influence of groups is proportional to the number of their members.

likely to be the most descriptively representative. The important point is that survey results are not inevitably the most representative measure of public opinion. Despite appearances to the contrary, they may not be even moderately representative.

OPINION SURVEYS AS A CHANNEL FOR INTEREST REPRESENTATION

Descriptive representation and political equality remain important standards by which to evaluate measures of public opinion (Beitz 1989; Christiano 1996; Mansbridge 1999b). If survey results fail a test of these standards, then using them to represent a public's views may be rightly questioned. But it should often – and perhaps usually – be the case that opinion givers as a group will be fairly representative of the population from which they were drawn. Moreover, if our concern is the representation of interests rather than of voices, then a descriptively representative sample of opinions may not be necessary so long as opinion givers represent the interests of a population. What about the political uses of surveys in these situations?

Opinion surveys can provide detailed public input to the political process that is available in no other form. Elections have been the traditional means for ordinary citizens to communicate their needs, wants, and values to governments through the selection of representatives, but because surveys seem in many ways superior to elections as a means of finding out what the public wants, they have come to be used extensively in democratic politics. Opinion polls are appealing because they are scientific – hence at least potentially nonideological – and because they are explicitly designed to reveal the public's will (Herbst 1993). Compared to traditional means of discerning public opinion, often through interest group representatives and party organizations, sample surveys provide a more reliable and valid measure of citizen preferences. Opinion polls also are thought to provide a more accurate portrait of public opinion than elections because surveys subsidize the costs of expressing opinions: they bring the poll to the citizen rather than the other way around.[7] In this way surveys are thought to avoid the tendency, noted by students of political participation, for economically and socially underprivileged citizens to self-select out of the active electorate (Conway 1991; Dalton 2002;

---

[7] A similar argument can be applied to forms of group activity, such as protests and petition campaigns, which mobilize citizens for direct action (Manin 1997: 171–3).

Rosenstone and Hansen 1993; Verba and Nie 1972; Verba, Schlozman, and Brady 1995; Wolfinger and Rosenstone 1980). Most important, surveys provide an information-rich measure of public opinion that is both explicit and detailed. Elections, by contrast, send blunt messages that are easily contestable and which generally provide only a limited amount of unambiguous political information (Conley 2001; Verba, Schlozman, and Brady 1995). Only through the medium of opinion surveys can a representative sample of the mass public communicate precise messages to political leaders. It is another question whether those leaders ought to pay any special attention to survey results.

There have always been political thinkers who were enamored of the theory of democracy but less than enthusiastic about rule by the masses. Such concerns form the basis of liberal conceptions of democracy and underlie the theoretical rationale for interest representation. The U.S. Constitution, with its limits on direct political involvement by ordinary citizens, is a prime example of such thought. But along the way there have also been some who believed that the public should have a direct impact on the running of government. Liberal and populist conceptions of representation both agree that the role of democratic government is to discern the public good and put that good into practice. Both also stress the need to be aware of what the public wants, although one sees public opinion as a potential impediment to the public good while the other sees the public's opinion as its ultimate arbiter.

While both the delegate and the trustee models place a premium on knowing what the public thinks – even Edmund Burke believed that trustees should be responsive to problems (but not solutions) communicated by constituents – they differ fundamentally in the role they assign to ordinary citizens in the process of legislating the public good. With its emphasis on limiting citizen involvement to voting in elections, the trustee model suggests a descriptive role for opinion surveys. By *descriptive* I mean using opinion surveys to reveal the distribution of attitudes, opinions, and beliefs in the mass public for purely informational purposes. This is a common way for politicians, media, and citizens to interpret polling data: warts and all, for better or worse, here is what the public happens to believe. Some of the common descriptive uses of survey data include:

- *Interpreting election results and public reactions to political events.* One of the common descriptive uses of opinion surveys is in the analysis of election outcomes and public reactions to political events. Opinion surveys, particularly exit polls, can help journalists interpret elections by shedding light on the intentions of voters (Dionne 1992; Lavrakas and Traugott 2000). Surveys used in this way also provide valuable feedback to political actors. Richard Nixon, for example, used private polls to determine whether his personal appearances on behalf of Republican candidates had enough of an impact on local constituencies to merit the time and effort spent in these pursuits (Jacobs and Shapiro 1995).

- *Revealing the climate of opinion.* Surveys provide a unique insight into the climate of opinion in which elections and issues are contested (Geer 1996; Henn 1998; Lang and Lang 1983; Shamir and Shamir 2000). This insight allows political actors and private citizens to take the opinions of others into consideration when making political decisions. For example, the Nixon administration relied on private polls to gauge the impact of negative media coverage about the president (Jacobs and Shapiro 1995). Media polls are used in a similar manner. By providing insight into the public's concerns, media polls on political issues give journalists the ability to decipher the campaign strategies developed by politicians from private surveys (Kagay 2000).

- *Marketing political policies and decisions.* One of the most common descriptive uses of opinion polls by political elites is to devise effective communication strategies for marketing political decisions and ideas (Cohen 1997; Crespi 1989; Garment, Fallows et al. 1980; Jacobs and Shapiro 2000; Maravall 1999). Political pollsters constantly search for just the right language to explain policies to the public or to frame political ideas. In the words of Richard Nixon (quoted in Jacobs and Shapiro 1995), opinion polls "let us know what obstacles we confront in attempting to sell a policy." During the debate over health care reform in 1994, members of Congress often used polling data to identify public misconceptions and determine which policy issues the public needed to be "educated" about (Shapiro, Jacobs, and Harvey 1995). During the 1990–1 Persian Gulf Crisis, the Bush administration also used polls to good effect in finding ways to justify the use of military force against Iraq (Mueller 1994: 117–8). When it became obvious that the administration's rationale for sending troops to the Persian Gulf was failing to generate public support, pollsters correctly discerned that emphasizing the plight of American hostages and the threat of Iraq's nuclear capability could rally the public behind military action.

- *Identifying winning issues.* Besides using surveys to package political decisions, candidates and elected officials routinely develop campaign platforms based on polling data about constituent preferences. Restricting the number of issues discussed in a campaign and positioning the candidate in line with the policy preferences of the median voter can be a wise electoral strategy (Davis, Hinich, and Ordeshook 1970; Downs 1957; Geer 1996). Evidence from the Johnson administration suggests that the president brought his policy stances in line with private poll results for the 1964 campaign, but then shifted to more of an opinion leadership strategy once he was elected to office (Jacobs and Shapiro 1993). In reviewing archival evidence from those years, Jacobs and Shapiro discovered that "the objective [of the Johnson campaign] was to create political momentum behind programs that already enjoyed popular support in order to propel the White House's policy agenda after election day."[8]

The delegate model, by contrast, with its emphasis on maximizing civic participation in governance, suggests a prescriptive role for opinion surveys. By *prescriptive* I mean using opinion polls to identify a course of action for government to follow or to define the boundaries of permissible government activity. Put another way, prescriptive uses of opinion surveys treat collective preferences as if they were collective decisions. It is important to point out that the prescriptive use of opinion surveys is not limited to those who interpret them as representing something like the will of the people. While some may subscribe to George Gallup's view of surveys as "sampling referenda" (Gallup and Rae 1940), the prescriptive uses of opinion polls do not require political actors to grant them what James Fishkin (1995: 162) calls "recommending force." The prescriptive uses of opinion surveys may result less from populist convictions than from political expediency: there are times when decision makers find it necessary or useful to defer to majority opinion, however misinformed, illogical, or unreasonable they perceive it to be. An important reason for this behavior was articulated by V. O. Key in his classic *Public Opinion and American*

---

[8] A similar strategy was attempted by Republican candidates to the U.S. House of Representatives in the 1994 elections. Newt Gingrich and other Republican leaders of the House touted that each item in their "Contract with America" was favored by a majority of Americans. After their electoral landslide, House Republicans claimed a mandate and began voting on the Contract's provisions. Only after public opposition began to mount did it become apparent that the Republican leadership had been given bad advice regarding some of the Contract's items – pollster Frank Luntz eventually admitted that he had never tested many of the issues beyond measuring support for simple advertising slogans ("GOP Pollster Never Measured Popularity of 'Contract,' Only Slogans," *Chicago Tribune*, 12 November 1995, Sec. 1, p. 11).

Democracy. Key wrote that public opinion communicated through surveys acts minimally "as a system of dikes which channel public action or which fix a range of discretion within which government may act or within which debate at official levels may proceed" (Key 1961: 552).[9] In other words, the opinion climate in which elites operate provides a critical check on the exercise of political power: surveys communicate not only what the public wants, but more important, what it will accept. These two ways of interpreting opinion surveys – one as revealing the will of the people, the other as revealing the boundaries of the public's acquiescence – can be used to strategic advantage by elites who wield polls as political weapons.

The available evidence suggests that political leaders often put opinion surveys to prescriptive ends, finding them especially useful for:

- *Formulating policy*. One way the opinion climate operates is to influence the development of public policy. Although it may be unusual for bureaucrats (Rich 1981) or legislators (e.g., Crespi 1989; Jacobs and Shapiro 2000; Shapiro, Jacobs, and Harvey 1995) to consult surveys when drafting laws or regulations, polls can sometimes have a powerful influence on policy development. Several studies of elite decision making have concluded that opinion surveys may be especially influential in constraining the processes of formulating and implementing foreign policy initiatives (Foyle 1999; Hinckley 1992; Marjenhoff 1991; Mueller 1994; Nacos, Shapiro, and Isernia 2000; Russett 1990; Sobel 2001; Wittkopf 1990).[10] One study of the Reagan and Bush administrations found that while foreign policy officials recognized that the public was inattentive to world affairs, these officials nevertheless sought to bring public input into the decision-making process because they felt that foreign policy initiatives were unworkable without broad public support (Powlick 1990). This perceived need for public support was driven by an upswing in congressional attention to foreign policy issues, aggressive news coverage of foreign affairs, and the historical lessons of the Vietnam War. The desire to avoid public disapproval

---

[9] In the same vein as Key, James Stimson (1991: 19–23) conceives of a "zone of acquiescence" defined by the public's ideological mood, within which policy changes are too small to arouse public attention. In this perspective, once policy moves too far to the left or right of the public's mood, the public becomes engaged and politicians are brought back into line.

[10] However, other research has concluded that government officials systematically misperceive American public opinion on foreign policy (Kull and Destler 1999).

is another incentive for the executive branch to keep an eye on policy preferences revealed in opinion surveys (Foyle 1999; Sobel 2001). According to Clinton pollster Stanley Greenberg, President Clinton decided against using a value-added tax to finance health care reform after seeing private polls that showed such a tax would be unpopular (Berke 1993). Greenberg also noted that opinion surveys convinced the Clinton administration to defend the North American Free Trade Agreement and to stand up to Ross Perot in a televised debate featuring Vice President Gore.

- *Identifying issues that require political action.* While opinion polls may not be so helpful to politicians in crafting policy – not least because of interest group pressure and predictable voting blocs in legislatures (Garment, Fallows et al. 1980) – they seem to be helpful in identifying broad policy agendas for legislative action (Cohen 1997). This use is entirely consistent with the trustee model of representation.[11] The Reagan White House used surveys to decide which issues should be given top priority for administration action (Maltese 1994: 185, 212). It also appears that members of Congress used opinion polls to influence the agenda for health care reform during the 103rd Congress (Shapiro, Jacobs, and Harvey 1995). Media polls are especially useful for introducing issues into the political limelight, since they speed up the process of bringing the public's concerns to the attention of politicians (Cantril 1991: 223). Some pollsters feel that media surveys should be put to even greater use in this regard. For example, Bud Lewis (1991: 80), former director of the *Los Angeles Times* poll, argues that "media polls have an obligation to explore more frequently what the country wants as a national agenda."

- *Applying or resisting political pressure.* Even when political actors arrive at issue positions without consulting opinion surveys, they often use polls to leverage their views by generating the impression of widespread public support (Herbst 1993). Rather than merely selecting

---

[11] No less an authority than Edmund Burke, famous advocate of the representative as trustee, felt that representatives should pay close attention to the problems articulated by the people even while disregarding the solutions they might suggest (Burke 1969; Pitkin 1967: Chapter 8). In Burke's view, "[T]he people are the masters. They have only to express their wants at large and in gross. We [members of Parliament] are the expert artists; we are the skillful workmen, to shape their desires into perfect form, and to fit the utensil to the use.... They are the sufferers, to tell the symptoms of the complaint; but we know the exact seat of the disease, and how to apply the remedy" (quoted in Pitkin 1967: 184).

popular issues to run on, political actors may employ survey results in this way as a resource for applying or resisting political pressure. For example, the Nixon administration used private polls in a defensive strategy to undermine the credibility of published surveys. It also attempted (with some success) to manipulate opinion results by lobbying the Gallup and Harris organizations to include favorably worded questions in their nationally syndicated surveys (Jacobs and Shapiro 1996). Poll numbers revealing Americans' distrust of the Soviet Union were used to tactical advantage by U.S. negotiators for the SALT treaty as a way to convince Soviet negotiators of their resolve to obtain verification measures (Garment, Fallows et al. 1980: 143). Interest groups frequently bolster their arguments to policymakers by supporting them with private survey data. This gives interest groups a strategic advantage in lobbying because politicians are often unable independently to validate or challenge the information contained in interest group polls (Garment, Fallows et al. 1980; Wilcox 1966). In a similar fashion, media polls provide reporters with an independent source of information about public opinion that protects them from being "spun" by politicians (Kagay 1991). Opinion surveys are especially influential in settling conflicts within political organizations. One study found that opinion polls were considered a valuable tactical resource by White House personnel in the Carter and Reagan administrations when trying to resolve internal disputes over matters of political strategy (Mattes 1992).

• *Holding politicians accountable to the public's preferences.* Polls are frequently used by media organizations to gauge the accountability of elected officials (Mann and Orren 1992). For example, a recent lead article on the front page of the *New York Times* (Seelye 1995) opened with this paragraph: "After months of hot oratory about the evils of career politicians, the House voted squarely against the will of the people tonight and rejected four proposals that would have limited the number of terms its members could serve." The news peg for this article was provided by a media poll which showed that term limits had majority support among Americans. This is one example of a general trend for journalists to oversimplify opinion data in ways that suggest the public has well-defined attitudes toward public affairs (Brady and Orren 1992; Cantril 1991: 52; Germond 1980). There are several reasons why journalists tend to use survey data in prescriptive ways. One is poor training. As recently as 1986, 42% of newspapers that commissioned their own surveys left reporters to analyze poll results without the assistance of trained consultants (Demers 1987). Another is the need to communicate complex data to lay audiences (Brady and Orren 1992). Pollsters' press releases can contribute to this tendency by summarizing survey data in very simple terms such as "Americans want this" or "The public is against that" (for some examples, see Mitchell 1980: 70–1).

The political uses of opinion surveys are as varied as the reasons for using them. What is important for our purposes is that political actors often use surveys strategically *as if* they represented the active voice of the people, even when in fact they believe that surveys provide, at best, merely information about the people.

Two thought experiments can help to focus the normative issues surrounding the uses of opinion polls for interest representation. In the first scenario I test the prescriptive role of opinion surveys by examining whether the collective preference of a representative group of opinion givers who are fully informed can be interpreted as the active voice of the people. In the second scenario I test the descriptive role of opinion surveys by asking whether the collective opinion of a representative group of opinion givers who are poorly informed can be used merely as one of many pieces of strategic information in the process of making a political decision. Answers to both of these questions will illuminate how appropriate, useful, and valid survey data are for the uses to which they are commonly put.

Polls as the Active Voice of the People

It is clear that the presence of information effects complicates the use of survey measures to represent the active voice of the people. Information asymmetries among groups in a society can have a significant influence on the shape of collective opinion. This influence is likely to be important when groups in a polity have competing interests, as well as when interests are contested, unclear, or unknown. The potential for information effects can be ignored only in cases where interests are unitary and all citizens act in accordance with those interests, or when political knowledge relevant to an issue is distributed equally within a population. The case of unitary interests functions as an ideal that is probably unrealizable in practice. The case of equal knowledge can be attainable but may be far from optimal: political information can be evenly distributed among groups when levels of knowledge are abysmally low.

In only two situations will information effects have no bearing at all on the quality of collective preferences. The first is when a population is fully informed. Previous chapters have used this term provisionally in relation to a specific index of political knowledge. But here, in a more general sense, by fully informed I mean that all information essential to understanding an issue is at uniformly high levels among the various groups in a population. The second situation, unrealizable in practice, is when a population is enlightened. By enlightened I mean that all information relevant to an issue is perfect, complete, and distributed at uniformly high levels among the various groups in a population. This definition of an enlightened population follows the thought experiments put forward by political philosophers who define interests as the choices people would make if they had full knowledge of the resulting consequences (Connolly 1972; Dahl 1989: 180–1, 358 fn. 3; Mansbridge 1983: 24–6). None of these philosophers expects any population (or individual) to achieve this standard, but only to try to approach it.

Because no individual or population can ever be fully enlightened, and because few individuals or populations are ever fully informed, we should always be wary of dignifying any collective preference with the term "will of the people," a phrase that suggests absolute validation. Several specific problems arise when we try to interpret public opinion measures in such a way.

No formal consent given by the population to be represented. No existing democratic polity consents or authorizes itself to be represented by a survey sample. In modern democracies, a public is taken to authorize its representatives and consent to be governed through elections. By contrast, in Athens and some other ancient democracies the public was taken to have authorized governance in part through representative bodies selected by lot. Several writers have suggested that modern democracies could benefit from such an arrangement (e.g., Dahl 1989; Fishkin 1991, 1995). As it stands, however, any interpretation of poll results as "the people's will" must come to grips with the fact that a public's randomly selected "representatives" can only informally represent larger groups in society. In a sense, these people unwittingly authorize themselves to stand for larger groups in society when they agree to participate in an opinion poll.

Respondents may be unaware that they represent others. When casting a vote in an election, voters understand that their actions are essentially political in nature. But because they are not formally authorized to represent, survey respondents are often unaware that their views will be used to represent the views of others and that their opinions could carry weight in the political process. Respondents might well answer a question differently if they saw themselves as representatives. Many respondents do answer differently depending on whether questions are seen as merely moral issues or as obviously political issues (Bourdieu 1979). For example, female survey respondents who had higher levels of education appeared to interpret poll questions about the hearings of Supreme Court nominee Clarence Thomas in the larger context of women's rights issues. Women with lower levels of education seemed to view these same questions as soliciting their own personal judgments about whether Thomas was guilty or innocent of sexual harassment (Herbst 1992).

Survey respondents can be thought of as what Jane Mansbridge (1983: 250–1) calls "informal representatives." These are people who unintentionally represent larger constituencies because of their voluntary participation in a political function, as the citizens who show up for a town meeting informally represent all the town's residents. As Mansbridge points out, the problem with informal representatives is that they may feel no obligation to act in the interests of others and are not held accountable for their actions. In the special case of sample surveys, opinion givers may not even be aware that they will be counted as representing larger groups in a society. Because the opinions given by respondents might change if they were aware of their status as representatives or knew a survey was to be used for political purposes, the fact that many respondents may be oblivious to the potential uses of their opinions presents a serious problem for interpreting survey results as the active voice of the people.

Survey results are not deliberative. At first glance it might seem that opinion surveys could fulfill the role assigned to legislatures by J. S. Mill in his *Considerations on Representative Government*. In Mill's view, the role of a legislature is to provide information about the public rather than to act or govern. The problem with using surveys in this way, as often has been pointed out, is that polls are not deliberative, and talking is exactly what Mill wanted legislatures to do. Jürgen Habermas (1989: 220–1; 1996a: 336) goes so far as to deny that the views collected by opinion polls can even be considered public opinions. In his view, individual public opinions must be formed consciously through active cognition rather than as unconscious reactions to symbols, and must be refined through a process of public debate. Because this rarely happens on a mass scale, Habermas dismisses the opinions of modern polities as "acclamation-prone," with today's democratic political systems giving rise to "an opinion climate instead of a public opinion" (1989: 217; for a more charitable interpretation of this development, see Manin 1997: 218–34).

Deliberation is often believed to perform several vital functions that, at least in theory, help to improve the quality of individual and collective preferences (Barber 1984; Fishkin 1991; Habermas 1996b; Nino 1996; although see Lupia 2002; Mansbridge 1999a). Ideally, uncoerced public deliberation could create a complete information environment in which the better argument prevails. Deliberation also can lead people to discover their interests as they move away from providing "top of the head" opinions to grapple seriously with political choices (Gastil 2000; Gastil and Dillard 1999; Price, Cappella, and Nir 2002). Because discussion will tend to clarify the root issues of a controversy, deliberation will sometimes create consensus as well as activate and create norms that orient participants to see themselves as part of larger communities rather than as isolated individuals (Gastil, Deess, and Weiser 2002; Miller 1992). These effects of deliberation were graphically demonstrated at the 1996 National Issues Convention, in which many participants in this deliberative poll reported changing their opinions through the process of discussing issues in small groups. The influence of deliberation also may have had led to significant changes in collective opinion on several issues (McCombs and Reynolds 1999). For all of its limitations, the results of this public experiment suggest that typical surveys provide an unrefined and therefore incomplete sense of the public will.[12]

Surveys create a public voice that is reactive rather than proactive.
Another difficulty with using opinion surveys as a measure of a public's will is that the range of issues over which a public can voice its views

---

[12] This is not to say that deliberation necessarily produces a "better" or more accurate group of opinions. Deliberative settings in the real world are probably never free of coercion, and the people who involve themselves in real-world deliberation are often grossly unrepresentative of the populations affected by their decisions (Bryan 1999). Moreover, arbitrary interpersonal dynamics within the deliberative setting can have undesirable effects on the development of consensus. This is also not to say that the results of opinion surveys are devoid of deliberative content. Page and Shapiro (1992: 362–6) suggest that the public engages in what they call "collective deliberation." The defining features of collective deliberation are its decentralization and its division of intellectual labor among various political actors. Especially important in this regard is the process of public deliberation occurring among and within mass media organizations, as was evidenced in news coverage of the Los Angeles riots of 1992, the opposition to Zoe Baird's nomination as U.S. attorney general, and U.S. involvement in the 1991 Gulf War (Page 1996; Page and Tannenbaum 1996).

is limited to whatever questions pollsters happen to ask. The problem, as Benjamin Ginsberg (1986) points out, is that "polling can create a misleading picture of the agenda of public concerns, for what appears significant to the agencies sponsoring polls may be quite different from the concerns of the general public" (81). A similar argument is made by Pierre Bourdieu (1979). Since surveys are sponsored by a variety of academic, business, media, and governmental interests, questions lacking immediate relevance to these sponsors will not normally be asked. Once in a while, however, rogue questions find their way into opinion surveys. In the days following the 1980 election of Ronald Reagan to the presidency, pollsters from CBS/*New York Times* asked a national sample whether they agreed that "The country needs more radical change than is possible through the ballot box." Incredibly, 6 out of 10 of those polled agreed with the statement. Yet the meaning of this collective preference remains unclear, for while it could be read variously as desiring revolution, guardianship, or merely spiritual renewal, the sponsors of the survey did not follow up on this question. Nor, apparently, has the question been repeated since.

By bracketing the scope of public opinion, polls may misrepresent the real concerns of many citizens who are denied a critical forum for their views (Lipari 2001). A similar argument could be made against the electoral system, which produces slates of candidates that are not themselves initially selected by the public. Party organizations and interest groups have a great deal of latitude in choosing campaign issues and candidates for office (e.g., Beck and Sorauf 1992; Eismeier and Pollock 1986; Ferguson 1991; Ferguson and Rogers 1986; Hall and Wayman 1990; Herrnson 1986; Przeworski, Stokes, and Manin 1999). Parties and many interest groups, of course, often adapt to public pressure over time. The degree to which such organizations depend on mass support provides a mechanism for public accountability, however imperfect that mechanism may be. Survey outfits, however, tend to be accountable only to their clients and sponsors (Miller 1995). The only obvious exception to this trend is polling done by media organizations: as mass media outlets compete for market shares, the polls they sponsor (like the stories they report) will tend to be geared toward the perceived interests of mass audiences (cf. Lewis 2001). Hence some survey organizations, at least, will be oriented like parties and interest groups to the needs, wants, and values of various segments of the mass public (cf. Manin 1997: 230). Yet even such an orientation cannot compensate for the inherent limitations of survey methods: surveyed opinions cannot be anything other than reactions to questions posed by others.

Aggregation procedures produce results that may be inconsistent with individual preferences. Two centuries of research into the mathematical properties of collective choices has shown that no method for aggregating preferences can satisfy even the minimal requirements one would wish for democratic rule (Arrow 1963; Black 1958; Mueller 1989; Riker 1982). In what is widely considered a classic in the field, William Riker (1982) writes that

> We should never take the results of any [aggregation] method always to be a fair and true amalgamation of voters' judgments. Doubtless the results often are fair and true; but, unfortunately, we almost never know whether they are or are not. Consequently, we should not generally assume that the methods produce fair and true amalgamations. We should think of the methods, I believe, simply as convenient ways of doing business, useful but flawed. This gives them all a place in the world, but it makes none of them sacrosanct. (113)

The sobering conclusion, says Riker, is that "we do not and cannot know what the people want" (238). Some scholars disagree, arguing that it is possible to design a robust voting system based on majority decisions over binary choices (Radcliff 1992, 1993) or to use a process of deliberation to select appropriate decision rules (Miller 1992).

Arrow cycling and other problems of social choice present important challenges to democratic theory, but what is possible may well be improbable, and imperfection should not be confused with chaos. A great many of the problems discovered by the social choice literature should be fairly (and perhaps extremely) rare in practice, in no small part because few people appear to have political preferences as rigid and well formed as this literature often presumes (Bartels 1998). Given what we now know about the psychology of preferences, the translation of latent to actual opinion through the framing of political choices (Entman and Herbst 2001; Key 1961; Schattschneider 1960; Zaller 1998) may be much more critical to democratic justice than the baroque curiosities of social choice theory. Nonetheless, the decision rules most commonly applied to survey data – majority and plurality rules using first preferences – have well-known flaws (see Mueller 1989; Riker 1982). The influence of dispersion effects in survey data adds to the potential that collective choices may not accurately reflect individual preferences.

These problems all point to the conclusion that even under ideal conditions, survey results cannot be equated in simple terms with the active voice of the people. Some of these objections are rooted in contemporary practices and could therefore be addressed through changes to the current ways of doing things. Democracies could legitimize representation by lot (Manin 1997), pollsters could instill opinion givers with the sense that they represent others; and pollsters could also make the survey process more deliberative.[13] Other problems are less correctable. Even when a population is fully informed and properly represented, it will always be impossible to determine whether its preferences are enlightened. Lacking control of its own agenda, the public voice as it appears in opinion polls may be distorted in a myriad of ways. And all known aggregation methods are liable to return a bad result from time to time.

Polls as Information about the People

If opinion surveys are likely to produce misleading statements of a public's will, then it would seem by default that polls must be used for informational purposes only. The legitimate political uses of polling might therefore include predicting vote intentions, selecting candidates worthy of support based on their popularity, planning campaign strategies, and designing legislative agendas. There is good evidence that political leaders often use survey data in precisely these ways (e.g., Clymer 1993; Crespi 1989; Jacobs and Shapiro 2000; Kolbert 1992; Shapiro, Jacobs, and Harvey 1995; Traugott 1992). Opinion polls used in these ways are given no exalted status as the people's voice. From a descriptive (as opposed to a prescriptive) standpoint, surveys merely relate what a population thinks, regardless of whether its preferences are uninformed or mistaken.

Using polls in this way might seem to be especially appropriate in cases where collective opinions are obviously influenced by information effects. For example, examining the collective preference in Figure 3.1 reveals that the appearance of majority support for more government stems from the lopsided distribution of opinions among ill-informed respondents. While the existence of information effects in these data undermines the possibility that the will of the people is to want more government services, knowing this does not mean that office seekers should simply disregard opinion surveys dealing with the scope of government. To the contrary, people seeking public office may want to shape their campaign platforms and communications strategies in ways that challenge or feed fuel to this

---

[13] Fishkin's work on deliberative polls aims to realize precisely these goals.

ill-informed opinion. Educating or pandering to the public in this way constitutes a descriptive use of opinion data.

The problem with using collective opinions to merely describe the characteristics of a population – even if those opinions are from a descriptively representative group of opinion givers – is that survey results are almost never merely informative. On the contrary, polling data are often used to influence decisions of one kind or another, and the political consequences of information-in-use are what complicate matters.

When survey results or other measures of public opinion are taken into account in the decision making processes of political actors, they can be seen as a proxy for the support or pressure that a public might manifest at the next election. In this sense, political actors who take counsel in survey results engage in what Jane Mansbridge (1996) calls "prospective representation" (see also Arnold 1993; Key 1961). Prospective representation means representing the preferences a public is likely to have at some point in the future. It occurs when political leaders take the anticipated reactions of their constituents into consideration when making political decisions. Several studies have explored how the anticipated reactions of constituents play into the decisions of political elites (Davison 1983; Fenno Jr. 1978; Herrera, Herrera, and Smith 1992; Mayhew 1974) as well as how this behavior among individual decision makers can explain the policy output of political institutions (Erikson, MacKuen, and Stimson 2002; Erikson, Wright, and McIver 1993: 247; Fiorina 1977; Stimson, MacKuen, and Erikson 1995; see also Page and Shapiro 1983; Wlezien 1995b). Contrary to theories of democracy that highlight the role of elections in political representation, these studies suggest that ongoing responsiveness between elections is a primary mode through which representation occurs. For example, when collective public opinion shifted more than a few percentage points, in nearly half of the cases documented by Page and Shapiro (1983) governmental policy soon came to reflect those changes.

To the extent that polls influence political decisions through the anticipatory reactions of political elites, it is inappropriate to think of them in descriptive terms alone. Indeed, only when there is no potential at all for a political decision to be swayed by survey results can information about a population's preferences be seen in purely descriptive terms. Political actors thus may unconsciously engage in a form of representative activity whenever they take survey data into account in the process of acting on behalf of others.

RECOGNIZING QUALITY IN OPINION SURVEYS

The opinion survey is one channel for political representation, however imperfect or informal. It may be inappropriate to think of survey results as the active voice of the people, but neither do they provide merely information about the people. Polls are at once descriptive and prescriptive; they produce both information and voice.

The critical issue thus becomes the quality of interest representation afforded by a given survey measure. While one could measure the quality of a collective opinion in many ways – for example, by comparing surveyed opinion with expert opinion, or by judging how accessible or salient the topic of a survey question is to average citizens, or by measuring the stability of opinion over time (see Price and Neijens 1997) – I have argued that one particularly useful standard is how close a collective preference comes to being fully informed. Collective preferences may be considered fully informed when they meet any of several criteria: when essential information is at uniformly high levels for all groups (the ideal case, but perhaps rare in practice), when simulated measures of fully informed opinion are consistent with measures of surveyed opinion, or when there is no substantial difference in the opinions of knowledgeable and ill-informed people who share the same demographic characteristics (see also Bartels 1990). Although this concept of quality does not approach the enlightened preferences standard in democratic theory, it is reasonably possible to operationalize it in quantitative terms. By this definition, a higher-quality collective preference is one that approximates what fully informed opinion might look like; a lower-quality preference is one that varies substantially from fully informed opinion. Survey results can thus be arranged on a hypothetical continuum from highest to lowest likelihood of interest representation, with those on the low end furthest removed from the active voice ideal, and those on the high end relatively more likely to provide good information about the people.

Use of this fully informed criterion does not eliminate dispersion effects by any means, nor does it guarantee equality of influence among individual respondents. Collective opinions meeting this standard may exhibit substantial inequality among groups and individuals. The absence of a substantial information effect in a collective opinion suggests only that such inequality may have little bearing on the shape of the collective preference.

Calling this standard a definition of quality is perhaps a misleading choice of words, because there is no reason to expect that high quality collective preferences – as defined here, any surveyed collective opinion that is essentially identical to a hypothetical fully informed collective opinion – are also enlightened preferences. In the 1992 ANES, for example, support for term limits on members of the U.S. Congress ran 81% in surveyed opinion and 80% in fully informed opinion, with less than 4% of respondents exhibiting inconsistent preferences. A similar pattern is found with the same question in the 1996 ANES data. Aside from the fact that a constitutional amendment would be required to put such a plan into effect – a key point surely missed by many supporters – it is not at all clear that term limits are either necessary (Stimson 1999) or effective for producing the various changes that proponents expect. For example, while the introduction of term limits seems to have increased the competitiveness of state legislative elections (Daniel and Lott 1997) and shifted legislative attention away from securing pork and onto producing state policy (Carey, Niemi, and Powell 1998), such changes have also had many unanticipated consequences, including increasing the number of costly special elections (Caress 1996) and diminishing the number of female legislators (Caress 1999). It is likely that states with term limits will not only have less power in Congress than states without them (Fett and Ponder 1993), but that term limits should tend to reduce the overall quality of representatives elected to legislatures (Mondak 1995a). In short, despite the fact that collective preferences on this issue are essentially free from information effects, the possibility that such preferences are enlightened seems highly unlikely given the decidedly mixed evidence on the benefits of term limits.

As this example makes clear, I am suggesting that the fully informed standard provides a necessary condition for collective interest representation, but not a sufficient condition. In terms of practical application, the percentage of inconsistent preferences or the size of gaps between surveyed and fully informed opinions can be used to assess only the likelihood that a collective preference *misrepresents* collective interests, with collective opinions having larger gaps being especially unlikely to represent collective interests. However, the opposite does not hold: the absence of such gaps should not be taken as a sign of enlightened preferences. We can think of this as a "negative" standard because it is only useful for identifying preferences with obvious representation problems brought about by information effects. It is of no help in identifying in a positive sense which preferences are closer to the enlightened preferences ideal.

The question that this criterion addresses is therefore not whether or when polls in fact represent the will of the people. To the contrary, the question is whether or when polls represent good information about the people, and the presence of substantial inequalities or information effects should tend to diminish this possibility. In this context, good information about the people means collective preferences that, if not descriptively representative, at least show signs of having a reasonable interest-bearing potential. Collective opinions with high levels of inequality and large information effects have particularly serious representation problems; those with either high levels of depletion and small information effects or minimal depletion and large information effects remain somewhat problematic; and collective opinions with little inequality and small information effects are least troubled by obvious representation problems.

To be sure, this criterion for quality in collective opinion is controversial. It is predicated on what Daniel Yankelovich (1991) calls "the epochal fallacy of our times," the notion "that good information automatically leads to good judgment" (10). He writes:

It would be perverse to deny that information is relevant to the quality of public opinion. But in a professional lifetime devoted to its study, I have come to the conclusion that equating quality opinion with being well informed is a serious mistake. Obviously, information plays some role in shaping public opinion. But often it is a minor role. To assume that public opinion is invariably improved by inundating people with information grossly distorts the role of information. A society operating on this assumption misconstrues the nature and purpose of public opinion in a democracy. (16)

Yankelovich is certainly correct in arguing that the informed opinion of policy experts is a poor standard against which to judge the quality of a public's collective preferences. Yet the definition of quality that he presents as a corrective to this view is normatively unsatisfying. Quality cannot simply be equated with "stable, consistent, and responsible" opinion, as Yankelovich suggests (Yankelovich 1991: 42; cf. Bennett 1990; Jacobs and Shapiro 2000: Chapter 9; Page and Shapiro 1992: 383–90). Measuring the quality of opinions only in terms of stability over time, internal consistency with other opinions a person holds, or "responsibility," by which Yankelovich means opinions that have emerged from a process of deliberation,[14] draws attention away from the content of those

---

[14] One problem with Yankelovich's emphasis on "responsible" opinion is that the political deliberation occurring in existing democracies is not the same as deliberation in a Habermasian "ideal speech situation" in which power is absent (Habermas 1975, 1984). Because power inequalities are always present in "real-world" deliberations, the process of discussing political views and exposing them to criticism is unlikely to produce a

opinions. From the standpoint of democratic theory, the defining quality of an opinion ought to be how accurately it reflects a person's interests.[15] As one of the most compelling definitions of interests to date is based on the preferences people would hold if they were fully informed about the consequences of their choices, it is difficult to envision an acceptable definition of quality in which information plays a minor role. Even if a collective preference is stable, consistent, and deliberative, it can hardly be considered a quality opinion if it misrepresents the interests of opinion givers.

By presenting this definition of quality in collective preferences, I am not suggesting that quality opinion should be interpreted as the will of the people. At best, the standard of fully informed opinion that I suggest provides only a rough measure of information effects, one that is likely to be flawed in a variety of ways. Yet some operational definition of quality is needed because, for better or worse, opinion polls are used extensively in the political process and their use is unlikely to be curtailed in the foreseeable future. As Lawrence Jacobs (1992) has pointed out, the more governments try to change public opinion, the more they become responsive to it. Without a set of criteria that can be used to identify survey results with obvious representation problems, all polls stand on equal ground because marginal percentages provide no obvious way to tell whether a collective preference represents what a public might really want. The primary value of this standard is to clarify when collective preferences might be based on thoughtful consideration of the issues. If opinion surveys are going to be used in the political process, this is valuable information for decision makers.

CAN SURVEYS BE DESIGNED TO IMPROVE THE QUALITY OF COLLECTIVE OPINIONS?

The low levels and uneven social distribution of political knowledge cause the results of many survey questions to fall short of the quality standard suggested here. If it were possible to design surveys to minimize the potential for information effects, the interpretation of survey results could be

---

"rational will" that reveals true consensus on common interests (Habermas 1975: 107–8).

[15] Although, of course, the liberal or subjective view holds that interests are revealed in and defined by expressed opinions. For problems with this view, see Bachrach 1975; Balbus 1971; Connolly 1972; Sunstein 1991.

greatly simplified. Instead of comparing the opinions of ill-informed respondents with those of knowledgeable respondents, one might construct
surveys in a way that would help to equalize the information resources
available to opinion givers.

Two potential remedies for information effects are unlikely to help
matters. First, polling organizations could design questions to reduce the
cognitive demands placed on survey participants, thereby making it easier for ill-informed respondents to provide meaningful opinions. Recent
work on question wording and order effects suggests that careful attention to survey design might help to minimize what may be meaningless
and apparently unmindful responses to the survey stimulus. But as shown
in Chapter 5, some of the most frequently discussed sources of response
effects appear to have little influence on the size of the gaps between surveyed and fully informed opinion. In light of these findings, it appears
that changes in questionnaire design may have limited potential to reduce
substantially the size of information effects. Second, survey organizations
might provide respondents with relevant facts and figures in the course
of the survey itself. Yet, as pointed out in Chapter 4, the survey environment is an ersatz context for the discovery of political interests. Since
this approach neglects the social construction of interests and the social
transmission of information, there is little reason to expect the resulting
collective opinion to be a better estimate of a population's fully informed
or enlightened preference.

A third potential countermeasure to information effects has been tested
extensively and found effective in raising the average information level of
opinion givers. It is also the most common method for pollsters to create
a pool of opinion givers who know what they're talking about: encouraging large numbers of people to give "don't know" and "no opinion"
responses. The rationale for this view is provided by studies which show
that between 20% and 30% of respondents will provide opinions on issues
they know nothing about unless encouraged to give a DK/NO response
(Bishop, Oldendick, and Tuchfarber 1983; Schuman and Presser 1981:
158). This behavior seems to be driven by the demand characteristics
of the survey interview. Less knowledgeable respondents apparently feel
pressured to answer questions even when they are unsure of their opinions
(Bishop, Tuchfarber, and Oldendick 1986). Using filter questions or other
means to encourage DK/NO responses thus can be seen as providing a
dual benefit: they let unopinionated respondents off the hook and thereby
increase the overall quality of collective opinion.

The findings from previous chapters provide mixed support for this view. Information effects were found to stem largely from the differences in opinion between knowledgeable and poorly informed opinion, but questions with higher levels of DK/NO responses did not tend to have smaller information effects than questions in which nearly all respondents give opinions. This is partly because such questions place greater cognitive demands on all respondents, thereby increasing the amount of random noise in substantive opinions, and partly because the opinions of knowledgeable respondents as a group tend already to resemble simulated measures of fully informed collective opinion. This latter finding suggests that surveyed opinion could be made to match fully informed opinion by intentionally increasing the amount of demographic misrepresentation in the pool of opinion givers through DK/NO prompts and filter questions (however, other means of achieving the same goal may produce less misrepresentation; see Adler 1984). At the same time, collective preferences with higher levels of respondent depletion are much less accurate in forecasting surveyed opinion trends than more inclusive measures of collective opinion. While these findings suggest no clear conclusions about whether filtering out all but the most knowledgeable respondents might produce higher quality collective preferences, they strongly suggest that the goals of descriptive representation and representation of interests may be at odds with one another.

In this light, the core question becomes whether the goal of descriptive representation can be sacrificed to achieve the greater goal of interest representation. The use of filter questions and "don't know" inducements to purge a sample of spurious opinions almost inevitably increases the degree of demographic misrepresentation and political inequality in the pool of opinion givers. The higher the rate of DK/NO responses, the higher the likelihood that descriptive representation and political equality will be compromised in survey results.

Although this sort of demographic misrepresentation may be seen today as a cause for concern, this has not always been the case. Electoral safeguards designed to filter out irresponsible and ill-conceived votes were widely approved of and even encouraged throughout the history of democratic rule (Manin 1997). This was especially true in what David Held (1987) calls "protective democracy," the liberal model of governance developed and refined in the writings of Locke, Montesquieu, Madison, Bentham, and John Stuart Mill. The basic idea was that certain groups of people should be excluded from the suffrage so that the common interests of society could be protected and discerned through the electoral process.[16] This is the model of democracy on which the United States was founded. The U.S. Constitution, by limiting direct elections to the House of Representatives and by leaving the qualifications of voters to be determined by the states, embodies the idea that the most informed and responsible members of society should represent the public rather than have the entire public represent itself.

The idea of counting some opinions as more valid than others thus has deep roots in democratic theory. Seen from this perspective, the use of filter questions and other means to increase the number of DK/NO responses can be seen as a reasonable and perfectly defensible way to refine measures of public opinion. As Bishop, Tuchfarber, and Oldendick (1986) observe, "The alternative is to create a spurious form of representativeness by minimizing the 'don't knows'." The problem is that maximizing the "don't knows" comes necessarily at the expense of political equality, and the political justification for this sacrifice passed away in the United States with the dawn of the Progressive movement in the early part of the 20th century. While the practice of filtering ill-informed respondents from the ranks of opinion givers is consistent with some models of democracy, it can also be seen as an anachronism at odds with the democratic forms and institutions in use today. The purpose behind restricting suffrage and siphoning off the least opinionated respondents is the same: to increase the quality of public opinion. Whether by literacy tests, poll taxes, and property requirements or by filter questions and DK/NO prompts, the effect is also the same: some groups of people with distinctive political interests inevitably lose representation within collective preferences.

Whether filter questions and other inducements should be used to create a relatively better-informed group of opinion givers depends on whether the fairness of the process or the quality of the result is held to be most important. If political equality is deemed most important, as it seems to be in many democratic societies today, then filter questions and "don't know" inducements should be avoided.[17] If the quality of opinion is most important, where by quality one means taking into account

---

[16] Rather than limit suffrage, Mill, in a twist, concluded that certain groups of intelligent and civic-minded people needed to be given extra votes. For an analysis of this view, see Beitz 1989: Chapter 2.

[17] I am not suggesting that *all* filter questions should be avoided. For example, filtering questions are often used intentionally to isolate a subsample of respondents with particular demographic or attitudinal characteristics. This conclusion only applies to efforts at producing a group of opinion givers that is especially knowledgeable.

only the opinions of minimally informed respondents, then the overrepresentation of certain demographic groups containing high proportions of well-informed opinion givers may pose no particular problem.

This tradeoff is complicated by the need to consider the representation of political interests, which takes us a step beyond mere descriptive representation of various demographic groups. If a situation arises in which all groups in a society share the same political interests, then political equality in the representation of preferences is less important. If, however, the political interests of two or more groups are in conflict, then democratic legitimacy rests on some approximation of political equality. When it is not clear whether interests are common or conflicting, then it must be assumed that political equality matters. And when political equality matters, the need for fair procedures disqualifies using the most knowledgeable citizens to define a population's preference.

This concern leads me to weigh the fairness of the process more heavily than the apparent quality of the result. Improving the quality of collective opinion by undermining descriptive representation and political equality – for this is often the result when respondents are encouraged to give nonsubstantive answers – can have serious drawbacks when survey results are used in the political process. Because the quality of collective opinion can be measured by any of several methods as the degree to which surveyed opinion approaches some semblance of fully informed opinion, it is unnecessary to use filter questions and other inducements to create a relatively more informed and strongly opinionated pool of opinion givers.

It may be possible to make the results of opinion surveys what many want them to be: wise, informed, and oriented to the common good. But to do this would require atavistic violations of democratic and liberal principles. We are left with polls that often fall short in quality but that may convey accurate information about a population's preferences, and a definition of fully informed opinion with which to test the quality of those preferences.

CONCLUSION

The low levels and uneven social distribution of political knowledge can be dismissed as a normative problem in only two ideal situations: when information costs as well as opportunities to become informed are the same for all members of a population, or when a population has common interests and all members give opinions in accordance with those interests. The first situation satisfies the conditions for political equality and descriptive representation in opinion surveys, the second treats these issues as irrelevant. But the first is unlikely to occur in mass politics, and there is no way to be sure if the second is ever the case. The critical question thus falls back to whether it is possible to identify the interests of all citizens. If this is not possible, then any inequities in the social distribution of political knowledge undermine the claim that survey results are necessarily egalitarian and representative.

Even when information asymmetries are minimal, opinion surveys remain unreliable indicators of the public will. But neither do they provide merely descriptive information about the public. Surveys and other measures of public opinion often become transformed through the anticipatory reactions of leaders into informal channels for political representation. Thus neither the "active voice" nor the "information only" perspective provides a satisfactory model for how opinion surveys should be used in the political process.[18]

In this light, I argue that the political uses of survey results should be guided by how well those results represent a public's fully informed preferences. Although this approach does nothing to correct representation problems, by calling attention to such problems it allows consumers of polling data to make informed decisions about how best to treat such data.

By drawing attention to the differences between surveyed and fully informed opinion, I am not advocating that estimates of fully informed opinion be used to guide policy, or that the opinions of the most informed citizens be given special consideration. The potential benefits of having collective opinion disproportionately influenced by informed opinion givers must be balanced against the likelihood that such measures will fail to represent all relevant interests. I am inclined to agree with Peter Bachrach (1975: 43) that "the task of determining the latent interests of the inarticulate rests exclusively with the inarticulate themselves." An appropriate response to information asymmetries is not to attend to paternalistic measures of what the public might want if it knew better, or to consult only the most knowledgeable citizens, but rather to encourage all citizens to discover and act on their interests. Until such time as this ideal becomes realized, measures of fully informed opinion can best be used to indicate when collective preferences are likely to be biased by information effects.

---

[18] A related perspective on limitations with both the trustee and delegate models, as applied to government responsiveness to surveyed preferences, is given in Jacobs and Shapiro 2000: Chapter 9.

8

What Surveys Can Tell Us about Public Opinion

> Is public opinion a beloved but unreal myth like the unicorn? Or a thing
> out there in the garden like an elephant, of which sight-impaired, competing
> methodologists measure different parts? Or a fuzzy set of probabilities like
> the electron, both wave and particle, perhaps of inherently uncertain loca-
> tion? Or does it include all of the above?...If we want to measure public
> opinion, we need to decide which of several meanings we are interested in.
>
> – Allen Barton (1998)

> The problem is not what public opinion is, but what different sets of beliefs
> lead us to do with it in the development and conduct of systems of politics.
>
> – David Minar (1960: 44)

When V. O. Key (1966) described the public as an "echo chamber," he
underscored the importance of political leadership to the quality of the
public's collective decisions. So long as the public was provided with good
information and clear alternatives, Key argued, it would make reasonable
and even responsible choices. This book has argued to the contrary that
the public as an echo chamber is not acoustically perfect, and that the
quality of collective preferences is not merely a function of the leadership
and information provided to citizens. The low levels and uneven social distribution of political knowledge ensure that collective preferences reflect
some voices better than others, and despite the optimism of revisionist
arguments to the contrary, the mass public is often unable to compensate
for its inattentiveness to politics.

The presence of information effects calls into question many of the
ways public opinion data are used by political leaders, journalists, and
citizens. Since the impact of information effects is observable and to some

extent predictable, it may be possible to improve on the standard uses of survey data by flagging those collective preferences with obvious representational problems. But the weight of evidence developed in preceding chapters also suggests the need to revise our expectations about the kind of contribution that collective preferences might provide to democratic politics. While some might conclude in light of these findings that surveys hinder rather than help democratic rule, it is also possible that opinion surveys are better suited to serve different roles or to provide other kinds of information than we seem to expect of them.

This final chapter summarizes the conclusions of this study and suggests ways that survey organizations, political leaders, and news outlets can change the manner in which they administer, interpret, and report opinion polls to address the impact of information effects. It then turns to the question of what roles (if any) collective preferences might usefully play in the governance of democracies.

MAJOR FINDINGS

While heuristic shortcuts, on-line processing, and collective rationality are often thought to help the mass public compensate for its unfamiliarity with public affairs, this study shows that their expected benefits often fail to materialize. Judgmental shortcuts and on-line processing may help citizens provide opinions more meaningful than they might otherwise be, but they do not compensate for want of political expertise. Because ill-informed survey respondents tend to behave differently than models of collective rationality expect them to, aggregating individual opinions turns out to be a surprisingly inefficient way to pool information dispersed across a mass public. Moreover, all of these potential remedies to the public's disengagement from politics overlook a fundamental problem: some kinds of people are more informed than others, and the social distribution of political knowledge bears on the quality of political representation provided by collective preferences.

There appear to be two primary mechanisms by which uneven levels of political knowledge undermine representation. The first is by affecting the demographic correspondence between a survey sample and the group of people who give substantive responses. Those poorly informed about politics tend to give "don't know" and "no opinion" responses at higher rates than more knowledgeable people. This tendency leaves the group of opinion givers disproportionately well educated, affluent, male, white, middle-aged, and partisan relative to the population they are supposed to represent. As a consequence, the particular needs, wants, and values expressed by these relatively knowledgeable groups tend to carry more numerical weight in collective preferences than they would if all voices in a population spoke in proportion to their numbers.

The second way that information asymmetries affect representation is by encouraging less knowledgeable respondents to rely on a limited number of prominent considerations when forming and expressing policy preferences. As a consequence, the opinions of ill-informed people are often quite similar to one another, and ill-informed opinion tends to distribute less evenly across response categories than well-informed opinion. Contrary to the predictions of collective rationality arguments, these dispersion effects generally cause the opinions of ill-informed rather than well-informed people to have an exaggerated influence over the shape of collective preferences.

Correcting for the low levels and uneven social distribution of political knowledge reveals that many collective policy preferences would look quite different if all respondents were equally well informed about politics. The biases in collective preferences brought about by information effects are most clearly revealed by simulating measures of fully informed opinion based on the actual opinions that respondents provide, although the degree of divergence in the opinions of ill- and well-informed respondents can also be used as a rough gauge of information effects. An analysis of these biases suggests that citizen disinterest in politics leads collective preferences to become more approving of politicians and political institutions, more isolationist in foreign policy, more accepting of governmental intervention in the economy, more desiring of a larger and more powerful federal government, and more conservative on social policy issues than they might appear if citizens were better acquainted with the realm of public affairs. These findings suggest that collective preferences often misrepresent the range of voices and interests in society, because the mix of voices giving opinions and the preferences expressed by many opinion givers might change if everyone had equally high levels of political knowledge.

Gaps between surveyed and fully informed opinion seem to be influenced less by depletion problems affecting the demographics of opinion givers than by convergence behavior among less knowledgeable respondents. Information effects in survey questions with relatively high levels of DK/NO responses are about the same size as those found in questions with low levels of DK/NO responses, but they tend to grow faster over time than those in questions with lower levels of group depletion.

However, the unique impact of group depletion is hard to pin down because it tends to occur in questions with higher levels of cognitive difficulty. Group depletion should increase the size of information effects, but questions with higher levels of cognitive difficulty produce noisy opinions among both ill- and well-informed respondents, which tend to diminish the size of information effects. Demographic misrepresentation in the ranks of opinion givers therefore may only appear to contribute minimally to the size of information effects. The impact of convergence behavior is more easily seen: the greater the differences in the distribution of well- and ill-informed opinion, the larger the size of the information effect. In part, this is because the mix of opinions held by the most knowledgeable respondents often approximates the shape of the fully informed collective opinion: the more that ill-informed opinion pulls the marginal percentages away from the shape of well-informed opinion, the less marginal percentages come to resemble fully informed collective preferences. Another reason for this tendency comes from the finding that large differences between ill- and well-informed opinion often result when the opinions of less knowledgeable respondents are more lopsided as a group than those of knowledgeable respondents. Information effects tend to be larger when the opinions of well-informed respondents distribute evenly across response options, because this allows the shape of ill-informed opinion to determine the collective preference.

Information effects arise from a variety of individual-level factors associated with or moderated by general political knowledge. The social distribution of policy-specific knowledge, differences in attitude structures and information processing strategies common to well- and ill-informed persons, levels of issue salience, and response instability produced by ambivalent attitudes all influence the size of information effects. In contrast, features of questionnaire design known to reduce the quality of responses were found to have little impact on the gaps between surveyed and fully informed opinion. Since it would be odd for the quality of collective preferences to be largely unrelated to the quality of questions posed to survey respondents, this finding suggests that question wording and ordering problems either produce essentially random errors in individual opinions, or that such problems produce systematic errors which influence ill- and well-informed opinion givers in similar ways. Some evidence was found to support the latter conclusion, confirming that the presence or absence of information effects is only one facet of representational quality in collective preferences.

Gaps between surveyed and fully informed opinions are also influenced by social processes of information diffusion and the information environments in which a population forms and updates its preferences. As a consequence, information effects can develop in unpredictable ways. For example, information effects tended to remain stable or grow in size over a period when the American population's average level of political knowledge was growing. Yet, they tended to diminish in size when popular interest in politics was piqued by presidential elections, and when news media raised the prominence of an issue on the public's agenda. In general, when the differences between surveyed and simulated fully informed opinions are small, future levels of surveyed opinion tend to remain stable. But when large gaps emerged between these measures, simulated opinions were decidedly inaccurate in predicting the direction or magnitude of future changes in surveyed opinion.

In light of these findings, it is hard to escape the conclusion that opinion surveys are frequently misused in democratic politics. The indiscriminate use of polls to represent what the public wants or is willing to accept is ill-advised, since some survey results better represent fully informed preferences than others, and even fully informed preferences are unlikely to be enlightened. Yet it is also misleading to think of opinion surveys as providing nothing but information about the people. Surveys can become a channel for political representation when leaders use opinion polls as descriptions of what the people think and feel. Because polls provide information that is both prescriptive and descriptive, the use of collective preferences in democratic politics should be guided by the quality of representation they provide. The degree of congruence between surveyed opinion and fully informed opinion provides one gauge of representational quality, but this standard is more useful for identifying representation problems than for suggesting when a collective preference might resemble something like the active voice of the people.

Taken together, these findings suggest the need for survey researchers, journalists, politicians, and citizens to identify and properly interpret survey results that have been influenced by the social distribution of political knowledge. In the following section, I suggest some ways to draw attention to representation problems in survey data. Although it might also be possible to improve the representational quality of collective preferences by retooling the methods of survey research, focusing on improvements to survey methods may highlight the wrong problems. To the extent that social inequalities in the kind and quantity of political information available to citizens are an enduring feature of democratic societies, then a solution to this problem is less likely to be found in reforming the standard practices of survey research than in reconsidering the uses of opinion surveys in democratic politics.

ADDRESSING ISSUES OF QUALITY IN OPINION SURVEYS

Many recommendations for improving the quality of surveyed opinion begin with the premise that the public's ignorance of politics is the problem. From this perspective, appropriate remedies to public inattentiveness include improving the quality of news coverage and political debates (Delli Carpini and Keeter 1996; Graber 1994, 2001; Rahn, Aldrich, and Borgida 1994), involving citizens in face-to-face deliberative processes (Fishkin 1991, 1995; Gastil 2000; Gastil and Dillard 1999), as well as increasing mobilization efforts, improving access to information, and providing more opportunities for civic education (Delli Carpini and Keeter 1996; Jacobs and Shapiro 2000; Nie, Junn, and Stehlik-Barry 1996; Rosenstone and Hansen 1993; Verba, Schlozman, and Brady 1995). All of these suggestions share the goal of making ordinary people better informed about politics, but they also share a common problem: the success of each of these solutions ultimately depends on changing the incentives that journalists, politicians, and ordinary citizens have in maintaining the present state of affairs. This laudable goal is certainly worth pursuing, but, like any solution to a collective action problem, is difficult to put into practice (Somin 1998; Weissberg 2001). We forget that the golden age of Athenian democracy, long heralded as a paragon of civic involvement (Arendt 1958), also had its share of popular disengagement from politics (Hansen 1991: Chapter 6; Splichal 1997: 28–9). After public shaming failed to raise turnout levels at the Assembly of the People – malingerers were fined and had their clothing daubed with red paint – the Greeks soon discovered that sizeable cash payments proved the most reliable means of guaranteeing enough attendance for a quorum. It is telling that the Pnyx – the meeting place of the Assembly – could, at best, accommodate only about a fifth of eligible citizens at one time (Hansen 1991: 130–2). Even Athenian expectations for popular involvement were never so high as to presume the *typical* citizen would show up to hear speeches and cast a vote.

Besides focusing attention on solutions that are difficult to achieve, the current debate over the significance of the public's low levels of knowledge tends to regress into sweeping generalizations about the quality of surveyed opinion. If only the public were better informed, a common lament goes, we could have more confidence that opinion surveys communicate something worth listening to. Recent efforts to challenge this view, bearing titles like *The Rational Public* (Page and Shapiro 1992) and *The Reasoning Voter* (Popkin 1991), have succeeded mainly by arguing that political knowledge should be relatively unimportant to the quality of collective opinion and election outcomes. These revisionist views give the impression that the public is able to compensate effectively for its low levels of knowledge. As I have argued at length, this optimism is frequently misplaced.

I am suggesting that the public's disengagement from political life should not be the defining problem in this debate. It is merely a fact. The fundamental problem lies in the ways that journalists, politicians, activists, and scholars interpret survey results in light or in spite of this fact. Polls fall short of the "active voice" standard, but they are more influential than the "information only" perspective suggests. Neither view reflects adequately the role of opinion surveys in democratic societies; neither grasps the essential fact that sometimes political knowledge matters, and sometimes it does not.

Instead of focusing on the public's lack of knowledge, producers and consumers of survey data would do well to determine when this lack of knowledge has a bearing on collective preferences. Toward this end I propose two ways to begin addressing issues of quality in collective preferences. Neither requires much additional effort or expenditure of resources on the part of survey organizations or those who report survey data. And because these recommendations are directed at pollsters, consultants, and journalists who interpret survey data for news media and political leaders, they avoid some of the collective action problems that plague well-intentioned remedies to the public's distaste for political information. However, these suggestions apply cosmetic fixes to a problem that invites a more foundational response. Later sections of this chapter will consider the larger and more difficult question of how opinion surveys might better enhance the quality of popular representation in democratic politics.

Include Knowledge Questions in Opinion Surveys as a Means to Estimate Quality in Collective Preferences

Despite the exuberance of George Gallup and other pioneers of the sample survey, opinion researchers and their critics have long cautioned against casually treating marginal percentages from this or that survey question as valid measures of what the people really want. One recurring concern since the beginning of the polling enterprise has been that the numerically precise measures of public opinion elicited by surveys can impart the patina of thoughtful consideration to what are essentially "doorstep opinions." One early critic of polling (Bernays 1945) cautioned that interpreting marginal percentages without also examining the extent to which respondents are knowledgeable about the subject of the question is "like diagnosing a patient by only reading the thermometer" (267a). Despite long-standing concerns over what Philip Converse later termed the "nonattitude" problem, most opinion surveys still contain few if any measures designed to tap knowledge of the issues placed before survey respondents.

Estimating information effects in collective preferences requires some measure of political knowledge. An emerging consensus suggests that since most people seem to be generalists when it comes to political knowledge, knowledge of specific issues can be predicted with some accuracy from a person's score on a test of general political knowledge consisting of only a few questions. Delli Carpini and Keeter (1993) have shown that a simple five-item index performs quite well next to longer scales. Nonetheless, it is also clear that general tests of political knowledge have their limitations. Some questions are more difficult than others, and the selection of items included in a knowledge scale thus has an important bearing on a population's apparent competence (Delli Carpini and Keeter 1996). The attempt to determine which facts are relevant to a given set of opinions is invariably political, and it may be difficult to ascertain which of the relevant facts are more important than others (Kuklinski, Quirk et al. 1998). Encouraging respondents to give "don't know" responses can make them seem less knowledgeable about politics than they actually are (Mondak 2000, 2001; Mondak and Davis 2001). Moreover, there is some evidence of heterogeneity in knowledge of specific issues (Delli Carpini and Keeter 1996; Iyengar 1986, 1990; Krosnick 1998; see also Nie, Junn, and Stehlik-Barry 1996), and policy-specific information can have a substantial impact on policy preferences that is independent from the effect of general political knowledge (Gilens 2001).

While such considerations invite further attention from researchers, direct measures of political knowledge nonetheless have several advantages over filter questions and other methods developed by survey practitioners to isolate relatively knowledgeable groups of respondents who hold firm opinions. A major drawback of using filter questions and "don't know" inducements is that they cause some respondents to be treated as missing. Aside from the depletion problems that these methods produce, the missing responses that might otherwise be recorded can be quite revealing. The use of filter questions thus eliminates a potentially important (and more descriptively representative) counterfactual measure of opinion.

Knowledge scales not only provide a way to distinguish between well- and ill-informed responses while creating fewer missing observations, but they also provide a useful measure of the volatility of collective preferences. One measure of volatility that has received attention in recent years is the "mushiness index" developed by Yankelovich, Skelly, and White (Asher 1988: 34–5; Yankelovich 1991: 34–7). This index consists of several follow-up responses to a question asking respondents to state their views on an issue. These follow-up questions tap the salience of the issue to respondents, the likelihood that respondents will change their views on the issue, how much respondents talk about the issue with other people, and how knowledgeable they feel about the issue. Although the mushiness index was found to perform quite well, it apparently never has been used since its development (Yankelovich 1991: 36). This is likely due to two problems. First, the mushiness index is simply too resource-intensive: asking four follow-up questions for every substantive question means that a survey can cover only one-fifth the number of issues it might otherwise explore. Second, although opinion mushiness can be indicated with something as simple as marking marginal percentages with an asterisk, the concept of opinion volatility is exceedingly difficult to communicate to lay audiences. Using knowledge measures to assess the quality of survey results has an edge in both of these areas. Including a few questions tapping knowledge of specific issues or an omnibus knowledge scale, which can be included at the end of a survey, is much less resource intensive than the mushiness index. Likewise, few journalists, political leaders, or lay audiences would have difficulty understanding a sentence like "Although the public as a whole is strongly opposed to raising taxes, a slight majority of the most knowledgeable citizens say they're willing to pay more to reduce the deficit."

The primary advantage of political knowledge questions over filters or other measures is the flexibility such questions allow for estimating various aspects of quality in a collective opinion. A single knowledge scale can be used to reveal dispersion effects brought about by differences in knowledge levels, estimate multiple shades of informed opinion by contrasting the group preferences of various information quartiles, and assess how well the mix of opinions given by the most knowledgeable respondents represents a hypothetical fully informed collective preference. One need not conduct a full-fledged simulation in order to estimate the effects of information asymmetries. A reasonable estimate can be obtained by simply comparing the differences of opinion between the most- and least-knowledgeable respondents. If the differences appear substantial, then the collective preference is likely to be influenced by information effects. When respondents at all levels of knowledge give roughly similar opinions, the collective preference is unlikely to be affected by information asymmetries. Because the influence of information effects can be seen by looking at a simple crosstabular display of opinions by knowledge level, measures of factual knowledge make it possible for consumers and producers of survey data to estimate when collective preferences might be influenced by such effects without resorting to the rather involved simulation procedure used here.[1]

Our confidence or dismay in the ability of citizens to comprehend political issues must be supported by evidence rather than intuition. To presume that a population either lacks or possesses a rudimentary understanding of public issues, or to hope that summing individual responses will reveal a population's considered opinion, is to misunderstand the nature of collective preferences. At a minimum, a short index or scale of political knowledge should be included in the standard set of demographics questions attached to any political opinion survey. Better still, pollsters might consider following opinion questions with policy-specific knowledge questions to clarify the factual basis from which opinions are offered. We want to know whether respondents understood what the questioners intended to ask them, and how well they were acquainted with the topic under investigation. As Leo Bogart observed, "The question of *what* people think about public issues is really secondary to the question of whether they think about them at all" (1967: 337, emphasis in original). Obviously, the scope and construction of such knowledge measures will be influenced by the purposes for which a survey is to be used. But without a direct measure of political knowledge, there is no reliable way to identify the presence and likely impact of information asymmetries in measures of surveyed opinion.

---

[1] Two widely available substitutes for direct measures of political knowledge – education and income level – give only the roughest approximations of information levels. Part of the reason is that the effects of education and income are likely to be confounded with other demographic characteristics and particular socialization experiences. Separating the effects of these various influences requires a direct measure of political knowledge.

Report Collective Preferences in Ways that Draw Attention to Issues of Quality and Representation

One of the fundamental problems with using opinion surveys in democratic politics is that they may seem to be one thing when they are not. Majority opinions may seem to be prescriptive measures of what the people want or will abide, when on closer inspection they seem more like artifacts of widespread confusion over the issues. The opposite is also true: majority preferences on new or obscure political issues may be summarily dismissed as ill-founded or shallow, when a more detailed analysis would show that people with high and low levels of relevant knowledge hold essentially the same opinions. One reason for this problem is careless reporting of survey results, especially the popular tendency to emphasize marginal percentages without discussing the underlying distributions of subgroup opinion. Another is the absence of a language with which consumers and producers of survey data can discuss issues of quality in collective preferences (Jacobs and Shapiro 2000; Price and Neijens 1997; Yankelovich 1991). Lacking such a language, users of survey data often fall into the habit of deferring to the judgment of experts, relying on their own intuition, or following prior expectations (from "you can't trust the polls" to "surveys tell it like it is") when evaluating the potential quality of poll results.

The methods outlined in this book for estimating fully informed opinion provide a way to identify some of the more obvious representation problems in collective opinions. It is often appropriate to describe the representational quality of survey results by contrasting the opinions of knowledgeable people with the opinions of less knowledgeable respondents or the collective preference of the entire group of opinion givers. To suggest that a collective opinion is free of obvious representational problems, it might be enough to say "Opinion polls show that people from all walks of life prefer term limits for members of Congress, and it seems to make little difference whether people are familiar with the issue or have heard hardly anything about it." Likewise, to raise the possibility that a measure of opinion is influenced by information effects, one need only say "Even though the public as a whole prefers that the government take a stronger stance in regulating the economy, support for free markets is higher among people who are more informed about national politics." Journalists occasionally describe opinion data in this way, and such reporting should be encouraged as a way to address issues of quality in language that lay persons can understand.

Another way of addressing the quality of survey results is to describe the knowledge levels of opinion givers, preferably by mentioning the percentage of opinion givers that know something about an issue or care about an issue a great deal. Yet while similar ideas have been suggested in recent years (e.g., Cantril 1991; Crespi 1989; Yankelovich 1991), it is still unusual to see journalists focus on these aspects of quality in survey data. Political consultants and survey researchers seem to be more attuned to such nuances, however, and the private survey information available to political leaders may be much more detailed in this regard than is the case for publicly-available data.[2]

One traditional gray area in the reporting of opinion data involves what Pierre Bourdieu (1990: 172) calls the "trauma, cross, and misery" of polling organizations: What to do with the respondents who give "don't know" or "no opinion" responses? In light of the representation problems imparted by uneven rates of item nonresponse, it seems inappropriate to omit the percentages of DK/NO responses when reporting survey results. Treating substantive responses from filtered questions as though they represented the entirety of a population's opinions is misleading because it obscures the potential for misrepresentation of voices. The general rule of thumb suggested by this study is that marginal percentages should be reported in terms of the entire sample of respondents rather than the pool of opinion givers. While it is interesting to know that two-thirds of opinion givers favor a particular policy, it is much more important to know that only half of respondents give substantive answers to the question.

Reporting survey results in ways that draw attention to indicators of quality helps to clarify the meaning of marginal percentages. Not only does discussion of quality issues properly focus attention on the potential usefulness of collective preferences, but it also draws attention to otherwise hidden dimensions of opinion data. For example, knowing that the most informed respondents tend to favor a policy that is opposed by the least informed suggests that relative levels of DK/NO responses may

---

[2] While many political pollsters have long conducted multivariate analyses using the latest statistical methods to plumb their data (Bruce and Wilcox 2000; Jacobs and Shapiro 1995), this is not always the case. For example, memos on public opinion given to President Clinton by advisor Dick Morris rarely went beyond simple marginal frequencies (Morris 1999), and pollster Frank Luntz convinced the Republican leadership in the U.S. House of Representatives that the 10 policy items comprising its "Contract with America" had overwhelming public support, revealing only later that his recommendations had been made on the basis of just a few focus group interviews (see note 8 in Chapter 7).

have important consequences for the shape of opinion marginals. Bringing issues of quality into discussions of survey results can help dispel the impression that the public has decisive opinions on a range of issues at the same time as it highlights instances where the public's opinions are deeply rooted and, perhaps, worth attending.

THE TWO MEANINGS OF PUBLIC OPINION

If, as this book has argued, collective rationality cannot be counted upon to deliver the mass public from various alleged deficiencies in its individual opinions, it might appear that the best systems of democratic rule should be those that minimize a polity's reliance on citizen input aside from the corrective hand of the occasional election (Somin 1998; Weissberg 2002a). The problem with this Schumpeterian conclusion lies in the premise that equates public opinion with the results of opinion surveys and, more broadly, that defines public opinion in utilitarian terms as the aggregation of individual preferences. Appreciating the limitations of this premise requires us to reconnect our contemporary understanding of public opinion to the meanings it carried before the age of the sample survey. The purpose of this exercise is not to separate the concept of public opinion from its present associations, but rather to enlarge and reinvigorate the term with a fuller sense of its foundational standing in democratic theory. Doing so opens a door of escape from the uncomfortable (and, I believe, false) conclusion that the usefulness of collective preferences to democratic processes depends on some version of collective rationality to imbue public opinion with more meaning than may be found in the opinions of individuals.

Largely due to the successes of survey research as a tool for social inquiry, popular use of the label "public opinion" has evolved since the advent of the sample survey nearly 70 years ago to denote aggregations of preferences relevant to public affairs that are expressed to survey interviewers in private by isolated individuals (P. E. Converse 1987; Ginsberg 1986; Glasser and Salmon 1995; Herbst 1993; Lee 2002; Sanders 1999). Yet the thoroughness of this transformation belies the fact that this is, in the long scheme of things, still a fairly new way of thinking about public opinion. When Frankfurt School sociologist Friedrich Pollock (1976: 230) questions whether public opinion is "a phenomenon of quantities," suggesting instead that it is a phenomenon of social forces, he invokes a conception of public opinion that predates the sample survey and that resonates deeply in the traditions of political philosophy. At the risk of greatly oversimplifying the genealogy of public opinion as a concept,[3] we can mark its development through three broad stages: from the earliest philosophical treatments of public opinion as an abstract force in society, developed in the writings of Locke, Bentham, Hume, Hegel, Madison, and Rousseau, but which can be traced back to ancient Roman and Greek political thought; to the mid 19th- and early 20th-century conceptions of public opinion as a sociological or discursive phenomenon, revealed ideally through active deliberation and arising from the competition among groups for social, economic, or political power, exemplified in the writings of Bryce, Tarde, Blumer, and Rogers, but carried on in the work of Bourdieu, Pateman, Barber, Fraser, and Habermas, among others; to the late 20th century vision of public opinion as a psychological phenomenon observed in the aggregation of individual preferences within a population or sample.

Two distinctions between past and current definitions of public opinion are especially relevant for the present discussion. First, up until the 1930s, the phenomenon of public opinion tended to be associated with action (including the expression of political opinions in public settings) or barriers to action rather than merely with a predisposition or readiness to act. In contrast, psychological interpretations of public opinion informed by survey research have tended to view attitudes rather than actions as the primary phenomenon of interest (Blankenship 1948). Second, while the earlier sociological conceptions of public opinion were concerned with action conducted by or in the service of interested groups rather than the population as a whole, the method of random sampling has cultivated a perspective which views public opinion as an attribute of unorganized masses or entire societies.[4] Thus while theorists in the century before the survey era tended to see public opinion as a form of social communication or control expressed through action that moderates or enhances the

---

[3] For histories of this conceptual transformation, see Bauer 1933; Berelson 1956; P. E. Converse 1987; Ginsberg 1986; Gunn 1995; Habermas 1989; Herbst 1993, 1995; Minar 1960; Noelle-Neumann 1984; Palmer 1936; Peters 1995; Price 1992; Speier 1950; Splichal 1999.

[4] In a limited sense, this shift in emphasis to public opinion as a collective property of entire societies draws current definitions closer to the much earlier philosophical interpretations of public opinion, which often equated public opinion with the force of social customs or habits common to a people and which tended to define political interests as a property of entire nations rather than of individuals. Yet the similarities cannot be stretched too far, for writers in the philosophical stage typically did not conceive of individual opinions as (potentially) interest-bearing preferences, an interpretation that flowed from later liberal theorists of democracy.

political power of organized groups, contemporary perspectives tend to see public opinion as a psychological construct expressed through words that predicts the likely behavior of unorganized groups (i.e., different *types* of individuals) and provides information about the political preferences of entire populations.

The limitations in this new way of thinking about public opinion are today more apparent than they were at first. Social scientists have long discarded the political agenda of early survey researchers who saw polls as an important tool for democratic reform (J. M. Converse 1987). In large part this change occurred as survey researchers became more familiar with the methodological limitations of polling and the characteristics of survey responses, which often did little to inspire confidence in the wisdom of the masses. Instead, surveys are today seen among social scientists primarily as an information-gathering tool, more useful for making sense of the public's attitudes and behaviors than for defining the public's priorities or giving authentic voice to its concerns (for exceptions, see Bennett 1990; Jacobs and Shapiro 2000; Kay 1998). Indeed, while academic parlance typically reserves the term public opinion for describing the surveyed attitudes or values of individuals, the classic (if abstract) understanding of public opinion as the power of popular sovereignty is still understood today, as it was to the contemporaries of Tocqueville and Bryce, as something which emerges from the currents of group politics. The disjuncture between these two meanings of public opinion is captured succinctly by Leo Bogart (1967):

A 1964 NORC survey reported by Charles Y. Glock and Rodney Stark found that 7 per cent of U.S. adults agreed that Hitler was right to try to kill all the Jews. We attribute no particular importance to this 7 per cent, which projects to some 8 million individuals, each one a potential mass murderer, because the sentiments they express to an interviewer are made individually without awareness of their collective strength. By contrast, we may feel enormous concern about the similarly small percentage of people who now vote for the neo-Nazi party in Germany, precisely because their opinions are crystallized and their political force is known. (335–6)

Although early survey researchers eventually were successful in appropriating the label of public opinion to describe the results of sample surveys, the functional forms of public opinion have remained essentially unchanged. We still tend to recognize the political manifestation of public opinion – by which we typically mean persuasive or coercive pressure brought against the state by actors who are not part of state institutions – in the mobilizing activities of political parties, the abiding power of pressure groups as intermediaries acting on behalf of particular interests, and the potential for agitation by social movements to bring about desired change from unresponsive institutions. What has changed since the rise of opinion polling is that we no longer tend to think of these activities as expressions of public opinion.

This double-mindedness is an important reason why contemporary students of politics have found it difficult to attribute much political legitimacy or usefulness to opinion polls, for it is clear by any measure that the organized activities of groups directed against key political decision makers carry far more power in the democratic process than do the private views of citizens unacquainted with one another, let alone organized for action or even caring much to inquire what all the ruckus is about. In this light, the hesitation among social scientists to seriously consider the results of opinion surveys as revealing something like the "will of the people" can be interpreted as arising from a healthy respect for the established channels of accountability and power in contemporary liberal democracies, rather than merely from an abiding distrust of the survey method for giving expression to the people's voice. To the extent that opinion polls seem to have little formal or substantive impact on the political process, then by equating the term public opinion with survey results we must conclude that public opinion so understood has little to do with popular sovereignty, the exercise of which we typically ascribe to groups and elections.

This conceptual tension provided the basis of a critique of the polling enterprise most forcefully advanced in the writings of Herbert Blumer (1948), Lindsay Rogers (1949), and Pierre Bourdieu (1979), who each attempted to wrest the label of public opinion from the product of survey research. The most thoroughgoing of these critiques was leveled by sociologist Herbert Blumer. Central to Blumer's (1948) criticism of the polling enterprise was the notion that the "sampling procedure forces a treatment of society as if society were only an aggregation of disparate individuals" (546). The core problem, in his view, is that "We do not know at all whether individuals in the sample represent that portion of structured society that is participating in the formation of public opinion on a given issue" (546), and "we know essentially nothing of the individual in the sample with reference to the significance of him or of his opinion in the public opinion that is being built up or which is expressing itself functionally in the operation of society" (546). In short, the position staked out by Blumer faults pollsters for the inability of the polling method to capture the way that public opinion actually works in society.

"If public opinion is to be studied in any realistic sense," Blumer wrote, "its depiction must be faithful to its empirical character" (543). From this perspective, according to Blumer, "in *any realistic sense* public opinion consists of the pattern of the diverse views and positions on the issue *that come to the individuals who have to act in response to the public opinion*" (545, italics in original).

More than 50 years have passed since the publication of Blumer's famous attack on opinion polling, and it speaks well for the shelf-life of an idea that the debate sparked by his critique remains heated to this day.[5] Yet despite the energy devoted to this debate, the continuing controversy over whether public opinion is best defined as the aggregation of individual preferences or as the "effective" expression of group-based opinion seems to have been largely emptied of its constructive potential. The most recent contributions to this debate are in many ways most remarkable for the starkness of their assertions and lack of engagement with the other side. For instance, the opening words of the 50th anniversary special issue of *Public Opinion Quarterly* was Eleanor Singer's (1987) celebratory proclamation that "Blumer was wrong," followed several years later by an equally blunt retort that "Blumer was right" (Salmon and Glasser 1995). More than a debate, these exchanges have all the salient qualities of a divorce proceedings: two camps unable or unwilling to work through what appear to be irreconcilable theoretical differences.

The debate is also remarkable for its one-sidedness. Despite the frequency with which Blumer's challenge is revisited by those critical of the modern polling enterprise, to my knowledge only one defender of the method has stepped forward in recent years to mount extended rebuttals in scholarly journals (P. E. Converse 1987; Converse 1996; see also Verba 1996). Writing in defense of survey research, Philip Converse (1987) pointed out that opinion polls had, since the days of Blumer's critique, become more closely and routinely perceived as public opinion by political actors, journalists, and the general public. While this argument in some ways misses Blumer's larger point, that talking about polls as public opinion doesn't mean that polls capture the actual processes of political influence at work between citizens and their representatives, Converse is surely correct that the ubiquity of opinion polling has conditioned people

---

[5] Blumer's critique is reflected or revisited in several recent contributions to the public opinion literature, including Bogart 1967; Bourdieu 1979; P. E. Converse 1987; Converse 1996; Crespi 1989, 1997; Ginsberg 1986, 1989; Glasser and Salmon 1995; Herbst 1993, 1998; Lemert 1992; Neuman 1986; Noelle-Neumann 1984; Price 1992; Splichal 1997.

to view polls as expressions of public opinion (Ginsberg 1986; Herbst 1993). This tendency, in Converse's view, appears to vindicate the polling enterprise in light of Blumer's critique:

If . . . any deflection whatever of behavior by the representative which arises as a result of some exposure to poll data, even the most vague "taking account of it," classifies as an instance of actual influence, then of course public opinion in poll form must be said to have a great deal of influence. And this kind of minimal influence must occur in very large doses among political practitioners, or it would be extremely hard to explain why such users pay many millions of dollars a year for this expensive class of information. (1987: S22)

In other words, Converse takes Blumer largely on his own terms but argues that the world has changed in 40 years. Moreover, Converse recognizes with Blumer that "public opinion as measured by sample surveys and public opinion 'effective' in the political arena, while often reasonably convergent, are hardly the same thing and can at times diverge remarkably" (S20). Converse adds, "What one makes of the discrepancy in normative terms, of course, cannot be solved empirically" (S21).

This last point illustrates what I believe is the major problem with the terms on which this debate over the identity of public opinion is being contested: at one level the participants are disagreeing over the definition of what constitutes public opinion as well as the empirical claim that polls have a palpable influence on politics, but at a deeper level the more fundamental disagreement can be seen as one over the political influence that polls ought to have relative to groups. A normative reading of this debate suggests that this deeper disagreement shows itself from time to time but never assumes a place of central importance in the arguments of either side.[6]

---

[6] For example, the essence of Converse's own contribution to the larger normative questions in this debate seems to be captured in the following sentence: "In the degree that values propel us to take a sober account of the opinion of all the people in forming policy outcomes – and they surely propel most of us a good distance in this direction – we *might as well* get a reasonably accurate reading of that opinion rather than entrusting it to a few local experts to guess at it" (S24, italics mine). This is hardly a rousing defense of the polling enterprise. Yet even this tentative justification begs the very question that I argue lies at the heart of this debate: Why might we want to "take a sober account of the opinion of all the people" in the first place?

Blumer addresses this question more directly, but his justification is nearly as perfunctory as that given by Converse. Blumer dismisses as a "normative plea" the idea that opinion polls yield a better picture of public opinion than "the confused, indefinite, slanted, and favor-ridden expressions of opinion that come ordinarily to the legislator, administrator or executive who has to act on public opinion" (548). In a now famous passage, Blumer concludes that "It is sufficient to note that if one seeks to justify polling as

It is precisely this neglected normative dimension that holds the promise of reconnecting these two ways of thinking about public opinion, for the debate over its meaning and definition obscures a fundamental normative tension between these two important conceptions of public opinion. The tension lies in the apparent tradeoff between representation of interests and representation of voices revealed in this study: the closer an indicator of collective opinion comes to representing all voices in a public, the less likely it will be to reflect the interests of that public. Put another way, the more descriptively representative the indicator of public opinion (surveys being the prime example of a descriptively representative indicator), the more likely the opinion it communicates will be ill-informed, unreflective, and otherwise wanting in quality, when quality is defined in terms of collective interest representation.

Resolving this tension requires a turn away from the recent tendency to identify public opinion with a particular method or channel of influence. Instead, we might do better to envision public opinion as a system of social indicators in which collective preferences and collective decisions, along with various types of individual and group activity, are seen as potentially offering different qualities or kinds of representation.[7] If polls are unlikely

---

a method of studying public opinion on the ground that the composition of public opinion *ought to be* different than what it is, he is not establishing the validity of the method for the study of the empirical world as it is. Instead, he is hanging on the coat-tails of a dubious proposal for social reform" (548).

This last statement, in my view, gets to the heart of the normative debate underlying the empirical one. Blumer elaborates on this last sentence in a footnote: "I refer to such a program as dubious because I believe the much needed improvement of public opinion in our society should be in the process by which public opinion organically functions, i.e., by arousing, organizing, and effectively directing the opinion of people who appreciate that they have an interest in a given issue. A reliance, instead, on a mere 'referendum' by an undifferentiated mass, having great segments of indifference and non-participation, is unlikely to offer a desirable public opinion. At the best, in my judgment, such a 'referendum' could operate as a corrective supplement and not as a substitute" (548). Here Blumer suggests some quality criteria that would seem to privilege group-based expressions of opinion, but these ideas are not subsequently developed in his critique.

[7] Although this general perspective resonated with social scientists of an earlier generation (e.g., Blumer 1946; Davison 1958; Key 1961; Lazarsfeld 1957; for a review, see Price 1992), it has fallen into disuse today (for exceptions, see Lee 2002; Shamir and Shamir 2000), and the public opinion literature has been impoverished by its neglect. Among the likely factors contributing to this shift are the rise of the mass society paradigm for understanding public opinion processes, the waning influence of sociological theory and waxing importance of psychological theory in orienting contemporary public opinion research, the ascendancy of the sample survey as a dominant tool of social inquiry, and the increased specialization of knowledge that has accompanied the development and expansion of social science disciplines over the last 50 years.

to disappear from the political landscape, and if polls are a channel for political representation – however informal this representation may be – then critics and defenders of the polling method would do well to focus on the kinds of representation that polls might best provide relative to other indicators of public opinion. Instead of asking what public opinion is, this approach would ask which indicators of public opinion should have political power in democratic societies, and which specific powers or roles each kind of public opinion should have. With particular regard to collective preferences revealed in opinion surveys, this approach could attempt to address two questions: What sort of opinion might surveys be particularly good at revealing, and which political functions might surveys be particularly suited to fulfill?

RECONSIDERING THE USES OF OPINION SURVEYS IN DEMOCRATIC POLITICS

How then to move the discussion forward to address the underlying normative issues at the heart of both the Blumer/Converse debate and the difficulty that many have in conceiving of opinion surveys as a potentially valuable form of democratic communication? Let me suggest four propositions that, taken together, can provide a basis for bracketing the important but seemingly intractable theoretical differences that have contributed to the entrenchment of current thinking on these matters:

1. Opinion polling is here to stay.
2. The presence of opinion polling is unlikely to diminish substantially the political power of group activity in democratic political systems.[8]
3. Organized groups provide a channel for political representation.
4. Opinion surveys provide a channel for political representation.

These four propositions taken together help to refocus attention on some key but underappreciated issues. First, if both groups and opinion

---

[8] One exception to this proposition is in reducing the legitimacy of claims that the policy positions espoused by organized groups represent the views of rank and file members or of broad categories of people defined by various demographic and attitudinal characteristics. One of the most palpable contributions that George Gallup's "sampling referenda" have made is to undermine the power of groups to define public opinion by claiming to embody it. At the same time, although Ginsberg (1986, 1989) argues that opinion polls generally undercut the power of organized groups, there is little evidence to date that group activities such as protest marches have dwindled as a consequence of the polling enterprise (Converse 1996).

surveys are likely to have a political impact in democratic societies, then the search for an umbrella definition of public opinion based on groups or polls is unlikely to be of much help in the attempt to understand the actual impact of groups, polls, and other channels of public opinion on political, economic, and civic institutions. Moreover, given that political polls are now commonplace and unlikely to decline in importance in the foreseeable future, the argument that poll results are something other than public opinion obscures the empirical reality that polls are often seen by journalists and political actors as indicators of public opinion (although this is not always the case; see Herbst 1998; Jacobs, Lawrence et al. 1998). This is not to say that the debate over definitions is trivial, just that it is limited in its potential for constructive contributions to pressing questions about the appropriate uses of opinion polls and other indicators of public opinion in the process of governance.

Second, if opinion polling is a channel for representation and if the survey enterprise is unlikely to eclipse the power of organized groups, then instead of trying to define public opinion in terms of either polls or groups we might do better to think of polls and groups as playing different roles within a larger system of socially constructed public opinion indicators.[9] To the extent that groups and opinion surveys are indeed channels for political representation, a systems perspective encourages us to attend not only to the kinds of power currently attributed to or exercised by various opinion indicators but also to the sorts of power these indicators ought to have given the strengths and limitations that each possesses as a vehicle for political representation and channel for political communication.

In short, this perspective helps to focus attention on the quality and type of representation afforded by each indicator, rather than whether one is generally better, more accurate, or more legitimate than the other. As Vincent Price (1992) observes, "To say that the ascendancy of polling helped to establish aggregate conceptions of public opinion is to say nothing about the inherent suitability of survey techniques as a mode of observation, only something about the typical way of interpreting such observations" (35). It is precisely in drawing attention to "the inherent suitability of survey techniques as a mode of observation" that normative theory can contribute to the polling enterprise. By recasting the Blumer/Converse

---

[9] The use of "socially constructed" should here be understood in the most narrow sense as recognizing that different phenomena come to be associated with the concept "public opinion" at different times by different people, rather than as a statement about whether public opinion exists "out there" independently of polls or other means of assessing it.

debate as a representation issue rather than a disagreement about the validity of opinion polling, the key question then becomes how much legitimacy polls and groups should be accorded for particular types of representation.

Descriptive Representation versus Interest Representation

To the extent that the development of fully informed or enlightened political preferences requires even a modest amount of relevant factual information, it would seem as a general rule that we should not expect measures of opinion that maximize descriptive representation to reveal the interests of an ill-informed population. Of course, any population should contain individuals who are knowledgeable about particular issues. The problem is that this sort of knowledge tends to be concentrated among groups already advantaged in the political system. Since these well-informed groups can be expected to have interests at least occasionally at odds with those of their ill-informed counterparts, it seems unlikely that any method for isolating only those people with informed preferences should produce measures of opinion that are descriptively representative of a population as a whole.

Thus a core tension with the use of opinion surveys as an input to the political process is that descriptive representation and interest representation are unlikely to obtain at the same time in the same measure. In general, collective preferences should tend either to misrepresent the demographic makeup of a population, or to misrepresent a population's fully informed needs, wants, and values. Moreover, the more egalitarian the indicator of public opinion – with opinion surveys in general being relatively more egalitarian than other indicators – the less likely the indicator will be effective, in Blumer's sense of having power in the political process. Outside of the election context, where the distribution of individual votes is formally recognized as decisive and authoritative, collective preferences are channels of representation that must themselves be represented by agents who convey and interpret measures of aggregate opinion to audiences or decision makers.

Despite these limitations, even the most hardened detractors of the polling method probably suspect that the kind of representation afforded by surveys must be good for something. Blumer himself suggested as much in a footnote to his famous 1948 critique, where he entertained the idea that "At the best, ... a [polling] 'referendum' could operate as a corrective supplement and not as a substitute [for organized group activity]" (548).

But given current thinking among political philosophers about the nature of political interests, the "something" that polls might be good for is unlikely to be interest representation, at least when defining interests in terms of preferences for one policy or another. There is good reason to expect that preferences articulated by mobilized groups will reflect underlying interests more completely than those expressed in opinion surveys of mass publics (Weissberg 2001, 2002a), in large part because group opinions undergo a filtering process brought about by preparing for and engaging in public deliberation with other groups (Mansbridge 1992). From this perspective, even defenders of the polling method might agree with Blumer that the quality of preferences represented by organized groups makes them deserving of special attention in the political system. The fact that opinion polls seem typically to be ignored in the policymaking process (Crespi 1989; Herbst 1998; Jacobs, Lawrence et al. 1998; Jacobs and Shapiro 2000; Rich 1981) may often be an appropriate response by decision makers seeking to legislate in the public's interest.

Yet, as is widely known, the primary defect of interest group pluralism is that all relevant interests are unlikely to be represented properly in the group process. In the famous words of political scientist E. E. Schattschneider, "The flaw in the pluralist heaven is that the heavenly chorus sings with a strong upper-class accent" (Schattschneider 1960: 34–5).[10] Given this fault with interest group pluralism, it seems desirable that indicators of public opinion that privilege interest representation should somehow be supplemented by indicators of public opinion that emphasize descriptive representation. But the solution does not seem to be elevating the standing of polls relative to groups as indicators of interest, or supposing that polls and groups can function interchangeably as indicators of public opinion, differing primarily in the accuracy of their claims (Gallup and Rae 1940). As Russell Neuman (1986) suggests, "There is a dynamic balance between the special talents of the political elite and the political system which generates the elite. It remains important to balance the specialized knowledge of the elite and the generalized common sense of the mass polity" (189). What then might usefully be represented by surveys in a balanced system of public opinion indicators?

---

[10] For a review of studies documenting biases in the interest group system, see Baumgartner and Leech 1998. One reason for bias in the group system is the uneven social distribution of skills and resources necessary for effectively leveraging power in the pluralist system (Rosenstone and Hansen 1993; Verba, Schlozman, and Brady 1995). Another reason is that some strata of society seem less aware of their interests than others, leaving those interests underrepresented among organized groups (Bachrach 1975).

By raising this question, I am not suggesting that surveys ought to be used as a channel of political representation. On the contrary, I suspect that surveys may not be well suited to the task of representing populations, and it is unclear to me how much the current limitations of the survey method as a representational vehicle can be improved upon. Rather, I am suggesting that surveys are already being used as a channel of representation, and that it may be nearly impossible to use survey data in the political process without engaging in some form of representational activity. If polls are already being used as a channel for political representation, and if polls are here to stay, then it seems appropriate to explore the most appropriate kinds of representation that polls could provide. It may be that the most appropriate kind of representation is merely the least damaging of all the inappropriate kinds of representation that polls could potentially afford. But even if the choice is among the better of undesirable outcomes, putting this question to the formidable intellectual talent on both sides of the Blumer/Converse debate seems likely to generate serious attention to the current and future uses of surveys in democratic politics. As a process of sustained deliberation is most likely to produce thoughtful answers to the question of what political functions surveys might be especially good for, the next section suggests some starting points for such a discussion.

WHAT CAN SURVEYS TELL US ABOUT PUBLIC OPINION?

To explore what sorts of opinions might usefully be represented by surveys in a balanced system of public opinion indicators, we might begin by reflecting on the sorts of opinions we should expect citizens to possess. Such reflection requires a normative theory of the citizen in a democratic society that specifies the political roles citizens play relative to other actors as well as the kinds of opinions necessary to fulfill those roles (Natchez 1985). Different theories of democracy will naturally emphasize different capacities of citizens (Beiner 1995; Held 1987; Thompson 1970), but a helpful point of departure for such an analysis is the five-stage model of democratic problem solving proposed by Vincent Price and Peter Neijens (1997). Their model, which identifies discrete periods during political deliberation when various actors might play different roles or contribute different kinds of information, provides a common framework for assessing the decision-making process that is easily adapted to different models of democracy. Price and Neijens suggest that collective decision making begins with an "elicitation of values" stage, in which a problem is defined along with the values and goals considered important in resolving the problem. Once the problem and relevant goals have been clarified, alternative solutions for addressing the problem are advanced and debated in the "development of options" stage, in which the number of possible options is reduced to a set of feasible alternatives. Once this winnowing process is completed, the pros, cons, and likely outcomes of each alternative are determined in the "estimation of consequences" stage. Having clarified the probable consequences of each alternative, the decision process advances to the "evaluation of alternatives" stage in which advocates for each proposal attempt to persuade others of its merits. Characterized by active public deliberation and heightened press coverage to the issue, this stage "is the phase that is most clearly identified as public discourse" (340) and is marked by widespread attention to the issue even among ordinary citizens. Public discussion over the merits of each proposed solution comes to a close at the fifth and final "decision" stage, when an individual, institutional, or collective decision selects one of the proposed solutions to remedy the problem.

Interest groups, politicians, news media, and other political actors are active within each of the five stages, and different models of democracy rely to various degrees on each actor to contribute in specific ways to the decision-making process. For example, liberal theories of democracy would tend to reserve a dominant role in the first three stages for experts, politicians, and interest groups. When it comes to the role of collective preferences in the larger decision-making process, Price and Neijens observe that opinion surveys were intended by their early proponents "to advance a particular aspect of quality – broad participation – at a particular phase of the decision-making process – the evaluation [of alternatives] stage" (352). Moreover, they note that with few exceptions, the potential for opinion polls to contribute to democratic decision making almost always has been understood to occur within the policy evaluation stage.

This was the role for surveys popularized by George Gallup (Gallup and Rae 1940), who adapted it from James Bryce (1891), and its impact is still seen today in the kinds of questions routinely put to the mass public by survey researchers, particularly in public interest polls (e.g., the Americans Talk Issues surveys) and media surveys. Questions like, "If it were a choice between these two items, which do you think President Clinton should do: cut the budget deficit or cut the taxes for the middle class?" (Harris), or "Do you think Congress should raise taxes to narrow the federal budget deficit even if George Bush does not ask for a tax increase, or not?"

(NBC/WSJ) position survey respondents as political "advisors" guiding politicians in their policy decisions. We might think of these as "what should they do" questions. A related type of evaluation question asks respondents to evaluate the motives, abilities, and past actions of political actors, as in "Who do you think is more serious about reducing the budget deficit, President Clinton or the Republicans in Congress?" (NBC) and "Who do you feel is most to blame for the budget impasse that has brought the federal government to a virtual halt, Congress or President Bush?" (*Washington Post*). These we might call "who's more popular, who's to blame" questions. A third category of "referendum" questions invites respondents to record their views on pressing issues of the day, as in "Do you favor or oppose the death penalty for persons convicted of murder?" (ANES). Most of the policy questions analyzed in earlier chapters were of this third variety.

Results from these three types of evaluation questions could potentially provide useful information about the climate of opinion in which the policy evaluation process takes place, but using them in a more prescriptive sense as a form of input to the policy-making process would seem to require that people giving answers have at least passing acquaintance with the objects being evaluated. This expectation quickly foundered when dashed against data by the first generation of survey researchers, a discovery that led Berelson, Lazarsfeld, and McPhee (1954: 311) to observe that "If the democratic system depended solely on the qualifications of the individual voter, then it seems remarkable that democracies have survived through the centuries." Giovanni Sartori (1965) put it more bluntly: "Let us be honest. The average voter is called on to make decisions on questions about which he knows nothing. In other words, he is incompetent" (78).

Despite the stir that this revelation caused among social scientists at the time, less attention was given then or since to the reasons why this discovery should be a cause for such profound disappointment. It is clear that polities benefit when political knowledge is high and evenly distributed, and that many shortcomings and inefficiencies in political systems could be remedied if ordinary citizens were more attentive to public affairs and, as a consequence, more aware of their political interests (Delli Carpini and Keeter 1996). But what core tenet of democratic theory is being offended by the public's apparent lack of civic-mindedness? Certainly the interests of many citizens will be at stake in any policy decision, but it is another thing to presume that democracy requires citizens to exercise vigilance over every interest they may have. The institutions of representative as opposed to direct democracy are designed precisely to avoid encumbering citizens with such an onerous responsibility. Rather, the cause for alarm seemed to be the (now apparently unrealistic) expectations of an informed citizenry developed in what is generally referred to as the "classical theory" of democracy. Lippmann (1922) disparaged the ideal of an "omnicompetent citizen" presumed by "those thinkers of the Eighteenth Century who designed the matrix of democracy" (162), Schumpeter ([1942] 1976) contrasted his realist view of democracy with an outmoded "eighteenth-century philosophy of democracy"[11] (250), and Berelson, Lazarsfeld, and McPhee (Berelson 1952; Berelson, Lazarsfeld, and McPhee 1954) confronted expectations from "the normative theory of political democracy" (Berelson 1952: 313) with the depressing results of opinion surveys. Yet, Carole Pateman's careful investigation of the works of Enlightenment and post-Enlightenment democratic theorists reveals that this "notion of a 'classical theory of democracy' is a myth" (Pateman 1970: 17). In contrast to popular rendering of this "classical" model, Pateman concludes that these earlier theorists were concerned with "the choice of good representatives (leaders) rather than the formulation of the electorate's opinion as such" (19) and with the "educative effect of participation" through which individuals developed the desirable attitudes and perspectives of the citizen.[12]

---

[11] Schumpeter writes: "The eighteenth-century philosophy of democracy may be couched in the following definition: the democratic method is that institutional arrangement for arriving at political decisions which realizes the common good by making the people itself decide issues through the election of individuals who are to assemble in order to carry out its will" (250).

[12] In describing the commonalities of the 18th century theorists of representative government, Pateman writes that their "theory of participatory democracy is built round the central assertion that individuals and their institutions cannot be considered in isolation from one another. The existence of representative institutions at national level is not sufficient for democracy; for maximum participation by all the people at that level socialization, or 'social training', for democracy must take place in other spheres in order that the necessary individual attitudes and psychological qualities can be developed. This development takes place through the process of participation itself. The major function of participation in the theory of participatory democracy is therefore an educative one, educative in the very widest sense, including both the psychological aspect and the gaining of practice in democratic skills and procedures. Thus there is no special problem about the stability of a participatory system; it is self-sustaining through the educative impact of the participatory process. Participation develops and fosters the very qualities necessary for it; the more individuals participate the better they become to do so. Subsidiary hypotheses about participation are that it has an integrated effect and that it aids the acceptance of collective decisions" (42–3). Pateman's emphasis on the educative role of participation in the work of these earlier theorists has since been challenged by Jane Mansbridge (1999a), who argues that while these writers expected some improvement

The ideal of the citizen informed about matters of policy seems to be of much more recent vintage than many students of public opinion recognize (Natchez 1985). Concern about the information necessary for effective citizenship in Revolutionary War-era America centered narrowly on awareness of the political rights and liberties threatened by the British Crown (Brown 1996). Rather than envisioning a citizenry capable of exercising considered judgment over matters of public policy, throughout most of the 19th century the elite debate over citizen competence in the United States focused on the boundaries of suffrage rights. While the informed citizen existed as an ideal that appeared from time to time in political rhetoric, its practical application was typically in service to the question of which citizens could be trusted to cast a competent vote (Brown 1996). According to Michael Schudson (1998), it was largely in response to the excesses of political corruption in the Gilded Age party system of the late 19th century that Progressive reformers elevated the ideal of the informed citizen to an exalted position in popular versions of "democratic theory." While it is unclear whether this "new textbook model of the citizen – independent, informed, public-spirited and above partisanship" (Schudson 1998: 197) popularized by Progressive-era reformers was solely responsible for coloring later interpretations of "classical democratic theory" by critics like Lippmann and Schumpeter, little doubt remains today that the apparent crisis in democratic theory ushered in by the discovery of an ill-informed public was both overstated and undersupported.

While the foundations of democratic theory are not shaken by the mass public's inattention to politics, the degree of indifference to public affairs nonetheless raises suspicions about the quality of its political evaluations and lowers expectations about the feasible scope of democratic rule. A large literature today suggests that the mass public can rely on a variety of aids to simplify the task of evaluating political candidates, and this work inspires greater faith in the quality of collective decisions registered in elections than did the early studies on voting behavior. The quality of collective preferences may be a different matter, and this book has documented ample reason for doubting the mass public's ability to exercise popular sovereignty through the medium of the opinion survey when that ability is conceived narrowly as skill in evaluating alternative policies. Yet

in citizens as a result of their participation, this "educative effect" was peripheral relative to other concerns and only vaguely discussed in the work of democratic theorists prior to John Stuart Mill.

policy evaluations are only one of many types of collective opinion that might be represented by surveys. Over the centuries political philosophers have envisioned a wide variety of alternative roles for citizens to play in democracies, and while different theories of democracy impose different demands on citizens, this philosophical work often suggests that the collective opinions of ordinary citizens could potentially make valuable contributions within the first stage of Price and Neijens' decision scheme. Three such roles for citizens are among the many that have been suggested by political philosophers: citizens might appropriately define the end goals of society, clarify and perhaps prioritize the values that should constrain the actions of political leaders, and identify problems for political action.

Ends Rather Than Means

A running theme in many theories of democracy is that citizen input can be more valuable in determining the ends that a society strives for than the means to attain those ends. Even James Bryce, the patron muse for Gallup's work on political opinion polling, suggests that what citizens can contribute to governance is less analysis of policy options than suggesting a general direction for government action: "It is therefore rather sentiment than thought that the mass can contribute, a sentiment grounded on a few broad considerations and simple trains of reasoning; and the soundness and elevation of their sentiment will have more to do with their taking their stand on the side of justice, honour, and peace, than any reasoning they can apply to the sifting of the multifarious facts thrown before them, and to the drawing of legitimate inferences therefrom" (Bryce 1891: Volume 2, 254). Bryce concludes that "public opinion can determine ends, but is less fit to examine and select means to those ends" (347).

More recent theories of democratic citizenship suggest similar roles for citizens. In Thomas Christiano's (1996) *The Rule of the Many*, the limits of citizen knowledge about politics are addressed by holding citizens responsible for choosing only the overall aims of society as well as the relative priority of those aims. Formal institutions such as legislatures and executives as well as informal political actors such as interest groups and parties are responsible for choosing the most appropriate means for realizing these ends. These actors are allowed to compromise and barter in the process of selecting means, but all trade-offs are to reflect the relative priorities that citizens assign to societal ends. Likewise, Robert Dahl (1989) holds that one of the five distinguishing features of a democratic system is the degree of control exercised over the political agenda by ordinary citizens: "The demos must have the exclusive opportunity to decide how matters are to be placed on the agenda of matters that are to be decided by means of the democratic process" (113). Dahl goes so far as to define popular sovereignty in terms of this criterion.

To the extent that surveys focus citizen attention on the means of the policy process rather than its ends, we might wonder whether the form of representation afforded by surveys accords with the roles that citizens play in democratic governance. If citizens are not responsible for developing opinions on particular pieces of legislation, then perhaps the fact that citizens seem not to have thought a great deal about such matters should come as no surprise. In this view, the focus of opinion polls might be placed more appropriately on gathering opinions about the larger ends of society, or on assessing the relative importance of items vying for space on the political agenda.

Values Rather Than Preferences

If it is more important for citizens to form judgments about societal goals rather than about the policies appropriate for attaining those goals, then eliciting a population's collective values rather than its collective preferences over competing policies might prove an especially useful application of the sampling method. Gallup himself emphasized this potential contribution, noting that "the ultimate values of politics and economics, the judgments on which public policy is based, do not come from special knowledge or from intelligence alone. They are compounded from the day-to-day experience of the men and women who together make up the society we live in. That is why public-opinion polls are important today" (Gallup and Rae 1940: 266). The study of values in public opinion research (for reviews, see Kinder 1998; Kinder and Sears 1985) traditionally has been eclipsed by the study of attitudes and preferences, despite findings that values structure the political preferences typically measured in surveys (Feldman 1988; Rokeach 1968), are more predictive of behavior than attitudes (Ball-Rokeach, Rokeach, and Grube 1984), and may be more central than attitudes in moderating framing effects and, more generally, the processes by which people use information to reach judgments (Bartels 1998; Hochschild 1981; Nelson, Clawson, and Oxley 1997; Sniderman and Theriault 1999). Values seem especially important as a means of assessing the concept of "latent opinion" developed by

V. O. Key (1961) to describe the preferences that a population would likely arrive at were it to become more engaged in and informed about public affairs (Entman and Herbst 2001; Zaller 1994, 1998).

An effort to sound the collective values of a population could focus on assessing the cultural climate in which preferences are produced (Bellah, Madsen et al. 1985; Hunter and Bowman 1996; McClosky and Zaller 1984; Wildavsky 1987), clarifying the tradeoffs between competing values in order to suggest the relative priority of one value relative to another in the eyes of a population (Abramson and Inglehart 1995; Ball-Rokeach, Rokeach, and Grube 1984; Christiano 1996; Inglehart 1997; Rokeach 1968, 1973; Sniderman, Fletcher et al. 1996), and examining the ways that a population applies value judgments when evaluating issues, events, or persons (Feldman 1988; Hochschild 1981; Marcus, Sullivan et al. 1995; McClosky and Zaller 1984). Each of these applications of survey sampling could profitably inform political representatives of a mass public's priorities during the initial "elicitation of values" stage of democratic decision making.

To suggest that this can be done is not to overlook the many challenges entailed in measuring and interpreting collective values. Different assumptions about the meaning of survey responses invite different interpretations of collective values (Clarke, Kornberg et al. 1999; Davis and Davenport 1999; Fischhoff 1991; Inglehart and Abramson 1999), and there is as yet little agreement over which cultural values or behaviors are most relevant to public life (Martin 1984). Moreover, it will be important to differentiate between judgments that assess current issues in light of particular values and judgments about the intrinsic worth or importance of the values themselves. The answer one gets when asking whether a policy is fair or unfair will depend to some extent on the respondent's level of familiarity with the policy, whereas answers to questions asking whether freedom is more important than equality should not depend on possession of special factual information. To be sure, the answers that respondents give to such questions may often covary with their level of political knowledge: while nearly all respondents answer value questions, the size of information effects in collective value judgments are often larger than in collective preferences over policy matters. Nonetheless, there may be good theoretical reasons to discount the relevance or apparent meaning of information effects in some kinds of collective value judgments. In the theory of justice put forward by John Rawls (1971), for example, claims to equality in matters of justice require only a capacity for moral personality, which Rawls defines as being capable of conceiving of one's own good and as possessing a sense of justice (504–12). Likewise, Christianity and many other world religions hold that all individuals are to some degree accountable for their actions because each has a basic level of competence and autonomy in matters of moral judgment. If the moral competence of persons – however derived – is held to be inviolable, then a case could be made for ignoring the presence of information effects in certain kinds of collective value judgments.

Problems Rather Than Solutions

Surveys of citizen opinion might also be more useful for identifying or clarifying problems for political action than solutions for political problems. Rather than being limited to defining the larger ends for society as a whole, in this view citizens might have a role in identifying which immediate problems should be the object of government attention. Such a role for citizens was suggested by Edmund Burke, the famous proponent of the trustee model of representation. Although Burke held the political opinions of ordinary citizens in low regard, he recognized that they were often better judges than their representatives of the problems government should address:

The most poor, illiterate, and uninformed creatures upon earth are judges of a *practical* oppression. It is a matter of feeling; and as such persons generally have felt most of it, and are not of an over-lively sensibility, they are the best judges of it. But for *the real cause*, or *the appropriate remedy*, they ought never to be called into council about the one or the other. They ought to be totally shut out; because their reason is weak; because, when once roused, their passions are ungoverned; because they want information; because the smallness of the property which individually they possess renders them less attentive to the consequence of the measures they adopt in affairs of the moment. (quoted in Pitkin 1969: 172, emphasis in original)

Similar arguments have been developed at greater length by a number of political philosophers from within a variety of democratic traditions. John Dewey (1927) understood that a social division of labor made reliance on experts inevitable to some degree. The proper use of experts, to Dewey, lay in recognizing the different roles played by the public and its representatives, and one of the foremost roles for the public was to direct the attention of government toward particular problems: "No government by experts in which the masses do not have the chance to inform the experts as to their needs can be anything but an oligarchy managed in the interests of the few" (208).[13] Ian Shapiro (1999) makes a similar point from a different perspective, arguing that people are better able to identify instances of injustice, when it happens or as they experience it, than they are to identify conditions of justice. His theory of democratic justice is predicated on this fundamental constraint of democratic practice. An especially thoroughgoing defense of the problem-identifying role is developed by Jürgen Habermas (1996a), who argues that public opinion "cannot 'rule' of itself but can only point the use of administrative power in specific directions" (300). The public sphere, he continues, ideally fulfills a particular set of functions for democratic rule:

I have described the political public sphere as a sounding board for problems that must be processed by the political system because they cannot be solved elsewhere. To this extent, the public sphere is a warning system with sensors that, though unspecialized, are sensitive throughout society. From the perspective of democratic theory, the public sphere must, in addition, amplify the pressure of problems, that is, not only detect and identify problems but also convincingly and *influentially* thematize them, furnish them with possible solutions, and dramatize them in such a way that they are taken up and dealt with by parliamentary complexes. Besides the "signal" function, there must be an effective problematization. The capacity of the public sphere to solve problems *on its own* is limited. But this capacity must be utilized to oversee the further treatment of problems that takes place inside the political system. (359, emphasis in original)

Habermas's conception of the public sphere is built upon a sociological or discursive model of public opinion,[14] and as with Blumer he argues that the functions of the public sphere cannot be carried out properly by opinion surveys. The problem with polls, according to Habermas, is that "the individual preferences expressed in opinion polls do not reliably reflect the actual preferences of the individuals polled, if by 'preferences' one means the preferences they *would* express after weighing the relevant

---

[13] Dewey (1927) concludes that "Inquiry, indeed, is a work which devolves upon experts. But their expertness is not shown in framing and executing policies, but in discovering and making known the facts upon which the former depend.... It is not necessary that the many should have the knowledge and skill to carry on the needed investigations; what is required is that they have the ability to judge of the bearing of the knowledge supplied by others upon common concerns" (209).

[14] Habermas (1996a) writes that "Public opinion is not representative in the statistical sense. It is not an aggregate of individually gathered, privately expressed opinions held by isolated persons. Hence it must not be confused with survey results. Political opinion polls provide a certain reflection of 'public opinion' only if they have been preceded by a focused public debate and a corresponding opinion-formation in a mobilized public sphere" (362). This argument is similar to the one advanced by Daniel Yankelovich (1991).

information and arguments. For the political transformation of values and attitudes is not a process of blind adaptation but the result of a constructive opinion- and will-formation" (1996: 336, emphasis in original). The basis of his concern is the potential disjuncture between surveyed opinion and enlightened preferences. However, the analysis in the preceding chapters shows not only that such disjunctures can be identified, but also that they may be less widespread than Habermas supposes. Although collective preferences may be less suited than organized associations of citizens to the task of communicating the urgency or priority of particular problems (i.e., the "effective problematization" function described by Habermas), polls might usefully aid the "signal" function of public opinion in Habermas's theory of the public sphere.

Translating the ideas of Burke, Dewey, and Habermas into practical terms requires some creativity on the part of survey researchers, as we might not expect Blumer's "undifferentiated mass" to have a clear understanding of what its collective problems might be. But several possibilities for addressing this concern already have been suggested. News organizations following the public journalism model have been using surveys to help identify community problems for several years. When used by newspapers and television stations for the purpose of discerning public concerns, quantitative polling methods are typically supplemented with qualitative means of assessing community opinions such as town hall meetings or citizen advisory boards (Rosen 1994, 1996). Such a joining of methods ensures a richness of opinion data that can be used to shape news agendas.

Much has been made of the fact that the mass public's perceptions of "most important problems" facing the nation are often influenced by the agenda of national news coverage (for reviews of the agenda-setting literature, see Dearing and Rogers 1996; McCombs, Shaw, and Weaver 1997; Protess and McCombs 1991). While such findings appear to undermine the potential for the mass public to contribute useful information about problems requiring governmental action, it may also be that students of survey data have been emphasizing the wrong kinds of questions. When inviting respondents to diagnose problems experienced collectively by everyone else, it would be surprising indeed if the collective answers to such questions did not reflect the agenda of news coverage. A different approach is suggested by Dewey, who reminds us that "Democracy must begin at home, and its home is the neighborly community" (213). Surveys might more fruitfully gather perceptions of local problems, perceptions that are especially likely to be informed by personal experience. Aggregate results to questions like "Have you ever been discriminated against in getting a job or promotion because of your race?" (CBS/NYT) provide unique forms of social information and compelling insights regarding the extent of social problems. In addition to serving Habermas's signal function by cataloguing the occurrence of events, experiences, or behaviors in a population – as is often done routinely by governmental bureaus, but less often recognized as a form of representational activity – survey methods can be used to enlist the personal experiences of respondents in ways that aid experts or representatives in diagnosing problems and developing appropriate solutions (Davison 1972). The British government has for some years relied on survey data from a "People's Panel" to improve the delivery of social services (Worcester 1998). The panel, composed of 5,000 citizens, is explicitly designed to supplement traditional forms of political representation by communicating the experiences of people who receive particular forms of government assistance back to the political representatives who oversee those programs. It may be that opinion surveys can be used in nontraditional ways such as these to improve the quality of information provided by citizens about societal problems.

CONCLUSION

After more than a half century of refinement, survey researchers have worked out many of the technical problems with opinion polling and at least adequately understand the remaining ones. Much less attention has been given to the appropriate political uses of the opinion survey in a mass democracy. Despite assurances by public opinion researchers that the public's low levels and uneven social distribution of political knowledge are relatively benign to the functioning of democracy, the mass public is often unable to make up for its inattentiveness. Because of this, the public's imperfect knowledge of politics has important consequences for the ways that opinion surveys are used in democratic politics. Public opinion polling can elevate the clear wishes of the few above the sometimes uncertain, fragmented, and ambivalent desires of the many. Some see this as a benefit. But when collective opinion fails to represent the voices and interests of all citizens in proportion to their numbers, opinion polling may provide a distorted view of public opinion.

One of the root problems with using surveys as a method for furthering popular sovereignty is that there has been no obvious way to tell when the opinions people give in surveys are "wrong" or "right," "good" or "bad," of high or low quality, or the degree to which they reflect political interests. While aspects of this problem can be clarified with empirical analysis, as this book has attempted to do, addressing it squarely requires that scholars engage in normative inquiry. Given the importance of this topic to democratic politics, its chronic neglect is a sobering testament to the determination of survey researchers for the past half-century to pursue a methodological agenda that allowed normative inquiry to wither on the vine. At the same time, as noted in the first chapter, the philosophical inquiries of political theorists have to this day conspicuously ignored the rise of opinion surveys as a form of collective expression. As a consequence of this neglect from both quarters, normative work in democratic theory is at least implicitly suspicious of surveys as meaningful indicators of public opinion and frequently dismissive of the possibility that they can somehow capture or convey political interests, often without giving sufficient attention to whether its expectations are grounded in fact. Likewise, empirical work tends casually to identify the results of sample surveys with the concept of public opinion, without sufficiently appreciating the normative problems inherent in the use of survey results as a channel for political representation.

Contemporary students of public opinion often seem to overlook the fact that at its most essential and abstract level, public opinion is the power of popular sovereignty, regardless of whether that power is active or passive, realized or unrealized, in the form of elections, polls, groups, or social control. At this root level, the critical questions are all normative and theoretical rather than descriptive or methodological, and tend to revolve around the problem of determining how popular sovereignty might be best exercised and realized. While by no means suggesting that opinion researchers should turn away from their current focus on the descriptive analysis of public opinion, I am persuaded that normative theories of citizenship and democracy generate a particularly appropriate set of questions for students of public opinion to concern themselves with.

To the extent that opinion polling matters politically, in large part it matters as a means to enhance or diminish popular sovereignty. Attention to the particular tasks or functions that opinion polling might best be suited can thus help to optimize the balance between elite and popular control of government. Of course, such attention by itself suggests no answers to thorny normative issues that are intertwined with popular sovereignty, such as the mechanisms through which this control should be carried out, the extent to which government activities should fall under the direct control of citizens, and the time lag over which popular control might best be brought into play (frequently and immediately, as with the delegate model of representation, or infrequently and over the longer term, in the case of the trustee model). Yet it may be that a renewed appreciation of these questions can move the debate over the political role of opinion surveys into a more fruitful season than seems currently to be the case.

The problem of popular sovereignty in democratic politics has traditionally invited three contradictory solutions: either the government must be run for the people, because they are unfit to rule; or the people must be better governed, to make them fit to rule; or the government should pay more attention to the people, because they only appear unfit to rule. This book shows that none of these offers a compelling response to the problem of popular disengagement from politics. The people's indifference toward public affairs complicates the effective exercise of popular sovereignty, but does not preclude it.

The cynicism of some who dismiss opinion polls as vacuous is unwarranted. On many issues the public provides collective preferences that are quite similar to fully informed opinions. At the same time, collective opinion is often a far cry from what it might look like if the mass public were better informed. The dynamics of preference aggregation thus present two challenges: to the extent that opinion surveys are seen as irrelevant to political decision making, we risk mistaking the public's reasoned judgment for what Hamilton called a "sudden breese of passion," and the democratic project must surely suffer as a result. But to the extent that surveys are taken at face value as accurate measures of public opinion, we risk misreading the voice of the few as the will of the many.

Appendix A: Political Knowledge Indices

The information measures used in this book are based on those constructed and tested by Delli Carpini and Keeter (1993, 1996). These indices are primarily additive measures of correct answers to factual knowledge questions, where a correct answer is assigned a value of 1 and an incorrect response or no answer is given a value of 0. They also incorporate a subjective assessment of respondent knowledge level made by the survey interviewer at the conclusion of the interview. Three kinds of factual knowledge items were used to construct these indices: relative location tests in which correct answers are constructed by comparing responses to two different questions, open-ended questions asking respondents to identify the job or political office held by a public figure, and closed-ended questions testing knowledge of changes in the federal budget deficit, constitutional powers of federal branches, which party held majority status in both houses of Congress, and which party was more conservative than the other. An example of a correct answer to a relative location test is placing the Republican Party as relatively more conservative than the Democratic Party on a seven-point ideology scale, regardless of where on the ideology scale a respondent actually placed the two parties.

POLITICAL KNOWLEDGE INDICES USED IN CHAPTERS 1–5

The 1988 knowledge index has a mean of 11.0, standard deviation of 5.2, maximum value of 21, and minimum value of 0 (Cronbach's alpha = .88). The index consists of 17 items: pre-election interviewer rating score (reverse coded), offices held by Jim Wright (13.9% correct answers), Ted Kennedy (69.0%), William Rehnquist (3.5%), Michail Gorbachev

(71.0%), George Schultz (38.8%), Margaret Thatcher (60.0%), and Yasser Arafat (36.8%); naming the majority party in the House (59.4%) and the majority party in the Senate (54.0%); identifying whether the federal budget deficit was smaller, the same, or larger than in 1980 (74.7%); identifying the relative position of Bush and Dukakis on ideology (55.8%) and the two parties on ideology (54.4%), government services (51.3%), national health insurance (44.3%), defense spending (57.5%), and job assurance (46.3%). Respondents in the lowest knowledge quartile averaged 2.0 correct answers out of 16 possible, while respondents in the highest knowledge quartile averaged 13.5 correct answers.

The 1992 knowledge index (displayed in Figure 1.1) has a mean of 12.7, standard deviation of 5.8, maximum value of 23, and minimum value of 1 (Cronbach's alpha = .89). The index consists of 19 items: post-election interviewer rating score (reverse coded), offices held by Dan Quayle (87.6% correct answers), William Rehnquist (8.4%), Boris Yeltsin (44.8%), and Tom Foley (25.7%); identifying which branch decides the constitutionality of laws (57.6%) and which branch nominates federal judges (57.9%); naming the majority party in the House (59.2%), the majority party in the Senate (51.0%), and the more conservative party (57.0%); identifying the relative position of the two parties on ideology (58.6%), government services (53.9%), defense spending (51.6%), and job assurance (57.8%); and identifying the relative position of Bush and Clinton on ideology (63.3%), government services (49.7%), defense spending (50.9%), job assurance (51.5%), and abortion (58.9%). Respondents in the lowest knowledge quartile averaged 2.5 correct answers out of 18 possible, while respondents in the highest knowledge quartile averaged 15.6 correct answers.

The 1996 knowledge index has a mean of 12.5, standard deviation of 4.8, maximum value of 21, and minimum value of 1 (Cronbach's alpha = .85). The index consists of 17 items: post-election interviewer rating score (reverse coded), offices held by Al Gore (87.8% correct answers), William Rehnquist (9.3%), Boris Yeltsin (64.7%), and Newt Gingrich (57.8%); identifying whether the federal budget deficit went up, down, or stayed the same during Clinton's term (29.2%); naming the majority party in the House (75.0%) and the majority party in the Senate (71.5%); identifying the relative position of the two parties on government services (64.1%), defense spending (48.6%), and environmental regulation (48.8%); and identifying the relative position of Clinton and Dole on government services (69.5%), job assurance (64.5%), health insurance (65.5%), environmental regulation (51.9%), affirmative action (60.8%), and abortion (58.4%). Respondents in the lowest knowledge quartile averaged 4.7 correct answers out of 16 possible, while respondents in the highest knowledge quartile averaged 14.2 correct answers.

POLITICAL KNOWLEDGE INDICES USED IN CHAPTER 6

In Chapter 6, each respondent's total number of correct answers was divided by the maximum possible score so that all knowledge indices could be standardized to range from 0 to 1.

The 1980 knowledge index has a mean of .53 and standard deviation of .25 (Cronbach's alpha = .78). The index consists of seven items: post-election interviewer rating score (reverse coded); naming the majority party in the House (62.0% correct answers); identifying the relative ideological locations of the two parties (41.4%); and locating the relative positions of the two parties on government services (43.6%), defense spending (44.1%), job assurances (41.1%), and government aid to blacks (46.0%).

The 1982 knowledge index has a mean of .51 and standard deviation of .26 (Cronbach's alpha = .81). The index consists of eight items: interviewer rating score (reverse coded); naming the majority party in the House (31.3% correct answers) and Senate (38.4%); identifying the relative ideological locations of the two parties (45.3%); and locating the relative positions of the two parties on government services (53.4%), defense spending (50.5%), job assurances (53.7%), and government aid to blacks (46.4%).

The 1984 knowledge index has a mean of .56 and standard deviation of .26 (Cronbach's alpha = .80). The index consists of eight items: post-election interviewer rating score (reverse coded); naming the majority party in the House (55.1% correct answers) and Senate (30.2%); identifying the relative ideological locations of the two parties (56.4%); and locating the relative positions of the two parties on government services (58.7%), defense spending (59.4%), job assurances (50.5%), and government aid to blacks (49.3%).

The 1986 knowledge index has a mean of .49 and standard deviation of .24 (Cronbach's alpha = .82). The index consists of 11 items: interviewer rating score (reverse coded); offices held by George Bush (77.2% correct answers), Caspar Weinberger (33.0%), William Rehnquist (13.5%), Tip O'Neill (56.3%), and Bob Dole (12.3%); naming the majority party in the House (33.3%) and Senate (47.8%); identifying the relative ideological locations of the two parties (52.6%); and locating the relative positions of the two parties on defense spending (61.2%) and government services (53.5%).

The 1988 knowledge index has a mean of .52 and standard deviation of .24 (Cronbach's alpha = .87). The index consists of 16 items, including all of those listed above except the relative location of the candidates on ideology.

The 1990 knowledge index has a mean of .46 and standard deviation of .23 (Cronbach's alpha = .84). The index consists of 13 items: interviewer rating score (reverse coded); offices held by Tom Foley (8.8% correct answers), Margaret Thatcher (49.8%), Dan Quayle (80.9%), William Rehnquist (4.2%), Michail Gorbachev (69.1%), and Nelson Mandela (15.4%); naming the majority party in the House (48.3%) and Senate (41.4%); identifying the relative ideological locations of the two parties (48.9%); and locating the relative positions of the two parties on government services (40.9%), defense spending (46.3%), and government aid to blacks (39.6%).

The 1992 knowledge index has a mean of .55 and standard deviation of .24 (Cronbach's alpha = .85). The index consists of 14 items, including all of those listed above except for the five relative location measures for Bush and Clinton.

The 1994 knowledge index has a mean of .55 and standard deviation of .25 (Cronbach's alpha = .86). The index consists of 13 items: interviewer rating score (reverse coded), offices held by Al Gore (79.2% correct answers), William Rehnquist (7.0%), Boris Yeltsin (46.1%), and Thomas Foley (34.2%); identifying which branch of the federal government was responsible for deciding the constitutionality of laws (56.9%) and for nominating federal judges (55.4%); naming the majority party in the House (73.0%) and Senate (65.6%); identifying the relative ideological locations of Republicans and Democrats (60.5%); and identifying the relative position of the parties on government services (49.7%), job assurances (54.6%), and government aid to blacks (48.8%).

The 1996 knowledge index has a mean of .58 and standard deviation of .22 (Cronbach's alpha = .78). The index consists of 11 items, including all of those listed above except for the six relative location items for Clinton and Dole.

The 1998 knowledge index has a mean of .58 and standard deviation of .24 (Cronbach's alpha = .81). The index consists of 11 items: interviewer rating score (reverse coded), offices held by Al Gore (88.4% correct answers), William Rehnquist (10.6%), Boris Yeltsin (49.7%), and

Newt Gingrich (59.9%); naming the majority party in the House (67.4%) and Senate (55.7%); identifying the relative ideological locations of Republicans and Democrats (60.8%); and identifying the relative position of the parties on government services (56.1%), abortion rights (45.9%), and environmental regulation (48.7%).

Appendix B: Methodology

Given the need to test for collective rationality in a wide variety of opinion distributions for which the sizes and shapes of the signal and noise distributions are known, a computer simulation was used to generate the raw data used for Chapter 2's analysis. The units of analysis in the simulation are collective opinion distributions made up of 1,500 respondents divided into signal and noise groups. The *signal distribution* is defined as the aggregated preferences of those hypothetical respondents possessing a balance of factually correct information. The *noise distribution* is defined as the aggregated opinions of those hypothetical respondents drawing from a balance of factually incorrect or misleading information as well as of those possessing no relevant information at all.

To assess how different ways of collapsing a given opinion distribution might affect the accuracy of signal estimates, opinion data were generated into a six-category response scale. Although it is unlikely that a six-point scale would be used in survey research, this response scale has a desirable property for studying the effects of aggregation: six categories can be collapsed directly into a dichotomous scale (treating the first three categories as one option and the second three categories as a second option) as well as into a three-point scale (with categories one and two as a first option, three and four as a middle option, and four and five as a third option). This makes it possible to directly compare estimates of a particular signal distribution aggregated into two, three, and six response categories.

Three signal-to-noise ratios were selected to model the effects of different signal strengths on the accuracy of signal estimates made from aggregate parameters. In the 25% signal condition, 375 respondents were assigned to the signal distribution and the rest to the noise distribution; in the 50% signal condition, 750 respondents were assigned to each group; and in the 75% signal condition, 1,125 respondents were assigned to the signal distribution and the remaining 375 to the noise distribution.

Three patterns of noise were used to generate distributions of ill-informed respondents. Ill-informed responses in the normal and skewed noise conditions were generated by treating them as binomial random variables, and noise patterns were calculated separately for the two-, three-, and six-category conditions. To model patterns of random noise, I calculated binomial probability distributions for each set of categories, with p equal to .5 in the normal noise condition and .65 in the skewed noise condition. In the six-category condition, the marginal percentages took the form .031/.156/.312/.312/.156/.031 for normal noise and .005/.048/.181/.336/.312/.116 for skewed noise (within each condition, the categories sum to 100%). In the three-category condition, the marginal percentages took the form .25/.5/.25 for normal noise and .12/.46/.42 for skewed noise. In the two-category condition, the marginal percentages took the form .5/.5 for normal noise and .35/.65 for skewed noise. Noise distributions were calculated separately for each of the two-, three-, and six-category conditions to avoid implausible patterns of ill-informed responses. For example, taking the six-category skewed noise pattern and condensing it into a dichotomous scale would channel noise responses into a .24/.76 split, an uncannily decisive pattern to be resulting from a random distribution process. Distributions of noise for a given signal-to-noise ratio were generated by multiplying the appropriate number of ill-informed respondents by the marginal percentages of the noise patterns.

For the data set to be as realistic as possible, it was important not only to sample all possible signal distributions but also to ensure that the probability distribution of signals was something like what might be expected in the real world. It seems reasonable that a much greater number of well-informed distributions should have a mean closer to the center of the range of responses than to either extreme. Put another way, given a properly designed survey question it is unlikely that well-informed respondents as a group should cluster with little or no variance at one extreme or another. The distribution of signals generated for the simulation was designed to meet this criterion. The set of signal distributions was created with a program compiled in C language, which is available from the author. This program generated a representative sample of all possible combinations of 750 respondents (representing the 50%

signal condition) across six categories. Given that without replacement, there are approximately 1.74^{17} possible combinations of 750 respondents across six categories, and that each successive combination represents a change in the position of just one respondent from that of the previous arrangement, the full set of combinations was deemed too impractical to use. Instead, a representative sample of these combinations was drawn to capture all possible signal distributions that were substantially different from one another. This was accomplished by generating the combinations in steps of 50 respondents, which narrowed the field to just more than 3.6 million possible combinations. To further reduce the number of distributions while maintaining a representative sample, only those combinations with a mean equal to 1 ($n = 1$), 2 ($n = 84$), 3 ($n = 433$), 4 ($n = 433$), 5 ($n = 84$) or 6 ($n = 1$) were retained for use in the simulation, resulting in 1,036 unique signal distributions. The means of the 1,036 signal distributions are normally distributed around a mean of 3.5, which is the midpoint of the six-category scale and also the mean shared by the normal and uniform noise conditions.

With 1,036 signal distributions represented in each of three noise conditions, three signal-to-noise ratios, and three category conditions, the data set for the simulation contains a total of 27,972 collective opinions. It should be noted that although "don't know" and "no opinion" responses are not considered in these data, the effects of item nonresponse as well as of filter questions can be simulated by assuming that filter questions and larger numbers of "don't know" responses increase the ratio of signal to noise in the grand distribution. In the tables presented in Chapter 2, the effect of adding a filter or increasing item nonresponse might be read as the effect in moving from (to give one example) a signal strength of 25% to one of 50%.

CHAPTER 3

Table 3.2. To determine whether the marginals of the highest or lowest knowledge quartile were more evenly dispersed across response categories, I calculated the degree to which each group's collective opinion deviated from a perfectly even distribution across response categories. The group with the smaller absolute deviation was judged to be more evenly distributed. Perfectly even distributions were defined as 50/50 splits in the case of dichotomous and 33/33/33 splits in the case of trichotomous questions. All questions not originally coded with two or three response options were recoded for this analysis into dichotomous or trichotomous distributions, as appropriate (details on individual questions are available from the author upon request). For dichotomous variables, the test statistic is

$$\text{Relative Dispersion} = \frac{(|50 - R1_{\text{low}}| + |50 - R2_{\text{low}}|)}{2}$$
$$- \frac{(|50 - R1_{\text{high}}| + |50 - R2_{\text{high}}|)}{2} \tag{1}$$

where $R1$ and $R2$ correspond to the percentage of responses in the first and second response categories, and high and low refer to the respective response distributions of the highest and lowest knowledge quartiles. For trichotomous questions, the statistic is

$$\text{Relative Dispersion}$$
$$= \frac{(|33.3 - R1_{\text{low}}| + |33.3 - R2_{\text{low}}| + |33.3 - R3_{\text{low}}|)}{2}$$
$$- \frac{(|33.3 - R1_{\text{high}}| + |33.3 - R2_{\text{high}}| + |33.3 - R3_{\text{high}}|)}{2} \tag{2}$$

A positive value means that responses from the highest knowledge quartile are more evenly dispersed across response categories; a negative value means that the lowest quartile is more evenly dispersed. This method was used so that both dichotomous and trichotomous questions could be compared under the same metric. Other potential test statistics, such as measures of kurtosis or skewness, are influenced by the number of response categories and were therefore considered inappropriate for estimating differences in dispersion across the entire range of questions.

Percentage-point differences between the opinions of the highest and lowest knowledge quartiles were calculated as follows. For dichotomous variables, the statistic is

$$\text{Relative Point Difference}_{\text{low}-\text{high}}$$
$$= \frac{(|R1_{\text{low}} - R1_{\text{high}}| + |R2_{\text{low}} - R2_{\text{high}}|)}{2} \tag{3}$$

For trichotomous variables, the statistic is

$$\text{Relative Point Difference}_{\text{low}-\text{high}}$$
$$= \frac{(|R1_{\text{low}} - R1_{\text{high}}| + |R2_{\text{low}} - R2_{\text{high}}| + |R3_{\text{low}} - R3_{\text{high}}|)}{2} \tag{4}$$

These statistics thus take the same scale as the point differences used in Page and Shapiro's (1992) *Rational Public* and have the added advantage of being directly comparable for both dichotomous and trichotomous variables. A point difference of zero means that both distributions are exactly the same; a difference of 100 means that they are exactly opposite. Across the 235 policy questions analyzed, relative point differences between quartiles range from 0.5 to 47.1, with a mean of 15.3 and standard deviation of 9.8.

Differences in modal preferences between the highest and lowest knowledge quartiles were determined by comparing which response category contained the largest number of responses for each quartile. Whenever the plurality preferences of high and low knowledge respondents occupied different response categories, these groups were coded as having different modal preferences.

CHAPTER 4

The method I use for simulating fully informed preferences extends the simulation approach developed by Bartels (1996) and by Delli Carpini and Keeter (1996). I use logistic regression to avoid the restrictive assumption that political information must have a linear relationship with preferences. Delli Carpini and Keeter use ordinary least squares to estimate parameters in their simulation; Bartels uses a probit model to estimate parameters, but later transforms those parameters in a way that assumes linearity of information effects. I also estimate fully informed preferences for people who give "don't know" and "no opinion" responses in the survey data, following the assumption that as information levels rise, the proportion of people who give opinions or turn out to vote should also rise. The logit model I use for simulating fully informed opinions in dichotomous questions is structured as follows:

$$prob \ (Y_i = 1) = \alpha + \beta_1 I_i + \Sigma \beta_k D_{ik} + \Sigma \delta_k (I_i \times D_{ik}) + e_i,$$

where Y_i is respondent i's policy preference (e.g., 1 for "favor", 0 for "oppose"), I_i is respondent i's score on a scale of political information, D_{ik} is respondent i's score on the kth demographic characteristic, $I_i \times D_{ik}$ is the product of respondent i's information score multiplied by respondent i's score on the kth demographic characteristic, and e_i is the error term for the ith observation. In this equation, β_1 is the coefficient for the information variable, β_k is the coefficient for the kth demographic characteristic, and δ_k is the coefficient for the kth interaction term. An ordered logit model that adds a second intercept parameter is used when estimating fully informed opinions in trichotomous questions.

After completing the four-step simulation procedure described in Chapter 4, the mean of the Y_i probabilities from hypothetically fully informed respondents are used to construct fully informed marginal percentages that can be compared directly to surveyed marginal percentages. It is important to note that the marginals resulting from this simulation process can be compared directly to the surveyed marginals only because they are operationalized as the mean of the individual probabilities that $Y_i = 1$ instead of the sum of the predicted values of Y_i. For example, if 60% of all respondents sharing a certain demographic profile favor a certain policy, each respondent has a probability of .6 for favoring the policy. The mean of these probabilities recovers the surveyed percentage in favor (.6 = 60%), but since the predicted value of Y_i for each respondent is 1 (because .6 > .5), estimates from predicted values would mistakenly show a group that is 100% in favor of the policy. The upshot is that most ordinary least squares applications (including the simulation method used in Delli Carpini and Keeter 1996) are less suited for estimating information effects than maximum likelihood applications because they introduce large amounts of error into such estimates.

The size of information effects in collective opinions was calculated by comparing the percentage-point differences between surveyed and fully informed collective opinions. For dichotomous questions, the statistic is

$$\text{Relative Point Difference}_{\text{S−FI}} = \frac{(|R1_S - R1_{\text{FI}}| + |R2_S - R2_{\text{FI}}|)}{2} \quad (5)$$

where S refers to surveyed opinion, and FI refers to the simulated fully informed opinion. For surveyed opinion, $R1$ and $R2$ correspond to the percentage of responses in the first and second response options. For fully informed opinion, $R1$ and $R2$ correspond to the mean of the fully informed Y_i probabilities (expressed as percentages) in each response category. In the case of trichotomous variables, the comparable statistic is

$$\text{Relative Point Difference}_{\text{S−FI}}$$
$$= \frac{(|R1_S - R1_{\text{FI}}| + |R2_S - R2_{\text{FI}}| + |R3_S - R3_{\text{FI}}|)}{2} \quad (6)$$

This statistic, which is directly comparable between dichotomous and trichotomous variables, takes a range of 0 to 100, with a point difference of 0 meaning that both distributions are exactly the same and a difference of 100 meaning that they are exactly opposite. Equivalent comparisons were used to determine the size of individual-level information effects.

It is important to point out that DK/NO and nonsubstantive responses volunteered by respondents are excluded when determining the marginal percentages of surveyed opinion used to calculate the size of these information effects. This choice serves to standardize the size of information effects across question formats. It also produces a more conservative estimate of information effects and a truer measure of the directional impact of information effects than would be the case if such responses were included when calculating surveyed marginal percentages. To illustrate the problem that this approach solves, consider a hypothetical question where a third of respondents favor a policy, a third oppose it, and a third give DK/NO responses. Counting the DK/NO responses as missing produces a marginal percentage of 50% in favor, while including them in the marginal percentages produces 33.3% in favor. Suppose the measure of fully informed opinion for this question, which uses predicted opinions for all respondents, shows 53% in favor. With DK/NO responses counted as missing in the surveyed data, the size of the effect amounts to only 3 percentage points. But when such responses are included in calculating surveyed marginals, the size of the information effect reaches 20 points. This illustrates the general point that questions with DK or NO prompts will tend, *ceteris paribus*, to produce larger information effects when DK/NO responses are included for calculating the distribution of surveyed opinion. Note also that counting DK/NO responses as part of surveyed marginals always decreases the size of marginal percentages for any substantive category, so long as at least some respondents give DK/NO responses. This tendency toward systematic bias makes it difficult to assess the directional impact of information effects on the distribution of substantive responses, which is another reason for excluding DK/NO responses from calculations of surveyed marginals when estimating the size of information effects.

Inconsistencies in surveyed and fully informed collective preferences were determined by noting when surveyed opinion had a different collective preference than simulated opinion. Each opinion distribution was coded as having either a majority preference in favor of one option, a plurality preference in favor of one option, or a tie between two options. In the case of dichotomous response scales, I considered a tie any marginals falling within plus or minus 3 percentage points of the 50% mark. For trichotomous response scales, a tie was coded for any marginals falling within plus or minus 3 percentage points of the 33.3% mark. It follows that a majority is defined as at least 53.5% of responses and a plurality as at least 36.3% of responses.

To illustrate how the fully informed collective preferences discussed in Chapter 4 were estimated, coefficients from the logistic regression that produced the data in Figure 4.1 are displayed in Table B.1. Including the constants and interaction terms, this model estimates a total of 52 parameters from ANES data. While this is a large number of parameters, the large sample sizes of the ANES studies (1,775 completed interviews in 1988, 2,255 in 1992, and 1,534 in 1996) should nevertheless ensure that these parameters exhibit the asymptotic properties of efficiency, unbiasedness, and normality (Aldrich and Nelson 1984: 53; also see discussion in King 1989: 74–80). The equation in Table B.1 represents a statistically significant improvement over the restricted model, but the table also reveals a relative paucity of significant coefficients. A similar pattern was found in the Bartels simulation of information effects in vote choices, where only between 14 and 24% of coefficients achieved conventional levels of significance (Bartels 1996: calculated from Tables 1, 4, 5, 6, 7, and 8). The reason for this pattern appears to be a collinearity problem stemming from the abundance of interaction terms that are correlated with political information scores as well as with the demographic variables. Most of this collinearity comes from the nature of the demographic variable clusters. For example, in the 1992 ANES Republican partisanship is correlated with Democratic partisanship at −.78. Likewise, living in a suburban area is correlated at −.57 with living in an urban area, and −.42 with living in a rural area. Intercorrelations like these that occur within variable clusters seem to account for most of the collinearity. The rest is due to associations between different variables. For example, the index of political knowledge is correlated at .56 with education and .42 with income. Being married is correlated at .42 with income and .33 with being a homeowner. All of this is complicated by the set of interaction terms, which are linearly but imperfectly related to both the information scale and the set of demographic terms. In spite of these associations, the theoretical approach to information effects adopted in this analysis dictates that all of these variables be included in the logit model. The result is a large number of insignificant coefficients, but the coefficients themselves should nonetheless be valid for the purposes to which they are put.

Examining the restricted form of this equation confirms that, absent the information and interaction terms, almost half of the coefficients attain conventional levels of significance (data not shown). Rerunning the regression using only the significant variable clusters identified in Table B.1

TABLE B.1. *Logit coefficients for support of abortion rights (1 = always permitted)*

Independent Variables	Main Effects		Interaction Effects (× Information)	
Information (1–23)	.167*	(.074)	...	...
Education (years)	.082	(.065)	.002	(.005)
Income (percentile)	.015*	(.006)	−.000	(.000)
Age (years)	−.003	(.012)	−.001	(.001)
Republican	.117	(.379)	−.066*	(.030)
Democrat	−.436	(.349)	.031	(.028)
Black	−.406	(.423)	.059	(.034)
Female	−.645*	(.304)	.065**	(.021)
Married	.203	(.316)	−.031	(.023)
Union family	−.119	(.392)	.001	(.028)
Homeowner	−.206	(.308)	.001	(.022)
Parent w/child at home	.066	(.312)	−.021	(.022)
Financially worse off	.445	(.284)	−.027	(.020)
Protestant	−.020	(.410)	−.067*	(.030)
Catholic	−.266	(.451)	−.066*	(.033)
Other religion	−.446	(.512)	−.020	(.038)
East	.986*	(.472)	−.063*	(.032)
Midwest	.365	(.479)	−.041	(.029)
South	.100	(.415)	−.041	(.028)
Urban	−.098	(.322)	−.000	(.022)
Rural	−.153	(.339)	.008	(.025)
Retired	1.101*	(.539)	−.055	(.039)
Homemaker	.749	(.446)	−.066	(.036)
Executive/Professional	.558	(.492)	−.038	(.032)
Clerical	.918	(.483)	−.055	(.037)
Technical/Sales	−.210	(.560)	.010	(.038)
Constant	−2.390*	(1.004)		

* $p < .05$
** $p < .01$
Note: Standard errors of parameter estimates are in parentheses.
Beginning log likelihood = −1348.8; Ending log likelihood = −1157.3.
N =1,953

produces no unexpected changes in the size or direction of coefficients. These findings suggest that the relatively large standard errors of many of the coefficients in the unrestricted equation should have little or no effect on the unbiasedness of the coefficients themselves.

A more substantial concern with the data shown in Table B.1 is the potential for specification error that comes from excluding attitudinal variables from the model. Given the need to exclude such obviously relevant measures as attitudes toward abortion and women's rights, in the analyses throughout this book I avoid any suggestion that the simulation model used here can *explain* individual-level opinions. Instead, I focus on what the model is intended to capture: differences in opinion between groups as well as the relationship between information and policy preferences within groups.

As a precaution, I also tested whether the presence of insignificant coefficients in Table B.1 affected the simulated marginal percentages. A second measure of fully informed collective opinion was estimated using a regression containing only the significant variable clusters from the reduced-form equation (i.e., education, income, age, partisanship, marital status, parental status, religious preference, region, and occupation, along with the information variable and the relevant interaction terms). The result of this alternative simulation was a fully informed collective preference that was 54.2% in favor of unrestricted abortion rights. Deviating by only 1.5 percentage points from the simulated marginals of the full equation, this result confirms the accuracy of the model shown in Table B.1 despite the frequency of insignificant coefficients. Similar results were obtained by rerunning the simulations for the examples in Figures 4.2, 4.3, and 4.4 using only significant variable clusters from the reduced form equations. It appears that the large standard errors of many coefficients in the unrestricted models do not substantially affect the simulation results.

CHAPTER 5

Figure 5.1. These charts display the relative dispersion statistics detailed in equation (1) along the *x*-axis, with the *y*-axis displaying collective information effects in the top chart and individual-level information effects in the bottom chart.

Table 5.2. The lopsidedness of opinions in the lowest and highest knowledge quartiles are calculated as in equations (1) and (2), except that separate calculations are made for each quartile. The lopsidedness statistic can thus take values ranging from 0 to 100, with 0 meaning that responses from the group are distributed perfectly evenly across response categories and a value of 100 meaning that the group opinion has no variance whatsoever, but is located completely within one of the response categories. Across the 235 questions analyzed here, the lopsidedness of the lowest knowledge quartile ranges from 0.1 to 57.4, with a mean of 23.0 and standard deviation of 12.9. The lopsidedness of the highest knowledge quartile ranges from 0.0 to 57.3, with a mean of 22.0 and standard deviation of 11.8. The lopsidedness scores of the highest and lowest quartiles have a moderate positive correlation, $r = .48$, $p < .001$.

CHAPTER 6

Simulations of fully informed opinion were conducted as described earlier, except that the set of independent variables was standardized to provide continuity in the simulation model from year to year. This involved eliminating measures of occupation for data series that begin with 1980, as the coding changed following the 1980 census. The reduced form models contain a total of 42 parameters, including a constant as well as knowledge, demographic, and interaction terms. All time series simulations included measures of political knowledge, education, income, age, partisanship, race, gender, martial status, occupation, religious affiliation, union membership, homeowner status, parental status, financial status, region, and type of community (i.e., urban or rural, with suburban as the contrast category). All knowledge indices used in this analysis range from 0 to 1 to correct for uneven scale lengths across years. Additional details about these knowledge indices are found in Appendix A.

Tables 6.2 and 6.3. Collective information effects reported in these tables were calculated using Equations (5) and (6). In this way, each survey question contributed a single observation per time period to the analysis, regardless of whether the question used a dichotomous or trichotomous response scale.

Table 6.4 The tests of predictive ability reported in this table and in Figure 6.5 require that data from survey questions with dichotomous response scales be constructed differently than questions with trichotomous response scales. Mapping trends for dichotomous variables like the abortion question used in Figure 6.3 is straightforward: with such data, one of the two response options can be selected to model over-time changes in aggregate opinion for that variable. Since in this kind of question the trend for one response option is a reverse image of the other, including data from both options would add no new information to the analysis. But the "hydraulic effect" for questions with trichotomous response options takes a different form because each of the response categories produces a distinctive trend that is not merely a reflection of any other. Yet, because collapsing any two trends produces the inverse of the third, including all three trends invites redundancy. To address this problem, for each trichotomous question the trend from the middle response option was omitted from the analysis. In this way, each dichotomous question produces a single data point in any given year (as illustrated in Figure 6.3.) while each trichotomous question produces two data points (as shown in Figure 6.5). Parsed out in this way, the data for analyzing trends consists of 361 observations (more specifically, 361 observations of surveyed data points, plus another 361 observations of fully informed data points). These observations represent trends from 27 unique questions repeated in identical form over as many as 10 time periods. The basic time lag in this analysis is two years.

As applied to these data, the Granger test is derived from the results of two regression equations:

$$S_t = \sum_{i=1}^{n} \alpha_i \, FI_{t-i} + \sum_{j=1}^{n} \beta_j \, S_{t-j} + u_{1t}$$

$$FI_t = \sum_{i=1}^{m} \lambda_i \, FI_{t-i} + \sum_{j=1}^{m} \delta_j \, S_{t-j} + u_{2t}$$

The first equation assesses the unique impact that lagged values of fully informed opinion have on surveyed opinion, controlling for lagged values of surveyed opinion, and the second equation assesses the unique impact that lagged values of surveyed opinion have on fully informed opinion, controlling for lagged values of fully informed opinion. In the first equation, we want to know whether entering the block of fully informed opinions produces a statistically significant improvement in predicting surveyed opinion, over and above the amount of variance explained by past values of surveyed opinion. In the second equation, we observe the same about surveyed opinion predicting future values of fully informed opinion. Four possible outcomes result from the test procedure. If fully informed opinion turns out to be a significant predictor in the first equation, but surveyed opinion is not significant in the second, we conclude that fully informed opinion Granger-predicts future values of surveyed opinion. If the opposite were to happen, we would conclude that surveyed opinion Granger-predicts future values of simulated opinion. If the variables of interest in both equations are significant, then this would be a case of mutual causality or feedback, an indeterminate relationship where each of the two variables simultaneously predict future values of the other. And finally, if neither of the variables proves to be a significant predictor, we would conclude that they are statistically unrelated to one another.

Figure 6.6. Pairing the 361 observations to code the type of change that occurred between t_1 and t_n measures of opinion produces 306 t_1/t_2 observations, a total reduced by the number of data pairs with time lags of greater than two years. Likewise, there are a total of 263 t_1/t_3 observations, 215 t_1/t_4 observations, and 169 t_1/t_5 observations.

References

Abramson, Paul R., and Ronald Inglehart. 1995. *Value Change in Global Perspective*. Ann Arbor: University of Michigan Press.

Achen, Christopher. 1975. Mass Political Attitudes and the Survey Response. *American Political Science Review* 69 (4):1218–31.

Adler, Kenneth P. 1984. Polling the Attentive Public. *Annals of the American Academy of Political and Social Science* 472 (March):143–54.

Aldrich, John, and Forrest Nelson. 1984. *Linear Probability, Logit, and Probit Models*. Beverly Hills: Sage.

Almond, Gabriel A. 1950. *The American People and Foreign Policy*. New York: Harcourt Brace.

Althaus, Scott L. 1996. Opinion Polls, Information Effects and Political Equality: Exploring Ideological Biases in Collective Opinion. *Political Communication* 13 (1):3–21.

———. 1998. Information Effects in Collective Preferences. *American Political Science Review* 92 (3):545–58.

———. 2001. Who's Voted in When the People Tune Out? Information Effects in Congressional Elections. In *Communication in U.S. Elections: New Agendas*, edited by R. P. Hart and D. Shaw. Lanham, MD: Rowman & Littlefield Publishers.

Althaus, Scott L., Jill A. Edy, and Patricia F. Phalen. 2002. Using the Vanderbilt Television Abstracts to Track Broadcast News Content: Possibilities and Pitfalls. *Journal of Broadcasting & Electronic Media* 46 (3):473–92.

Alvarez, R. Michael, and John Brehm. 1995. American Ambivalence towards Abortion Policy: Development of a Heteroskedastic Probit Model of Competing Values. *American Journal of Political Science* 39 (4):1055–82.

———. 1997. Are Americans Ambivalent towards Racial Policies? *American Journal of Political Science* 41 (2):345–74.

———. 1998. Speaking in Two Voices: American Equivocation about the Internal Revenue Service. *American Journal of Political Science* 42 (2):418–52.

————. 2002. *Hard Choices, Easy Answers: Values, Information, and American Public Opinion.* New York: Princeton University Press.

Alwin, Duane F., and Jon A. Krosnick. 1991. The Reliability of Survey Attitude Measurement: The Influence of Question and Respondent Attributes. *Sociological Methods & Research* 20 (1):139–81.

Appelbaum, Lauren D. 2001. The Influence of Perceived Deservingness on Policy Decisions Regarding Aid to the Poor. *Political Psychology* 22 (3):419–42.

Arendt, Hannah. 1958. *The Human Condition.* Chicago: University of Chicago Press.

Arnold, R. Douglas. 1993. Can Inattentive Citizens Control Their Elected Representatives? In *Congress Reconsidered,* edited by L. Dodd and B. Oppenheimer. Washington, DC: Congressional Quarterly.

Arrow, Kenneth. 1963. *Social Choice and Individual Values.* 2nd ed. London: Yale University Press.

Asher, Herbert. 1988. *Polling and the Public: What Every Citizen Should Know.* Washington, DC: CQ Press.

Austen-Smith, David, and Jeffrey S. Banks. 1996. Information Aggregation, Rationality, and the Condorcet Jury Theorem. *American Political Science Review* 90 (1):34–45.

Avey, M.J. 1989. *The Demobilization of American Voters.* New York: Greenwood.

Bachrach, Peter. 1967. *The Theory of Democratic Elitism: A Critique.* Boston: Little, Brown and Company.

————. 1975. Interest, Participation, and Democratic Theory. In *Participation in Politics,* edited by J. R. Pennock and J. Chapman. New York: Lieber-Atherton.

Bachrach, Peter, and Morton S. Baratz. 1962. Two Faces of Power. *American Political Science Review* 56 (4):947–52.

Baer, Denise, and Michael Bositis. 1988. *Elite Cadres and Party Coalitions: Representing the Public in Party Politics.* New York: Greenwood.

Bagdikian, Ben. 1990. *The Media Monopoly.* 3rd ed. Boston: Beacon Press.

Balbus, Isaac D. 1971. The Concept of Interest in Pluralist and Marxian Analysis. *Politics and Society* 1 (February):151–77.

Ball-Rokeach, Sandra J., Milton Rokeach, and Joel W. Grube. 1984. *The Great American Values Test: Influencing Behavior and Belief through Television.* New York: Free Press.

Barabas, Jason. 2002. Another Look at the Measurement of Political Knowledge. *Political Analysis* 10 (2):209.

Barber, Benjamin. 1984. *Strong Democracy.* Berkeley: University of California Press.

Bartels, Larry M. 1988. *Presidential Primaries and the Dynamics of Public Choice.* Princeton, NJ: Princeton University Press.

————. 1990. Public Opinion and Political Interests. Paper presented at the annual meeting of the Midwest Political Science Association, at Chicago, IL.

————. 1991. Constituency Opinion and Congressional Policy Making: The Reagan Defense Buildup. *American Political Science Review* 85 (2):457–74.

————. 1996. Uninformed Votes: Information Effects in Presidential Elections. *American Journal of Political Science* 40 (1):194–230.

————. 1998. Democracy with Attitudes. Paper presented at the annual meeting of the American Political Science Association, Sep. 3–6, at Boston, MA.

————. 2000. Partisanship and Voting Behavior, 1952–1996. *American Journal of Political Science* 44 (1):35–50.

Barton, Allen H. 1998. Public Opinion as Unicorn, Elephant, or Electron: What Concept Corresponds to Our Indicators? Paper presented at the annual meeting of the American Association for Public Opinion Research, May 14–17, at St. Louis, MO.

Bauer, Wilhelm. 1933. Public Opinion. In *Encyclopedia of the Social Sciences*, edited by E. R. A. Seligman. New York: Macmillan.

Baumgartner, Frank R., and Beth L. Leech. 1998. *Basic Interests: The Importance of Groups in Politics and in Political Science*. Princeton, NJ: Princeton University Press.

Bay, Christian. 1965. *The Structure of Freedom*. New York: Atheneum.

Beck, Paul Allen, and Frank Sorauf. 1992. *Party Politics in America*. Seventh ed. New York: HarperCollins.

Beiner, Ronald, ed. 1995. *Theorizing Citizenship*. Albany, NY: SUNY Press.

Beitz, Charles R. 1989. *Political Equality: An Essay in Democratic Theory*. Princeton, NJ: Princeton University Press.

Bellah, Robert N., Richard Madsen, William M. Sullivan, Ann Swidler, and Steven M. Tipton. 1985. *Habits of the Heart: Individualism and Commitment in American Life*. Berkeley: University of California Press.

Bennett, Stephen E. 1988. "Know-Nothings" Revisited: The Meaning of Political Ignorance Today. *Social Science Quarterly* 69 (2):476–90.

————. 1989. Trends in Americans' Political Information, 1967–1987. *American Politics Quarterly* 17:422–35.

————. 1993. Out of Sight, Out of Mind: Americans' Knowledge of Party Control of the House of Representatives, 1960–1984. *Political Research Quarterly* 46 (March):67–80.

————. 1994. The Persian Gulf War's Impact on Americans' Political Information. *Political Behavior* 16:179–201.

————. 1995a. Americans' Knowledge of Ideology, 1980–1992. *American Politics Quarterly* 23 (3):259–78.

————. 1995b. Comparing Americans' Political Information in 1988 and 1992. *Journal of Politics* 57 (2):521–32.

————. 1996. "Know-Nothings" Revisited Again. *Political Behavior* 18 (3): 219–33.

Bennett, Stephen E., Richard S. Flickinger, and Staci L. Rhine. 2000. Political Talk over Here, over There, over Time. *British Journal of Political Science* 30:99–119.

Bennett, Stephen E., and David Resnick. 1990. The Implications of Nonvoting for Democracy in the United States. *American Journal of Political Science* 34 (3):771–802.

Bennett, W. Lance. 1990. Toward a Theory of Press-State Relations in the United States. *Journal of Communication* 40 (2):103–25.

————. 1993. Constructing Publics and Their Opinions. *Political Communication* 10 (2):101–20.

Bennett, W. Lance, and Jarol Manheim. 1993. Taking the Public by Storm: Information, Cueing, and the Democratic Process in the Gulf Conflict. *Political Communication* 10:331–52.

Berelson, Bernard. 1952. Democratic Theory and Public Opinion. *Public Opinion Quarterly* 16 (3):313–30.

———. 1956. The Study of Public Opinion. In *The State of the Social Sciences*, edited by L. D. White. Chicago: University of Chicago Press.

Berelson, Bernard, Paul Lazarsfeld, and William McPhee. 1954. *Voting: A Study of Opinion Formation in a Presidential Campaign.* Chicago: University of Chicago Press.

Berinsky, Adam J. 1999. The Two Faces of Public Opinion. *American Journal of Political Science* 43 (4):1209–30.

———. 2000. The Search for the Voice of the People: Public Opinion Polling and Political Representation in America. Ph.D. dissertation, Department of Political Science, University of Michigan, Ann Arbor.

———. 2002. Silent Voices: Social Welfare Policy Opinions and Political Equality in America. *American Journal of Political Science* 46 (2):276–87.

Berke, Richard L. 1993. Clinton Advisor Says Polls Had a Role in Health Plan. *New York Times*, December 9, A17.

Bernays, Edward L. 1945. Attitude Polls – Servants or Masters? *Public Opinion Quarterly* 9 (3):264–8.

Birch, Anthony H. 1971. *Representation.* New York: Praeger.

———. 1993. *The Concepts and Theories of Modern Democracy.* New York: Routledge.

Bishop, George, Robert Oldendick, and Alfred Tuchfarber. 1983. Effects of Filter Questions in Public Opinion Surveys. *Public Opinion Quarterly* 47 (Winter):528–46.

Bishop, George, Alfred Tuchfarber, and Robert Oldendick. 1986. Opinions on Fictitious Issues: The Pressure to Answer Survey Questions. *Public Opinion Quarterly* 50 (Summer):240–50.

Black, Duncan. 1958. *The Theory of Committees and Elections.* New York: Cambridge University Press.

Blankenship, A. B. 1948. What Is Public Opinion? *International Journal of Opinion and Attitude Research* 2 (2):201–6.

Blumer, Herbert. 1946. Collective Behavior. In *New Outlines of the Principles of Sociology*, edited by A. M. Lee. New York: Barnes & Noble.

———. 1948. Public Opinion and Public Opinion Polling. *American Sociological Review* 13 (5):542–54.

Bogart, Leo. 1967. No Opinion, Don't Know, and Maybe No Answer. *Public Opinion Quarterly* 31 (3):331–44.

Bourdieu, Pierre. 1979. Public Opinion Does Not Exist. In *Communication and Class Struggle*, edited by A. Mattelart and S. Siegelaub. New York: International General.

———. 1990. Opinion Polls: A "Science" without a Scientist. In *In Other Words: Essays towards a Reflexive Sociology*, edited by P. Bourdieu. Stanford, CA: Stanford University Press.

Boyd, Richard. 1989. The Effects of Primaries and Statewide Races on Voter Turnout. *Journal of Politics* 51 (3):730–9.

Brady, Henry E., Sidney Verba, and Kay L. Schlozman. 1995. Beyond SES: A Resource Model of Political Participation. *American Political Science Review* 89 (2):271–94.

Brady, Henry, and Gary Orren. 1992. Polling Pitfalls: Sources of Error in Public Opinion Surveys. In *Media Polls in American Politics*, edited by T. Mann and G. Orren. Washington DC: Brookings Institution.

Brehm, John. 1993. *The Phantom Respondents: Opinion Surveys and Political Representation*. Ann Arbor: University of Michigan Press.

Brown, Richard D. 1996. *The Strength of a People: The Idea of an Informed Citizenry in America, 1650–1870*. Chapel Hill, NC: University of North Carolina Press.

Bruce, John, and Clyde Wilcox. 2000. Pollsters, Political Scientists, and Affect: Comparing the Treatment of Emotional Response. *Votes & Opinions* 3 (2): 8–31.

Bryan, Frank M. 1999. Direct Democracy and Civic Competence: The Case of the Town Meeting. In *Citizen Competence and Democratic Institutions*, edited by S. Elkin and K. Soltan. University Park, PA: University of Pennsylvania Press.

Bryce, James. 1891. *The American Commonwealth*. New York: Macmillan.

Burke, Edmund. 1969. The Representative as Trustee. In *Representation*, edited by H. Pitkin. New York: Atherton Press.

Campbell, Angus, Phillip Converse, Warren Miller, and Donald Stokes. 1960. *The American Voter*. New York: John Wiley and Sons.

Cannel, C., P. Miller, and L. Oksenberg. 1981. Research on Interviewing Techniques. In *Sociological Methodology 1981*, edited by S. Leinhardt. San Francisco: Jossey-Bass.

Cantril, Albert. 1991. *The Opinion Connection: Polling, Politics, and the Press*. Washington DC: CQ Press.

Caress, Stanley M. 1996. The Impact of Term Limits on Legislative Behavior: An Examination of a Transitional Legislature. *PS Political Science & Politics* 29 (4):671–6.

———. 1999. The Influence of Term Limits on the Electoral Success of Women. *Women & Politics* 20 (3):45–63.

Carey, John M., Richard G. Niemi, and Lynda W. Powell. 1998. The Effects of Term Limits on State Legislatures. *Legislative Studies Quarterly* 23 (2): 271–300.

Carmines, Edward, and James Kuklinski. 1990. Incentives, Opportunities, and the Logic of Public Opinion in American Political Representation. In *Information and Democratic Processes*, edited by J. Ferejohn and J. Kuklinski. Urbana, IL: University of Illinois Press.

Carmines, Edward, and James Stimson. 1980. The Two Faces of Issue Voting. *American Political Science Review* 74 (March):78–91.

Chaiken, Shelly. 1980. Heuristic Versus Systematic Information Processing and the Use of Source Versus Message Cues in Persuasion. *Journal of Personality and Social Psychology* 39 (5):752–66.

Chaiken, Shelly, and Alice H. Eagly. 1993. *The Psychology of Attitudes.* Fort Worth, TX: Harcourt Brace Jovanovich College Publishers.

Chaiken, Shelly, Akiva Liberman, and Alice H. Eagly. 1989. Heuristic and Systematic Information Processing Within and Beyond the Persuasion Context. In *Unintended Thought,* edited by J. Uleman and J. Bargh. New York: Guilford Press.

Chaiken, Shelly, and Durairaj Maheswaran. 1994. Heuristic Processing Can Bias Systematic Processing: Effects of Source Credibility, Argument Ambiguity, and Task Importance on Attitude Judgment. *Journal of Personality and Social Psychology* 66 (3):460–73.

Chen, Serena, and Shelly Chaiken. 1999. The Heuristic-Systematic Model in Its Broader Context. In *Dual-Process Theories in Social Psychology,* edited by S. Chaiken and Y. Trope. New York: Guilford.

Chong, Dennis. 1993. How People Think, Reason, and Feel about Rights and Liberties. *American Journal of Political Science* 37 (3):867–99.

Christiano, Thomas. 1990. Freedom, Consensus, and Equality in Collective Decision Making. *Ethics* 101 (October):151–81.

———. 1996. *The Rule of the Many: Fundamental Issues in Democratic Theory.* Boulder: Westview Press.

Clarke, Harold D., Allan Kornberg, Chris McIntyre, Petra Bauer-Kaase, and Max Kaase. 1999. The Effect of Economic Priorities on the Measurement of Value Change: New Experimental Evidence. *American Political Science Review* 93 (3):637–47.

Clymer, Adam. 1993. Poll Takers Say It Was the Economy, Stupid; but Future is Less Clear. *New York Times,* 24 May 1993, A12.

Cohen, Jeffrey E. 1997. *Presidential Responsiveness and Public Policy-Making: The Public and the Policies that Presidents Choose.* Ann Arbor: University of Michigan Press.

Condorcet, Nicolas Caritat de. 1785. *Essai sur L'application de L'analyse a la Probabilitié des Decisions Rendues a la Pluralite des Voix.* New York: Chelsea Publishing Company, 1972.

———. 1995. Excerpts from *An Essay on the Application of Analysis to the Probability of Decisions Rendered by a Plurality of Votes,* 1785. In *Classics of Social Choice,* edited by I. McLean and A. Urken. Ann Arbor: University of Michigan Press.

Conley, Patricia H. 2001. *Presidential Mandates: How Elections Shape the National Agenda.* Chicago: University of Chicago Press.

Connolly, William E. 1972. On "Interests" in Politics. *Politics and Society* 2 (4): 459–77.

———. 1993. *The Terms of Political Discourse.* 3rd ed. Princeton, NJ: Princeton University Press.

Conover, Pamela Johnston, Stanley Feldman, and Kathleen Knight. 1986. Judging Inflation and Unemployment: The Origins of Retrospective Evaluations. *Journal of Politics* 48 (3):565–88.

———. 1987. The Personal and Political Underpinnings of Economic Forecasts. *American Journal of Political Science* 31 (3):559–83.

Converse, Jean M. 1976. Predicting No Opinion in the Polls. *Public Opinion Quarterly* 40 (Winter):515–30.

———. 1987. *Survey Research in The United States: Roots and Emergence 1890–1960.* Berkeley: University of California Press.

Converse, Philip E. 1962. Information Flow and the Stability of Partisan Attitudes. *Public Opinion Quarterly* 26:578–99.

———. 1964. The Nature of Belief Systems in Mass Publics. In *Ideology and Discontent*, edited by D. Apter. New York: Free Press.

———. 1970. Attitudes and Nonattitudes: Continuation of a Dialogue. In *The Quantitative Analysis of Social Problems*, edited by E. Tufte. Reading, Mass.: Addison-Wesley.

———. 1987. Changing Conceptions of Public Opinion in the Political Process. *Public Opinion Quarterly* 51 (S):S12–S24.

———. 1990. Popular Representation and the Distribution of Information. In *Information and Democratic Processes*, edited by J. Ferejohn and J. Kuklinski. Urbana: University of Illinois Press.

———. 1996. The Advent of Polling and Political Representation. *PS: Political Science & Politics* 29 (4):649–57.

———. 2000. Assessing the Capacity of Mass Electorates. *Annual Review of Political Science* 3:331–53.

Converse, Philip E., and George B. Markus. 1979. Plus Ca Change...The New CPS Election Study Panel. *American Political Science Review* 73 (1): 32–49.

Converse, Philip E., and Roy Pierce. 1986. *Political Representation in France.* Cambridge, MA: Belknap Press of Harvard University Press.

Conway, Margaret. 1991. *Political Participation in the United States.* 2nd ed. Washington, DC: CQ Press.

Cook, Fay Lomax, and Edith J. Barrett. 1992. *Support for the American Welfare State: The Views of Congress and the Public.* New York: Columbia University Press.

Cote, Joseph A., and Ronald Buckley. 1987. Estimating Trait, Method, and Error Variance: Generalizing across 70 Construct Validation Studies. *Journal of Marketing Research* 24 (August):315–18.

Craig, Stephen C., James G. Kane, and Michael D. Martinez. 2002. Sometimes You Feel Like a Nut, Sometimes You Don't: Citizens' Ambivalence about Abortion. *Political Psychology* 23 (2):285–301.

Cranston, Maurice. 1991. Condorcet, Marie Jean. In *The Blackwell Encyclopaedia of Political Thought*, edited by D. Miller. Oxford: Basil Blackwell.

Crespi, Irving. 1989. *Public Opinion, Polls, and Democracy.* Boulder: Westview Press.

———. 1997. *The Public Opinion Process.* Mahwah, NJ: Lawrence Erlbaum Associates.

Cutler, Fred. 1999. Jeremy Bentham and the Public Opinion Tribunal. *Public Opinion Quarterly* 63 (3):321–46.

———. 2002. The Simplest Shortcut of All: Sociodemographic Characteristics and Electoral Choice. *Journal of Politics* 64 (2):466–90.

Dahl, Robert A. 1956. *A Preface to Democratic Theory.* Chicago: University of Chicago Press.

———. 1989. *Democracy and Its Critics.* New Haven: Yale University Press.

Dahl, Robert, and Charles Lindblom. 1953. *Politics, Economics and Welfare.* Chicago: University of Chicago Press.

Dalton, Russell J. 2002. *Citizen Politics.* 3rd ed. New York: Chatham House.

Daniel, Kermit, and John R. Lott. 1997. Term Limits and Electoral Competitiveness: Evidence from California's State Legislative Races. *Public Choice* 90 (1):165–84.

Danielian, Lucig H., and Benjamin I. Page. 1994. The Heavenly Chorus: Interest Group Voices on TV News. *American Journal of Political Science* 38 (4): 1056–78.

Davis, Darren W., and Christian Davenport. 1999. Assessing the Validity of the Postmaterialism Index. *American Political Science Review* 93 (3):649–64.

Davis, Otto, Melvin Hinich, and Peter Ordeshook. 1970. An Expository Development of a Mathematical Model of the Electoral Process. *American Political Science Review* 64:426–48.

Davison, W. Phillips. 1958. The Public Opinion Process. *Public Opinion Quarterly* 22 (2):91–106.

———. 1972. Public Opinion Research as Communication. *Public Opinion Quarterly* 36 (3):311–22.

———. 1983. The Third-Person Effect in Communication. *Public Opinion Quarterly* 47:1–15.

Dearing, James W., and Everett M. Rogers. 1996. *Agenda-Setting.* Thousand Oaks, CA: Sage Publications.

Delli Carpini, Michael X., and Scott Keeter. 1991. Stability and Change in the U.S. Public's Knowledge of Politics. *Public Opinion Quarterly* 55:583–612.

———. 1992. An Analysis of Information Items on the 1990 and 1991 NES Surveys. Report to the Board of Overseers for the National Election Studies.

———. 1993. Measuring Political Knowledge: Putting First Things First. *American Journal of Political Science* 37 (4):1179–1206.

———. 1996. *What Americans Know about Politics and Why It Matters.* New Haven, CT: Yale University Press.

DeLuca, Tom. 1995. *The Two Faces of Political Apathy.* Philadelphia: Temple University Press.

Demers, David P. 1987. Use of Polls in Reporting Changes Slightly Since 1978. *Journalism Quarterly* 64 (Winter):839–42.

Dewey, John. 1927. *The Public and Its Problems.* New York: H. Holt and Company.

Dimock, Michael A. 1998. Political Knowledge and the Political Environment: Reassessing Trends in Partisanship, 1960–1996. Paper presented at the annual meeting of the American Political Science Association, Sept. 3–6, at Boston.

Dion, Robert L. 2000. The Strategic Framing of Political Issues: The Case of the Gays in the Military Debate. Ph.D. dissertation, Department of Political Science, Indiana University, Bloomington.

Dionne, E.J. 1992. The Illusion of Technique: The Impact of Polls on Reporters and Democracy. In *Media Polls in American Politics*, edited by T. Mann and G. Orren. Washington, DC: Brookings Institution.

Downs, Anthony. 1957. *An Economic Theory of Democracy.* New York: Harper Collins.

Duch, Raymond M., Harvey D. Palmer, and Christopher J. Anderson. 2000. Heterogeneity in Perceptions of National Economic Conditions. *American Journal of Political Science* 44 (4):635–52.

Edelman, Murray. 1988. *Constructing the Political Spectacle*. Chicago: University of Chicago Press.

Eismeier, Theodore, and Philip Pollock III. 1986. Strategy and Choice in Congressional Elections: The Role of Political Action Committees. *American Journal of Political Science* 30:197–213.

Eliasoph, Nina. 1998. *Avoiding Politics*. New York: Cambridge University Press.

Entman, Robert M., and Susan Herbst. 2001. Reframing Public Opinion as We Have Known It. In *Mediated Politics: Communication in the Future of Democracy*, edited by W. L. Bennett and R. M. Entman. Cambridge: Cambridge University Press.

Epstein, Edward. 1973. *News from Nowhere*. New York: Vintage.

Erikson, Robert S., Michael B. MacKuen, and James A. Stimson. 2002. *The Macro Polity*. New York: Cambridge University Press.

Erikson, Robert S., Gerald C. Wright, and John P. McIver. 1993. *Statehouse Democracy: Public Opinion and Policy in the American States*. Cambridge: Cambridge University Press.

Estlund, David M., Jeremy Waldron, Bernard Grofman, and Scott L. Feld. 1989. Democratic Theory and the Public Interest: Condorcet and Rousseau Revisited. *American Political Science Review* 83 (4):1317–40.

Faulkenberry, G. David, and Robert Mason. 1978. Characteristics of Nonopinion and No Opinion Response Groups. *Public Opinion Quarterly* 42: 533–43.

Feick, Lawrence. 1989. Latent Class Analysis of Survey Questions that Include Don't Know Responses. *Public Opinion Quarterly* 53:525–47.

Feld, Scott L., and Bernard Grofman. 1988. Ideological Consistency as a Collective Phenomenon. *American Political Science Review* 82 (3):773–88.

Feldman, Stanley. 1988. Structure and Consistency in Public Opinion: The Role of Core Beliefs and Values. *American Journal of Political Science* 32 (2):416–40.

———. 1989. Measuring Issue Preferences: The Problem of Response Instability. In *Political Analysis*, edited by J. Stimson. Ann Arbor: University of Michigan Press.

———. 1995. Answering Survey Questions: The Measurement and Meaning of Public Opinion. In *Political Judgment: Structure and Process*, edited by M. Lodge and K. M. McGraw. Ann Arbor: University of Michigan Press.

Fenno Jr., Richard. 1978. *Home Style: House Members in Their Districts*. Boston: Little, Brown.

Ferguson, Thomas. 1991. An Unbearable Lightness of Being – Party and Industry in the 1988 Democratic Primary. In *Do Elections Matter?*, edited by B. Ginsberg and A. Stone. Armonk, NY: M.E. Sharpe.

Ferguson, Thomas, and Joel Rogers. 1986. *Right Turn: The Decline of the Democrats and the Future of American Politics*. New York: Hill and Wang.

Fett, Patrick J., and Daniel E. Ponder. 1993. Congressional Term Limits, State Legislative Term Limits and Congressional Turnover: A Theory of Change. *PS Political Science & Politics* 26 (2):211–6.

Finkel, Steven E., and Edward N. Muller. 1998. Rational Choice and the Dynamics of Collective Political Action: Evaluating Alternative Models with Panel Data. *American Political Science Review* 92 (1):37–49.

Fiorina, Morris. 1977. *Congress: Keystone of the Washington Establishment.* New Haven, CT: Yale University Press.

Fischhoff, Baruch. 1991. Value Elicitation: Is There Anything in There? *American Psychologist* 46 (8):835–47.

Fishkin, James S. 1991. *Democracy and Deliberation: New Directions for Democratic Reform.* New Haven, CT: Yale University Press.

———. 1995. *The Voice of the People: Public Opinion and Democracy.* New Haven, CT: Yale University Press.

Fishkin, James S., and Robert C. Luskin. 1999. Bringing Deliberation to the Democratic Dialogue. In *The Poll with a Human Face: The National Issues Convention Experiment in Political Communication,* edited by M. McCombs and A. Reynolds. Mahwah, NJ: Lawrence Erlbaum Associates.

Fiske, Susan T., Richard R. Lau, and Richard A. Smith. 1990. On the Varieties and Utilities of Political Expertise. *Social Cognition* 8 (1):31–48.

Fiske, Susan T., and Shelley E. Taylor. 1991. *Social Cognition.* 2nd ed. New York: McGraw-Hill.

Foyle, Douglas C. 1999. *Counting the Public In: Presidents, Public Opinion, and Foreign Policy.* New York: Columbia University Press.

Francis, Joe, and Lawrence Busch. 1975. What We Now Know about "I Don't Knows". *Public Opinion Quarterly* 39 (2):207–18.

Gallup, George, and Saul Rae. 1940. *The Pulse of Democracy: The Public Opinion Poll and How It Works.* New York: Greenwood Press.

Galston, William A. 2001. Political Knowledge, Political Engagement, and Civic Education. *Annual Review of Political Science* 4:217–34.

Gamson, William. 1992. *Talking Politics.* New York: Cambridge University Press.

Gans, Herbert. 1979. *Deciding What's News: A Study of CBS Evening News, NBC Nightly News, Newsweek, and Time.* New York: Pantheon.

Garment, Leonard, James Fallows, Susan B. King, Paul Warnke, Robert B. Hill, Warren Mitofsky, and Patrick Caddell. 1980. The User's Perspective: A Round Table on the Impact of Polls. In *Polling on the Issues,* edited by A. Cantril. Washington DC: Seven Locks Press.

Gastil, John. 2000. *By Popular Demand: Revitalizing Representative Democracy through Deliberative Elections.* Berkeley: University of California Press.

Gastil, John, E. Pierre Deess, and Phil Weiser. 2002. Civic Awakening in the Jury Room: A Test of the Connection Between Jury Deliberation and Political Participation. *Journal of Politics* 61 (2):585–95.

Gastil, John, and James P. Dillard. 1999. Increasing Political Sophistication through Public Deliberation. *Political Communication* 16 (1):3–23.

Geer, John G. 1996. *From Tea Leaves to Opinion Polls: A Theory of Democratic Leadership.* New York: Columbia University Press.

Genova, B.K.L., and Bradley S. Greenberg. 1979. Interests in News and the Knowledge Gap. *Public Opinion Quarterly* 43 (1):79–91.

Germond, Jack. 1980. The Impact of Polling on Journalism. In *Polling on the Issues,* edited by A. Cantril. Washington DC: Seven Locks Press.

Gigerenzer, Gerd, and Reinhard Selten, eds. 2001. *Bounded Rationality: The Adaptive Toolbox*. Cambridge, MA: MIT Press.

Gigerenzer, Gerd, Peter M. Todd, and the ABC Research Group. 1999. *Simple Heuristics that Make Us Smart*. New York: Oxford University Press.

Gilens, Martin. 1999. *Why Americans Hate Welfare*. Chicago: University of Chicago Press.

———. 2001. Political Ignorance and Collective Policy Preferences. *American Political Science Review* 95 (2):379–96.

Ginsberg, Benjamin. 1986. *The Captive Public*. New York: Basic Books.

———. 1989. How Polling Transforms Public Opinion. In *Manipulating Public Opinion: Essays on Public Opinion as a Dependent Variable*, edited by M. Margolis and G. Mauser. Pacific Grove, CA: Brooks/Cole Publishing.

Glasser, Theodore L., and Charles T. Salmon, eds. 1995. *Public Opinion and the Communication of Consent*. New York: Guilford Press.

Gosnell, Harold F. 1940. The Polls and Other Mechanisms of Democracy. *Public Opinion Quarterly* 4 (2):224–8.

Graber, Doris A. 1988. *Processing the News: How People Tame the Information Tide*. 2nd ed. White Plains: Longman.

———. 1994. Why Voters Fail Information Tests: Can the Hurdles Be Overcome? *Political Communication* 11 (4):331–46.

———. 2001. *Processing Politics: Learning from Television in the Internet Age*. Chicago: University of Chicago Press.

Granger, C.W.J. 1969. Investigating Causal Relations by Econometric Models and Cross-Spectral Methods. *Econometrica* 37 (3):424–38.

Grofman, Bernard, and Scott L. Feld. 1988. Rousseau's General Will: A Condorcetian Perspective. *American Political Science Review* 82 (2):567–76.

Grofman, Bernard, and Guillermo Owen. 1986a. Condorcet Models, Avenues for Future Research. In *Information Pooling and Group Decision Making*, edited by B. Grofman and G. Owen. Greenwich, CT: JAI Press.

———, eds. 1986b. *Information Pooling and Group Decision Making*. Greenwich, CT: JAI Press.

Grofman, Bernard, and Julie Withers. 1993. Information-Pooling Models of Electoral Politics. In *Information, Participation, and Choice*, edited by B. Grofman. Ann Arbor: University of Michigan Press.

Groves, Robert. 1989. *Survey Errors and Survey Costs*. New York: John Wiley & Sons.

Gujarati, Damodar N. 1995. *Basic Econometrics*. 3rd ed. New York: McGraw Hill.

Gunn, J. A. W. 1995. "Public Opinion" in Modern Political Science. In *Political Science in History: Research Programs and Political Traditions*, edited by J. Farr, J. S. Dryzek and S. T. Leonard. New York: Cambridge University Press.

Habermas, Jürgen. 1975. *Legitimation Crisis*. Translated by T. McCarthy. Boston: Beacon Press.

———. 1984. *The Theory of Communicative Action*. Translated by T. McCarthy. 2 vols. Boston: Beacon Press.

———. 1989. *The Structural Transformation of the Public Sphere: An Inquiry into a Category of Bourgeois Society.* Translated by T. Burger and F. Lawrence. Cambridge, MA: M.I.T Press.

———. 1996a. *Between Facts and Norms: Contributions to a Discourse Theory of Law and Democracy.* Translated by W. Rehg. Cambridge, MA: The MIT Press.

———. 1996b. Three Normative Models of Democracy. In *Democracy and Difference: Contesting the Boundaries of the Political,* edited by S. Benhabib. Princeton, NJ: Princeton University Press.

Hall, Richard, and Frank Wayman. 1990. Buying Time: Moneyed Interests and the Mobilization of Bias in Congressional Committees. *American Political Science Review* 84:798–820.

Haller, H. Brandon, and Helmut Norpoth. 1994. Let the Good Times Roll: The Economic Expectations of U.S. Voters. *American Journal of Political Science* 38 (3):625–50.

Hallin, Daniel. 1986. *The "Uncensored War": The Media and Vietnam.* Berkeley: University of California Press.

Hansen, Mogens H. 1991. *The Athenian Democracy in the Age of Demosthenes: Structure, Principles, and Ideology.* Oxford, UK: Blackwell.

Hartley, Thomas, and Bruce Russett. 1992. Public Opinion and the Common Defense: Who Governs Military Spending in the United States? *American Political Science Review* 86 (4):905–15.

Hastie, Reid, and Bernadette Park. 1986. The Relationship Between Memory and Judgment Depends on Whether the Judgment Task Is Memory-Based or On-Line. *Psychological Review* 93 (3):258–68.

Heise, David R. 1969. Separating Reliability and Stability in Test-Retest Correlation. *American Sociological Review* 34 (1):93–101.

Held, David. 1987. *Models of Democracy.* Stanford, CA: Stanford University Press.

Henn, Matt. 1998. *Opinion Polls and Volatile Electorates: Problems and Issues in Polling European Societies.* Aldershot, U.K.: Ashgate.

Herbst, Susan. 1992. Surveys in the Public Sphere: Applying Bourdieu's Critique of Opinion Polls. *International Journal of Public Opinion Research* 4 (3): 220–229.

———. 1993. *Numbered Voices: How Opinion Polling Has Shaped American Politics.* Chicago: University of Chicago Press.

———. 1995. On The Disappearance of Groups: 19th- and Early 20th-Century Conceptions of Public Opinion. In *Public Opinion and the Communication of Consent,* edited by T. L. Glasser and C. T. Salmon. New York: Guilford.

———. 1998. *Reading Public Opinion: Political Actors View the Democratic Process.* Chicago: University of Chicago Press.

Herman, Edward, and Noam Chomsky. 1988. *Manufacturing Consent: The Political Economy of the Mass Media.* New York: Pantheon Books.

Herrera, Cheryl, Richard Herrera, and Eric Smith. 1992. Public Opinion and Congressional Representation. *Public Opinion Quarterly* 56:185–205.

Herrnson, Paul. 1986. Do Parties Make a Difference? The Role of Party Organizations in Congressional Elections. *Journal of Politics* 48:589–615.

Hetherington, Marc J. 1996. The Media's Role in Forming Voters' National Economic Evaluations in 1992. *American Journal of Political Science* 40 (2): 372–95.

———. 2001. Resurgent Mass Partisanship: The Role of Elite Polarization. *American Political Science Review* 95 (3):619–31.

Higgins, E. Tory. 1996. Knowledge Activation: Accessibility, Applicability, and Salience. In *Social Psychology: Handbook of Basic Principles*, edited by E. T. Higgins and A. W. Kruglanski. New York: Guilford.

Hill, Jennifer L., and Hanspeter Kriesi. 2001. An Extension and Test of Converse's "Black-And-White" Model of Response Stability. *American Political Science Review* 95 (2):397–413.

Hill, Kim Quaile, and Angela Hinton-Andersson. 1995. Pathways of Representation: A Causal Analysis of Public Opinion-Policy Linkages. *American Journal of Political Science* 39 (4):924–35.

Hill, Kim Quaile, and Jan E. Leighley. 1992. The Policy Consequences of Class Bias in State Electorates. *American Journal of Political Science* 36 (2):351–65.

Himmelstein, Jerome, and James McRae. 1988. Social Issues and Socioeconomic Status. *Public Opinion Quarterly* 52:492–512.

Hinckley, Ronald H. 1992. *People, Polls, and Policymakers: American Public Opinion and National Security*. New York: Lexington.

Holbrook, Allyson L., Melanie C. Green, and Jon A. Krosnick. 2003. Telephone Versus Face-to-Face Interviewing of National Probability Samples with Long Questionnaires: Comparisons of Respondent Satisficing and Social Desirability Response Bias. *Public Opinion Quarterly* 67 (2):79–125.

Hochschild, Jennifer L. 1981. *What's Fair? American Beliefs about Distributive Justice*. Cambridge, MA: Harvard University Press.

Huckfeldt, Robert. 2001. The Social Communication of Expertise. *American Journal of Political Science* 45 (2):425–38.

Huckfeldt, Robert, Paul Allen Beck, Russell J. Dalton, and Jeffrey Levine. 1995. Political Environments, Cohesive Social Groups, and the Communication of Public Opinion. *American Journal of Political Science* 39 (4):1025–54.

Huckfeldt, Robert, and John Sprague. 1995. *Citizens, Politics, and Social Communication: Information and Influence in an Election Campaign*. New York: Cambridge University Press.

Hunter, James Davison, and Carl Bowman. 1996. The State of Disunion: 1996 Survey of American Political Culture Executive Summary. Charlottesville, VA: In Media Res Educational Foundation.

Inglehart, Ronald. 1997. *Modernization and Postmodernization: Cultural, Economic, and Political Change in 43 Societies*. Princeton, NJ: Princeton University Press.

Inglehart, Ronald, and Paul R. Abramson. 1999. Measuring Postmaterialism. *American Political Science Review* 93 (3):665–77.

Iyengar, Shanto. 1986. Whither Political Information. Report to the Board of Overseers and Pilot Study Committee, National Election Studies.

———. 1990. Shortcuts to Political Knowledge: The Role of Selective Attention and Accessibility. In *Information and Democratic Processes*, edited by J. Ferejohn and J. Kuklinski. Urbana, IL: University of Illinois Press.

————. 1991. *Is Anyone Responsible? How Television Frames Political Issues.* Chicago: University of Chicago Press.

Jackman, Simon, and Paul M. Sniderman. 2002. The Institutional Organization of Choice Spaces: A Political Conception of Political Psychology. In *Political Psychology,* edited by K. R. Monroe. Mahwah, NJ: Lawrence Erlbaum.

Jacobs, Lawrence. 1992. The Recoil Effect: Public Opinion and Policymaking in the U.S. and Britain. *Comparative Politics* 24:199–217.

Jacobs, Lawrence R., Eric D. Lawrence, Robert Y. Shapiro, and Steven S. Smith. 1998. Congressional Leadership of Public Opinion. *Political Science Quarterly* 113 (1):21–41.

Jacobs, Lawrence R., and Robert Y. Shapiro. 1993. The Public Presidency, Private Polls, and Policymaking: Lyndon Johnson. Paper presented at the annual meeting of the American Political Science Association, September 2–5, at Washington DC.

————. 1995. The Rise of Presidential Polling: The Nixon White House in Historical Perspective. *Public Opinion Quarterly* 59:163–95.

————. 1996. Presidential Manipulation of Polls and Public Opinion: The Nixon Administration and the Pollsters. *Political Science Quarterly* 110 (4):519–38.

————. 2000. *Politicians Don't Pander: Political Manipulation and the Loss of Democratic Responsiveness.* Chicago: University of Chicago Press.

Jacoby, William G. 2000. Issue Framing and Public Opinion on Government Spending. *American Journal of Political Science* 44 (4):750–67.

Judd, Charles M., and James W. Downing. 1990. Political Expertise and the Development of Attitude Consistency. *Social Cognition* 8 (1):104–24.

Kagay, Michael. 1991. The Use of Public Opinion Polls by the New York Times: Some Examples from the 1988 Presidential Election. In *Polling and Presidential Election Coverage,* edited by P. Lavrakas and J. Holley. Newbury Park: Sage Publications.

Kagay, Michael R. 2000. Continuing Evolution in the Use of Public Opinion Polls by The New York Times: The 1996 Presidential Election Experience. In *Election Polls, The News Media, and Democracy,* edited by P. J. Lavrakas and M. W. Traugott. New York: Chatham House.

Katz, Elihu, and Paul Lazarsfeld. 1955. *Personal Influence: The Part Played by People in the Flow of Mass Communications.* Glencoe, IL: Free Press.

Kay, Alan F. 1998. *Locating Consensus for Democracy: A Ten-Year U.S. Experiment.* St. Augustine, FL: Americans Talk Issues.

Keeter, Scott, Carolyn Miller, Andrew Kohut, Robert M. Groves, and Stanley Presser. 2000. Consequences of Reducing Nonresponse in a National Telephone Survey. *Public Opinion Quarterly* 64:125–48.

Key, V.O. 1950. *Southern Politics in State and Nation.* New York: Knopf.

————. 1961. *Public Opinion and American Democracy.* New York: Knopf.

————. 1966. *The Responsible Electorate.* New York: Random House.

Kim, Joohan, Robert O. Wyatt, and Elihu Katz. 1999. News, Talk, Opinion, Participation: The Part Played by Conversation in Deliberative Democracy. *Political Communication* 16 (4):361–85.

Kinder, Donald R. 1998. Opinion and Action in the Realm of Politics. In *The*

Handbook of Social Psychology, edited by D. T. Gilbert, S. T. Fiske and G. Lindzey. Boston: McGraw Hill.

Kinder, Donald R., and Don Herzog. 1993. Democratic Discussion. In *Reconsidering the Democratic Public*, edited by G. Marcus and R. Hanson. University Park, PA: Pennsylvania State University Press.

Kinder, Donald R., and D. Roderick Kiewiet. 1981. Sociotropic Politics: The American Case. *British Journal of Political Science* 11:129–61.

Kinder, Donald R., and Lynn M. Sanders. 1990. Mimicking Political Debate with Survey Questions: The Case of White Opinion on Affirmative Action for Blacks. *Social Cognition* 8 (1):73–103.

Kinder, Donald R., and David O. Sears. 1985. Public Opinion and Political Action. In *Handbook of Social Psychology*, edited by G. Lindzey and E. Aronson. New York: Random House.

King, Gary. 1989. *Unifying Political Methodology: The Likelihood Theory of Statistical Inference*. Cambridge: Cambridge University Press.

Kirk, Roger E. 1990. *Statistics: An Introduction*. Fort Worth: Hold, Rinehart and Winston.

Klapper, Joseph. 1960. *The Effects of Mass Communication*. Glencoe, IL: Free Press.

Kleppner, Paul. 1982. *Who Voted? The Dynamics of Electoral Turnout, 1870–1980*. New York: Praeger.

Knäuper, Bärbel. 1999. Age Differences in Question and Response Order Effects. In *Cognition, Aging, and Self-Reports*, edited by N. Schwarz, D. C. Park, B. Knäuper and S. Sudman. Philadelphia: Psychology Press.

Knoke, David. 1979. Stratification and the Dimensions of American Political Orientations. *American Journal of Political Science* 23 (4):772–91.

Knoke, David, Lawrence Raffalovich, and William Erskine. 1987. Class, Status, and Economic Policy Preferences. *Research in Social Stratification and Mobility* 6:141–58.

Knowles, Eric S., and Brenda Byers. 1996. Reliability Shifts in Measurement Reactivity: Driven by Content Engagement or Self-Engagement? *Journal of Personality and Social Psychology* 70 (5):1080–90.

Kolbert, Elizabeth. 1992. Test Marketing a President. *New York Times*, 30 August 1992, I: 8ff.

Krause, George A., and Jim Granato. 1998. Fooling Some of the Public Some of the Time? A Test for Weak Rationality with Heterogeneous Information Levels. *Public Opinion Quarterly* 62 (2):135–51.

Krosnick, Jon A. 1991. Response Strategies for Coping with the Cognitive Demands of Attitude Measures in Surveys. *Applied Cognitive Psychology* 5: 213–36.

———. 1998. Review of *What Americans Know about Politics and Why It Matters*, by Michael Delli Carpini and Scott Keeter. *Annals of the American Academy of Political and Social Science* 559 (September):189–91.

———. 1999a. Maximizing Questionnaire Quality. In *Measures of Political Attitudes*, edited by J. P. Robinson, P. R. Shaver and L. S. Wrightsman. San Diego, CA: Academic Press.

———. 1999b. Survey Research. *Annual Review of Psychology* 50:537–67.

Krosnick, Jon A., and Duane F. Alwin. 1987. An Evaluation of a Cognitive Theory of Response-Order Effects in Survey Measurement. *Public Opinion Quarterly* 51 (2):201–19.

———. 1988. A Test of the Form-Resistant Correlation Hypothesis: Ratings, Rankings, and the Measurement of Values. *Public Opinion Quarterly* 52: 526–38.

Krosnick, Jon A., Matthew K. Berent, and David S. Boniger. 1994. Pockets of Responsibility in the American Electorate: Findings of a Research Program on Attitude Importance. *Political Communication* 11:391–411.

Krosnick, Jon A., and Laura A. Brannon. 1993. The Impact of the Gulf War on the Ingredients of Presidential Evaluations: Multidimensional Effects of Political Involvement. *American Political Science Review* 87 (4):963–75.

Krosnick, Jon A., and Leandre R. Fabrigar. 1997. Designing Rating Scales for Effective Measurement in Surveys. In *Survey Measurement and Process Quality*, edited by L. Lyberg, P. Biemer, M. Collins, E. de Leeuw, C. Dippo, N. Schwarz and D. Trewin. New York: John Wiley.

———. forthcoming. *Designing Great Questionnaires: Insights From Psychology*. New York: Oxford University Press.

Krosnick, Jon A., and Donald R. Kinder. 1990. Altering the Foundations of Support for the President through Priming. *American Political Science Review* 84:497–512.

Krosnick, Jon A., and Michael A. Milburn. 1990. Psychological Determinants of Political Opinionation. *Social Cognition* 8 (1):49–72.

Kuklinski, James H., and Norman L. Hurley. 1994. On Hearing and Interpreting Political Messages: A Cautionary Tale of Citizen Cue-Taking. *Journal of Politics* 56 (3):729–51.

Kuklinski, James H., and Paul J. Quirk. 2000. Reconsidering the Rational Public: Cognition, Heuristics, and Mass Opinion. In *Elements of Reason: Cognition, Choice, and the Bounds of Rationality*, edited by A. Lupia, M. D. McCubbins and S. L. Popkin. New York: Cambridge University Press.

———. 2001. Conceptual Foundations of Citizen Competence. *Political Behavior* 23 (3):285–311.

Kuklinski, James H., Paul J. Quirk, Jennifer Jerit, and Robert F. Rich. 2001. The Political Environment and Citizen Competence. *American Journal of Political Science* 45 (2):410–24.

Kuklinski, James H., Paul J. Quirk, Jennifer Jerit, David W. Schwieder, and Robert F. Rich. 2000. Misinformation and the Currency of Democratic Citizenship. *Journal of Politics* 62 (3):790–816.

Kuklinski, James H., Paul J. Quirk, David W. Schwieder, and Robert F. Rich. 1998. "Just the Facts, Ma'am": Political Facts and Public Opinion. *Annals of the American Academy of Political and Social Science* 560 (November):143–54.

Kull, Steven, and I. M. Destler. 1999. *Misreading the Public: The Myth of a New Isolationism*. Washington DC: Brookings.

Kwak, Nojin. 1999. Revisiting the Knowledge Gap Hypothesis: Education, Motivation, and Media Use. *Communication Research* 26 (4):385–413.

Ladha, Krishna K. 1992. The Condorcet Jury Theorem, Free Speech, and Correlated Votes. *American Journal of Political Science* 36 (3):617–34.

Lane, Robert. 1962. *Political Ideology: Why the American Common Man Believes What He Does*. New York: Free Press.

Lang, Gladys Engel, and Kurt Lang. 1983. *The Battle for Public Opinion: The President, the Press, and the Polls during Watergate*. New York: Columbia University Press.

Lau, Richard R., and David P. Redlawsk. 1997. Voting Correctly. *American Political Science Review* 91 (3):585–98.

———. 2001. Advantages and Disadvantages of Cognitive Heuristics in Political Decision Making. *American Journal of Political Science* 45 (4):951–71.

Lavrakas, Paul J., and Michael W. Traugott, eds. 2000. *Election Polls, the News Media, and Democracy*. New York: Chatham House.

Lazarsfeld, Paul F. 1957. Public Opinion and the Classical Tradition. *Public Opinion Quarterly* 21 (1):39–53.

Lazarsfeld, Paul F., Bernard Berelson, and Helen Gaudet. 1948. *The People's Choice: How the Voter Makes Up His Mind in a Presidential Campaign*. 2nd ed. New York: Columbia University Press.

Lazarsfeld, Paul F., and Robert K. Merton. 1948. Mass Communication, Popular Taste and Organized Social Action. In *The Communication of Ideas: A Series of Addresses*, edited by L. Bryson. New York: Harper and Brothers.

Lee, Taeku. 2002. *Mobilizing Public Opinion: Black Insurgency and Racial Attitudes in the Civil Rights Era*. Chicago: University of Chicago Press.

Leege, David C., and Lyman A. Kellstedt, eds. 1993. *Rediscovering the Religious Factor in American Politics*. Armonk, NY: M.E. Sharpe.

Lemert, James. 1992. Effective Public Opinion. In *Public Opinion, the Press, and Public Policy*, edited by J. D. Kennamer. Westport, CT: Praeger.

Lessler, Judith T., and Barbara H. Forsyth. 1996. A Coding System for Appraising Questionnaires. In *Answering Questions: Methodology for Determining Cognitive and Communicative Processes in Survey Research*, edited by N. Schwarz and S. Sudman. San Francisco: Jossey-Bass.

Lewis, I. A. (Bud). 1991. Media Polls, the Los Angeles Times, and the 1988 Presidential Election. In *Polling and Presidential Election Coverage*, edited by P. Lavrakas and J. Holley. Newbury Park: Sage Publications.

Lewis, Justin. 2001. *Constructing Public Opinion: How Political Elites Do What They Like and Why We Seem to Go Along with It*. New York: Columbia University Press.

Lichter, S. Robert, Stanley Rothman, and Linda Lichter. 1986. *The Media Elite: America's New Powerbrokers*. New York: Hastings House.

Lin, I-Fen, and Nora Cate Schaeffer. 1995. Using Survey Participants to Estimate the Impact of Nonparticipation. *Public Opinion Quarterly* 59:236–58.

Lipari, Lisbeth. 2001. Voice, Polling, and the Public Sphere. In *Politics, Discourse, and American Society: New Agendas*, edited by R. P. Hart and B. H. Sparrow. Lanham, MD: Rowman & Littlefield.

Lippmann, Walter. 1922. *Public Opinion*. New York: Free Press.

———. 1925. *The Phantom Public*. New York: MacMillan.

———. 1955. *The Public Philosophy*. Boston: Little, Brown.

Lockerbie, Brad. 1991. The Influence of Levels of Information on the Use of Prospective Evaluations. *Political Behavior* 13 (3):223–35.

Lodge, Milton, and Kathleen M. McGraw, eds. 1995. *Political Judgment: Structure and Process*. Ann Arbor: University of Michigan Press.

Lodge, Milton, Kathleen M. McGraw, and Patrick Stroh. 1989. An Impression-Driven Model of Candidate Evaluation. *American Political Science Review* 83 (2):399–419.

Lodge, Milton, Marco R. Steenbergen, and Shawn Brau. 1995. The Responsive Voter: Campaign Information and the Dynamics of Candidate Evaluation. *American Political Science Review* 89 (2):309–26.

Lord, Frederic M. 1980. *Applications of Item Response Theory to Practical Testing Problems*. Hillsdale, NJ: Lawrence Erlbaum Associates.

Lord, Frederic M., and Melvin R. Novick. 1968. *Statistical Theories of Mental Test Scores*. Reading, MA: Addison-Wesley.

Lukes, Steven. 1974. *Power: A Radical View*. London: Macmillan Press.

Lupia, Arthur. 1994. Shortcuts Versus Encyclopedias: Information and Voting Behavior in California Insurance Reform Elections. *American Political Science Review* 88 (1):63–76.

———. 2002. Deliberation Disconnected: What It Takes to Improve Civic Competence. *Law and Contemporary Problems* 65:133–50.

Lupia, Arthur, and Mathew D. McCubbins. 1998. *The Democratic Dilemma: Can Citizens Learn what They Need to Know?* New York: Cambridge University Press.

Luskin, Robert. 1987. Measuring Political Sophistication. *American Journal of Political Science* 31 (4):856–99.

———. 1990. Explaining Political Sophistication. *Political Behavior* 12 (4):331–61.

———. 2002. From Denial to Extenuation (and Finally Beyond): Political Sophistication and Citizen Performance. In *Thinking about Political Psychology*, edited by J. H. Kuklinski. New York: Cambridge University Press.

MacKuen, Michael. 1990. Speaking of Politics: Individual Conversational Choice, Public Opinion, and the Prospects for Deliberative Democracy. In *Information and Democratic Processes*, edited by J. A. Ferejohn and J. H. Kuklinski. Urbana, IL: University of Illinois Press.

MacKuen, Michael B., Robert S. Erikson, and James A. Stimson. 1992. Peasants or Bankers? The American Electorate and the U.S. Economy. *American Political Science Review* 86 (3):597–611.

Madison, James. [1787] 1982. Federalist No. 10. In *The Federalist Papers*, edited by G. Wills. New York: Bantam Books.

Maltese, John Anthony. 1994. *Spin Control: The White House Office of Communications and the Management of Presidential News*. 2nd ed. Chapel Hill: University of North Carolina Press.

Manin, Bernard. 1997. *The Principles of Representative Government*. New York: Cambridge University Press.

Mann, Thomas, and Gary Orren. 1992. To Poll or Not to Poll . . . and Other Questions. In *Media Polls in American Politics*, edited by T. Mann and G. Orren. Washington DC: Brookings Institution.

Mansbridge, Jane J. 1983. *Beyond Adversary Democracy*. Chicago: University of Chicago Press.

———. 1992. A Deliberative Theory of Interest Representation. In *The Politics of Interests: Interest Groups Transformed*, edited by M. P. Petracca. Boulder, CO: Westview Press.

———. 1996. Rethinking Representation. Unpublished manuscript.

———. 1999a. On the Idea that Participation Makes Better Citizens. In *Citizen Competence and Democratic Institutions*, edited by S. L. Elkin and K. E. Soltan. University Park, PA: Pennsylvania State University Press.

———. 1999b. Should Blacks Represent Blacks and Women Represent Women? A Contingent "Yes". *Journal of Politics* 61 (3):628–57.

———, ed. 1990. *Beyond Self Interest*. Chicago: University of Chicago Press.

Maravall, José María. 1999. Accountability and Manipulation. In *Democracy, Accountability, and Representation*, edited by A. Przeworski, S. C. Stokes and B. Manin. New York: Cambridge University Press.

Marcus, George E., W. Russell Neuman, and Michael MacKuen. 2000. *Affective Intelligence and Political Judgment*. Chicago: University of Chicago Press.

Marcus, George E., John L. Sullivan, Elizabeth Theiss-Morse, and Sandra L. Wood. 1995. *With Malice Toward Some: How People Make Civil Liberties Judgments*. New York: Cambridge University Press.

Marjenhoff, William A. 1991. Public Opinion and Reagan Foreign Policy-Making. Ph.D. dissertation, Department of Political Science, Pennsylvania State University.

Markus, Gregory, and Philip Converse. 1979. A Dynamic Simultaneous Equation Model of Electoral Choice. *American Political Science Review* 73 (4):1055–70.

Martin, Elizabeth. 1984. Cultural Indicators and the Analysis of Public Opinion. In *Surveying Subjective Phenomena*, edited by C. F. Turner and E. Martin. New York: Russell Sage Foundation.

Mattes, Robert B. 1992. The Politics of Public Opinion: Polls, Pollsters, and Presidents. Ph.D. dissertation, Department of Political Science, University of Illinois, Urbana-Champaign.

Mayer, William G. 1993. *The Changing American Mind: How and Why American Public Opinion Changed between 1960 and 1988*. Ann Arbor: University of Michigan Press.

Mayhew, David. 1974. *Congress: The Electoral Connection*. New Haven: Yale University Press.

McClosky, Herbert. 1958. Conservatism and Personality. *American Political Science Review* 52:27–45.

McClosky, Herbert, and John Zaller. 1984. *The American Ethos: Public Attitudes toward Capitalism and Democracy*. Cambridge, MA: Harvard University Press.

McCombs, Maxwell, and Amy Reynolds, eds. 1999. *The Poll with a Human Face: The National Issues Convention Experiment in Political Communication*. Mahwah, NJ: Lawrence Erlbaum Associates.

McCombs, Maxwell, Donald L. Shaw, and David Weaver, eds. 1997. *Communication and Democracy: Exploring the Intellectual Frontiers in Agenda-Setting Theory*. Hillsdale, NJ: Lawrence Erlbaum Associates.

McGraw, Kathleen M., and Neil Pinney. 1990. The Effects of General and Domain-Specific Expertise on Political Memory and Judgment. *Social Cognition* 8 (1):9–30.

McGuire, William J. 1969. The Nature of Attitudes and Attitude Change. In *Handbook of Social Psychology*, edited by G. Lindzey and E. Aronson. Reading, MA: Addison-Wesley.

McKelvey, Richard, and Peter Ordeshook. 1990. Information and Elections: Retrospective Voting and Rational Expectations. In *Information and Democratic Processes*, edited by J. Ferejohn and J. Kuklinski. Urbana, IL: University of Illinois Press.

McLean, Iain, and Arnold B. Urken, eds. 1995. *Classics of Social Choice*. Ann Arbor: University of Michigan Press.

Mebane, Walter R. 1994. Fiscal Constraints and Electoral Manipulation in American Social Welfare. *American Political Science Review* 88 (1):77–94.

Meyers, Marian J. 1994. Defining Homosexuality: News Coverage of the Repeal the Ban Controversy. *Discourse & Society* 5 (3):321–44.

Miller, David. 1992. Deliberative Democracy and Social Choice. *Political Studies* XL:54–67.

Miller, Joanne M., and Jon A. Krosnick. 1996. News Media Impact on the Ingredients of Presidential Evaluations: A Program of Research on the Priming Hypothesis. In *Political Persuasion and Attitude Change*, edited by D. C. Mutz, P. M. Sniderman and R. A. Brody. Ann Arbor: University of Michigan Press.

Miller, Nicholas R. 1986. Information, Electorates, and Democracy: Some Extensions and Interpretations of the Condorcet Jury Theorem. In *Information Pooling and Group Decision Making*, edited by B. Grofman and G. Owen. Greenwich, CT: JAI Press.

Miller, Nicholas R. 1996. Information, Individual Errors, and Collective Performance: Empirical Evidence on the Condorcet Jury Theorem. *Group Decision and Negotiation* 5:211–28.

Miller, Peter V. 1995. The Industry of Public Opinion. In *Public Opinion and the Communication of Consent*, edited by T. L. Glasser and C. T. Salmon. New York: Guilford.

Miller, Warren. 1988. *Without Consent: Mass-Elite Linkages in Presidential Politics*. Lexington: University Press of Kentucky.

Miller, Warren, and M. Kent Jennings. 1987. *Parties in Transition: A Longitudinal Study of Party Elites and Party Supporters*. New York: Russell Sage Foundation.

Minar, David. 1960. Public Opinion in the Perspective of Political Theory. *Western Political Quarterly* 13 (1):31–44.

Mitchell, Robert C. 1980. Polling on Nuclear Power: A Critique of the Polls after Three Mile Island. In *Polling on the Issues*, edited by A. Cantril. Washington D.C.: Seven Locks Press.

Mondak, Jeffery J. 1993a. Public Opinion and Heuristic Processing of Source Cues. *Political Behavior* 15 (2):167–92.

———. 1993b. Source Cues and Policy Approval: The Cognitive Dynamics of Public Support for the Reagan Agenda. *American Journal of Political Science* 37 (1):186–212.

———. 1994a. Cognitive Heuristics, Heuristic Processing, and Efficiency in Political Decision Making. In *Research in Micropolitics*. Greenwich, CT: JAI Press.

————. 1994b. Question Wording and Mass Policy Preferences: The Comparative Impact of Substantive Information and Peripheral Cues. *Political Communication* 11 (2):165–83.

————. 1995a. Elections as Filters: Term Limits and the Composition of the U.S. House. *Political Research Quarterly* 48 (4):701–27.

————. 1995b. *Nothing to Read: Newspapers and Elections in a Social Experiment.* Ann Arbor: University of Michigan Press.

————. 2000. Reconsidering the Measurement of Political Knowledge. *Political Analysis* 8 (1):57–82.

————. 2001. Developing Valid Knowledge Scales. *American Journal of Political Science* 45 (1):224–38.

Mondak, Jeffery J., and Belinda Creel Davis. 2001. Asked and Answered: Knowledge Levels when We Will Not Take "Don't Know" for an Answer. *Political Behavior* 23 (3):199–224.

Monroe, Alan D. 1979. Consistency between Policy Preferences and National Policy Decisions. *American Politics Quarterly* 7:3–18.

————. 1998. Public Opinion and Public Policy, 1980–1993. *Public Opinion Quarterly* 62 (1):6–28.

Moore, Wilbert E., and Melvin M. Tumin. 1949. Some Social Functions of Ignorance. *American Sociological Review* 14 (6):787–95.

Morris, Dick. 1999. *Behind the Oval Office: Getting Reelected against All Odds.* Revised ed. Los Angeles: Renaissance Books.

Mueller, Dennis C. 1989. *Public Choice II.* Cambridge: Cambridge University Press.

Mueller, John. 1994. *Policy and Opinion in the Gulf War.* Chicago: University of Chicago Press.

Mutz, Diana C. 1998. *Impersonal Influence: How Perceptions of Mass Collectives Affect Political Attitudes.* New York: Cambridge University Press.

Mutz, Diana C., and Paul S. Martin. 2001. Facilitating Communication across Lines of Political Difference: The Role of the Mass Media. *American Political Science Review* 95 (1):97–114.

Nacos, Brigitte L., Robert Y. Shapiro, and Pierangelo Isernia, eds. 2000. *Decisionmaking in a Glass House: Mass Media, Public Opinion, and American and European Foreign Policy in the 21st Century.* Lanham, MD: Rowman & Littlefield.

Nadeau, Richard, and Richard G. Niemi. 1995. Educated Guesses: The Process of Answering Factual Knowledge Questions in Surveys. *Public Opinion Quarterly* 59:323–46.

Narayan, Sowmya, and Jon A. Krosnick. 1996. Education Moderates Some Response Effects in Attitude Measurement. *Public Opinion Quarterly* 60 (1): 58–88.

Natchez, Peter B. 1985. *Images of Voting/Visions of Democracy.* New York: Basic Books.

Nelson, Thomas E., Rosalee A. Clawson, and Zoe M. Oxley. 1997. Media Framing of a Civil Liberties Conflict and Its Effect on Tolerance. *American Political Science Review* 91 (3):567–83.

Nelson, Thomas E., and Donald R. Kinder. 1996. Issue Frames and Group-Centrism in American Public Opinion. *Journal of Politics* 58 (4):1055–78.

Neuman, W. Russell. 1986. *The Paradox of Mass Politics: Knowledge and Opinion in the American Electorate.* Cambridge, MA: Harvard University Press.

———. 1998. The Nature of Issue Publics. Paper presented at the annual meeting of the American Political Science Association, Sep. 3–6, at Boston, MA.

Neuman, W. Russell, Marion Just, and Ann Crigler. 1992. *Common Knowledge: News and the Construction of Social Meaning.* Chicago: University of Chicago Press.

Nie, Norman, and Kristi Andersen. 1974. Mass Belief Systems Revisited: Political Change and Attitude Structure. *Journal of Politics* 36 (August):541–91.

Nie, Norman H., Jane Junn, and Kenneth Stehlik-Barry. 1996. *Education and Democratic Citizenship in America.* Chicago: University of Chicago Press.

Nie, Norman, Sidney Verba, and John Petrocik. 1979. *The Changing American Voter.* Enlarged ed. Cambridge, MA: Harvard University Press.

Nino, Carlos S. 1996. *The Constitution of Deliberative Democracy.* New Haven: Yale University Press.

Nisbett, Richard E., and Lee Ross. 1980. *Human Inference: Strategies and Shortcomings of Social Judgment.* Englewood Cliffs, NJ: Prentice-Hall.

Nisbett, Richard E., and Timothy DeCamp Wilson. 1977. Telling More than We Can Know: Verbal Reports on Mental Processes. *Psychological Review* 84 (3):231–59.

Noelle-Neumann, Elisabeth. 1984. *The Spiral of Silence: Public Opinion – Our Social Skin.* Chicago: University of Chicago Press.

Olson, Mancur. 1965. *The Logic of Collective Action: Public Goods and the Theory of Groups.* Cambridge: Harvard University Press.

Ottati, Victor, and Robert Wyer. 1990. The Cognitive Mediators of Political Choice: Toward a Comprehensive Model of Political Information Processing. In *Information and Democratic Processes,* edited by J. Ferejohn and J. Kuklinski. Urbana, IL: University of Illinois Press.

Page, Benjamin I. 1978. *Choices and Echoes in Presidential Elections.* Chicago: University of Chicago Press.

Page, Benjamin I. 1996. *Who Deliberates? Mass Media in Modern Democracy.* Chicago: University of Chicago Press.

Page, Benjamin I., and Robert Y. Shapiro. 1983. Effects of Public Opinion on Policy. *American Political Science Review* 77:175–90.

———. 1992. *The Rational Public: Fifty Years of Trends in Americans' Policy Preferences.* Chicago: University of Chicago Press.

———. 1993. The Rational Public and Democracy. In *Reconsidering the Democratic Public,* edited by G. Marcus and R. Hanson. University Park, PA: Pennsylvania State University Press.

———. 1999. The Rational Public and Beyond. In *Citizen Competence and Democratic Institutions,* edited by S. L. Elkin and K. E. Soltan. University Park, PA: Pennsylvania State University Press.

Page, Benjamin I., and Jason Tannenbaum. 1996. Populistic Deliberation and Talk Radio. *Journal of Communication* 46 (2):33–54.

Palmer, Paul. 1936. The Concept of Public Opinion in Political Theory. In *Essays in History and Political Theory*. New York: Russell & Russell.

Parenti, Michael. 1986. *Inventing Reality: The Politics of the Mass Media*. New York: St. Martin's Press.

Pateman, Carole. 1970. *Participation and Democratic Theory*. London: Cambridge University Press.

Patterson, Thomas. 1980. *The Mass Media Election: How Americans Choose Their President*. New York: Praeger.

Payne, Stanley L. 1951. *The Art of Asking Questions*. Princeton: Princeton University Press.

Peters, John D. 1995. Historical Tensions in the Concept of Public Opinion. In *Public Opinion and the Communication of Consent*, edited by T. L. Glasser and C. T. Salmon. New York: Guilford.

Petty, Richard E., and John T. Cacioppo. 1986. *Communication and Persuasion: Central and Peripheral Routes To Attitude Change*. New York: Springer-Verlag.

Petty, Richard E., and Duane T. Wegener. 1999. The Elaboration Likelihood Model: Current Status and Controversies. In *Dual-Process Theories in Social Psychology*, edited by S. Chaiken and Y. Trope. New York: Guilford.

Pitkin, Hanna. 1967. *The Concept of Representation*. Berkeley: University of California Press.

———, ed. 1969. *Representation*. New York: Atherton Press.

Pollock, Friedrich. 1976. Empirical Research into Public Opinion. In *Critical Sociology*, edited by P. Connerton. New York: Penguin.

Popkin, Samuel L. 1991. *The Reasoning Voter: Communication and Persuasion in Presidential Campaigns*. Chicago: University of Chicago Press.

———. 1993. Information Shortcuts and the Reasoning Voter. In *Information, Participation, and Choice*, edited by B. Grofman. Ann Arbor: University of Michigan Press.

Popkin, Samuel L., and Michael A. Dimock. 1999. Political Knowledge and Civic Competence. In *Citizen Competence and Democratic Institutions*, edited by S. L. Elkin and K. E. Soltan. University Park, PA: Pennsylvania State University Press.

———. 2000. Knowledge, Trust, and International Reasoning. In *Elements of Reason: Cognition, Choice, and the Bounds of Rationality*, edited by A. Lupia, M. D. McCubbins and S. L. Popkin. New York: Cambridge University Press.

Powlick, Philip J. 1990. The American Foreign Policy Process and the Public. Ph. D. dissertation, Department of Political Science, University of Pittsburgh.

Presser, Stanley, and Howard Schuman. 1980. The Measurement of a Middle Position in Attitude Surveys. *Public Opinion Quarterly* 44 (1):70–85.

Price, Vincent. 1992. *Public Opinion*. Newbury Park: Sage.

———. 1999. Political Information. In *Measures of Political Attitudes*, edited by J. P. Robinson, P. R. Shaver and L. S. Wrightsman. San Diego: Academic Press.

Price, Vincent, Joseph N. Cappella, and Lilach Nir. 2002. Does Disagreement Contribute to More Deliberative Opinion? *Political Communication* 19 (1): 95–112.

Price, Vincent, and Peter Neijens. 1997. Opinion Quality in Public Opinion Research. *International Journal of Public Opinion Research* 9 (4):336–60.

———. 1998. Deliberative Polls: Toward Improved Measures of "Informed" Public Opinion? *International Journal of Public Opinion Research* 10 (2):145–76.

Price, Vincent, and David Tewksbury. 1997. News Values and Public Opinion: A Theoretical Account of Media Priming and Framing. In *Progress in Communication Sciences*, edited by G. Barnett and F. Boster. London: Ablex Publishing.

Price, Vincent, and John Zaller. 1993. Who Gets the News? Alternative Measures of News Reception and Their Implications for Research. *Public Opinion Quarterly* 57:133–64.

Prior, Markus. 2002. Political Knowledge after September 11. *PS: Political Science & Politics* 35 (3):523–9.

Protess, David L., and Maxwell McCombs, eds. 1991. *Agenda Setting: Readings on Media, Public Opinion, and Policymaking*. Hillsdale, NJ: Lawrence Erlbaum Associates.

Przeworski, Adam, Susan C. Stokes, and Bernard Manin, eds. 1999. *Democracy, Accountability, and Representation*. New York: Cambridge University Press.

Radcliff, Benjamin. 1992. The General Will and Social Choice Theory. *Review of Politics* 54 (1):34–49.

———. 1993. Liberalism, Populism, and Collective Choice. *Political Research Quarterly* 46 (1):127–55.

Rahn, Wendy M. 1993. The Role of Partisan Stereotypes in Information Processing about Political Candidates. *American Journal of Political Science* 37 (2):472–96.

Rahn, Wendy M., John H. Aldrich, and Eugene Borgida. 1994. Individual and Contextual Variations in Political Candidate Appraisal. *American Political Science Review* 88 (1):193–99.

Rahn, Wendy M., and Katherine J. Cramer. 1996. Activation and Application of Political Party Stereotypes: The Role of Television. *Political Communication* 13 (2):195–212.

Rapoport, Ronald. 1982. Sex Differences in Attitude Expression: A Generational Explanation. *Public Opinion Quarterly* 46:86–96.

Rasinski, Kenneth. 1989. The Effect of Question Wording on Public Support for Government Spending. *Public Opinion Quarterly* 53:388–94.

Rawls, John A. 1971. *A Theory of Justice*. Cambridge, MA: Belknap Press.

Rich, Robert F. 1981. *Social Science Information and Public Policy Making*. San Francisco: Jossey-Bass.

Riker, William. 1982. *Liberalism against Populism: A Confrontation between the Theory of Democracy and the Theory of Social Choice*. Prospect Heights, IL: Waveland Press.

Rogers, Everett M. 1995. *Diffusion of Innovations*. 4th ed. New York: Free Press.

Rogers, Lindsay. 1949. *The Pollsters: Public Opinion, Politics, and Democratic Leadership*. New York: Alfred A. Knopf.

Rogers, Theresa F. 1989. Interviews by Telephone and in Person: Quality of Responses and Field Performance. In *Survey Research Methods: A Reader*, edited by E. Singer and S. Presser. Chicago: University of Chicago Press.

Rokeach, Milton. 1968. *Beliefs, Attitudes, and Values: A Theory of Organization and Change*. San Francisco: Jossey-Bass Inc.

———. 1973. *The Nature of Human Values*. New York: Free Press.

Rosen, Jay. 1994. Making Things More Public: On the Political Responsibility of the Media Intellectual. *Critical Studies in Mass Communication* 11 (December):362–88.

———. 1996. *Getting the Connections Right: Public Journalism and the Troubles in the Press.* New York: Twentieth Century Fund Press.

Rosenstone, Steven J., and John Mark Hansen. 1993. *Mobilization, Participation, and Democracy in America.* New York: Macmillan.

Rothman, Stanley, and S. Robert Lichter. 1987. Elite Ideology and Risk Perception in Nuclear Energy Policy. *American Political Science Review* 81 (2):383–404.

Rousseau, Jean-Jacques. [1762] 1973. *The Social Contract and Discourses.* London: J. M. Dent & Sons.

Rugg, Donald, and Hadley Cantril. 1944. The Wording of Questions. In *Gauging Public Opinion*, edited by H. Cantril. Princeton: Princeton University Press.

Russett, Bruce M. 1990. *Controlling the Sword: The Democratic Governance of National Security.* Cambridge, MA: Harvard University Press.

Salmon, Charles T., and Theodore L. Glasser. 1995. The Politics of Polling and the Limits of Consent. In *Public Opinion and the Communication of Consent*, edited by T. L. Glasser and C. T. Salmon. New York: Guilford Press.

Sanders, Lynn M. 1999. Democratic Politics and Survey Research. *Philosophy of the Social Sciences* 29 (2):248–280.

Sartori, Giovanni. 1965. *Democratic Theory.* London: Frederick Praeger.

———. 1987. *The Theory of Democracy Revisited.* Chatham, New Jersey: Chatham House.

Schattschneider, E. E. 1960. *The Semisovereign People: A Realist's View of Democracy in America.* New York: Harcourt Brace Jovanovich.

Schlesinger, Mark, and Richard R. Lau. 2000. The Meaning and Measure of Policy Metaphors. *American Political Science Review* 94 (3):611–26.

Schudson, Michael. 1998. *The Good Citizen: A History of American Civic Life.* New York: Free Press.

Schuman, Howard, and Jean M. Converse. 1971. The Effects of Black and White Interviewers on Black Responses in 1968. *Public Opinion Quarterly* 35(1): 44–68.

Schuman, Howard, and Stanley Presser. 1980. Public Opinion and Public Ignorance: The Fine Line Between Attitudes and Nonattitudes. *American Journal of Sociology* 85 (5):1214–25.

———. 1981. *Questions and Answers in Attitude Surveys: Experiments on Question Form, Wording, and Context.* New York: Academic Press.

Schuman, Howard, and Jacqueline Scott. 1987. Problems in the Use of Survey Questions to Measure Public Opinion. *Science* 236 (May 22):957–9.

Schuman, Howard, Charlotte Steeh, Lawrence Bobo, and Maria Krysan. 1997. *Racial Attitudes in America: Trends and Interpretations.* Cambridge, MA: Harvard University Press.

Schumpeter, Joseph. [1942] 1976. *Capitalism, Socialism, and Democracy.* Reprint, New York: Harper & Row.

Schwarz, Norbert, and Seymour Sudman, eds. 1996. *Answering Questions: Methodology for Determining Cognitive and Communicative Processes in Survey Research.* San Francisco, CA: Jossey-Bass.

Seeley, Thomas D. 2001. Decision Making in Superorganisms: How Collective Wisdom Arises from the Poorly Informed Masses. In *Bounded Rationality: The Adaptive Toolbox*, edited by G. Gigerenzer and R. Selten. Cambridge, MA: MIT Press.

Seelye, Katharine Q. 1995. House Turns Back Measures to Limit Terms in Congress. *New York Times*, March 30, A:1.

Shamir, Jacob, and Michal Shamir. 1997. Pluralistic Ignorance across Issues and over Time: Information Cues and Biases. *Public Opinion Quarterly* 61 (2):227–60.

———. 2000. *The Anatomy of Public Opinion*. Ann Arbor: University of Michigan Press.

Shapiro, Ian. 1999. *Democratic Justice*. New Haven: Yale University Press.

Shapiro, Robert Y. 1998. Public Opinion, Elites, and Democracy. *Critical Review* 12 (4):501–28.

Shapiro, Robert Y., Lawrence R. Jacobs, and Lynn K. Harvey. 1995. Influences on Public Opinion toward Health Care Policy. Paper presented at the annual meeting of the Midwest Political Science Association, April 6–8, at Chicago, IL.

Shepard, Alicia C. 1993. Did the Networks Sanitize the Gay Rights March? *American Journalism Review* 15 (July/August):27–9.

Sigal, Leon. 1973. *Reporters and Officials: The Organization and Politics of Newsmaking*. Lexington, Mass: D.C. Heath and Co.

Sigelman, Lee, and Ernest Yanarella. 1986. Public Information on Public Issues: A Multivariate Analysis. *Social Science Quarterly* 67 (2):402–10.

Simon, Herbert A. 1957. *Models of Man*. New York: Wiley.

Singer, Eleanor. 1987. Editor's Introduction. *Public Opinion Quarterly* 51 (Special):S1–S3.

Singer, Eleanor, and Stanley Presser, eds. 1989. *Survey Research Methods: A Reader*. Chicago: University of Chicago Press.

Singer, Eleanor, and Howard Schuman. 1988. Controversies. *Public Opinion Quarterly* 52 (4):576–81.

Sinnott, Richard. 2000. Knowledge and the Position of Attitudes to a European Foreign Policy on the Real-to-Random Continuum. *International Journal of Public Opinion Research* 12 (2):113–37.

Smith, Eric R.A.N. 1989. *The Unchanging American Voter*. Berkeley: University of California Press.

Smith, Eric, and Peverill Squire. 1990. The Effects of Prestige Names in Question Wording. *Public Opinion Quarterly* 54 (1):97–116.

Smith, Renée M. 1993. Information Diffusion and the Dynamics of Public Support for Presidents. Paper presented at the Annual Meeting of the Midwest Political Science Association, April 14–17, 1993, at Chicago, Illinois.

Smith, Tom W. 1978. In Search of House Effects: A Comparison of Responses to Various Questions by Different Survey Organizations. *Public Opinion Quarterly* 42 (4):443–63.

———. 1987. That Which We Call Welfare by Any Other Name Would Smell Sweeter: An Analysis of the Impact of Question Wording on Response Patterns. *Public Opinion Quarterly* 51 (1):75–83.

Sniderman, Paul M. 2000. Taking Sides: A Fixed Choice Theory of Political Reasoning. In *Elements of Reason: Cognition, Choice, and the Bounds of Rationality*, edited by A. Lupia, M. D. McCubbins, and S. L. Popkin. New York: Cambridge University Press.

Sniderman, Paul, Richard Brody, and Philip Tetlock. 1991. *Reasoning and Choice: Explorations in Political Psychology*. New York: Cambridge University Press.

Sniderman, Paul M., Joseph F. Fletcher, Peter H. Russell, and Philip E. Tetlock. 1996. *The Clash of Rights: Liberty, Equality, and Legitimacy in Pluralist Democracy*. New Haven: Yale University Press.

Sniderman, Paul M., and Sean M. Theriault. 1999. The Dynamics of Political Argument and the Logic of Issue Framing. Unpublished manuscript, Stanford University.

Sobel, Richard. 2001. *The Impact of Public Opinion on U.S. Foreign Policy Since Vietnam*. New York: Oxford University Press.

Somin, Ilya. 1998. Voter Ignorance and the Democratic Ideal. *Critical Review* 12 (4):413–58.

Speier, Hans. 1950. Historical Development of Public Opinion. *American Journal of Sociology* 55 (4):376–88.

Splichal, Slavko. 1997. Political Institutionalisation of Public Opinion through Polling. *Javnost: The Public* 4 (2):17–37.

———. 1999. *Public Opinion: Developments and Controversies in the Twentieth Century*. Lanham, MD: Rowman & Littlefield.

Steele, Janet E. 1997. Don't Ask, Don't Tell, Don't Explain: Unofficial Sources and Television Coverage of the Dispute over Gays in the Military. *Political Communication* 14 (1):83–96.

Sterne, Simon. 1969. The Representational Likeness. In *Representation*, edited by H. Pitkin. New York: Atherton Press.

Stimson, James A. 1975. Belief Systems: Constraint, Complexity and the 1972 Election. *American Journal of Political Science* 19 (3):393–417.

———. 1990. A Macro Theory of Information Flow. In *Information and Democratic Processes*, edited by J. Ferejohn and J. Kuklinski. Urbana, IL: University of Illinois Press.

———. 1991. *Public Opinion in America: Moods, Cycles, and Swings*. Boulder, CO: Westview Press.

———. 1999. Party Government and Responsiveness. In *Democracy, Accountability, and Representation*, edited by A. Przeworski, S. C. Stokes, and B. Manin. New York: Cambridge University Press.

Stimson, James A., Michael B. MacKuen, and Robert S. Erikson. 1995. Dynamic Representation. *American Political Science Review* 88 (3):543–65.

Sturgis, Patrick J. 2003. Knowledge and Collective Preferences: A Comparison of Two Approaches to Estimating the Opinions of a Better Informed Public. *Sociological Methods & Research* 31 (4).

Sunstein, Cass R. 1991. Preferences and Politics. *Philosophy & Public Affairs* 20 (1):3–34.

Swabey, Marie C. 1937. *Theory of the Democratic State*. Cambridge, MA: Harvard University Press.

Tanur, Judith M., ed. 1992. *Questions about Questions: Inquiries into the Cognitive Bases of Surveys*. New York: Russell Sage Foundation.

Taylor, Shelly E., and Susan Fiske. 1978. Salience, Attention, and Attribution: Top of the Head Phenomena. In *Advances in Social Psychology*, edited by L. Berkowitz. New York: Academic Press.

Thompson, Dennis F. 1970. *The Democratic Citizen: Social Science and Democratic Theory in the Twentieth Century*. New York: Cambridge University Press.

Tichenor, P.J., G.A. Donohue, and C.N. Olien. 1970. Mass Media Flow and Differential Growth in Knowledge. *Public Opinion Quarterly* 34 (2): 159–70.

Tourangeau, Roger, Lance J. Rips, and Kenneth Rasinski. 2000. *The Psychology of Survey Response*. New York: Cambridge University Press.

Traugott, Michael. 1992. The Impact of Media Polls on the Public. In *Media Polls in American Politics*, edited by T. Mann and G. Orren. Washington, DC: Brookings Institution.

Tuchman, Gaye. 1978. *Making News: A Study in the Construction of Reality*. New York: Free Press.

Vanishing Voter Project. 2000. *Americans Are Forgetting Some of What They Knew about Bush and Gore* [Electronic]. The Joan Shorenstein Center on the Press, Politics, and Public Policy, Harvard University 2000a [cited December 20 2000]. Available from http://www.vanishingvoter.org/releases/04-21-00.shtml.

———. 2000. *Americans' Support of Presidential Candidate Drops as Their Campaign Interest Declines* [Electronic]. The Joan Shorenstein Center on the Press, Politics, and Public Policy, Harvard University 2000b [cited December 20 2000]. Available from http://www.vanishingvoter.org/releases/05-02-00.shtml.

Verba, Sidney. 1996. The Citizen as Respondent: Sample Surveys and American Democracy. *American Political Science Review* 90 (1):1–7.

Verba, Sidney, Nancy Burns, and Kay Lehman Schlozman. 1997. Knowing and Caring about Politics: Gender and Political Engagement. *Journal of Politics* 59 (4):1051–72.

Verba, Sidney, and Norman Nie. 1972. *Participation in America: Political Democracy and Social Equality*. Chicago: University of Chicago Press.

Verba, Sidney, Kay Lehman Schlozman, and Henry E. Brady. 1995. *Voice and Equality: Civic Voluntarism in American Politics*. Cambridge, MA: Harvard University Press.

Verba, Sidney, Kay Lehman Schlozman, Henry Brady, and Norman Nie. 1993. Citizen Activity: Who Participates? What Do They Say? *American Political Science Review* 87 (2):303–18.

Viswanath, K., and John R. Finnegan. 1996. The Knowledge Gap Hypothesis: Twenty-Five Years Later. In *Communication Yearbook 19*, edited by B. Burleson. Thousand Oaks, CA: Sage Publications.

Viswanath, K., Emily Kahn, John R. Finnegan, James Hertog, and John D. Potter. 1993. Motivation and the Knowledge Gap: Effects of a Campaign to Reduce Diet-Related Cancer Risk. *Communication Research* 20 (4):546–63.

Warren, Kenneth F. 2001. *In Defense of Public Opinion Polling*. Boulder, CO: Westview.

Weatherford, M. Stephen. 1983. Economic Voting and the "Symbolic Politics" Argument: A Reinterpretation and Synthesis. *American Political Science Review* 77 (1):158–74.

Weissberg, Robert. 1976. *Public Opinion and Popular Government*. Englewood Cliffs, NJ: Prentice-Hall.

———. 2001. Democratic Political Competence: Clearing the Underbrush and a Controversial Proposal. *Political Behavior* 23 (3):257–84.

———. 2002a. *Polling, Policy and Public Opinion: The Case Against Heeding the "Voice of the People"*. New York: Palgrave-Macmillan.

———. 2002b. The Problem with Polls. *The Public Interest* 148 (Summer):37–48.

Wheeler, Michael. 1976. *Lies, Damn Lies, and Statistics: The Manipulation of Public Opinion in America*. New York: Dell.

Wilcox, Walter. 1966. The Congressional Poll – and Non-Poll. In *Political Opinion and Electoral Behavior*, edited by E. Dreyer and W. Rosenbaum. Belmont, CA: Wadsworth Publishing.

Wildavsky, Aaron. 1987. Choosing Preferences by Constructing Institutions: A Cultural Theory of Preference Formation. *American Political Science Review* 81 (1):3–21.

Wiley, David E., and James A. Wiley. 1970. The Estimation of Measurement Error in Panel Data. *American Sociological Review* 35 (1):112–17.

Wittkopf, Eugene R. 1990. *Faces of Internationalism: Public Opinion and American Foreign Policy*. Durham, NC: Duke University Press.

Wittman, Donald. 1989. Why Democracies Produce Efficient Results. *Journal of Political Economy* 97 (6):1395–1424.

———. 1995. *The Myth of Democratic Failure: Why Political Institutions Are Efficient*. Chicago: University of Chicago Press.

Wlezien, Christopher. 1995a. Dynamics of Representation: The Case of U.S. Spending on Defense. *British Journal of Political Science* 26 (Part1):81–103.

———. 1995b. The Public as Thermostat: Dynamics of Preferences for Spending. *American Journal of Political Science* 39 (4):981–1000.

Wlezien, Christopher B., and Malcolm L. Goggin. 1993. The Courts, Interest Groups, and Public Opinion about Abortion. *Political Behavior* 15 (4): 381–405.

Wolfinger, Raymond, David Glass, and Peverill Squire. 1990. Predictors of Electoral Turnout: An International Comparison. *Policy Studies Review* 9 (3): 551–74.

Wolfinger, Raymond, and Steven Rosenstone. 1980. *Who Votes?* New Haven: Yale University Press.

Worcester, Robert M. 1998. The People's Panel. Paper presented at the annual meeting of the American Association for Public Opinion Research, May 14–17, at St. Louis.

Wyatt, Robert O., Elihu Katz, and Joohan Kim. 2000. Bridging the Spheres: Political and Personal Conversation in Public And Private Spaces. *Journal of Communication* 50 (1):71–92.

Yankelovich, Daniel. 1991. *Coming to Public Judgment: Making Democracy Work in a Complex World*. Syracuse, NY: Syracuse University Press.

Zaller, John. 1985. Pre-Testing Information Items on the 1986 NES Pilot Survey. Report to the National Election Study Board of Overseers.

———. 1991. Information, Values, and Opinion. *American Political Science Review* 85 (4):1215–37.

———. 1992a. *The Nature and Origins of Mass Opinion.* New York: Cambridge University Press.

———. 1992b. Political Awareness and Susceptibility to Elite Influence on Foreign Policy Issues. Paper presented at the annual meeting of the American Political Science Association, Sept. 3–6, at Chicago, IL.

———. 1994. Positive Constructs of Public Opinion. *Critical Studies in Mass Communication* 11:276–87.

———. 1996. The Myth of Massive Media Impact Revived: New Support for a Discredited Idea. In *Political Persuasion and Attitude Change*, edited by D. C. Mutz, P. M. Sniderman and R. A. Brody. Ann Arbor: University of Michigan Press.

———. 1998. Coming to Grips with V. O. Key's Concept of Latent Opinion. Paper presented at the annual meeting of the American Political Science Association, Sep. 3–6, at Boston, MA.

Zaller, John, and Stanley Feldman. 1992. A Simple Theory of the Survey Response: Answering Questions Versus Revealing Preferences. *American Journal of Political Science* 36 (3):579–616.

Index